Understanding Barthes,
Understanding Modernism

Understanding Philosophy, Understanding Modernism

The aim of each volume in **Understanding Philosophy, Understanding Modernism** is to understand a philosophical thinker more fully through literary and cultural modernism and consequently to understand literary modernism better through a key philosophical figure. In this way, the series also rethinks the limits of modernism, calling attention to lacunae in modernist studies and sometimes in the philosophical work under examination.

Series Editors:
Paul Ardoin, S. E. Gontarski, and Laci Mattison

Volumes in the Series:
Understanding Bergson, Understanding Modernism
Edited by Paul Ardoin, S. E. Gontarski, and Laci Mattison

Understanding Deleuze, Understanding Modernism
Edited by S. E. Gontarski, Paul Ardoin, and Laci Mattison

Understanding Wittgenstein, Understanding Modernism
Edited by Anat Matar

Understanding Foucault, Understanding Modernism
Edited by David Scott

Understanding James, Understanding Modernism
Edited by David H. Evans

Understanding Rancière, Understanding Modernism
Edited by Patrick M. Bray

Understanding Blanchot, Understanding Modernism
Edited by Christopher Langlois

Understanding Merleau-Ponty, Understanding Modernism
Edited by Ariane Mildenberg

Understanding Nietzsche, Understanding Modernism
Edited by Douglas Burnham and Brian Pines

Understanding Derrida, Understanding Modernism
Edited by Jean-Michel Rabaté

Understanding Adorno, Understanding Modernism
Edited by Robin Truth Goodman

Understanding Flusser, Understanding Modernism
Edited by Aaron Jaffe, Rodrigo Martini, and Michael F. Miller

Understanding Marx, Understanding Modernism
Edited by Mark Steven

Understanding Barthes, Understanding Modernism
Edited by Jeffrey R. Di Leo, and Zahi Zalloua

Understanding Bakhtin, Understanding Modernism (forthcoming)
Edited by Philippe Birgy

Understanding Badiou, Understanding Modernism (forthcoming)
Edited by Arka Chattopadhyay and Arthur Rose

Understanding Zizek, Understanding Modernism (forthcoming)
Edited by Jeffrey R. Di Leo and Zahi Zalloua

Understanding Nancy, Understanding Modernism (forthcoming)
Edited by Cosmin Toma

Understanding Cavell, Understanding Modernism (forthcoming)
Edited by Paola Marrati

Understanding Barthes, Understanding Modernism

Edited by
Jeffrey R. Di Leo and Zahi Zalloua

BLOOMSBURY ACADEMIC
NEW YORK • LONDON • OXFORD • NEW DELHI • SYDNEY

BLOOMSBURY ACADEMIC
Bloomsbury Publishing Inc
1385 Broadway, New York, NY 10018, USA
29 Earlsfort Terrace, Dublin 2, Ireland

BLOOMSBURY, BLOOMSBURY ACADEMIC and the Diana logo are trademarks
of Bloomsbury Publishing Plc

First published in the United States of America 2022
This paperback edition published 2024

Copyright © Jeffrey R. Di Leo, Zahi Zalloua, and Contributors, 2022

Cover design: Eleanor Rose
Cover image © Getty Images

All rights reserved. No part of this publication may be reproduced or transmitted in any form or by any means, electronic or mechanical, including photocopying, recording, or any information storage or retrieval system, without prior permission in writing from the publishers.

Bloomsbury Publishing Inc does not have any control over, or responsibility for, any third-party websites referred to or in this book. All internet addresses given in this book were correct at the time of going to press. The author and publisher regret any inconvenience caused if addresses have changed or sites have ceased to exist, but can accept no responsibility for any such changes.

Library of Congress Cataloging-in-Publication Data
Names: Di Leo, Jeffrey R., editor. | Zalloua, Zahi Anbra, 1971- editor.
Title: Understanding Barthes, understanding modernism /
edited by Jeffrey R. Di Leo and Zahi Zalloua.
Description: New York : Bloomsbury Academic, 2022. | Series: Understanding philosophy, understanding modernism | Includes bibliographical references and index. |
Summary: "Explores and illuminates Roland Barthes' profound impact on our understanding of literary modernism"– Provided by publisher.
Identifiers: LCCN 2022001331 (print) | LCCN 2022001332 (ebook) | ISBN 9781501367403 (hardback) | ISBN 9781501393518 (paperback) | ISBN 9781501367410 (epub) | ISBN 9781501367427 (pdf) | ISBN 9781501367434
Subjects: LCSH: Barthes, Roland–Criticism and interpretation. | Barthes, Roland–Influence. | Modernism (Literature) | Literature–Philosophy. | Philosophy, Modern–20th century.
Classification: LCC P85.B33 U529 2022 (print) | LCC P85.B33 (ebook) |
DDC 801/.95092–dc23/eng/20220410
LC record available at https://lccn.loc.gov/2022001331
LC ebook record available at https://lccn.loc.gov/2022001332

ISBN: HB: 978-1-5013-6740-3
PB: 978-1-5013-9351-8
ePDF: 978-1-5013-6742-7
eBook: 978-1-5013-6741-0

Series: Understanding Philosophy, Understanding Modernism

Typeset by Deanta Global Publishing Services, Chennai, India

To find out more about our authors and books visit www.bloomsbury.com and sign up for our newsletters.

Contents

List of Figures	vii
Series Preface	viii
Acknowledgments	ix

Introduction *Jeffrey R. Di Leo and Zahi Zalloua* — 1

Part I Mapping Barthes

1. Roland Barthes's Myth of Photography *Jean-Michel Rabaté* — 15
2. Barthes and the Search for Rigor *Thomas Pavel* — 33
3. Barthes and the French Classics *Michael Moriarty* — 42
4. Pleasure in Paradigm: *Sade, Fourier, Loyola* *Rudolphus Teeuwen* — 55
5. Understanding Barthes, Understanding Proust *Thomas Baldwin* — 70
6. Take Two: Barthes and Film in the Age of *Mythologies* *Steven Ungar* — 84
7. Barthes, Bazin, and Écriture *Dudley Andrew* — 103
8. Barthes's Hedonism *Jeffrey R. Di Leo* — 116

Part II Legacies and Afterlives

9. Point Counterpoint: Derrida's "The Deaths of Roland Barthes" *Brian O'Keeffe* — 137
10. Objects of Desire: *Chosisme* after Object-Oriented Ontology *Zahi Zalloua* — 151
11. Orpheus Turning: The Reader to Come in *Camera Lucida* *Daniel T. O'Hara* — 173
12. No Wish to "Understand" nor to "Grasp": Opacity in the Work of Roland Barthes and Édouard Glissant *Andy Stafford* — 186
13. Roland Barthes and Don DeLillo on Living Together/Apart *Herman Rapaport* — 206
14. Barthes: Visual Culture and Homosexual Sociabilities *Magali Nachtergael* — 223

Part III Glossary

15. Author *Andy Stafford* — 239
16. Codes *Andy Stafford* — 241
17. Haiku *Brian O'Keeffe* — 245

18	*Jouissance* Andy Stafford	248
19	The Neutral *Andy Stafford*	250
20	Readerly/Writerly *Warren Motte*	253
21	Sign *Dinda L. Gorlée*	256
22	Semiology *Dinda L. Gorlée*	259
23	Structuralism *Dinda L. Gorlée*	262
24	*Studium/Punctum* Andy Stafford	265
25	Work/Text *Gerald Prince*	267

Notes on Contributors   271
Index   275

Figures

6.1	Marlon Brando in *Julius Caesar*, directed by Joseph L. Mankiewicz	87
6.2	*Battleship Potemkin*, directed by Sergei M. Eisenstein	88
6.3	*Battleship Potemkin*, directed by Sergei M. Eisenstein	89
6.4	Charlie Chapin in *Modern Times*, directed by Charlie Chaplin	90
6.5	Charlie Chapin in *Modern Times*, directed by Charlie Chaplin	90
6.6	Greta Garbo in *Queen Christina*, directed by Rouben Mamoulian	91
6.7	Greta Garbo in *Ninotchka*, directed by Ernst Lubitsch	92
6.8	Aubrey Hepburn in *Sabrina*, directed by Billy Wilder	92
6.9	Marlon Brando and Eva Marie Saint in *On the Waterfront*, directed by Elia Kazan	97

Series Preface

Sometime in the late twentieth century, modernism, like philosophy itself, underwent something of an unmooring from (at least) linear literary history in favor of the multiperspectival history implicit in "new historicism" or, say, varieties of "presentism." Amid current reassessments of modernism and modernity, critics have posited various "new" or alternative modernisms—postcolonial, cosmopolitan, transatlantic, transnational, geomodernism, or even "bad" modernisms. In doing so, they have not only reassessed modernism as a category but also, more broadly, rethought epistemology and ontology, aesthetics, metaphysics, materialism, history, and being itself, opening possibilities of rethinking not only which texts we read as modernist but also how we read those texts. Much of this new conversation constitutes something of a critique of the periodization of modernism or modernist studies in favor of modernism as mode (or mode of production) or concept. Understanding Philosophy, Understanding Modernism situates itself amid the plurality of discourses, offering collections focused on key philosophical thinkers influential both to the moment of modernism and to our current understanding of that moment's genealogy, archeology, and becomings. Such critiques of modernism(s) and modernity afford opportunities to rethink and reassess the overlaps, folds, interrelationships, interleavings, or cross-pollinations of modernism and philosophy. Our goal in each volume of the series is to understand literary modernism better through philosophy as we also better understand a philosopher through literary modernism. The first two volumes of the series, those on Henri Bergson and Gilles Deleuze, have established a tripartite structure that serves to offer both accessibility to the philosopher's principle texts and to current new research. Each volume opens with a section focused on "conceptualizing" the philosopher through close readings of seminal texts in the thinker's oeuvre. A second section, on aesthetics, maps connections between modernist works and the philosophical figure, often surveying key modernist trends and shedding new light on authors and texts. The final section of each volume serves as an extended glossary of principal terms in the philosopher's work, each treated at length, allowing a fuller engagement with and examination of the many, sometimes contradictory, ways terms are deployed. The series is thus designed both to introduce philosophers and to rethink their relationship to modernist studies, revising our understandings of both modernism and philosophy, and offering resources that will be of use across disciplines, from philosophy, theory, and literature, to religion, the visual and performing arts, and often to the sciences as well.

Acknowledgments

We would like to thank the contributors to this volume for sharing their chapters and insights with us. Thanks also go to Vikki Fitzpatrick for her administrative assistance; to Keri Ruiz for the help she has given us in preparing this manuscript for production; and to Orlando Di Leo for his assistance with the frame grabs in Chapter 6. At Bloomsbury, we owe a debt of gratitude to Paul Ardoin, S. E. Gontarski, and Laci Mattison, the editors of this series, *Understanding Philosophy, Understanding Modernism*. Their helpful suggestions and steadfast encouragement at every stage of this project were most appreciated. Finally, thanks as well to Haaris Naqvi and Rachel Moore of Bloomsbury for steering this manuscript through the publication process.

Introduction

Jeffrey R. Di Leo and Zahi Zalloua

In her 1968 preface for the English translation of Roland Barthes's first book, *Writing Degree Zero* (1953), Susan Sontag described him as "[a] man of prodigious learning, unflagging mental energy, and acutely original sensibility, [who] has established his credentials as aesthetician, literary and theatre critic, sociologist, metapsychologist, social critic, historian of ideas, and cultural journalist."[1] Moreover, only fifteen years after his first book, Sontag had already dubbed him "a rare breed of intellectual virtuoso" comparable to Theodor Adorno, Kenneth Burke, and Karl Kraus.[2] She finds him to be "the most consistently intelligent, important, and useful critic—stretching that term—to have emerged anywhere in the last fifteen years."[3] Yet if Sontag is right that Barthes stretches the term "critic" (and we think she is), then to call him a *philosopher*, as we do—and she later does—also stretches the term "philosopher," especially for those within the academy. The question though of whether this philosophical stretching is a good thing or not depends on your audience.

Like Adorno, Burke, and Krauss, who each in their own way rejected the academic separation of aesthetics, history, sociology, and philosophy, Barthes too never allowed academic specialization to determine his philosophical character or intellectual process. When Sontag returns fifteen years later to comment on the complete career of the now recently deceased Barthes, she describes him not only as a "teacher, man of letters . . . connoisseur of strong ideas, [and] protean autobiographer" but also as a "moralist" and "philosopher of culture."[4] The latter two designations are important especially in the United States and the United Kingdom where academic philosophy in the second half of the twentieth century was loathe to welcome Barthes into their ranks.

But perhaps the same can be said of France too, where he was only elected to a chair at the Collège de France in March of 1976, a mere four years to the month of his death in 1980. And even here, it appears that the election process was initiated by him, rather than from Michel Foucault, who is sometimes said to have initiated his candidacy.[5] In fact, in his report on Barthes's candidacy, Foucault does not use the idolic language of Sontag to describe him:

> His appeal might seem to be limited to the trendy, as they say. But any historian would accept that fashions, enthusiasms, fads, or even exaggerations can, at a given moment, reveal the existence of more deep-rooted and fertile cultural phenomena. These voices, these few voices heard today outside the universities,

do they not form part of contemporary history? And should we not welcome them among us?[6]

Furthermore, it was Foucault who suggested that Barthes's chair in the French academy be in the somewhat arcane, if non-existent, academic discipline of "literary semiology."[7] While this term points to an earlier phase of his career exemplified by *Elements of Semiology* (1964) and *The Fashion System* (1967), it was one that by Barthes's own accounting was far behind him in 1976.

It was surpassed first by his "textuality" phase with the publications of *S/Z* and *Empire of Signs* in 1970 and *Sade, Fourier, Loyola* in 1971. In *S/Z*, for example, he gave a close reading of Balzac's *Sarrasine*, which was accomplished by the utilization of five "codes": the cultural, hermeneutic, proairetic, semantic, and symbolic. It became a signature event in the history of textual analysis because he also claimed that the codes he used to read this 1830 novella could differ in number and kind from one reading to the next. But just as critics and philosophers were beginning to grapple with the bold structural positions of his textualist phase, Barthes's work took another turn when he entered his "morality" phase with the publications of *The Pleasure of the Text* in 1972 and *Roland Barthes by Roland Barthes* in 1975.[8]

The designation—chair in "literary semiology"—was created especially for a writer for whom Foucault, based on his report to the aforementioned academy, regarded as someone from "outside" of the academy—and as most definitely someone other than a "philosopher." Even if one writes off Foucault's assessment of Barthes's worthiness to be welcomed "among *us*"—that is, among the distinguished membership of the French academy—as tainted by the bad terms between them that had festered for over ten years, the description of Barthes's work by Foucault as merely "trendy," that is, a "fashion" or a "fad," is one that would have been fully embraced by academic philosophy in the United States and the United Kingdom at the time. Moreover, one cannot help but feel a sense a cruelness in Foucault's use of "fashion" to describe Barthes's intellectual contributions when *The Fashion System* (1967) is often regarded as the crowning achievement of his semiological investigations.

This is why Sontag's assessment of Barthes—that is, the view of an outsider to the academy in general *and* academic philosophy in particular, albeit a formidable and widely respected observer of intellectual life—is valuable in helping to establish his place as a philosopher. Sontag's designation of him as a "moralist" serves to establish a connection between the type of philosophy Barthes practices to one with roots in ancient Greek philosophy, and extending into the moral philosophies of André Gide and Jean-Paul Sartre, whom she calls the two most influential writer-moralists of the twentieth century in France.[9] Fittingly, one of Barthes's first articles, published in 1942, over a decade before his first book, is on Gide; and in *Writing Degree Zero*, he argued against the positions of Sartre's "What Is Literature?" (1948), and advocated for *writing* (*écriture*), a term that bridges two other terms: language and style.[10] So too are both with him at the end: the last essay he published before he died was on Gide's journal writing, which was philosophically important to his notion of morality;[11] and his final book, *Camera Lucida: Reflections on Photography* (1980), where he showcases the paired notions of *spectrum* and *punctum*, which are an important part of his philosophical legacy, was inspired by Sartre's *The Imaginary* (1940) as well as Sontag's *On Photography* (1977).

Additionally, her designation of him as a "philosopher of culture" suggests a connection between his work and not only with the sociologies of everyday life of Henri Lefebvre and Michel de Certeau but also with critiques of mass culture from Adorno and Max Horkheimer to Jean Baudrillard. The combination of his work in both of these directions along with his contributions to the philosophy of language via his work in social mythology, textuality, *and* semiology ensure a preeminent place for his thought among philosophers who have significantly contributed to our understanding of modernity.

The unique combination of moralist and philosopher of culture gives Barthes's work an enduring quality that Sontag recognized back in 1982 when she claimed "of all of the intellectual notables who have emerged since World War II in France, Roland Barthes is the one whose work I am most certain will endure."[12] Now, forty years later, while some might quibble over whose work, for example, is the "most certain" to endure of a group of postwar French thinkers that includes Jacques Derrida, Michel Foucault, Julia Kristeva, and Jacques Lacan, no thinking person would disagree as to *whether* Barthes's will endure—because it has.

By the time Barthes passed away in March of 1980, he had already published a great amount of material that established him as one of the leading philosophers of the second half of the twentieth century. The designation "philosopher" here comes not from academic philosophy, where he has been widely viewed pejoratively as a "postmodern" philosopher or a "theorist," which are both code words among professional philosophers for a "non-philosopher." Rather, it comes from those who value his daring engagements with the ways in which modern culture manifests itself in or constitutes readers and writers. His professional crime seems to be that he wrote about writers and culture that appealed to a wide and dedicated readership, rather than to just the specialized readership of academic philosophy. He made philosophy a way of living one's life through insightful observation and fragmentary writing—with the latter perhaps being the most alienating aspect of his philosophical methodology to academic philosophers.

In addition to the voluminous work he published during his lifetime, he also left behind an extensive posthumous corpus that includes the five-volume *Œuvres complètes* (2002), the "outing" *Incidents* (1987), six full collections of teaching notes, two diaries, notes, and drafts for *Roland Barthes by Roland Barthes*, *A Lover's Discourse*, and *Camera Lucida*, and letters, notes, and short texts recently published as *Album* (2015). This posthumous material not only adds more nuance and depth to his philosophical achievements but also provides a wealth of resources to understanding dimensions of Barthes that were largely not available to scholars prior to his death.

Neil Badmington has called these works his "afterlives" and introduces them to us in his excellent book, *The Afterlives of Roland Barthes* (2016). Just as the recent publication of Foucault's, Derrida's, and Deleuze's lectures have provided an entirely new lens from which to view their philosophical contributions, Barthes posthumous publications are providing an opportunity to rethink his legacy as well. In our case, this material is especially useful in piecing together the legacies of his modernism and the full scope of his philosophical vision. So, just based on the recent volume of work by and on Barthes in the forty-plus years that have passed since his death, including the recent establishment of a journal dedicated to the study of his work,[13] it is clear that it was not just a "fad" as Foucault insinuates in his comment to the academy, but rather constituted something more enduring as Sontag speculated.

Moreover, unlike Adorno whose star has at best flickered in the fifty years since his death, Barthes has only shown more brightly. As one might recall, in the final year of his life, when Adorno was giving the first of his lectures on "An Introduction to Dialectical Thinking" to nearly 1,000 students at the Institute for Social Research at the Goethe–University Frankfurt, a few of them infamously rushed the podium. Three showered him with flower pedals and bore their breasts. After the incident, which came to be known as the *Busenaktion* ("breast action"), Adorno fled the room, whereupon students then distributed a leaflet which said, "Adorno as an Institution is Dead."[14] This occurred in 1969, the year *after* Sontag compared Barthes to Adorno. One wonders if she had written her preface a year later whether Barthes would have been compared to a philosopher whom students at the time were declaring "institutionally dead." But then again, Barthes was already *effectively* institutionally dead in 1969 as it would be another seven years before he would be elected to the French academy. Moreover, it might be argued that the enduring quality of his work is in large part due to his outsider role relative to the academy for most of his career.

As the chapters in this volume demonstrate, we are only now beginning to appreciate the enduring quality of his philosophical achievement. Understanding modernism through the work of Barthes is a journey through the incredibly wide range of twentieth-century thought that he engaged, developed, and inspired. Between 1950 and 1980, Barthes's work had an enormous impact on many different schools of thought including existentialism, structuralism, semiotics, Marxism, cultural studies, media studies, reception theory, and post-structuralism. His background in classics and philology matched by a methodology adapted from linguistics, psychoanalysis, and the social sciences resulted in a decidedly modern approach to literature and culture that eventually contributed as well to opening the door to postmodern thinking. Along the way, he built a philosophical portfolio that will endure long after many of the dominant academic philosophers of the 1960s and 1970s are long forgotten or even worse—left for dead by their students. Rather than Adorno, Burke, and Krauss, the company he keeps today is in line with the best philosophical work of Lacan, Foucault, and Derrida. And like them, his work continues to have a contested relationship with professional philosophy, particularly in the United States and the United Kingdom.

Mapping Barthes

The first part of *Understanding Barthes, Understanding Modernism*, "Mapping Barthes," is devoted to assessing the modern literary and philosophical contributions by Barthes prior to 1980, and primarily through the work published during his lifetime. It covers all of the major periods of his development from *Writing Degree Zero* (1953) to *Camera Lucida* (1980).

In "Roland Barthes's Myth of Photography," Jean-Michel Rabaté opens the collection with an assessment of the path of Barthes's work on the image over the span of his career. Barthes is often invoked by theoreticians of photography and film, as shown by Kaja Silverman's *The Miracle of Analogy* (2015), and many others. However, as is often argued, Barthes did change his position between the publication of *Mythologies* in 1957 and *Camera Lucida* in 1980, to the point that the later essays seem to contradict the first explorations. He moved from a rhetorical analysis of ideology to a deliberately "naïve" or "sentimental" analysis of the impact of family photographs. Rabaté not only finds this view to be reductive but also argues that it fails to explain the appeal Barthes has kept for various specialists of the image.

In this chapter, Rabaté traces Barthes's evolution in his various essays on photography. He suggests a deeper continuity between the debunking of "myths" underpinning images used by publicity, the semiology of a "message without a code," and the autobiographical exploration of the *"punctum,"* a detail speaking with an insistent and intimate voice in which the drama of loss and absence is replayed. In the process, he reconstructs the genealogy of Barthes's approaches to photography in order to make sense of his final confrontation with phenomenology. A "photogenic" thread is shown to connect the analyses of political mystification in *Mythologies*, the workings of systems of signs, and the ontology of loss and spectrality marking the final meditations.

The next chapter, by Thomas Pavel, turns to Barthes's *On Racine* (1963), a book where he argues for the priority of "text" over authorial intention. This argument, which is also made in other works by Barthes, is in many ways the centerpiece of his modern approach to writers and writing, if not also the philosophical locus of his methodology. In "Barthes and the Search for Rigor," Pavel distinguishes between, on the one hand, the inspiring use of modernist critical approaches sensitive to general properties of literary works—structural analysis and Sartre's existentialist view of theatrical plots—which allow Barthes to capture important aspects of Racine's tragedies and, on the other hand, the limited attention Barthes pays to Racine's own literary background, the moral psychology represented in his works, and the multiple differences between his plays. Pavel concludes by suggesting that when one examines past periods and cultures, one should also find out the specificity of their own message, rather than mostly focus on what we are interested in hearing.

Michael Moriarty continues discussion of some of the philosophical implications of his work in *On Racine* by considering it within the context of Barthes's overall engagement with the French classics. In "Barthes and the French Classics," Moriarty points out that in an early essay Barthes explores the pleasures of reading the literature of the seventeenth century. In his 1960s discussions of seventeenth-century texts, he plays down the issue of pleasure. *On Racine* aims to make the texts remote from, rather than connecting them with, our experience. In his essays on the moralists La Rochefoucauld and La Bruyère, Barthes emphasizes the difference between their worldview and that of a modern reader; yet he argues that their approach to writing raises issues of continuing relevance. Traces of the moralists' concerns can be seen in Barthes's own writing from the mid-1970s on, both in his preoccupations and in his approach to style. Moriarty's conclusion reviews Barthes's different approaches to the encounter with texts from the past.

In "Pleasure in Paradigm: *Sade, Fourier, Loyola,*" Rudolphus Teeuwen explores the absolute newness and delight these writers offer Barthes as a reader. Teeuwen claims that Barthes's delight consists of language spurning accepted ideological sense. Instead, Sade, Fourier, and Loyola arrange broken-up pieces of their first languages into paradigms of new second languages, defiantly nonreferential. The three authors delight because they realize Barthes's own aspiration for newness and allow him to read them in new ways. For Teeuwen, Barthes's new way of reading is that of "cruising" the text: reading a text primed for the excitement of first encounters, of experiencing new aspects each time he cruises it. The pleasure of this repeated experience of newness is allied with the pleasure of identifying and enjoying an author's personal charms and amiabilities, aspects of authorial style or personality of which new traces can be found again and again in repeated readings of a text.

Thomas Baldwin's "Understanding Barthes, Understanding Proust" continues the discussion of Barthes's philosophy of literature. He cleverly uses an early essay by Barthes on the novels of Jean Cayrol to glean insight on the literary modernism of Marcel Proust. In his 1952 article, "Jean Cayrol and His Novels," Barthes argues that classical art reduces the world to a structure of relations. In what Barthes calls the "classical-Romantic complex," the material stuff of the world is experienced as a distant spectacle, rather than as part of a human environment. Things are different, he says, in Cayrol's modern novels, where matter misbehaves and overcomes a classical, ideal distance. Barthes, however, does not refer to Proust—or to his masterpiece of literary modernism, *À la recherche du temps perdu*—in the article on Cayrol. Nevertheless, given Barthes's alignment of Proust elsewhere with both classical and modern authors (including Cayrol), Baldwin asks whether the distinctions he draws in this article can be made to bear upon Proust's work in particular and Barthes's philosophical understanding of modernism in general.

The next two chapters turn our attention from Barthes's philosophy of literature to his philosophy of film. In doing so, they also take us back to the work he did in the early phases of his career. This period extends from the essays he wrote in the early 1940s through the 1957 publication of *Mythologies*. Of particular note during this period is the publication of a series of essays on topics ranging from the Romans in films and wrestling to the face of Garbo and steak and chips in 1953, the same year his first book, *Writing Degree Zero*, was published. These essays dealt with the "myths" of everyday French life as revealed by culture and mass media—"myths" that Barthes regarded as suppressing the historicity of struggle in favor of the timelessness of nature.

Mythologies would become his first work in semiology, which he would formally introduce later in *Elements of Semiology* in 1964, a work that in turn demonstrated in some depth his debt to the linguistics of Ferdinand Saussure and A. J. Greimas. But just as semiology blossomed as a field in part through the influence of Barthes's early work, so too did cultural studies, albeit much later. Arguably, semiology hit its stride institutionally in the 1970s, whereas cultural studies would peak in the 1990s, some twenty years later. Still, both fields of study persist into the present, with many of their devotees continuing to attest to the formative impact of Barthes's early work on their respective fields.

In "Take Two: Barthes and Film in the Age of *Mythologies*," Steven Ungar examines the ten short texts on film topics Barthes wrote from 1943 through the 1957 publication of *Mythologies*. It does this in conjunction with an auto-critique of a 1989 piece in which Ungar explored what he referred to at the time as Barthes's resistance to film. Ungar also conducts a close reading of "A Sympathetic Worker," a piece Barthes devoted to Elia Kazan's 1954 feature, *On the Waterfront*. He concludes by setting Barthes's remarks on Kazan's film alongside concurrent reviews by Chris Marker and André Bazin, the latter of whom becomes the subject of the next chapter.

Dudley Andrew's "Barthes, Bazin, and Écriture" digs even deeper into the somewhat unexpected parallels between the careers of Barthes and Bazin, and the topics that drew their attention. They both became well-known critics after the Second World War with Bazin initially being the more famous of the two. Occasionally, they even wrote for the same journals and on the same films. Both were marked by photography and both prioritized the term *écriture*, which entered their critical vocabularies at virtually the same moment, the end of 1947. Bazin shaped his ideas about authorship and adaptation around cinematic *écriture*, while Barthes made *écriture* the topic of his first book. Perhaps, claims Andrew, thanks to Barthes, Bazin's subtle treatment of adaptations by directors like René Clément affected the discourse of Truffaut and Rohmer and perhaps their films later on.

Finally, in the last chapter in this section, Jeffrey R. Di Leo takes up the philosophical significance of Barthes becoming an unapologetic proponent of hedonism in literary studies. In "Barthes's Hedonism," Di Leo explains that Barthes stood alone among literary theorists in his own time—and now ours—in his explicit engagement with the hedonic tradition. In this chapter, Di Leo examines his engagement with this "very old tradition," which Barthes says in *The Pleasure of the Text* (1973) "has been repressed by nearly every philosophy; we find it defended only by marginal figures, Sade, Fourier; for Nietzsche, hedonism is a pessimism." Di Leo, on the other hand, addresses how hedonism becomes an optimism in the hands of Barthes and explores its roots in the aesthetic hedonism and journal writing of André Gide. In sum, to view Barthes as a hedonist is not only to regard him as a philosopher but also to understand how he adapted this ancient philosophy to his own needs as well as to those of modernity.

Legacies and Afterlives

The chapters in Part II, "Legacies and Afterlives," focus both on the posthumously published material and on the legacies of his work after his death in 1980. This later work has attracted attention, for example, in conjunction with notions of the neutral, gay writing, and critiques of everyday life.

In "Point Counterpoint: Derrida's 'The Deaths of Roland Barthes,'" Brian O'Keeffe discusses Jacques Derrida's "The Deaths of Roland Barthes," a text written in 1981 that offers a powerful assessment of Barthes's work, particularly *Camera Lucida*. Derrida's text proves to be an excellent way to open out many aspects of the Barthesian corpus, including posthumously published work such as *How to Live Together* (2013), his 1976–7 seminar at the Collège de France. By the same token—and not insignificantly— "The Deaths of Roland Barthes" puts Barthes in philosophical dialogue with Derrida. For O'Keeffe, this dialogue is one well-worth staging, especially since the question of legacies and afterlives is a theme common to both Derrida and Barthes, as well as one directly examined in Derrida's essay. Still, "The Deaths of Roland Barthes" has been largely ignored by both Derrida scholars and Barthes specialists. O'Keeffe's aim is accordingly to insist on the importance of this essay and to use it as a different way to engage with Barthes's work.

In "Objects of Desire: *Chosisme* after Object-Oriented Ontology," Zahi Zalloua turns our attention to Barthes's early essays on Alain Robbe-Grillet's poetics of the "new novel." Barthes describes Robbe-Grillet's art as *chosiste*—thing-oriented, or *chose*-oriented. This way of writing purports to liquidate the instrumentality of the object, making it appear as an "optical resistance." Barthes's *chosiste* approach finds much resonance with the proponents of the contemporary movement of Object-Oriented Ontology (OOO). And yet it also differs from OOO to the extent that Barthes's *chosisme* does not so much get rid of the subject in favor of a flat ontology (the anti- or posthumanism of OOO) as foreground the object and its entanglement with desire. Thus, Barthes's subsequent texts on *écriture*, argues Zalloua, focused more and more on this entanglement with desire and its pleasures.

Like Zalloua, Daniel T. O'Hara reveals yet another way in which Barthes's critical legacy continues to resonate in contemporary theory. In "Orpheus Turning: The Reader to Come in *Camera Lucida*," O'Hara analyzes closely the performance of self-irony in this posthumous text. Barthesian self-irony resembles the best of modernist self-irony. It is lyric and philosophical at the highest levels, even as it anticipates the "affective turn"[15] in contemporary criticism with its celebration of pathos, pity. The text would recreate its reader, as it would its author, along the lines of a never-seen photo of his mother, as if death itself were the only-begotten muse-reader appropriate for the future in which photography will replace literature as the dominant mode of art available to all.

The next chapter in this section is "No Wish to 'Understand' nor to 'Grasp': Opacity in the Work of Roland Barthes and Édouard Glissant" by Andy Stafford. Though Barthes and Glissant crossed paths in the mid-1950s as members of the editorial board of Maurice Nadeau's journal *Les Lettres Nouvelles*, any similarities, convergences, or parallels in their work did not emerge until the 1970s. Indeed, Glissant's thought is often linked to the Deleuzian rhizomatic, rather than the Barthesian *romanesque*. However, Barthes's writings in the wake of May 1968 begin to develop, just like Glissant's in the 1970s, a critique of science that involves a theorization of opacity. At the same time, as Glissant promotes postcolonial notions of the opaque in a variety of publications across the 1970s that are then collected into *Le Discours antillais* (1981), Barthes theorizes the "NVS," the "non-vouloir-saisir" (no wish to grasp) in *A Lover's Discourse* (1977), having ended *The Empire of Signs* (1970) with the "aucun vouloir-saisir" (no will-to-seize) of Japanese culture. If "opacity" becomes a key term in Glissant's critique of Western acts of "com-prendre"—in which anthropology's attempts to "comprendre" (understand) other cultures are seen to lead only to "prendre" (take/own)—Barthes strives to theorize the opacity of the other person. Stafford here aims to answer the resultant question: Is the opacity of the person the same as the opacity of cultures?

In "Roland Barthes and Don DeLillo on Living Together/Apart," Herman Rapaport situates aspects of Roland Barthes's 1976-7 seminar *How to Live Together* (2013) with Don DeLillo's novel *Falling Man* (2007). Central to both texts is the theme of living together/apart. Methodologically, Rappaport operationalizes Barthes's tropological critical approach as an interpretant whereby to analyze *Falling Man*, which, like Barthes's text, consists of numerous fragments of everyday experience concerning living together/apart, which are constructed figuratively. *Falling Man*, in turn, functions as an interpretant for Barthes's seminar consisting of an alphabetized list of tropes outlined and described by telegraphic commentary intended for future elaboration and development. Given that *How to Live Together* lacks an overall argument or thesis, apart from the insight that sociality can be broken down into a tropology of figures, a literary interpretant such as *Falling Man* is useful as a means of elucidating Barthes's seminar. A close reading of aspects of *Falling Man* exposes how Barthes and DeLillo are in an implicit interlocution that validates their understanding of the contemporary human condition in which we share.

The final chapter in Part II is "Barthes: Visual Culture and Homosexual Sociabilities" by Magali Nachtergael. Little attention has been paid to Barthes's gay visual culture and community and its potential influence on his writings. But when focusing on Barthes's relationships with art, artists, and visual culture, it appears that Barthes "situated" himself and his discourses in the margins. From the sanatorium to *Camera Lucida*, he theorized this marginal position while maintaining that his point of view was avowedly personal, if not that of an observer of his time. Starting with Barthes's thinking within the frame of visual studies, and then gay and queer studies, Nachtergael revisits some of his concepts (the neutral, the *mathesis singularis*, and the Marxist legacy in the background) and repositions his theoretical legacy in contemporary visual culture and theory.

Part II is followed by a Glossary, which continues to revisit more of Barthes's concepts. The contributions by Dinda Gorleé ("Sign," "Semiology," and "Structuralism"), Warren Motte ("Readerly/Writerly"), Brian O'Keeffe ("Haiku"), Gerald Prince ("Work/Text"), and Andy Stafford ("Author," "Codes," "Jouissance," "The Neutral," and "Studium/ Punctum") are presented here to both complement the work in Parts I and II as well as to fill in some of the more obvious philosophical gaps in the preceding material, particularly as related to the conceptual inventory Barthes utilizes to understand modernity.

Notes

1. Susan Sontag, "Preface," in Roland Barthes, *Writing Degree Zero* [1953], trans. Annette Lavers and Colin Smith (New York: Hill and Wang, 1968), vii.
2. Ibid.
3. Ibid.
4. Susan Sontag, "Writing Itself: On Roland Barthes," in *A Barthes Reader*, ed. and intro. Susan Sontag (New York: Hill and Wang, 1982), vii.
5. Louis-Jean Calvet, *Roland Barthes: A Biography*, trans. Sarah Wykes (Bloomington, IN: Indiana University Press, 1995), 212.
6. Ibid., 212–13.
7. Ibid., 213.
8. Roland Barthes, *Roland Barthes by Roland Barthes*, trans. Richard Howard (New York: Hill and Wang, 1977), 145.
9. Sontag, "Writing Itself," xix.
10. Roland Barthes, "On Gide and His Journal [1942]," trans. Richard Howard, in *A Barthes Reader*, ed. Susan Sontag (New York: Hill and Wang, 1982), 3–17.
11. Roland Barthes, "Deliberation [1979]," in *A Barthes Reader*, 479–95.
12. Ibid., vii.
13. The journal *Barthes Studies* (ISSN 2058-3680) is an open-access, independent, peer-reviewed journal for research in English on the work of Roland Barthes. The inaugural volume appeared on November 12, 2015, which is Barthes's 100th birthday. A new volume of the journal is published annually on November 12. Its editor is Neil Badmington, and several members of its editorial board are contributors to this volume: Thomas Baldwin, Magali Nachtergael, Jean-Michel Rabaté, and Andy Stafford. For more details, see http://sites.cardiff.ac.uk/barthes/. Last accessed March 3, 2021.
14. See Peter Gordon, "The Utopian Promise of Adorno's 'Open Thinking,' Fifty Years On," *The New York Review*, August 5, 2019. https://www.nybooks.com/daily/2019/08/05/the-utopian-promise-of-adornos-open-thinking-fifty-years-on/.
15. See, for example, Patricia Ticineto Clough and Jean Halley, eds., *The Affective Turn: Theorizing the Social* (Durham, NC: Duke University Press, 2007).

Bibliography

Badmington, Neil. *The Afterlives of Roland Barthes*. New York and London: Bloomsbury, 2016.

Barthes, Roland. *Album: Unpublished Correspondence and Texts* [2015]. Trans. Jody Gladding. Ed. Éric Marty. New York: Columbia University Press, 2018.

Barthes, Roland. *Camera Lucida: Reflections on Photography* [1980]. Trans. Richard Howard. New York: Vintage Classics, 2020.

Barthes, Roland. *Comment Vivre Ensemble: Simulations romanesques de quelques espaces quotidiens. Cours et séminaires au Collège de France 1976–1977*. Ed. Claude Coste. Paris: Seuil/IMEC, 2002.

Barthes, Roland. *Elements of Semiology* [1964]. Trans. Annette Lavers and Colin Smith. New York: Hill and Wang, 1968.

Barthes, Roland. *Empire of Signs* [1970]. Trans. Richard Howard. New York: Hill & Wang, 1982.

Barthes, Roland. *The Fashion System* [1967]. Trans. Matthew Ward and Richard Howard. New York: Hill and Wang, 1983.

Barthes, Roland. *How to Live Together: Novelistic Simulations of Some Everyday Spaces—Notes for a Lecture Course and Seminar at the Collège de France (1976-1977)*. Trans. Kate Briggs. New York: Columbia University Press, 2013.

Barthes, Roland. *Incidents* [1987]. Trans. Teresa Lavender Fagen. London and New York: Seagull Books, 2010.

Barthes, Roland. *A Lover's Discourse: Fragments* [1977]. Trans. Richard Howard. London: Jonathan Cape, 1979.

Barthes, Roland. *Mythologies: The Complete Edition, In a New Translation* [1957]. Trans. Richard Howard. New York: Hill and Wang, 2012.

Barthes, Roland. *Œuvres complètes*. Ed. Éric Marty. 2nd ed. 5 vols. Paris: Gallimard, 2002.

Barthes, Roland. *On Racine* [1963]. Trans. Richard Howard. New York: Hill and Wang, 1964.

Barthes, Roland. *The Pleasure of the Text* [1973]. Trans. Richard Miller. New York: The Noonday Press, 1975.

Barthes, Roland. *Roland Barthes by Roland Barthes* [1975]. Trans. Richard Howard. New York: Hill and Wang, 1977.

Barthes, Roland. *Sade, Fourier, Loyola* [1971]. Trans. Richard Miller. Baltimore: Johns Hopkins University Press, 1976.

Barthes, Roland. *Writing Degree Zero* [1953]. Preface by Susan Sontag. Trans. Annette Lavers and Colin Smith. New York: Hill and Wang, 1968.

Calvet, Louis-Jean. *Roland Barthes: A Biography*. Trans. Sarah Wykes. Bloomington, IN: Indiana University Press, 1995.

Clough, Patricia Ticineto, and Jean Halley, eds. *The Affective Turn: Theorizing the Social*. Durham, NC: Duke University Press, 2007.

DeLillo, Don. *Falling Man*. New York: Scribner, 2007.

Derrida, Jacques. "The Deaths of Roland Barthes [1981]." In *Psyche: Inventions of the Other, Volume 1*. Ed. Peggy Kamuf and Elizabeth G. Rottenberg. Stanford: Stanford University Press, 2007. 264–97.

Glissant, Édouard. *Le Discours antillais*. Paris: Editions du Seuil, 1981.

Gordon, Peter. "The Utopian Promise of Adorno's 'Open Thinking,' Fifty Years On." *The New York Review*, 5 August 2019. https://www.nybooks.com/daily/2019/08/05/the-utopian-promise-of-adornos-open-thinking-fifty-years-on/. Last accessed 2 March 2021.

Sartre, Jean-Paul. *The Imaginary: A Phenomenological Psychology of the Imagination* [1940]. Revisions and historical introduction by Arlette Elkaïm-Sartre. Trans. and philosophical introduction by Jonathan Webber. New York: Routledge, 2004.

Sartre, Jean-Paul. "What Is Literature?" [1948]. In *"What Is Literature?" and Other Essays*. Intro. Steven Ungar. Cambridge, MA: Harvard University Press, 1988. 21–246.

Silverman, Kaja. *The Miracle of Analogy, or The History of Photography, Part 1*. Stanford: Stanford University Press, 2015.

Sontag, Susan. *On Photography*. New York: Farrar, Straus and Giroux, 1977.

Sontag, Susan. "Preface." In Roland Barthes, *Writing Degree Zero* [1953]. Trans. Annette Lavers and Colin Smith. New York: Hill and Wang, 1968. vii–xxi.

Sontag, Susan. "Writing Itself: On Roland Barthes." In *A Barthes Reader*. Ed. and intro. Susan Sontag. New York: Hill and Wang, 1968. vii–xxxviii.

Part I

Mapping Barthes

1

Roland Barthes's Myth of Photography

Jean-Michel Rabaté

Analogy and Photogeny

In her superb book on the history of photography, *The Miracle of Analogy* (2015), Kaja Silverman begins her survey of the medium with Roland Barthes's *Camera Lucida*.[1] Her analysis of how photography is founded on an analogy with the world disregards the usual considerations of the technical medium's cultural or technological filters. Her general approach is indebted to Barthes's analyses. Silverman is aware that Barthes's rethinking of photography in *Camera Lucida* was prepared by essays, all influential, the main one being "The Photographic Message" dating from 1961. I would like to take the measure of a displacement that some readers saw as a recantation. Whereas in the essays of the 1950s and the 1960s, Barthes insisted on the mythological nature of the photograph, famously defining photography as a "message without a code,"[2] and then went on to explain that photography cannot for all that be taken as purely "denotative," that its objectivity had to be "mythical";[3] his last book contradicts his earlier semiotic point of view. In *Camera Lucida*, stating that he is and has always been a "realist," he writes:

> The realists, of whom I am one and of whom I was already one when I asserted that the Photograph was an image without code—even if, obviously, certain codes do inflect our reading of it—the realists do not take the photograph for a "copy" of reality, but for an emanation of *past reality*: a *magic*, not an *art*.[4]

In 1980, which is the date of the publication of the latter book, Barthes's last one, since he died a few months after, he mentions "the image" and not a "message." This slight shift betrays a considerable terminological change. If Barthes did change his position between 1957 and 1980, to the point that the later essays seem to contradict the first explorations, this change is not a recantation but a modified inflexion, a new intonation. As Borges stated: "Perhaps universal history is the history of the various intonations of a few metaphors."[5] Similarly, Barthes's thinking moved insensibly, via serial intonations of a few metaphors, from a rhetorical analysis of ideology to deliberately naïve or sentimental analyses of the impact of family photographs. We need to follow this evolution so as to understand the continuity between the debunking of "myths" underpinning images used by publicity, the semiology of a "message without a code," and the autobiographical exploration of the "*punctum*," a detail speaking with an insistent and intimate voice in which the drama of loss and absence is replayed. A genealogy of Barthes's approaches to photography is needed in order to make sense of the shift from semiology to phenomenology.

Most commentators point to the 1970 "Third Meaning"[6] essay about a few of Eisenstein's film stills for *Ivan the Terrible*, in which Barthes developed the notion of a supplementary (third) meaning appearing in stray details envisaged outside denotation (the description of reality, the first meaning) or connotation (the meanings encoded by various systems of values, the cultural encoding of the second meaning). His original thesis was established both from a film, as the details from Eisenstein's images had first to be contextualized in the whole film's narrative, and from equivalents of still photographs. However, it is impossible to make sense of Barthes's later theory of photography without having followed his progression through images, his evolving understanding of their different codes, and his analysis of the powerful personal impact that images exert on him.

The importance of the visual field for Barthes appears as early as 1952, when he began publishing his "mythologies."[7] If Barthes defined myth as a "type of speech" in the synthetic analysis entitled "Myth Today,"[8] he nevertheless used one photograph from *Paris Match* to explain the redoubled structure of the myth. We see a young black soldier saluting the French flag on the cover of the weekly magazine. The image shapes a patriotic "myth" in which French nationalism both reveals and conceals its colonialist and exploitative nature.[9] First, we have to read the image, which entails that we recognize the flag and the uniform, and also see that the boy is not only black but also young, a child almost who nevertheless wears a French uniform. The complex suggestions force us to participate in the unfolding of the myth of the empire. The editors of that *Paris Match* issue felt that the photograph needed a caption; it stated: "The nights of the Army. The young Diouf has come from Ouagadougou with his friends, children from military personnel in French Africa, to open the show the French Army presents in the Palais des Sports this week."[10] Barthes explains that he reads *Paris Match*, an illustrated weekly on the Right, just because he finds it at his barber's, as if he had to excuse his indulging in popular illustrated weeklies.

The image allowed him to make a main point: here was a sign saying that a black soldier salutes the French flag that then turns into a second-order signifier; this time it asserts that France is a great empire to which the sons of its exploited minions pay homage. No need to know anything more about the young Diouf, who came all the way from Ouagadougou to Paris. Diouf is neither a symbol nor an allegory of French colonialism, but a myth. His smiling face does not interest us for anthropological reasons, as if we were trying to connect him with other African types, or because we find him cute. Diouf remains flat and nameless because he illustrates the pure form of the myth:

> the Negro who salutes is not the symbol of the French Empire: he has too much presence, he appears as a rich, fully experienced, spontaneous, innocent,

indisputable image. But at the same time this presence is tamed, put at a distance, made almost transparent; it recedes a little, it becomes the accomplice of a concept which comes to it fully armed, French imperiality: once made use of, it becomes artificial (*empruntée*).[11]

I highlight two terms, *indiscutable* and *empruntée*, noting that the latter also means "borrowed." Barthes avoids a theoretical danger, the risk of seeing his concept of myth conflated with that of a "symbol." Why would such an analysis be damaging or misleading? Romantic notions of the symbol or of allegory would entail that a true or fictitious biography of the young hero would be composed, before making him rise to the level of a superior value, like that of the nation. By refusing such a movement, Barthes leaves us with an enigmatic signifier that is almost devoid of meaning. It remains in an expectation because it lies in wait for meaning to be provided by the axis or the plane of the signified: "this history which drains out of the form will be wholly absorbed by the concept."[12] The concept of French imperiality suffices to restore a narrative to an image devoid of direction or depth. Barthes concludes that this process ushers in "a chain of causes and effects, motives and intentions. Unlike the form, the concept is in no way abstract: it is filled with the situation. Through the concept, it is a whole history which is implanted in the myth."[13] These formulations are tricky, especially when Barthes explains later in "Myth Today" that myth coming from the Right is even more devoid of history than when it comes from the Left. But are there even left-wing mythologies? These hesitations are crucial when we read those pages with *Camera Lucida* in mind.

I will be looking at a few sections of "mythologies" in order to assess how the new translation, accompanied by relevant images, has modified our understanding not only of what constitutes a "myth" for Barthes but also of its ontology insofar as it is linked with the Image. What has changed since we began reading *Mythologies* in English? The new translation by Richard Howard, plus the insertion of the photographs discussed by Barthes, make different contexts appear, and they become more relevant in the essays hinging around images.

It is extremely hard to make sense of the "Iconography of Abbé Pierre"[14] without the picture of the celebrated priest. Here again, Barthes is discussing a cover of *Paris Match*; the magazine announced that the priest had been given 120 million francs, 20,000 covers, 12,000 sweaters, 10,000 trousers, 8,000 overcoats, 7,000 shoes, and 2,000 shirts to help the poor and homeless.[15] The cover presents the priest with his long beard and unkempt hair hugging a little girl in need of protection. *Paris Match* still surveys the "passionate life of the apostle of homeless people." Barthes must have seen this cover at his barber's, which is why he zeroes in on the hair. He brilliantly expatiates on how the hairstyle portrays a modern saint:

> Abbé Pierre's haircut, visibly conceived to achieve a neutral equilibrium between short hair (an indispensable convention to avoid notice) and shaggy hair (a suitable condition to manifest scorn for other conventions), here joins the capillary archetype of sanctity: the saint is above all a being without formal context; the idea of fashion is antipathetic to the idea of sanctity.[16]

Barthes lays out the fundamental rule of semiotics: there is no neutrality among signs, for there are only signs of neutrality. The hair of the famous priest is a token, highly recognizable as such, inscribing him in a series of priestly figures, from the evil Frolo of the *Hunchback of Notre-Dame*, who was clean-shaven, probably because glabrous rhymes with scabrous, whereas the beloved Father Charles de Foucauld, who lived and died among the Tuaregs in the Sahara, had a nicely pointed beard.

It seems that the impetus for these "mythologies" was provided by regular visits to Barthes's hairdresser, which explains why one of these vignettes analyzes the way Romans are classified according to their hairstyle by Hollywood. The text begins thus: "In Mankiewicz's *Julius Caesar*, all the male characters wear bangs."[17] This becomes self-evident when we look at the promotion image created by Mankiewicz, when his film was released in 1953.[18] It has seven profiles, five men beginning with Marlon Brando, James Mason and John Gielguld, then Deborah Kerr and Greer Garson. The effect of a Roman frieze is convincing and forces viewers to focus on the weird bangs and fringes falling with several types of curls on their foreheads. Barthes notes ironically that bald Romans didn't exist and that the hairdresser was the film's principal artisan.[19] Even if the actors look like Hollywood stars, their bangs signify a link with a mythical Romanity. French spectators can only laugh, finding "comical the mixture of these gangster-sheriffs with the little Roman fringe: rather like an excellent music-hall gag."[20] Sweat is added as a corrective to the faces so as to reintroduce seriousness: sweat is read by Barthes not as a sign of the excessive heat of Roman summers but as a symptom of moral drama: "we are meant to be in the sign of an agonizingly laborious virtue, i.e. in the very locus of tragedy, which perspiration is intended to represent."[21] The Roman cogito would be condensed in the phrase: "to sweat is to think!"[22] Then there is one exception—one does not sweat, it is Caesar, which means that Caesar does not think; he will pay dearly for his mindlessness. Barthes deconstructs elegantly these ambiguous signs, all calling up the mixture of deliberately unkempt hair and virile beard in Abbé Pierre's portraits.

Reading Barthes's critique of Abbé Pierre's studious attempt at looking natural, which concludes with a Marxist appeal to social justice instead of charity,[23] we may forget that the iconic French priest had already appeared earlier in a context dominated by images and by film. In "The Poor and the Proletariat," Barthes examines Charlie Chaplin's 1953 decision to give half the sum of money he had obtained from a Soviet jury to the same Abbé Pierre.[24] Jacqueline Guittard's illustrated edition of Barthes's text shows Abbé Pierre sitting in front of Charlie Chaplin at the hotel Crillon in Paris.[25] Chaplin had just been awarded the International Peace Prize from an organization masterminded by the Soviet government. We see him smiling, his full shock of white hair reflected in a huge mirror. Seated near him, Abbé Pierre has tamed the exuberance of his hair and beard. Chaplin wears a suit and tie, the priest a military parka, a dirty coat; he holds a walking stick resembling a shepherd's crook from biblical times. To that pious image, Barthes grafts memories of Chaplin's *Modern Times*, hinting that he transformed the proletariat into the sentimental notion of "the poor." Barthes believes that Chaplin never considered the proletariat politically, unlike Brecht, who did. If Chaplin showed alienation and made fun of cops and bourgeois, he addressed a "primitive proletarian, still external to the Revolution."[26] The essay rejects the alliance between an apparently well-off Hollywood filmmaker and a poor French priest: "In short, this is why Chaplin's poor man triumphs over everything: because he eludes every temptation, rejects every sponsorship and never invests in man except as man alone. His anarchy, politically questionable, may represent in art the most efficient form of revolution."[27] Indeed, Chaplin was a few years ahead of his last film, the notorious 1957 *A King in New York*, which was banned by the American censors for allegedly endorsing communist ideals.

Barthes is even more scathing about "The Great Family of Man,"[28] Edward Steichen's photographic exhibition that had been shown at the Musée d'Art Moderne in 1956. Barthes skewers the spurious unanimity of "all men" presented in a mythical manner, as if, despite differences of appearances and customs, all men, women, and children were bound to follow the same course. He denounces the good feelings supposed to be induced by a show predicated on an erasure of historical and cultural tensions, marred by grandiloquent and sententious captions. Steichen's sentimental syncretism is taken to task for revealing a reduction of History to Nature—those two archrivals always capitalized by Barthes, who then asks pointedly why no picture represents Emmett Till, murdered a year earlier at the age of fourteen for having allegedly whistled at a white woman: "why not ask the parents of Emmett Till, the young black murdered by white men, what *they* think of *the great family of men?*"[29] Unlike the black boy saluting the French flag, this absence is all the more revealing. Barthes then hones in on a French scene: the North African inhabitants of "Barbès" in Paris who had had a scuffle with the police in August 1955. They too wonder what's their link with the "family of man."

Is Barthes aiming at shock effects with these images? It is enough to look at his essay on "Shock Photos"[30] to realize that he rejects this type of gut-level appeal. We find the executed Guatemalan looters in a double page, once more taken from *Paris Match*. Four photos are compassionately blurred, although unhappily wrongly captioned in the English translation. What photo 9 presents as the execution of Guatemalan communists is in fact an execution of looters who had been caught red-handed by the army. Barthes begins his essay by referring to Geneviève Serreau, who was addressing a more political exhibition. What is quite startling is the equanimity of the caption's tone. Catching the very instant when the four looters are struck by a volley of bullets, the journalist comments impassibly: "In this photo, which evokes an engraving by Goya, we see the last spasms of the men condemned to death, riddled with bullets. They had been caught looting farms."[31] Another insert explains that given this hurried and final form of justice, 700 people asked for political asylum to various embassies in the capital, and that the ambassador from San Salvador had to rent a villa in order to sort out the reds (Communists) from the White (Rightists).

These horrifying images were shown in a series of "Shock Photos" displayed at the Galerie d'Orsay. One finds side by side an Austrian goalkeeper jumping desperately and missing the ball, the screaming face of Adnan Malki's fiancée after his assassination in Syria, French cops with raised truncheons, columns of prisoners marching, soldiers and fields of skulls, and so on. In this case, Barthes sensibly rejects the forceful imposition of one type of "overconstructed" horror[32] on the viewer. He explains why these images fail to touch or reach us:

> This is because, as we look at them, we are in each case dispossessed of our judgment: someone has shuddered for us, reflected for us, judged for us; the photographer has left us nothing—except a single right of intellectual acquiescence: we are linked to these images only by a technical interest; overindicated by the artist himself, for us they have no history, we can no longer *invent* our own reception of this synthetic nourishment, already perfectly assimilated by its creator.[33]

To this saturated meaning, Barthes opposes historical paintings like the well-known portrait of Napoleon crossing the Alps by Jean-Louis David. From 1801 to 1805, David made no less than five versions of this famously idealized picture. Barthes praises the romantic heroization of the French leader in the name of art:

> painters have left to movement the amplified sign of the unstable, what we might call the *numen*, the solemn shuddering immobilization of a pose nonetheless impossible to fix in time; it is this motionless exaggeration of the ineffable—which will later, in the cinema, be called *photogeny*—which is the very site where art begins.[34]

I want to stress the curious oxymorons used here: "*le transissement solennel d'une pose pourtant impossible à installer dans le temps*," and "*majoration immobile de l'insaisissable.*"[35] Both complex phrases combine the freezing of time and the impossibility of something like a snapshot, given the slow composition technique of paintings in 1805. Barthes may have known that the emperor had refused to sit for the painting, requesting instead an idealized version of who he was. David obliged, and asked his son to pose; the result was indeed staggering, but he felt the need to redo the painting four more times. The result has very little to do with History: Is it pure Myth, or is it Art? Barthes tends to categorize these paintings as Art because of an excess in sheer expressivity, of what he calls the "*entêtement de l'expression, que l'on pourrait aussi appeler rhétorique.*"[36] Howard translates as "that persistence of expression that we might also call rhetorical," downplaying what should be the "stubbornness" or the "obstinacy of expression," terms that will find a new context with the "third meaning."

The reference to Art exemplifies Barthes's refusal to let a legible signified be thrust in front of his eyes—however, in this case, he makes just an exception for a series of "news-agency photographs," those that were included in issues of *Paris Match*. So, we are back to Malki's fiancée and the executed Guatemalan looters. Here again, a similar stubbornness appears: "*où le fait surpris éclate dans son entêtement*," or, as Howard translates, quite adequately this time, "where the fact, surprised, explodes in all its stubbornness."[37] What is it that explodes so suddenly? It is the curious discrepancy between the images and the texts that accompany them, which creates another type of "scandal" than that of Napoleon perilously perched on a rearing horse; this time, it is the fact in the "very obviousness of its obtuse nature."[38] The images appear calmer than the apparent neutrality of the written captions. Truly, they are "inferior to their legend,"[39] both irreducible to mythologization and less captivating than the words chosen to document state terror.

It is therefore the very banality, as Hannah Arendt spoke of the "banality of evil," that shocks: spectators need to take a more active role, to supplement these blank testimonies of horror with a personal assessment. The photographer disappears, he too being "inferior" to his legend. This may be why the anonymous narrator of *Paris Match* notes that an onlooker is taking a photograph of the dead bodies riddled with bullets. Barthes's conclusion is superb: "Here we are indeed concerned with that critical catharsis Brecht demands, and no longer, as in the case of painting, with an emotive purgation: thus perhaps we can rediscover the two categories of the epic and the tragic. The literal photograph introduces us to the scandal of horror, not to horror itself."[40] Barthes's genius is to touch on what strikes any viewer who is captivated by these awful images; indeed, there is a scandal in the scene; such a scandal is conveyed by Barthes's apparently bland and acquiescing mode of writing. We imagine for a minute that we return to normalcy when we see a priest blessing the dead, soldiers getting ready for more killings, a crowd of onlookers slightly disappointed and eager for more blood, and a local photographer moving away with his huge Stetson hat and his camera in his hand. In fact, we have reached a point beyond terror and pity; we become ethical or "critical" subjects. Our anger is fully political for it cannot be "purified" by any catharsis.

The same sense of scandal continues when we move to less disheartening images, one such being a "pink dinner" provided by *Elle*, unhappily rendered in a black-and-white image in the new translation of *Mythologies*. However, even deprived of its sickening and eye-popping pink hue, the food presented on those pages betrays an excess of glazing: layers upon layers of sauces, icing, jellies, creams, custards, white chocolate drippings, spilled honey, or any available transparent and sticky substance will cover all dishes with a universal sheet of liquid coating. Why is it that, like fashion, the recipes of the previous generation are so dismally anti-erotic? This culinary kitsch transmigrates effortlessly from one cookbook to the next. Barthes, who was a gourmet, demonstrates that the cuisine sold by *Elle* to its low-income readers, the majority, in fact, is a dream of impossible consumption. In this case, obviously, the reader will never learn how to cook. It may be because the viewer's gaze has been fed by an excess of shiny surfaces, a phantasmatic surfeit meant to signify bourgeois luxury.

Barthes was disgusted by the obscene display of gelatinous surfaces, which corresponds to his nausea facing a pseudo-nature always invoked by myth. The best evocation of this instinctive recoil is to be found in the synthetic section of *Mythologies*:

> What is sickening in myth is its resort to a false nature, its superabundance of significant forms, as in these objects which decorate their usefulness with a natural appearance. This will to weigh the signification with the full guarantee of nature cause a kind of nausea: myth is too rich, and what is in excess is precisely its motivation.[41]

Myth is defined as fake luxury, an overlay of decoration whose function is to play at being natural by erasing the historical forces needed for such a production. Just as an excess of sugary glazing reiterates that we are facing "comfort food," a kitschy decoration hiding, say, a toilet seat disguised in a plastic rendition of forest moss, betrays a desperate attempt at reintroducing a pseudo-natural motivation: whatever happens takes place because it follows its deep essence, and one cannot do anything in front of a fate settled once for all—here is the pernicious ideological message of myth for Barthes.

However, one might object that these mythical images remain mythical even when they betray their artificiality. The constructedness in mythical images appears even in the iconic faces of movie stars. Barthes tries to understand the common point of the portraits coming from the Harcourt Studios. The faces of Gérard Philippe, Danielle Darrieux, Jean Marais, and Danièle Delorme exhibit all the same sublimated features presenting an idealized face, in order to "capture this unearthly beauty."[42] Barthes pretends to believe in this magic:

> as if this countenance, floating between the stage's crude earth and the "town"'s radiant sky, could be only momentarily caught by surprise, ravished from its natural intemporality, then devoutly abandoned to its solitary and regal course; sometimes maternally plunged earthward, sometimes ecstatically upraised, the actor's face seems to unite with his celestial home in an ascension without haste and without muscles, quite contrary to an onlooking humanity which, belonging to a different zoological class and capable of movements only by legwork (and not by face), must return to its residence on foot.[43]

Whether ascending to a mystical sky or keeping a steady link with mother earth, sublimation elevates the lit and transfigured visages to a loftier realm abstracted from daily cares and social relations. What is funny in this soft parody is that Barthes uses the rhetoric of "photogeny" that has marked the first wave of film criticism in France.

The concept of "photogeny" had been coined by Louis Delluc, a remarkable film critic and director who published his book *Photogénie* in 1920, one year before publishing the first book written (in French) about Charlie Chaplin. Jean Epstein developed the term in influential essays on film in the late 1920s. For Delluc, the aim of film and photography is to make visible the beauty that is already contained in the world. For Epstein, film turns into a new epistemology because it ushers in a new type of knowledge, unveiling an essence of things and beings that could not be perceived otherwise given their fluctuating appearances.[44] With different emphases, Delluc and Epstein define "photogeny" less as a quality possessed by actors and faces than as the almost magical power that images and film have of transforming people and things. The ephemeral intensity that burns the image in their early films testifies to this positive meaning of "photogeny."

Barthes attempts to debunk the effect of the concept by exposing its mechanism, which boils down to the production of an ethereal illusion: the actor becomes a myth after he or she has been separated from terrestrial limitations, rendered almost divine, soaring up in the painted paradise of alienated imaginations. Two counterexamples are those photographers who do not sublimate their portraits; these are two women, Thérèse Le Prat and Agnès Varda. If Le Prat remained conventional with her iconic portraits of singers and stars like Juliette Gréco, Jeanne Moreau, Jean-Louis Barrault, and Louis Jouvet that one finds in her 1952 *Autres Visages d'Acteurs*, Agnès Varda had already started her career as an irreverent, mocking, and innovative photographer. She had become Jean Vilar's official photographer when he directed the Théâtre National Populaire, whose productions elicited rave reviews from Barthes.

One exception is Greta Garbo. In "Garbo's face," Barthes once more discusses a film, *Queen Christina* this time, so as to establish a contrast between Garbo's idealized, formidable, hieratic features and Audrey Hepburn's vivacious mobility suggesting either a child-woman or a cat-woman.[45] For once, Barthes does not cavil or object to the undeniable attraction of Garbo's face. Comparing it with a "snowy" mask, he zooms in on the eyes, presented as "two rather tremulous wounds."[46] However, Chaplin's funny face somehow adheres to his unmitigated praise: "Even in its extreme beauty, this face not drawn but rather sculptured in smooth and friable matter, i.e. both perfect and ephemeral, calls up Chaplin's flour-white complexion, his vegetally dark eyes, his totemic visage."[47] Barthes appreciates the abstract, desexualized appearance of her superb features, but then operates a surprising superposition of Charlie Chaplin and Greta Garbo. However, there is no sneer here, only admiration for both, which proves that Garbo's face is not just a mask. The fact that hers is a "face" is confirmed by our wish to link her imaginatively with other faces: "the mask is merely an addition of lines, the face is above all a thematic recall, some lines evoking other lines."[48] This openness to the others ensures that Garbo's beauty never turns into a petrifying Medusa's head; she embodies a reassuring transition "from terror to charm."[49]

In all these essays, what is at stake is a variable use of the term "photogeny," which finally comes to the fore in "Electoral photogeny."[50] We return to political satire here, a satire that does not spare anyone. Barthes comments on what was then a new device, the insertion of personal photographs showing the likeness of political candidates in poster and leaflets. They were distributed before the 1956 election for a new Parliament after the collapse of the Mendès-France government in 1955. One discovers a young Le Pen, whose first name was only Jean and not yet Jean-Marie then. He is featured alone in the National Union list, whereas the Communist Party had two candidates, one a distant aunt of mine, Maria Rabaté, the other Roger Garaudy, later pilloried by Louis Althusser.[51] Maria Rabaté and Roger Garaudy were elected, for this was a time when the Communist Party got more than one-fourth of the French votes. These elections were marked by violent actions from the extreme right, as they were enraged by Pierre Mendès-France socialist orientation; the spokesman for the Right was Pierre Poujade, a populist leader skewered regularly in *Mythologies*.

Barthes evinces a sharp understanding of how photographs construct social reality: "Photography's conventions themselves are replete with signs. The full-face shot accentuates the candidate's realist outlook, especially if he is furnished with 'focalizing' spectacles. . . . A three-quarter pose, more common, suggests the tyranny of an ideal: the gaze dissolves nobly into the future."[52] His attention is captured at first by the way photographs render these candidates more human, closer to us. They convey a certain style, and let us guess details about their private lives that had been concealed in earlier campaigns. To this, Barthes adds that they allow us to see the candidates' ideology.[53] However, having stated this, Barthes does not fall back on a neo-Marxist position that would entail a critique of the bourgeois ideology. Here, in the indiscriminate use of personal pictures for the aims of a campaign, he sees that the candidates all want to come closer to their constituencies, and wish to elicit if not immediately a "conversion" to their ideas, at least pave the way to a "complicity" with what they represent:

> the campaign photo is a mirror that reflects the familiar, the known, it proposes to the elector his own effigy clarified, magnified, proudly elevated into a type. Moreover, it is this glorification which quite precisely defines *photogeny*: the elector finds himself simultaneously expressed and heroized, he is invited to elect himself, to weigh the mandate he is about to give with a veritable physical transference: he is delegating his "race."[54]

The term "race" can surprise; the quotes show that it is the slang use Barthes is evoking: it means something like "people whose gut reactions are identical with mine." What he is describing comes close to Freud's analysis of mass hypnosis in "Group Psychology and the Analysis of the Ego," a text in which Freud showed how crowds get so entranced by a leader's personality that all is handed over to him without any condition or critical judgment. Political hypnosis has taken place, here performed by the magic of photography reduced to "photogeny." The genius of photography, its *"malin génie,"* Descartes would say, is to delude by releasing those shiny and captivating images that all exert their power unconsciously, via *"photogénie."* What works positively for the face of Greta Garbo takes on a more sinister aspect in the context of politics. Barthes sees photography as the pure inverse of politics: "To the degree that photography is an ellipsis of language and the condensation of an ineffable social reality, it constitutes an anti-intellectual weapon and tends to dodge 'politics' (i.e., a body of problems and solutions) for the sake of a 'lifestyle'—a sociomoral status."[55]

This analysis anticipates Louis Althusser's famous description of ideology as a button-holding interpellation, a notion anticipated by what Barthes called an "adhomination"—from "ad hominem"—that is a direct address that catches you not only because you have to say who you are, but in the very saying you become the other's puppet.[56] This concept is deployed in "Myth Today," when Barthes untangles the specific mechanism by which History is transformed into Nature: "We now understand why, *in the eyes of the myth consumer*, the intention, the adhomination of the concept can remain manifest, without however, appearing to have an interest in the matter: what causes mythical speech to be uttered is perfectly explicit, but it is immediately frozen into something natural (*transie dans une nature*)."[57] Like photography, myth neither hides nor excessively displays appearances: appearing to provide pure appearances, it distorts them in fact by resorting to the naturalizing trick of which any publicity photograph can be an example.

Thanks to a more accurate translation and to an edition that includes images, we can connect the dots and understand Barthes's progression when he moved from the critical debunking of "myths" underpinning images used by publicity to more complex semiological analyses of "messages without a code," and finally to the autobiographical exploration of why certain images reveal a *"punctum,"* a detail speaking with an insistent and intimate voice. Barthes ended his trajectory with a phenomenology of the poignantly emotive "punctum" contained in some photos not as a recantation of his first theorizing, but an awareness that ideology critique had had its day, had become boring and predictable. The multicolored thread that connects Barthes's earlier analyses of mystified pictures in *Mythologies*, his reconstruction of the workings of systems of signs, and the poignantly autobiographical meditations of *Camera Lucida* leads us to this awareness.

The Ontology of the "Point"

A lot has been said about Barthes's "return" to realism, phenomenology, the Imaginary, and Sartrian models: death and his own inclinations reconciled Barthes with Sartre (both died in 1980). The concept of the "Phantom," the thing resurrected but not exactly at the right place, corresponds to what Barthes expects of photography. In keeping with Balzac's innate fear that each photograph his friend Nadar would take might steal some layer in his private and precious spectral emanations, Barthes describes the triangle composed by the photographer, the object, and the observer as a sort of Ghost Dance:

> The *Operator* is the Photographer. The *Spectator* is ourselves, all of us who glance through collections of photographs—in magazines and newspapers, in books, albums, archives. . . . And the person or thing photographed is the target, the referent, a kind of little simulacrum, any *eidolon* emitted by the object, which I should like to call the *Spectrum* of the Photograph, because this word retains, through its root, a relation to "spectacle" and adds to it that rather terrible thing which is there in every photograph: the return of the dead.[58]

A convergence of two obsessions marks the later Barthes: a return to the form of the journal and an exploration of family photographs at a time of deep mourning for his mother. Barthes, despite surprising theoretical about-faces, nevertheless remained steadfast in his effort to abide by an ethics of signs announced in *Mythologies*. In *Camera Lucida*, he has the courage to speak of himself, of his own idiolectal choices, likes, and dislikes, hoping that his tone will be just and touch us. When he distinguishes the *Operator*, the *Spectator*, and the *Spectrum*, this pseudoscientific terminology aims at releasing a "ghost," which defines photography as the "spectro-graphy" performed by a camera. *Camera Lucida* requires a narrative in the first person, and in the past tense:

I collected in a last thought the images that had "pricked" me (since this is the action of the *punctum*), like that of the black woman with the gold necklace and the strapped pumps. In each of them, inescapably, I passed beyond the unreality of the thing represented, I entered crazily into the spectacle, into the image, taking into my arms what is dead, what is going to die, as Nietzsche did.[59]

It is only on the antepenultimate page of *Camera Lucida* that we realize that the treatise on Photography is closer to the *Journal of a Madman*, a man crazed by grief and mourning. A hint had been given early on, during a discussion of the doubling effect of photography: "Even odder: it was *before* Photography that men had the most to say about the vision of the double. Heautoscopy was compared with an hallucinosis; for centuries this was a great mythic theme. But today it is as if we repressed the profound madness of Photography."[60] Such a madness can only be revealed by a subject aware of his own fascination and of a deeper madness underlying this fascination. The "madness" of photography consists in making us see death as the main referent. The central question becomes not "Who am I?," but "Am I alive or dead—when I see a photograph, or when I am (become) a photograph?" In order to reach this disquieting question, Barthes needs first to prick or pierce the equanimity of a purely cultural (entropic) contemplation. For this, he has to produce his first rhetorical machinery, the opposition between the *studium* and the *punctum*.

Such a binary is not reached immediately in *Camera Lucida*, for it is only after Barthes has stated his dissatisfaction with previous discourses on photography as an art or a genre that he can state his desire to stick to the particular. Thanks to the deictic of photography, he reaches an "ontological desire" connecting the image to its source, the person or object that are absent by definition. It is only after asserting his main thesis, using phenomenological terms which are quite new to his pen that he can elaborate a "structural rule."[61] Noticing that he is struck, interested, "hailed" only by certain photographs, he wonders what it is in a photograph that attracts his eye. Starting from a picture by Koen Wessing depicting Nicaraguan soldiers patrolling in a poor village while two nuns pass by, the presence side by side of these "discontinuous elements"[62] yields a main rule: a detail will focus one's attention. Hence the opposition between a *studium* reducing photography to generality (connotations, politics, history of art, referential or documentary value) and the *punctum* which shoots out like an arrow and pierces the subject, seizing upon the subjective cathexis of the eye. The decision to wait for an "accident" that can "prick" him leads to remarkable discussions of several photographs.

This movement toward a subjective glance is less surprising than it seems, given the drift already sketched in *Mythologies*. The *punctum* provides a rationale for a subjective decentering identical with the flash of meaning, a visual flash that turns into a "floating flash,"[63] which allows Barthes to present his private mythology of the image. As we have seen, the *punctum* develops the notion of the "third meaning," this "non-concept" devoid of any semantic stability and iterability. It catches the moment when an image produces a nonmeaning that touches viewers because of some formal properties. With the *punctum*, the point touches the viewer by revealing that one need not fear: the enormous catastrophe has already taken place. Barthes's critical discourse only adds what was already there. "Last thing about the *punctum:* whether or not it is triggered, it is an addition: it is what I add to the photograph and *what is nonetheless already there.*"[64]

Any attempt to systematize the "details" seen by Barthes in the photographs he likes would be idle; Barthes shares with Freud the idea that details are the main gates to insight. From a single detail, one can reconstruct both the effect and the affect of a work of art, as Freud showed with the Moses of Michelangelo. However, despite the private or subjective elements exposed, Barthes's "points" cannot be reduced to psychobiography. Often, indeed, his *punctum* calls up homosexuality, as when a boy's hand caresses de Brazza's thigh. But precisely because this curious gesture is a little too obvious, the *punctum* will have to be elsewhere. In the case of the black woman's strapped shoes, Barthes revises his judgment and has to come up with another explanation—which implies that the *punctum* is not immediate, but needs a certain temporality to unfold itself:

> this photograph has *worked* within me, and later on I realized that the real *punctum* was the necklace she was wearing; for (no doubt) it was the same necklace (a slender ribbon of braided gold) which I had seen worn by someone in my own family, and which, once she died, remained shut up in a family box of old jewelry (this sister of my father had never married, lived with her mother as an old maid, and I had always been saddened whenever I thought of her dreary life).[65]

Barthes could not have admitted more openly the private nature of these associations. They require an entire family romance to be understood. A complex Freudian game of displacement—from shoes to neck, a similar buckle or band—and condensation (locked box equals enforced sterility) is at work here. If the straps on the shoes do not mean much to most viewers and appear as a "private" *punctum,* Barthes's reelaboration shows the necklace to be a token of sterility. It allegorizes how strong family "attachments" can ruin a life: a new insight into the role of the straps is provided. In the same way, although Barthes comments at length on the picture of his mother when she was five, and opposes it to two other pictures—one from 1913, another where she is holding her son, Roland, which is reproduced in *Roland Barthes by Roland Barthes* with the somewhat ironical caption of "The demand for love"[66]—we cannot see the central picture of the mother. As Barthes says, the image would remain pure *studium* for the outside observer and could never emblematize the love invested in it.

The first part of this double essay whose structure is carefully constructed so as to give twice twenty-four elegiac "songs" concludes with the idea that the referent of all photographs is Death. The second part leads to the referent of all photographs as the Mother. These two mothers mingle and mesh. In the pages where Barthes comments on his mother's absent photograph, he only gives us a portrait by Nadar. This beautiful woman with white hair is simply presented by the caption as: "Nadar: The Artist's Mother (or Wife)."[67] A few pages later, we find the moving admission: "Ultimately I experienced her, strong as she had been, my inner law, as my feminine child. Which was my way of resolving Death."[68] Barthes becomes both his own father (he never knew him since he died in the First World War when he was one year old) and his own mother by a strange logical twist. The mother becomes the *punctum* par excellence: she embodies the culmination of particularity. To reengender his mother, Barthes needs to write about her this strange narrative, his meditation on a single photograph of her as a child. However, there is no redemption given the loss of any dialectical recuperation of the dead object: "From now on I could do no more than await my total, undialectical death. That is what I read in the Winter Garden Photograph."[69]

Another photograph confirms this idea. In the first part of the essay, Barthes describes an old Mozarabic house from the Grenada Alhambra by Charles Clifford. The photograph touches Barthes but he cannot find a true *punctum* in it. He can only confess: "[T]his old photograph (1854) touches me: it is quite simply *there* that I should like to live."[70] Explicating the wish to "inhabit" pictures, Barthes then links these places to a maternal function. They embody a regressive desire to return to the mother's womb:

> Looking at these landscapes of predilection, it is as if I *were certain* of having been there or of going there. Now Freud says of the maternal body that "there is no other place of which one can say with so much certainty that one has already been there." Such then would be the essence of the landscape (chosen desire): *heimlich*, awakening in me the Mother (and never the disturbing Mother).[71]

One can highlight the Freudian elements of this photograph, which depicts a house resembling a tattooed body with its elaborate yet-faded Arab fresco, the two windows serving as eyes, and the huge arch bringing to mind human legs. It takes some time to discover a young boy sitting on a slab, his back pressed against the right-hand side of the house. Dwarfed by the enormity of the building, he stares into the void, while one can see behind, in the distance, a cypress tree and then, quite distinctly, three white crosses. This house is nothing but the entrance to a cemetery: heimlich already contained the unheimlich as the return of inevitable Death. Yet this Death, if it is not dialectical, can be tamed an instant, incorporated within a sweet regressive fantasy which carries the subject back to somewhere in himself.[72]

In stark contrast to this almost lyrical tone in the midst of an elegiac mode, the abrupt announcement of the Mother's death marks a rupture in the book at the beginning of the second part: "Now, one November evening shortly after my mother's death, I was going through some photographs."[73] The Mother's image, even more than her death, remains "undialectical." It cannot be transformed into Hegelian negativity, a Proustian search for a Lost Time, or the Sartrian recapturing of an *eidos* in a flash of the imagination. On the contrary, its two dimensions and glossy paper only testify to a certain "Nevermore" of the reality that "That has been."

Barthes bypasses the optical apparatus of the *camera obscura* that led to photography in order to stress the chemical operation of emulsions fixated on paper:

> For the *noeme* "That-has-been" was possible only on the day when a scientific circumstance (the discovery that silver halogens were sensitive to light) made it possible to recover and print directly the luminous rays emitted by a variously lighted object. The photograph is literally an emanation of the referent. . . . A sort of umbilical

cord links the body of the photographed thing to my gaze: light, though impalpable, is here a carnal medium, a skin I share with anyone who has been photographed.[74]

Barthes relishes the thought that the silver in the emulsion remains somewhat alive. Photography participates in some magical transubstantiation (light becomes metal), and thus avers the consubstantiality of the gaze to its object. The striking image of the umbilical cord suggests a bond belonging to the mystical. If photography is a resurrection and a haunting by the means of a bidimensional image, could we not say that the inventor of photography was not Niepce or Talbot, but Veronica? Noting that the wonder and astonishment he experiences in front of photographs comes nothing short of the religious, Barthes adds: "Photography has something to do with resurrection: might we not say of it what the Byzantines said of the image of Christ which impregnated St. Veronica's napkin: that it was not made by the hand of man, *acheiropoeitos*?"[75] Barthes goes further when he states that each and every photograph performs an ontological proof, "a proof no longer merely induced: the proof-according -to-St.-Thomas-seeking-to-touch-the-resurrected-Christ."[76] This proof would reconcile Saint Thomas, the skeptic who needed to touch the wound, and Veronica, the pitiful woman who preserved an image imprinted by Jesus's own blood. The *punctum* belongs to the mystical realm; it is always an arrow shot from God at an ecstatic St. Theresa.

The Holy Shroud of Jesus might be the conceptual model upon which photography is founded, as Georges Didi-Huberman argues when he studies the paradoxical nature of this object whose fabrication cannot be explained.[77] The Holy Shroud offers a negative image of a man, Christ or not Christ, at a time when photography had not been invented. It was only in 1898, when Secundo Pia was asked to photograph the *sudarium*, that one saw a man's face appear. The photograph represents a positive image that would have been produced by a volume applied on a Veil; it has been dated from the fourteenth century. If most specialists believe that the shroud was fabricated at that time in Burgundy, nobody can explain the technique by which the print was made. Thus, the shroud embodies an absolute Myth: it is the pure concept of an authentic fake, a fabrication through which the theological and technological mysteries of transubstantiality and consubstantiality merge. Barthes's distinction is to usher in a mystical mode of writing, a writing that takes place by itself, a writing that would be the direct inscription of traces on paper while testifying to the reality of an event. Like a haiku, it points to what remains outside any commentary.

Notes

1 Kaja Silverman, *The Miracle of Analogy, or The History of Photography, Part 1* (Stanford: Stanford University Press, 2015).
2 Roland Barthes, "The Photographic Message," in *Image-Music-Text*, trans. Stephen Heath (London: Fontana/Collins, 1977), 17.
3 Ibid., 19.

4   Roland Barthes, *Camera Lucida*, trans. Richard Howard (New York: Hill and Wang, 1981), 88.
5   Jorge Luis Borges, "Pascal's Sphere," in *Selected Non-Fictions*, trans. Esther Allen, Suzanne Jill Levine and Eliot Weinberger (New York: Penguin, 1999), 353.
6   Roland Barthes, "The Third Meaning: Research Notes on Some Eisenstein Still," in *Image-Music-Text*, trans. Stephen Heath (London: Fontana, 1977), 52–68.
7   I use the new translation by Richard Howard, Roland Barthes, *Mythologies, The Complete Edition, in a New Translation* (New York: Hill and Wang, 2012). I have modified some translations and signal it in parentheses.
8   Barthes, "Myth Today," in Roland Barthes, *Mythologies, The Complete Edition*, 217.
9   Ibid., 225.
10 Caption on the cover of *Paris Match* for June 25–July 2, 1955, reproduced Barthes *Mythologies*, édition illustrée établie par Jacqueline Guittard (Paris: Seuil, 2010), 248.
11 Barthes, *Mythologies, The Complete Edition*, 228.
12 Ibid.
13 Ibid.
14 Ibid., 53–5.
15 Barthes, *Mythologies* illustrated, 61.
16 Barthes, *Mythologies, The Complete Edition*, 53.
17 Ibid., 19.
18 See Barthes, *Mythologies* illustrated, 24.
19 Barthes, *Mythologies, The Complete Edition*, 19.
20 Ibid., 20.
21 Ibid.
22 Ibid., 21.
23 Ibid., 55.
24 Ibid., 35.
25 See Barthes, *Mythologies* illustrated, 38.
26 Barthes, *Mythologies, The Complete Edition*, 36.
27 Ibid., 57, modified.
28 Ibid., 196–9.
29 Ibid., 197.
30 Ibid., 116–18.
31 *Paris Match*, number 276, Paris (July 10, 1954), 24.
32 Barthes, *Mythologies, The Complete Edition*, 116.
33 Ibid., 116–17.
34 Ibid., 117, trans. modified.
35 Roland Barthes, *Mythologies* (Paris: Seuil, 1957), 120. Howard renders "*majoration*" as "overvaluation," which is misleading, since this brings us back to the term used for a bad imposition of prethought meaning as in banal shock photos.
36 Barthes, *Mythologies*, 120.
37 Barthes, *Mythologies, The Complete Edition*, 118.
38 Ibid.
39 Ibid.
40 Ibid.
41 Ibid., 236.
42 Ibid., 16.
43 Ibid., modified.

44 See the analyses of David Bordwell, *French Impressionist Cinema: Film Culture, Film Theory and Film Style* (New York: Arno Press, 1980); and of Richard Abel, *The French Cinema. The First Wave 1915-1929* (Princeton, NJ: Princeton University Press, 1984).
45 Barthes, *Mythologies, The Complete Edition*, 74-5.
46 Ibid., 73.
47 Ibid., modified.
48 Ibid., 74.
49 Ibid.
50 Ibid., 181-3.
51 See Barthes, *Mythologies* illustrated, 194-5.
52 Barthes, *Mythologies, The Complete Edition*, 183.
53 Ibid., 182.
54 Ibid.
55 Ibid., 181.
56 Louis Althusser, "Ideology and Ideological State Apparatuses" in *Lenin and Philosophy and other Essays*, trans. Ben Brewster (London: NLB, 1971), 121-76.
57 Barthes, *Mythologies, The Complete Edition*, 240.
58 Barthes, *Camera Lucida*, 9.
59 Ibid., 118-17.
60 Ibid., 12-13.
61 Ibid., 23.
62 Ibid.
63 Ibid., 53.
64 Ibid., 55.
65 Ibid., 53.
66 Roland Barthes, *Roland Barthes par Roland Barthes* (Paris: Seuil, 1975), 7.
67 Barthes, *Camera Lucida*, 68.
68 Ibid., 72.
69 Ibid.
70 Ibid., 38.
71 Ibid., 40.
72 Ibid.
73 Ibid., 63.
74 Ibid., 80-1.
75 Ibid., 82.
76 Ibid., 80.
77 Georges Didi-Huberman, "The Index of the Absent Wound (Monograph on a Stain)," *October: The First Decade 1978–1986*, eds. A. Michelson, R. Krauss, D. Crimp, and J. Copjec (Cambridge, MA: MIT Press, 1987), 39-57.

Bibliography

Abel, Richard. *The French Cinema: The First Wave 1915-1929*. Princeton, NJ: Princeton University Press, 1984.

Althusser, Louis. *Lenin and Philosophy and Other Essays*. Trans. Ben Brewster. London: NLB, 1971.

Barthes, Roland. *Camera Lucida*. Trans. Richard Howard. New York: Hill and Wang, 1981.
Barthes, Roland. *Image-Music-Text*. Trans. Stephen Heath. London: Fontana/Collins, 1977.
Barthes, Roland. *Mythologies*. Paris: Seuil, 1957.
Barthes, Roland. *Mythologies: The Complete Edition, In a New Translation*. Trans. Richard Howard. New York: Hill and Wang, 2012.
Barthes, Roland. *Roland Barthes par Roland Barthes*. Paris: Seuil, 1975.
Bordwell, David. *French Impressionist Cinema: Film Culture, Film Theory and Film Style*. New York: Arno Press, 1980.
Borges, Jorge Luis. *Selected Non-Fictions*. Trans. Esther Allen, Suzanne Jill Levine and Eliot Weinberger. New York: Penguin, 1999.
Didi-Huberman, Georges. "The Index of the Absent Wound (Monograph on a Stain)." In *October: The First Decade 1978–1986*. Eds. A. Michelson, R. Krauss, D. Crimp, and J. Copjec. Cambridge, MA: MIT Press, 1987. 39–57.
Guittard, Jacqueline, ed. *Barthes Mythologies*. Paris: Seuil, 2010.
Silverman, Kaja. *The Miracle of Analogy, or The History of Photography, Part 1*. Stanford: Stanford University Press, 2015.

2

Barthes and the Search for Rigor

Thomas Pavel

It is not easy to formulate a coherent description and evaluation of all Roland Barthes's critical writings, given that this most flexible and versatile French critic of the last century often changed his approach to literary studies, always joining the best, most recent theoretical trend, even if this meant abandoning his previous theoretical opinions. His writings, moreover, mix wonderfully perceptive insights with statements that are less satisfying, if not even invalid. For this reason, some of his works, in particular his book *On Racine*, have been the target of severe criticisms, often blind to their true merits, yet at the same time justified, at least up to a certain point.

The present volume being devoted to the links between Barthes and modernism, one should emphasize the most interesting and durable aspects of these links. In order to avoid, nevertheless, the Manichean attitude that either promotes past authors to the status of unfailing geniuses or considers them as dangerous wrongdoers, the present chapter will try to distinguish between Roland Barthes, the incredibly insightful modern critic, and Roland Barthes, the disciple of new theories to which he enthusiastically adhered without always fully understanding their implications. In most cases, the literary acumen of the great critic is dazzling. His theoretical works, usually serious and trustworthy, succeed in raising important issues yet sometimes neglect crucial aspects of the topics they examine.

It is equally relevant to distinguish between the stable aspects of Barthes's writings and the various choices they successively put forward. After the Second World War, some rebellious French writers and thinkers were *committed intellectuals* who dedicated themselves to a given political cause and never abandoned it. Jean-Paul Sartre, for instance, adhered at some point to the communist ideal and remained faithful to it until the end of his life. By contrast, the options of *avant-garde intellectuals*, usually in agreement with the most recent trends, changed as soon as intellectual life took a new turn.

Roland Barthes belonged to the second type. He was certainly rebellious, as proven by the Marxist background of his early essays as well as by the structuralism of his next stage, both directly defying the traditional historicism of academic French literary studies. His rebellion, however, never took drastic forms, since even as an opponent of the dominant trends Barthes's main talent was the invention of beautiful, striking ideas rather than coherent action. His taste for beauty and his hesitancy to act later made him publish a moving essay, *Fragments of a Lover's Discourse*, which unexpectedly allies erudition and sensibility, and, in his last courses at the College de France, allowed him to confess his desire, never fully satisfied, of writing a novel. Philippe Roger's monograph[1] has perceptively described the aesthetic orientation of all Barthes's writings, from the earliest to the latest. A constant love of beauty, on the one side, and a passionate yet fleeting adhesion to new theories and methods, on the other side, guided Barthes's intellectual career. In order to examine their interaction, let us consider a few aspects of his book *On Racine*, published in 1963.[2]

It includes three studies: a description of the universe evoked in Racine's tragedies, a performance review of *Phaedra* at the Théâtre National Populaire, Paris, and, finally, a polemical rejection of literary history. This last study annoyed the historians of literature and made them react quite strongly; reading it almost sixty years after its publication, one discovers pertinent remarks as well as disconcerting leaps into the unknown.

Under the title *History or Literature?* this last section begins by quoting a French Radio program that paralleled historical events and musical works composed at the same date, for instance, "1789: the Convening of the General Estates, the recall of Necker, concerto nr. 4 in C minor for strings by B. Galuppi."[3] Naïve and touching in Barthes's view, this kind of juxtaposition raises the old problem of the links between history and art works. Hegel, Hippolyte Taine, Karl Marx, and their disciples (Barthes himself having earlier been one of them) were certain to have solved it by showing that during any given period all historical events and all philosophical and artistic achievements manifest the same worldview. Barthes notices, however, that at a closer look history and literary history look like two continents barely communicating with each other. Would it be in any way possible to improve the traffic between them? Yes, he answers, especially if one does not forget that a literary work is *something else* than its history and that, accordingly, the history of literature as an institution is different from the history of literature as a creative activity. To study the latter, Barthes concluded, one needs an additional discipline that would examine literary creation using a psychological method. Several versions of this discipline did in fact exist at that time, each studying literary works independently of their historical and biographical context: the British and American New Criticism, the Russian and Czech structural poetics, and German stylistics. French critics and scholars were at that time just beginning to discover them.

Barthes, however, did not think of existing methods. He rather envisaged building a new discipline in which the study of literature both as an institution and as a creative art would converge with each other by relying on the conviction that within the general economy of society the task of literature consists in institutionalizing subjectivity. As often in his writings, the argument, plausible and persuasive up to this point, soon reaches enigmatic conclusions. Literature having the paradoxical task of bringing together a public institution and personal subjectivity, literary critics need to recognize, first, that they cannot just *tell the truth* and, second, that their writings are, in some sense, part of literature. At the same time, critics must realize that their knowledge should become systematic. Thus, the artistic side of Barthes promotes the inability to tell the plain truth—a poetic admission—and the sense of belonging to literature. And yet, surprisingly, the critic has the duty to obey the discipline of a system, as practitioners of human sciences need to do. How can one reconcile these contradictory requirements?

A similar tension between the clarity of critical insights and the exuberance of the theoretical drive is perceptible in the description of Racine's universe, whose first part, *The Structure*, offers a magnificent reading of his tragedies. Barthes—fortunately one dares say—does not pay too much attention to the rules of neoclassical poetics, to the religious debates in France in the seventeenth century, or to the social organization of the Old Regime. The first sentence, "There are three Mediterraneans in Racine: Classical, Hebrew and Byzantine," brings together the horizons of *Phèdre*, *Athalie*, and *Bajazet*. He continues: "The great tragic places are arid lands, squeezed between the sea and the desert, shade and sun raised to an absolute state." In Greece, a country that Barthes had never seen, "[t]he sun produces a landscape that is pure, distinct, depopulated.... The Racinian habitat knows only one dream of flight: the sea, the ships."[4] These close-ups, immersed in light, seduce the reader.

The tragic space includes a concealed chamber, "the invisible and dreadful place where Power lurks."[5] In *Britannicus*, it is Nero's room, in *Esther* the palace of Assuerus, in *Athalie* the Holy of Hollies where the Hebrew God lives. The stage is just an Antechamber, a treacherous path on which characters (propelled by a tragic wind, one might add) complain about their misfortune and debate their improbable choices. Power remains invisible and the stage is the site of fear, separated from the Chamber by the Door, a menacing barrier, dangerous to cross, as in *Britannicus*, where the main character loses his life when he joins the banquet offered by Nero in the invisible Chamber. Occasionally, Barthes continues, when Power spies on the characters huddled together in the Antechamber, the Veil or the listening Wall replaces the Door, as happens, again in *Britannicus*, when Nero, hidden behind a Veil, listens to the conversation between Britannicus and his beloved Junia. As for the Outside—the third tragic place—it runs behind the Antechamber and it shelters death, since it takes in the characters condemned by Power. Roxane tells Bajazet to *go out*, thus condemning him to death; similarly, those who commit suicide expire outside the stage, as does Atalide, again in *Bajazet*. Can one recognize here the neoclassical rule of decorum, according to which characters should never die in front of the spectators? Barthes answers "no" because, by focusing on the artistic meaning of this rule, he assumes that "What propriety rejects in carnal death is an element alien to tragedy, an 'impurity,' the density of a reality scandalous."[6]

Characters threatened by Power run into the Outside Space, without being sure that the escape would succeed. It is in this space that the major decisions that lead to crucial actions are made. In *Bajazet*, for instance, the order to execute both Roxane, the sultan's infidel concubine, and the young prince she loves comes from far away, from the absent sultan. Efficient actions rarely begin on the stage, except those decided by the Power, as when Theseus, in *Phaedra*, condemns Hippolytus to death. As for the main characters, they are never capable to trigger an event. As Barthes puts it, "everything leads to the tragic site, but everything is locked there."[7]

Concerning the anthropological meaning of these tragedies, Barthes thinks that they rely on an old fable according to which the human horde, dominated by the strongest male, offers him its women and sons. The father rules (Amurat, Mithridates, Theseus), brothers are enemies (Nero and Britannicus, Pharnace and Xiphares in *Mithridates*), sons (Britannicus, Bajazet, Hippolytus) are destroyed by the cruelty of the ruling male. Are they *characters* in the present acceptation of the term? Racine's contemporaries rightly called them *actors*, that is, masks personifying types or functions rather than individuals, Barthes notes, thus detecting the specificity of the *mimesis* in French neoclassical tragedies. Paying little attention to concrete details, this mimetic approach places its objects at certain level of generality: the tyrant, the hostile brother, the persecuted son, a level that in the twentieth century became the target of structural analysis of folktales and literary plots, an approach strongly supported by Barthes in France.

The propensity to define general types also applies to the motivation of the characters' actions. According to Barthes, Racine's tragedies stage the conflict between two kinds of love. On the one side, the sisterly Eros is calmly based on mutual confidence between lovers raised together and bound by a long-term friendship (Britannicus and Junia, Bajazet and Atalida); on the other side, the Eros-Event, a violent passion, arises suddenly during an unexpected encounter (Nero and Junia, Roxana and Bajazet) and is never shared. In *Phaedra*, one might add, Hippolytus and Aricia's love is, like the sisterly Eros, mutual and innocent; yet, like the Eros-Event, it is born when the two characters unexpectedly meet. As soon as they confess their mutual feelings, they are able to obliterate the old mutual hatred between their families. As Barthes, however, understood so well, Hippolytus and Aricia's flight could not possibly succeed since Power, represented here by Theseus deluded by Phaedra, decides to end Hippolytus's life.

According to Barthes, unshared love at first strike obeys a rather simple logic, labeled "fundamental relationship," which makes visible the authority always present in the Eros-Event. Formulated as a diagram that predicts Barthes's impending structuralist turn, this relationship requires that

A has all power over B
A loves B who does not love A,
A representing Nero, Roxana and Phaedra, while B are Junia, Bajazet, and Hippolytus.

One should, however, add that a second relationship, equally fundamental in Racine's tragedies, underlies sisterly Eros, called in Racine's time "benevolent love" (*amor benevolentiae*). Barthes does not go into the details of this second type of link, but if one follows his method, it would take the following form:

B (Junia, Bajazet, Hippolytus) loves C (Britannicus, Atalida, Aricia)
B has no legal or state-power over C.

Barthes's analysis focuses on the links between A and B, emphasizing its two main aspects: the asymmetry of power ("[o]ne is powerful, the other one is subject, one is a tyrant, the other one a captive") and the spatial contiguity ("A and B are confined in the same place") in order to conclude that "[i]t is ultimately the tragic site that establishes the tragedy" and "Aside from this arrangement . . . the conflict always remains unmotivated."[8] With his usual elegance, Barthes then formulates an unexpected thesis according to which "[t]he radicalism of the tragic solution derives from the simplicity of the initial problem: the entire tragedy seems to consist of a vulgar *not enough room for two*. The tragic conflict is a crisis of space."[9] And because this space remains closed, he continues, the relationship is immovable, the tragedy's task being, precisely, the representation of this immobility.

Thus, Racine is promoted (or, perhaps, demoted?) to the rank of precursor of Jean-Paul Sartre's theater, in particular of the closed space one cannot leave and of the dead-end situation, both present in Sartre's best-known play *No Exit* (1944). As Tiphaine Samoyault's beautiful biography of Barthes[10] explains, the author of *Being and Nothingness* was both a model and a counter-model for Barthes, who often took deliberately anti-Sartrian positions. Yet, however different their theoretical views might have been, the influence of Sartre's "dramaturgy of situations" and, in particular, of his 1944 play on the first part of *On Racine* is real. Barthes himself signals it when he states that "according to the classical Sartrian schema, it is B's liberty that A seeks to possess by force; in other words, he is engaged in an insoluble paradox: if he possesses, he destroys, if he releases, he frustrates himself."[11] Sartre's theater, which guided Barthes's insights about the features of Racine's tragic space and about the ways in which its elements—the Chamber, the Antechamber, the Outside Space—organize the action, has also, thanks to the simplicity of its conflicts, inspired Barthes's interpretations of Racine's plot structures.

And yet, the tendency to simplify the issues involved in Racine's plots and state that their conflict is always unmotivated may have gone too far. Modernism tempts critics to generalize retroactively its practices, but it might be better to examine what past writers actually intended to do. One of the features of French neoclassical tragedies, Racine's in particular, was the addition of love-stories to Greek and Roman classical plots. This innovation, already present in the theater of the Spanish Golden Age, breaks down the old Aristotelian unity of action. Barthes seems aware of it when he describes the *two* kinds of love present in Racine's theater. Subsequently, however, he neglects to ask how these kinds of love *together* organize and motivate the play's action. Way beyond the "crisis of space" and "immobility," the "*not enough room for two*" (Barthes's appealing insight), which generates the tragic conflict, should not be considered "vulgar" given that the holder of Power hopes to find room *in the heart* of his beloved. The metaphorical use of "room" here signals a love rivalry, visible both in *Britannicus* and in *Phaedra*. In these two tragedies, the powerful lover already knows or soon finds out that the person who inspires his/hers Eros-Event is a faithful partner in a different, sisterly Eros. A therefore takes revenge by sending either B (Hippolytus) or C (Britannicus) to death. As for the question "Who would be sacrificed, B or C?" its answer consists in choosing the man (Britannicus, Bajazet, Hippolytus) and sparing the woman (Junia, Atalida, Aricia). The disappointed lover does not kill his rival just in order to assert his Power (with a capital P), but rather acts because he/she senses the limits of his/her power (with non-capital p) to inspire love.

This awareness, moreover, does not always have the same background. In *Britannicus*, Nero and his half-brother do not only vie for the heart of Junia; they also compete for the imperial crown. Nero is quite worried about it, given that his mother Agrippina, his *true* rival who raised him to the imperial throne only in order for *her* to reign, might, in case of a conflict, support Britannicus and his legitimate claim to power. As Racine himself explains in the play's second preface (1674), the tragedy is no less about Agrippina's fall into disgrace than about the death of Britannicus. Equally important, Nero does not act as a monster from the very beginning, but gradually adopts this role, the play showing, again according to its author, the birth of a monster. This is, most likely, the reason why Nero's love for Junia, whom he meets by chance, does not seem inevitable. On the contrary, as M. Adereth, editor and commentator of this play, noted long ago, the dialogue between Nero and his confident Narcissus emphasizes the hesitations of the young emperor. Telling Narcissus about his unexpected meeting with Junie, Nero confesses:

> Je ne sais si cette négligence,
> Les ombres, les flambeaux, les cris et le silence,
> Et le farouche aspect de ses fiers ravisseurs,
> Relevaient de ses yeux les timides douceurs . . .[12]

and adds:

> Mais je m'en fais peut-être une trop belle image,
> Elle m'est apparue avec trop d'avantage:
> Narcisse, qu'en dis–tu?[13]

M. Adereth comments: "Which lover has ever asked this kind of question at the very moment when he imagines himself in love for the rest of his life?" (my translation) Quoted by René Pommier,[14] one of the most severe critics of Barthes's book, M. Adereth's question brings a revealing detail to light: Nero's love for Junia, far from having the strength of an "absolute event," as Barthes describes it, rather looks like a whim. Guided by the generality of his notions, often adequate, Barthes does not always take into account the specific details of individual tragedies, just as modernism often thinks in general terms and dismisses details.

Yet, Barthes's reference to Sartre's dramaturgy helps us understand a less-commented aspect of *Britannicus*. Nero wants to master Junia's *freedom*, either by trying to intimidate her or by threatening to execute her beloved Britannicus. Surveillance of the most personal form of liberty takes place during the scene of the Veil (to use Barthes's term), when Nero, after requiring Junia to abandon Britannicus, "Si ses jours vous sont chers, éloignez-le de vous, / Sans qu'il ait aucun lieu de me croire jaloux,"[15] hides and watches the conversation between the two lovers. It is one of the rare moments when Racine's theater seems to foresee twentieth-century tyrannies, which, as Sartre knew so well, secretly supervised not only the actions but also the conversations and the thoughts of their subjects.

Phaedra's conflict as well is only partially faithful to Barthes's diagram. Is Phaedra a tyrant? Is Hippolytus her subject? Does she have full power over him? Is their relationship "unmovable"? Does the play represent this immobility? Not quite. Consumed with passion, Phaedra loses her will to live: "Je ne me soutiens plus, la force m'abandonne."¹⁶ When she confesses her passion to her confident Oenone, Phaedra feels even weaker, more abandoned. Things *change*, however, since in this tragedy action relies less on "immobility" than on false news and the return of the truth. The rumor of Theseus's death gives Phaedra the courage to seek Hippolytus's alliance, even his love. The same rumor unites Hippolytus with Aricia under the protection of benevolent love.

By declaring her passion to Hippolytus in this new situation, Phaedra, far from acting as a tyrant, surrenders herself to her victor: "Voilà mon cœur. C'est là que ta main doit frapper,"¹⁷ she tells him. When she later learns that Theseus is alive, she first wants to kill herself but soon realizes that she must live in order to defend her reputation: "Mourons: de tant d'horreurs qu'un trépas me délivre" and, two verses later, "Je ne crains que le nom que je laisse après moi."¹⁸ In his *History and Literature*, Barthes argued that nonhistoricist studies of literature should follow a psychological method. If so, rather than applying to several tragedies the same general diagram, he could have examined the winding behavior of *Phaedra*'s characters and the variety of their psychological states. This way he might have taken into account the nuances of the conflict: in Racine's play, as in Euripides and Seneca's versions, Phaedra takes revenge by accusing Hippolytus of having attempted to rape her. In Racine's version, however, she regrets her lie and, ready to acknowledge her own guilt, she asks Theseus to spare his son. Her husband's answer lets her know, however, that Hippolytus courts another woman. Left alone on stage, Phaedra confesses that she might have told Theseus the truth if she did not learn about Aricia: "Peut-être si la voix ne m'eût été coupée/L'affreuse vérité me serait échappée."¹⁹ Thanks to this reversal, in the end an *indirect* revenge takes place, carried out by a sea monster sent by Neptune at Theseus's request. Although he is the Power holder, Theseus does not act like a tyrant, especially since he does not know that his son is innocent. The difference between *Phaedra* and *Britannicus*'s denouements is considerable.

If Theseus is not a tyrant, why does he act so brutally? A killer of monsters, nomadic, always in love, allied with the god Neptune, Theseus incarnates the energy of the heroic age. In his *New Science*, first published in 1725 and reissued in 1730, Giambattista Vico described the heroic age as a time of violence, polytheism, and polygamy. The civilized age that came after it was, by contrast, a time of peace, monotheism, and monogamy. In Racine's *Phaedra*, a similar distinction separates, on the one hand, the amorous exploits of indomitable Theseus, a hero worthy of mythological legends and ancient tragedies and, on the other hand, the sisterly Eros, chaste, calm, and faithful, protected by a single God without a name, that unites Hippolytus and Aricia. Their love was probably inspired by that of Theagenes and Chariclea, the protagonists of Heliodorus's *Ethiopian Story* (second or third century CE), one of the most admired literary works in the seventeenth century, a work that Racine had read and reread as a teenager. As for Phaedra, in Racine's tragedy she hesitates. Conquered as a young woman by the heroic Theseus, she is now consumed by an illegitimate passion kindled by Venus, the pagan goddess of love. Yet the young man who attracts her incarnates the new age: chaste, dignified, faithful, Hippolytus inherits from his father only his physical beauty. Heroic brutality seems to triumph, since the ancient god massacres the young Hippolytus, but Phaedra, in the grip of remorse, poisons herself and, before dying, confesses the truth. Theseus, until then an enemy of Aricia's family, gives up violence and accepts the peaceful, monogamous choice of Hippolytus by hoping that "[s]on amante aujourd'hui me tienne lieu de fille."[20]

Barthes's illuminating interpretations, in particular those present in the section devoted to the structure of Racine's tragedies, would have been even more convincing if the generality of his approach would have been more sensitive to the individual diversity of the plays and to the moral psychology of their characters—an important concern of neoclassical writers. Besides, as Barthes himself suggested, the priority given to literary creativity should not leave out the institutional aspects of literary culture: the artistic worldview and the literary preferences of a past period.

Likewise, one can certainly welcome artistic and intellectual modernity, its criticism of past historical periods, its interest in abstract approaches to meaning, and its sense that details do not always matter. Reflecting on Barthes's *On Racine*, however, one realizes that when one examines past periods and cultures, one needs to pay attention to what *they* have to say rather than hear what *we* want to hear. Abstract approaches are certainly helpful, but so is attention to nuances. Artistic forms, so praised by modernists, have always been important, but, as Barthes's readings of Racine remind us, one should never forget what artistic and literary works aim at telling us.[21]

Notes

1 Philippe Roger, *Roland Barthes, Roman* (Paris: Livre de poche, 1986).
2 Roland Barthes, *On Racine*, trans. Richard Howard (New York: Hill and Wang, 1964).
3 Ibid., 153.
4 Ibid., 3.
5 Ibid.
6 Ibid., 5.
7 Ibid., 7–8.
8 Ibid., 25.
9 Ibid., 26.
10 Tiphaine Samoyault, *Roland Barthes: Biographie* (Paris: Seuil, 2015), passim.
11 Barthes, *On Racine*, 26.
12 "Perhaps her negligée, / The shadows, torches, shouts, and the silence / And the wild looks of those violent men / Set of the timid softness of her eyes . . ." in Jean Racine, *Britannicus, Phaedra, and Athalia*, trans. C. H. Sisson (Oxford: Oxford World Classics, 2001), 23.

13 "But perhaps my imagination flattered her; / Perhaps she is not really so beautiful. / Narcissus, what do you think?" Ibid., 23.
14 René Pommier, *Le Sur Racine de Roland Barthes* (Paris: SERES, 1988), 105.
15 "If you value his life, break with him now, / Without his having cause to think me jealous." Racine, *Britannicus, Phaedra, and Athalia*, 32.
16 Act I, scene 3, v. 154. "I cannot manage for my strength has gone." Ibid., 84.
17 Act II, scene 5, v. 704. "Here is my heart. It is there your hand should strike." Ibid., 103.
18 Act III, scene 3, v. 857, 860. "Let me die and this death save me from these horrors . . . / All I fear is the name I leave behind me." Ibid., 109.
19 Act IV, scene 5, v. 1201–2. "Perhaps if I had not been interrupted / The truth in all its horror would have come out." Ibid., 120.
20 Act V, scene 7, v. 1654. "Let her he loved be welcome as my daughter." Ibid., 135.
21 A slightly different French version of this chapter was published in Jean-Pierre Bertrand, éd., *Roland Barthes: continuités* (Paris: Christian Bourgois, 2017), 147–63.

Bibliography

Barthes, Roland. *On Racine*. Trans. Richard Howard. New York: Hill and Wang, 1964.
Pommier, René. *Le Sur Racine de Roland Barthes*. Paris: SERES, 1988.
Racine, Jean. *Britannicus, Phaedra, and Athalia*. Trans. C. H. Sisson. Oxford: Oxford World Classics, 2001.
Roger, Philippe. *Roland Barthes, Roman*. Paris: Livre de poche, 1986.
Samoyault, Tiphaine. *Roland Barthes: Biographie*. Paris: Seuil, 2015.

3

Barthes and the French Classics

Michael Moriarty

In 1971, Barthes was interviewed by Jean Thibaudeau for the avant-garde journal *Tel Quel*. Questioned about his debt to eighteenth-century writers, he replied, "I have read (no doubt regrettably) more Bossuet than Diderot." Why "regrettably" ("hélas")? And why "no doubt" ("sans doute"), as if he were toning down his regret by expressing it as a concession to his interlocutor's expectations? Surely because he knows that, in the eyes of *Tel Quel* readers, he ought to like Diderot, a lot: Diderot, the materialist, the atheist, the writer of subversive fiction with a pornographic twist (*Les Bijoux indiscrets*, *La Religieuse*). Yet, he admits, the language of eighteenth-century writing (save that of Sade) leaves him cold: the language of a progressive age has less relish for him than that of its authoritarian predecessor, as embodied by Jacques-Bénigne Bossuet (1627–1704), bishop and preacher to the king and the aristocracy.[1] In other words, there is a disconnection between his ideological preferences (or perhaps between his awareness of where ideological orthodoxy lies) and his literary response to the texts of the seventeenth century. This chapter explores some of the ambiguities and complexities of that response.

Taking Pleasure in the Classics

Barthes's enthusiasm for the seventeenth-century classics is manifested in one of his earliest published works, "Plaisir aux Classiques," which appeared in *Existences*, the journal of the students' sanatorium to which he was confined by tuberculosis for much of the war years.[2] From the examples he cites, which often take the form of quotations, it is clear that by "classiques" he means principally the canonical writers of the seventeenth and eighteenth centuries (he refers also to Michelet and Hugo, but very much en passant and without quotation).[3] The anthology of twenty-four quotations with which his article finishes draws preponderantly on the seventeenth century (sixteen examples). There are seven from the eighteenth century (plus one from Fontenelle, who belongs more or less half to each). But five of these are from writers (Vauvenargues and Chamfort) who are successors of the seventeenth-century moralists. There is one from Rousseau and one from Voltaire. Barthes's use of the term "classiques" does not imply any necessary relationship to the literary-historical concept of French "classicism," which he mentions but does not discuss in detail.[4] In what follows, I use the word "classics" in a sense close to that of Barthes, to designate the canonical authors of the seventeenth century, and thus leave out of consideration Barthes's writings on nineteenth- and twentieth-century authors, important though many of these were to him, Proust above all.[5]

One of the prime reasons Barthes cites for reading these classics is that modern writers (he cites several examples, including Proust) set such store by them. The fact that they, whom we admire for other reasons, admire the classics suggests that if we do not ourselves admire them, we must be missing something. What we are missing is, first of all, pleasure, of various kinds. First, these writers appeal to the reader's subjective experience: we recognize in their works our own selves and our own feelings. We can read a generalization by La Bruyère or a line of Racine as if the point of them were to mirror the bitterness or the passionate love we are currently feeling.[6] There is a degree of irony in Barthes's celebration of this aspect of the experience of reading the classics: "I feel myself chosen; the artist is discovering me; he sings of me, of my suffering, my joy, my curiosity." He is the Echo of a Narcissus (myself), who is unable to speak.[7] For there is an element of self-deception, of bad faith, in all of this. The classical text is a "pure mirror" but it has been lit up ("enflammé") by ourselves.[8] We have projected our own self-discovery, our own narcissistic self-contemplation, onto the text. The image of the mirror is all the more appropriate because seventeenth-century *moraliste* writers are themselves much given to images of reflection.[9]

Barthes's language thus already distances us from the apparent purport of his discourse. And indeed he follows this with a more explicit judgment of value: to reflect the reader is probably not the "most noble" function of literature. Yet the pleasure, for all that it is questionable, is not denied or effaced: it is "seductive."[10] Seduced by the not-quite-noble or, at any rate, the not-most-noble, Barthes is already affirming his split subjectivity, his refusal to efface pleasure with the eraser of moral judgment. Indeed his dubiously noble pleasure has a heuristic value, for it is that which enables him to discover the particular seductive appeal of classic art: its presentation of and appeal to subjectivity in a resolutely impersonal and general discourse.[11]

Barthes cites other reasons for valuing the classical writers: they do not try to say everything, and are thus open to fresh interpretations; their style is the product of a rich rhetorical culture; their works are manageable in scale, thus easier to reconcile with a life outside reading; they enrich our experience of contemporary writing. The first two, in particular, are picked up in his later work, in a radical reinterpretation of a classical writer (*Sur Racine*) and in the treatise on rhetoric.[12]

Questioning the Classics

Barthes emerged after the war from his sanatorium into a harsher ideological climate, in which the humanism and hedonism of writings like "Plaisir aux Classiques" would have been withered by the blasts of Marxism and existentialism. And his early writings, especially those later gathered together into *Le Degré zéro de l'écriture*, partake of this new atmosphere, as when he pronounces that "classical writing is obviously the writing of a class" (the bourgeoisie).[13] The ideological analysis has an effect that the moral judgments quoted earlier seemed not to have: to foreclose the possibility of pleasure in the writing.

In Barthes's writings of the 1950s, references to the classical writers often serve a satirical purpose, being applied to elements of popular culture, as if in anticipation of his later argument that so-called mass culture ("la culture dite de masse") is founded on the degenerate survival of the Aristotelian conception of rhetoric that underpins classical literature also.[14] Both classical literature and modern popular culture allegedly depend on the notion of character as a fixed essence (a notion inimical to both the philosophies—Marxism and existentialism—that Barthes at this stage supports).[15] A critique of the press reviews of Sartre's play *Nekrassov* excoriates the bourgeois humanist critics whose idea of the "complexity" of the human soul derives from La Rochefoucauld.[16] The dismissive allusion to La Rochefoucauld in a discussion of Sartre betokens an awareness that respect for classical literature can inhibit a necessary engagement with contemporary thought. And this is very much the case Barthes makes in *Sur Racine*.

This is not the place to discuss *Sur Racine* at any length. My point here is simply to gauge the distance Barthes has traveled from "Plaisir aux Classiques." In one perspective, the distance seems very great: he now argues that we must give up the attempt to find ourselves in Racine's theater: "What there is of us that can be found there is not the better part either of Racine or of ourselves." Insofar as his theater can engage us, it must be by its otherness.[17] He is speaking specifically here of theatrical productions, but his analyses of the texts are conducted in the same spirit; his anthropological and psychoanalytical references are aimed at making Racine's characters unrecognizable as their old familiar selves, and at inhibiting the attempt to find ourselves in them.[18] At the same time, he is maintaining his earlier position that, because the classical writers do not try to say everything, they are open to fresh interpretations. That is why he can reject the accusation that it is illegitimate to open up, as he does, the symbolic dimensions of the Racinian text.[19]

Rereading the *Moralistes*

In the 1960s, however, Barthes produced two remarkable essays on the moralists La Rochefoucauld and La Bruyère.[20] Both of them (like "L'Homme Racinien," the essay that forms most of *Sur Racine*) were originally prefaces to editions of the texts.[21] They show Barthes exploring the problem I began by alluding to, of how to come to terms with a literary text based on or advocating a worldview different from, or perhaps antithetical to, one's own.

In both these essays, Barthes makes implicit concessions to Sartre's view of seventeenth-century literature as hamstrung by its predominantly psychological and ethical perspectives, its taking for granted of established solutions to religious, metaphysical, political, and social problems.²² He focuses on its inbuilt restrictions: its class basis; its neutralization of the political; and its promotion of a psychology that is simply the obverse of that neutralization. With its cynical account of human nature and motivation, La Rochefoucauld's *Maximes* may appear to be a subversive text: but it is as if polite society has itself set up the subversive spectacle for its own benefit, and the subversive effect itself is strictly limited to the psychological domain.²³

Likewise, La Bruyère's vision reduces the people to pure objects, devoid of the characteristics ascribed to members of the privileged social groups;²⁴ his submission to the cult of the monarch cuts across what would today be called a systematically demystifying attitude;²⁵ we no longer think of a person's "character" as reducible to a simple character-type.²⁶ He, at least, cannot be accused of foregrounding the psychological at the expense of the social: he represents human beings much more in social than in psychological terms.²⁷ Moreover, "character" is not an individual property, since every individual "character" is defined by the person's relationship to a given category, or set of overlapping categories, such as age, social origin, wealth, and vanity.²⁸ Nonetheless, Barthes suggests that we no longer accept that a single writer can encompass the totality of a social world that we require to be broken down into the domains of different disciplines such as sociology, literary criticism, and psychoanalysis.

Yet Barthes's account of the two writers goes well beyond ideological critique. In both essays, Barthes draws a dividing line between two kinds of reading. The description of the first kind harks back to "Plaisir aux Classiques": we take pleasure in finding ourselves reflected in the moralist's text. We open La Rochefoucauld's *Maximes*, and pick a maxim at random, appropriating it to our own mood or situation. In the second kind of reading, we treat the book sequentially, but then we find not ourselves but the author, a man of his time, with his obsessions.²⁹ Likewise, we can read La Bruyère in quest of a generalization that will perfectly express our resentment against our fellow-humans; or in order to register all that separates his world from our own, in order the better to understand ourselves.³⁰

Whereas in "La Bruyère" Barthes espouses the second approach, in "La Rochefoucauld" he adopts a third approach, a sort of synthesis of the first two: analyzing the structure of the individual maxim, and in that light analyzing the content of the collection. But in both cases, the first approach, centered on the reader's subjectivity and pleasure, is set aside.

Barthes's analysis of La Rochefoucauld focuses on aspects of the text that disturb the relationship between the time of reading and the time of writing. In the two kinds of reading he began with, one time had clear primacy over another. In the first, I, as I am now, find myself reflected in the text; its historicity disappears. In the second, I am aware primarily of the author as a seventeenth-century man; my own experience becomes irrelevant.

The most obvious way in which this situation is complicated is when the reader becomes aware, intermittently, of La Rochefoucauld's "strange" modernity, his capacity to go beyond the philosophical framework of his time, which recognizes only immobile essences, to something like a dialectical pattern of thought: good can come out of evil, changes of quantity produce changes of quality; essences are transformed by praxis. Unfortunately, moral considerations then intervene to block the dialectical progress (*OC* IV, 37–8).[31] This kind of perception is a commonplace of mid-twentieth-century Marxist writing, which celebrates earlier writers and thinkers to the extent to which they "anticipate" Marxist truth, especially the concept of dialectics (think of Lucien Goldmann); it is not particularly Barthesian.

Far more interesting, and more distinctive, is the result of Barthes's attempt to unpick the basic structural patterns of the maxim. He uses it to evoke a symbolic dimension beyond the letter of the text (and thus perhaps immune to the historical-ideological critique). In other words, Barthes is not just seeking to expose the structure of the text as an object to be contemplated; he is using the structural model to illuminate our unconscious response as readers; and the unconscious, from a Freudian point of view, is outside time.

There are two dominant strands of this symbolism. The first is religious. Take maxim 89: "Everyone complains of their memory, and no one of their judgement."[32] The structure of the maxim, says Barthes, is a combination of "star-words" ("mots-vedettes"), terms denoting substances or essences ("complains," "memory," "judgement") and weaker terms that establish a relationship between the key terms. This alternation of strong and weak elements has a certain metrical quality, which imparts to it a certain oracular character.[33] Moreover, the relationships between the terms are often quantitative, as in "We have more strength than willpower" (the opening of maxim 30) or "People's happiness or unhappiness depends no less on their temperament than on fortune" (maxim 61). The author is thus weighing objects against one another and announcing the results; a certain iconographical tradition represents this as a divine activity.[34] The image reflects a certain fascination on Barthes's part with ancient Greek and Roman religion and ritual.[35] But Barthes immediately tones down the religious connotations: La Rochefoucauld's thinking, derived from a "rationalist movement," is profane; he is not a god, not even a priest, but a chemist—yet after all, Barthes goes on to say, in our collective imagination the gap between these two figures, the priest and the chemist, is not so great.[36] There is a perceptible degree of uncertainty in Barthes's language here, but it registers an essential ambiguity in his subject's work. We may know, and Barthes certainly knew, that some of La Rochefoucauld's claims (for instance, that the pagans' virtues were inspired by self-love) were emphasized by Augustinian and in particular Jansenist writers;[37] but when actually reading the *Maximes*, most readers do not feel that they are dealing with a religious thinker, as they would with Pascal or even La Bruyère.[38]

In any case, the transmutation of the religious into the scientific is reversed a few pages later, in the discussion of self-love (*amour-propre*), the most powerful factor in La Rochefoucauld's universe, the root of all the passions. Self-love is a quasi-chemical substance that turns out to have magical powers, just as passion (which is just a form of self-love) is a busy and tormenting deity.[39] This mobilization of cultural archetypes suggests a certain unconscious resonance in our response to La Rochefoucauld, which transcends our acute sense of the historical and ideological limitations of his work.

The second strand of imagery is not archetypal in the sense of dealing with figures from our cultural imaginary, like the god, the priest, or the scientist: it is initially thematic and substantial, in the sense these terms bear in Barthes's reading of Michelet: that is, it evokes an attitude to certain qualities of matter.[40] Yet behind these qualities, a figure takes shape, but not that of a human or divine agent, like a priest or a god or a chemist, but of a nonhuman object of phantasy, the insect: the maxim is hard, gleaming, and fragile, like the prothorax of an insect; and it terminates in a cluster of words that functions like an insect's stylet, or piercing mouthpart. Barthes calls this latter element of the maxim its "pointe."[41] The *pointe* is a component of the maxim's structure, but with a distinctive effect: to introduce affect and pleasure into what might appear as a neutral purely conceptual structure.[42] It is an utterance that highlights the processes by which it creates meaning: it turns meaning into spectacle.[43] Thus, in maxim 107 ("It is a form of flirtatiousness to point out that one never goes in for flirtatiousness") the *pointe*, the effect of surprise, comes from the displacement of the obvious meaning of a reported utterance by the antithetical meaning (the speaker is unwittingly saying "I am a flirt"). It is the spectacular nature of the *pointe* that constitutes its pleasure.[44]

We see how Barthes has taken us, through what is intended to be a purely structural analysis of the maxim as a form, beyond the antithesis he constructed in the opening sentences. There the options seemed to be either rediscovering ourselves in an individual maxim, as individuals in our own time, or encountering the author in his own time. Barthes's analysis of the structure of the maxim discloses a spectacle of meaning that bypasses the opposition past/present: we seem to make contact with a prehistorical past state of language.[45] There is perhaps something uncanny in this. And there is perhaps something uncanny in another aspect of the text, which is linked to another of the recurrent formal features of the *Maximes*: the relation of restrictive identity ("*x* is nothing but *y*"), exemplified in maxim 15: "Clemency on the part of rulers is often nothing but a political move to win their subjects' affection." An apparently impressive virtue is reduced to an unimpressive reality. Barthes argues, however, that the reduction, in a way, undoes itself. For the second term of the maxim, which denotes the reality, is of its nature the predicate. It is the mask or the appearance that is the subject of the discourse. La Rochefoucauld represents moral virtues as mere illusions ("songes"), but as the grammatical subject of the maxims, they are still center stage, and resist all attempts to expel them. This, Barthes suggests, gives the *Maximes* a certain nightmarish quality.[46] In struggling with the nightmare, we are again projected into a time that is neither our own nor La Rochefoucauld's.

Indeed, the spectacle of meaning has a tragic as well as a pleasurable side. Barthes began, as we saw, by noting that we can, we do, on one level read the *Maximes* for ourselves. But, as the end of his essay suggests, in so doing we are unwittingly asking the tragic and potentially fatal question: "Who am I?"[47] The reply takes the "terrifying funereal" form of the formula of restrictive identity ("nothing but"); yet the answer is unreliable, since we can never rid ourselves of the specter of virtue.[48] It is as if La Rochefoucauld has uncovered the law of the symbolic that governs human life, that is, on one level, that all our actions are doomed to carry unconscious significations, and that the processes of this signification can be formalized in rigorously impersonal fashion, and also the law of the imaginary, that they must appear to the agent to be other than they are, to be manifestations of an essential moral self, which is nothing other than the dream of virtue. But the form of the maxim has another dimension besides its deathly quality. In the interplay of question and answer, the answer does not quite correspond to the question; for the question "Who am I?" is answered not in the second person ("You are (this or that))" but in the third ("This is nothing but that"). There is something ludic in this discrepancy, reminiscent of the riddle as a form of salon entertainment. This, for Barthes, is the true timelessness of La Rochefoucauld: the discoveries of the *Maximes* may date, but their basic project remains, saying as it does that "play comes into contact with the death of the subject."[49] This is hardly the thought we should have arrived at by reading the *Maximes* as messages to ourselves or as a record of La Rochefoucauld's views. Reading La Rochefoucauld is thus not necessarily pleasurable in the ways set out in "Plaisir aux Classiques"; but it offers a powerful imaginative experience that bridges the gap between his time, and his worldview, and ours.

But La Rochefoucauld also concerns us in another way. He is not a writer, inasmuch as his project is to speak the truth. In that sense, he prefigures the modern intellectual, the more so in that the role allotted him by society itself is to challenge its own way of life.[50] He thus becomes a figure of Barthes's own self-interrogation as to his social role, in roughly contemporary texts like "Écrivains et écrivants" (1960) and the 1963 preface to *Essais Critiques*. And this is true also of La Bruyère. When we have taken stock of all that separates us from him, we realize that (unlike La Rochefoucauld) he is a writer ("écrivain"), and this is his true claim on our interest.[51] He concerns us as a writer partly because of his own reflection on the status and ethics of literary activity. First, he writes about writing (as a craft, a technique) and about the writer, the man of letters, who is open to the social world, without being part of social life.[52] Second, he sees the writer's activity as a response to the state of the language that he has inherited but that does not determine his activity, which is rather a result of deliberate choice. The writer in this sense is exercising his responsibility, in a distinctively modern way. Third, though La Bruyère's aim was certainly to instruct, the effect of his work is not didactic; he is modern in the sense that he opens up questions, rather than giving answers; he points to problems, rather than using them to advocate particular solutions.[53]

If Barthes plays down or denies the relevance to us of the moralists' message, it is clear that he finds relevance in their situation *qua* intellectual or *qua* writer, to his own. This line of thought has been explored in great depth by Claude Coste in *Roland Barthes moraliste*. Tracking Barthes throughout his career, and bringing out the ethical concerns of his writing, Coste presents him as a twentieth-century reincarnation (*mutatis mutandis*) of the seventeenth-century moralist.[54] Naturally enough, he draws frequently and to good effect on Barthes's essays on La Rochefoucauld and La Bruyère.[55] He makes a convincing case for seeing the moralists as inspirations for Barthes's own writing.

Barthes praises La Bruyère in a way that suggests such a connection:

> *Les Caractères* is a marvelous collection of substances, places, customs, attitudes; within it human beings are almost continually taken charge of by an object or

an incident: clothing, gait, tears, colors, make-up, faces, foodstuffs, landscapes, furniture, visits, baths, letters, etc.[56]

This profusion is a source of pleasure to the reader, but it also perhaps appealed specifically to the writer of *Mythologies*, where, again, human beings are represented against a multifarious background of objects and behavior patterns. And the words "object" and "incident" look forward also to later writings. This is obvious enough in the case of the latter, which features as a title of a posthumously published work;[57] but as regards the former, it is equally clear. In *Roland Barthes par Roland Barthes*, Barthes notes his tendency, "out of consideration for the reader," to introduce sensuous objects, sometimes a slew of sensuous objects, into an intellectual disquisition.[58] But this is exactly how La Bruyère imparts density and flavor to his moralist discourse.

In *Le Plaisir du texte*, Barthes identifies the first phase in the quest for a materialist theory of the subject as consisting in a ruthless critique of the illusions with which the imaginary subject surrounds itself. In this, he states, the classical moralists excel.[59] But in *Roland Barthes par Roland Barthes*, there is a certain rehabilitation of the imaginary subject. Barthes discusses how he thinks of himself, how he may appear to others, while aware of the pitfalls of this enterprise: the risk of producing a static portrait of a supposedly unitary and coherent personality (the supreme illusion of the imaginary). In order to keep the risk of a false coherence at bay, he practices an aesthetic of discontinuity, of the fragment, reminiscent of the fragmentary writing of the moralists (while being perfectly aware of the limitations of this strategy).[60]

At the same time, Barthes sets about rejecting discursive arrogance, not only that of the doxa, the so-called common opinion, but also that of the discourses of abstract theory ("la Science") and political militancy that aim to challenge the doxa, and exult in their triumphs over it.[61] In reaction to this, Barthes aims to establish an ethic and aesthetic of care for the reader. And in this there is something classical. The "consideration for the reader" of which he spoke earlier is a classical value—Barthes's language here is very reminiscent of La Bruyère's, when he speaks of choosing to write in a certain way "on account of the good opinion one has of one's readers."[62] We saw also that Barthes observes that his own writing repeatedly exhibits certain procedures (such as the construction of opposing terms (denotation/connotation, *lisible/scriptible*, and so forth)) the point of which is simply to enable him to say something: he calls these "figures" a term that deliberately echoes the figures of traditional rhetoric. If this modus operandi is in keeping with a semiological approach, that approach itself preserves something of traditional rhetoric. After all, Barthes is writing, like the practitioner of rhetoric, as if writing were a matter of finding procedures to represent a preexisting idea; in short, he is writing "classically" ("j'écris classique"), and the texts he produces, with their clearly marked sentence structures, are readable ("lisible").[63] In the late essay "L'Image," he promotes readability as a value, associating it with the writer's work on sentence structure and syntax, and he ventures to suggest, with all kinds of oratorical precautions, that "no one can ever say how much love (for the other, the reader) there is the writer's working on the sentence."[64]

We have seen Barthes exploring various ways in which we can approach literature from the past, even if we do not accept the author's worldview. We can, as in *Sur Racine*, distance ourselves from the text by describing it in a language, that of present-day theory, entirely alien to the author's. We can trace the operation of archetypal resonances that constitute the text's imaginative appeal, beyond any conceptual or ideological agenda; we can find in it a questioning of our own identity, as in "La Rochefoucauld." We can use the author's reflections on his or her situation as a writer to illuminate our own, as in "La Bruyère." In all these cases, we are setting aside or devaluing the experience of which Barthes spoke in "Plaisir aux Classiques" of finding ourselves addressed, very personally, by the text. But in his very late writing, we find a rehabilitation of this experience. Speaking of reading Pascal, he says, "to love literature [. . .] is to believe, is to see, that this is a living human being who speaks, as if their body were beside me; [. . .] it is to find that these old words ('Wretchedness of humanity,' 'Concupiscence,' and so forth) perfectly express the things that are presently in me, it is *not to feel the need for another language.*"[65] From "Pleasure in the Classics" to "loving literature," Barthes went on both a very long and a very short journey, which suggests that fully to understand the modern we need at times to turn to the early modern.

Notes

1 Roland Barthes, "Réponses," in *Œuvres complètes*, ed. Éric Marty, 2nd ed., 5 vols (Paris: Gallimard, 2002), III, 1023–44 (1039). All references are to this edition (hereafter *OC*). All translations from Barthes and other authors are my own.
2 Barthes, "Plaisir aux Classiques," *Existences*, 1944 (*OC* I, 57–67).
3 Ibid., 67.
4 Ibid., 60.
5 This is not necessarily how Barthes continued to use the term: he later refers to Sade, Flaubert, and Proust as his favorite "classical" authors ("Réponses," 1033).
6 Barthes, "Plaisir aux Classiques," 57.
7 Ibid., 57–8.
8 Ibid., 58.
9 See, for instance, La Fontaine's eulogy of La Rochefoucauld in "L'Homme et son image," *Fables*, I.11, in *Fables*, ed. Marc Fumaroli, 2 vols (Paris: Imprimerie Nationale, 1985).
10 Barthes, "Plaisir aux Classiques," 58.
11 Ibid.
12 Barthes, "L'Ancienne Rhétorique: Aide-mémoire," *OC* III, 527–601.
13 Barthes, *Le Degré zéro de l'écriture*, *OC* I, 169–225 (206). There are various problems involved in identifying "classical" writing as bourgeois, but this is not the place to discuss them.
14 Barthes, "L'Ancienne Rhétorique," 599–600.
15 See Barthes, "Le Monde où l'on catche," *Mythologies, suivi de "Le Mythe, aujourd'hui,"* *OC* I, 671–870 (686). Molière and Racine are alluded to on page 679, and Molière again on page 682. See also Barthes, "Folies-Bergère," *OC* I, 234–44 (238), for the comparison of popular culture and classical literature. There is a good discussion

of references to classical literature in *Mythologies* in Claude Coste, *Roland Barthes moraliste* (Villeneuve-d'Ascq: Presses Universitaires du Septentrion, 1998), 90–1.

16 Barthes, "Nekrassov juge de sa critique" [1955], in *OC* I, 599–604 (601).

17 Barthes, "Dire Racine," in *Sur Racine*, *OC* II, 53–196 (174).

18 Barthes admits in the interview with Jean Thibaudeau that, since he doesn't like Racine, in order to write on him he had to force himself to inject his personal problems of "amorous alienation." Annette Lavers, however, wisely warns us against taking these apparently damaging admissions too literally (*Roland Barthes: Structuralism and After* [London: Methuen, 1982], 180).

19 Barthes, *Critique et vérité*, *OC* II, 757–801 (777–9).

20 Barthes, "La Rochefoucauld: *Réflexions ou Sentences et Maximes*" [1961], in *Nouveaux Essais Critiques* [1972], *OC* IV, 25–40; Barthes, "La Bruyère" [1963], in *Essais Critiques* [1964], *OC* II, 473–87. For divergent conceptions of the *moraliste* genre, see Odette de Mourgues, *Two French Moralists: La Rochefoucauld and La Bruyère* (Cambridge: Cambridge University Press, 1978), and Louis Van Delft, *Le Moraliste classique: essai de définition et de typologie* (Geneva: Droz, 1982); more recently, see also Bérengère Parmentier, *Le Siècle des moralistes: de Montaigne à La Bruyère* (Paris: Seuil, 2000).

21 On Barthes's prefaces, see Antoine Compagnon, "Barthes and Commissioned Writing," in *Interdisciplinary Barthes*, ed. Diana Knight, *Proceedings of the British Academy* 228 (New York: Oxford University Press, 2020), 205–30.

22 Jean-Paul Sartre, *Qu'est-ce que la littérature?* (Paris: Gallimard, 1948), 104. For a criticism of this view, see Michael Moriarty, *Fallen Nature, Fallen Selves: Early Modern French Thought II* (Oxford: Oxford University Press, 2006), 5–9.

23 Barthes, "La Rochefoucauld," 39. The opposition between, on the one hand, the pre-Freudian psychological approach to human behavior, with its recourse to the concept of individual character, and, on the other, political and ideological approaches, and the preference given to the latter kind, is a constant of Barthes's writing in the 1950s and 1960s. See Michael Moriarty, *Roland Barthes* (Cambridge: Polity Press, 1991), 45–6, 65–6, 94–5.

24 Barthes, "La Bruyère," 479–80.

25 Ibid., 482. La Bruyère bitterly denounces the disruptive social influence of new money, especially in the chapter "Des biens de fortune"; but his ideal vision of society is as a static hierarchy, with a paternal monarch at the top. See François-Xavier Cuche, *Une Pensée sociale catholique: La Bruyère, Fleury, Fénelon* (Paris: Le Cerf, 1991).

26 Barthes, "La Bruyère," 477.

27 Ibid., 475.

28 Ibid., 476. This conception is Aristotelian in origin, as Barthes would have known: see Aristotle, *Rhetoric*, 2.12.1-2 (1388b31-1389a2). The fullest account of the notion of character used by early modern moralists is that of Louis Van Delft, *Littérature et anthropologie: nature humaine et caractère à l'âge classique* (Paris: Presses Universitaires de France, 1993).

29 Barthes, "La Rochefoucauld," 25.

30 Barthes, "La Bruyère," 474–5.

31 For another reference to the intermittent modernity of the text, see page 39.

32 That is, everyone admits to having a poor memory, no one to having poor judgment. Barthes does not give the numbers of the maxims he quotes.

33 Barthes, "La Rochefoucauld," 27.
34 Ibid., 29.
35 Compare the allusions to the *numen*, the nod of the head by which the god signifies his will (Barthes, "Puissance et désinvolture," *Mythologies*, OC I, 726) and to the Roman art of divination by the flight of birds (Barthes, *S/Z*, OC III, 119-345 [§ VII, 129]).
36 Barthes, "La Rochefoucauld," 29.
37 Ibid., 35.
38 For discussions of this ambiguity, see Jean Lafond, *La Rochefoucauld: Augustinisme et literature* [1977], 3rd ed. (Paris: Klincksieck, 1986) and Michael Moriarty, *Disguised Vices: Theories of Virtue in Early Modern French Thought* (Oxford: Oxford University Press, 2011), 253-75, 359-82.
39 Barthes, "La Rochefoucauld," 36.
40 Barthes, "Lecture de Michelet," in *Michelet*, OC I, 291-450 (430-1).
41 Barthes, "La Rochefoucauld," 26.
42 Ibid., 31.
43 Ibid., 33. Barthes seems to be using the term in one of its possible seventeenth-century senses: a *pointe d'esprit* is "a thought that surprises us by some imaginative subtlety, by some play on words" ("une pensée qui surprend par quelque subtilité d'imagination, par quelque jeu de mots") (*Dictionnaire de l'Académie Française*, first edition (1694), s.v. pointe, https://artflsrv03.uchicago.edu/philologic4/publicdicos /query?report=bibliography&head=point. Accessed July 27, 2020. "Conceit" in its poetic sense might be an English equivalent.
44 Barthes, "La Rochefoucauld," 31-2. The term *spectacle* links the maxim to one of the central preoccupations of Barthes's work; he observes that "spectacle" is the universal category through which he perceives the world (*Roland Barthes par Roland Barthes*, OC IV, 575-771 (749)).
45 Ibid., 32-3.
46 Ibid., 38.
47 Barthes cites Ériphile, the tragic anti-heroine of Racine's *Iphigénie*, to whom an oracle has predicted that she cannot discover who she is without dying and who kills herself when her identity is revealed. Claude Coste discusses this passage suggestively (*Roland Barthes moraliste*, 157).
48 Barthes, "La Rochefoucauld," 40.
49 Ibid.
50 Ibid., 39.
51 Barthes, "La Bruyère," 483. To call La Bruyère an "écrivain" is by no means anachronistic. Partly by his own reflections on writing, he played a role in the emergence of a relatively autonomous literary field (see Alain Viala, *Naissance de l'écrivain: sociologie de la littérature à l'âge classique* (Paris: Minuit, 1985)).
52 Again, Barthes's insight is historically very pertinent. By defining writing as a craft at the outset of his text (La Bruyère, *Les Caractères*, "Des ouvrages de l'esprit," 3), La Bruyère is rejecting the then widespread idea (associated with the notion of the *honnête homme*) that it should be one gentlemanly accomplishment among others. See Pascal, *Pensées*, 647, 605, 587 (Lafuma's numbering)/532, 502, 486 (Sellier's numbering)/547, 517, 500 (Le Guern's numbering).
53 Barthes, "La Bruyère," 486-7. There is, one suspects, an implicit contrast with the modern writer whose commitment (*engagement*) takes a straightforwardly ideological form.

54 Coste, *Roland Barthes moraliste*, 15, 89, 115–16, 206, 267–8.
55 See Coste 55, 58, 127–8, 134, 157, 165–6 for references to these essays.
56 Barthes, "La Bruyère," 483.
57 The volume published as *Incidents* (Paris: Éditions du Seuil, 1987) contains a section with the same title, which I take to be Barthes's own.
58 Barthes, *Roland Barthes par Roland Barthes*, 709–10.
59 Barthes, *Le Plaisir du texte*, *OC* III, 217–64 (257).
60 Barthes, *Roland Barthes par Roland Barthes*, 672. Coste emphasizes the difference between the Barthesian fragment and those of the *Maximes* and the *Caractères*, where the fragment is a part of a totality (134).
61 Ibid., 627.
62 La Bruyère, *Les Caractères*, "Des ouvrages de l'esprit," 57. The point is not exactly the same: while conceding that we write in order to be understood, La Bruyère is suggesting that to go beyond the obvious, to resort to subtlety and implication, is a sign of respect for the reader.
63 Barthes, *Roland Barthes par Roland Barthes*, 669. The rhetorical conception of the relationship between language and thought as mutually external (we have a picture in our mind, and we aim to convey it in words) is referred to in "L'Ancienne Rhétorique," A.7.4 (*OC* III, 557).
64 Barthes, "L'Image," *OC* V, 512–19 (514).
65 Barthes, *La Préparation du roman (I et II): Cours et séminaires au Collège de France (1978–1979 et 1979–1980)*, ed. Nathalie Léger (Paris: Seuil, 2003), 353 (Barthes's italics). Compare the discussion of passages in Tolstoy and Proust and the "moment of truth" in Barthes, "Longtemps je me suis couché de bonne heure," *OC* V, 469–70 (467–8). See also Lucy O'Meara, *Roland Barthes at the Collège de France* (Liverpool: Liverpool University Press, 2012), 169.

Bibliography

Aristotle. *"Art" of Rhetoric*. Ed. and trans. J. H. Freese. Loeb Classical Library. Cambridge, MA: Harvard University Press and London: Heinemann, 1926.

Barthes, Roland. *La Préparation du roman (I et II): Cours et séminaires au Collège de France (1978–1979 et 1979–1980)*. Ed. Nathalie Léger. Paris: Seuil, 2003.

Barthes, Roland. *Œuvres complètes [OC]*. 2nd ed. 5 vols. Ed. Éric Marty. Paris: Gallimard, 2002.

Compagnon, Antoine. "Barthes and Commissioned Writing." In *Interdisciplinary Barthes*. Ed. Diana Knight. *Proceedings of the British Academy 228*. New York: Oxford University Press, 2020. 205–30.

Coste, Claude. *Roland Barthes moraliste*. Villeneuve-d'Ascq: Presses Universitaires du Septentrion, 1998.

Cuche, François-Xavier. *Une Pensée sociale catholique: La Bruyère, Fleury, Fénelon*. Paris: Le Cerf, 1991.

Dictionnaire de l'Académie Française. First edition (1694). https://artfl-project.uchicago.edu/content/dictionnaires-dautrefois.

La Bruyère, Jean de. *Les Caractères*. Ed. Emmanuel Bury. Le Livre de Poche Classique. Paris: Librairie Générale Française, 2004.

Lafond, Jean. *La Rochefoucauld: Augustinisme et literature* [1977]. 3rd ed. Paris: Klincksieck, 1986.
La Fontaine, Jean de. *Fables*. Ed. Marc Fumaroli. 2 vols. Paris: Imprimerie Nationale, 1985.
La Rochefoucauld, François VI, duc de. *Réflexions ou Sentences et maximes morales et Réflexions diverses*. Ed. Laurence Plazenet. Paris: Champion, 2005.
Moriarty, Michael. *Disguised Vices: Theories of Virtue in Early Modern French Thought*. Oxford: Oxford University Press, 2011.
Moriarty, Michael. *Fallen Nature, Fallen Selves: Early Modern French Thought II*. Oxford: Oxford University Press, 2006.
Moriarty, Michael. *Roland Barthes*. Cambridge: Polity Press, 1991.
de Mourgues, Odette. *Two French Moralists: La Rochefoucauld and La Bruyère*. Cambridge: Cambridge University Press, 1978.
O'Meara, Lucy. *Roland Barthes at the Collège de France*. Liverpool: Liverpool University Press, 2012.
Parmentier, Bérengère. *Le Siècle des moralistes: de Montaigne à La Bruyère*. Paris: Seuil, 2000.
Sartre, Jean-Paul. *Qu'est-ce que la littérature?* Paris: Gallimard, 1948.
Van Delft, Louis. *Le Moraliste classique: essai de définition et de typologie*. Geneva: Droz, 1982.
Van Delft, Louis. *Littérature et anthropologie: nature humaine et caractère à l'âge classique*. Paris: Presses Universitaires de France, 1993.
Viala, Alain. *Naissance de l'écrivain: sociologie de la littérature à l'âge classique*. Paris: Minuit, 1985.

4

Pleasure in Paradigm

Sade, Fourier, Loyola

Rudolphus Teeuwen

In his manifesto *Suprematism*, part 2 of his book *The Non-Objective World*, Kasimir Malevich writes,

> When in the year 1913, in my desperate attempt to free art from the ballast of objectivity, I took refuge in the square form and exhibited a picture which consisted of nothing more than a black square on a white field, the critics, and along with them, the public sighed "Everything we loved is lost. We are in a desert."[1]

This desert is a world of painting consisting of lines and shapes without subject matter or imitated reality, a grammar of pure painting without obligation to "things." Malevich had the courage to go into that desert of objectlessness that throws off the "dead weight of the world" and, as he puts it in an essay, "I have transformed myself into the zero of form and dragged myself out of Academic Art's whirlpool of trash."[2] For all their differences—Malevich looking to Bergson, Barthes to Saussure; Malevich often a mystic, Barthes seldom one; Malevich a painter and theoretician, Barthes a theoretician and writer—what stands out is how both Malevich and Barthes turn away from representation of the world in favor of radical newness, "the zero of form."

Sade, Fourier, Loyola is the book in which Barthes celebrates radical newness and presents it as offering a reader the delight that, Barthes presumes, must have animated the three authors. The three devise a second language, made up of material from their first language, but unlike the first language not meant for communication. The second languages of the three authors combine known words and grammatical categories from their first languages but in ways that do not make acceptable social, ideological, philosophical, or political sense. In order not to make such sense, the first step of the three must be to isolate themselves and the language they are developing from the world. All three therefore seek forms of retreat: Sade has libertines imprison their victims; Fourier creates in the phalanstery a way of living together that is not the family, village, or city; and Loyola organizes a religious retreat in which, undisturbed by the world, exercitants learn to formulate a request that might elicit an answer from

God. The three second languages consist, like any language, of basic units and rules for combining them. For Sade, the units are body postures, sites of pleasure, and sexual acts described and dissertated upon; for Fourier, human passions (of which he declares there are exactly 1,620) reciprocally exercised in such a way that the description of Harmony, Fourier's new world, will realize a continual sweetness of sensual pleasure; for Loyola, prayers, visions, and tears that amount to the formulation of an ultimate request of God. These units are combined according to rules the three authors design, rules that make them inventors of languages or "logothetes," as Barthes has it.[3]

The three logothetes retreat from referentiality, that which turns writing into a "whirlpool of trash." Stripped of public language, ideology, sociolect (of "doxa" as Barthes calls it), their deserts flower with new charms and pleasures of language. To Barthes, Fourier's charm, for instance, is the anacoluthon, "that sudden twisting of the syntagm," the exhilarating non-sequitur of a logical-grammatical side-jump, the error that makes for unforeseen combinations in his mania for calculations, geometrical progression, and taxonomy.[4] Sade's charms include that "most elegant of figures, chiasmus" in a sentence like "She obtains from this lovely girl's fingers the same services her tongue renders to me." The chiasmus in this sentence, "(*obtain . . . / . . . render*)," makes that "the paradigm becomes the condition of pleasure," one that depends on the "intelligence, both mental and complicit, of syntax."[5]

Loyola offers Barthes less pleasure. Whereas Fourier and Sade feel congenial to him in the way they write and think—Barthes's work more and more assumes a similar rhapsodic quality in the last decade of his life—Loyola does not. Barthes only appreciates Ignatius after he has stripped the saint of mysticism and spirituality: "what I get from Loyola's life are not the saint's pilgrimages, visions, mortifications, and constitutions, but only his 'beautiful eyes, always a little filled with tears.'"[6] Once he has defrocked and materialized the Jesuit, Barthes can turn Ignatius's asceticism into the objectlessness of his language, a language he can take pleasure in: "For Ignatius, every human act is by nature paradigmatic," and includes the operation of "*proairesis*, which consists in disposing points of bifurcation in the project of a line of conduct, in examining both perspectives, in choosing one and not the other, and then in moving on."[7] This step-by-step pushing forward of language to a next formulation by means of bifurcation leads to a moment of perfect balance between final alternatives that can be tipped one way or the other only by God: God must now speak, or His silence be accepted. God must provide the object to Ignatius's language whittled down to a final bifurcation of yes or no. Ignatius's paradigm of bifurcations does not constitute a system of signifiers but solicits a single binary sign: God's answer ("yes"/"no"), or his silence.

So, the three writers gain the freedom to use words that never need alight on preestablished meaning. Barthes shows how they, each in his own way, exploit this freedom by using *many* words: they invent classifications which cut up their specific obsessions (eroticism, utopia, spirituality) with a neatness that requires such endlessness of detail, clarification, and reordering and that allows such profusion of captivating exceptions that the resulting discourse expands deliriously toward endlessness. This expansive embrace of order and exception yields the idiosyncratic tics of language, chiasmus (Sade), anacoluthon (Fourier), and proairesis (Loyola), that delight Barthes. The new language of Sade is "a vast discourse founded in its own repetitions (and not those of others), paid out in details, surprises, voyages, menus, portraits, configurations, proper nouns, etc."[8] Fourier and Loyola produce vast discourses of their own, also based on unique repetitions of their own, "and not those of others," also requiring an "etc." to signal that the detailing of this enumerative vastness could always have gone on.

Sade, Barthes explains, is subversive not because he writes "what shocks public opinion, morality, the law, the police," but because he invents "a paradoxical (pure of any *doxa*) discourse: *invention* (and not provocation) is a revolutionary act: it cannot be accomplished other than in setting up a new language."[9] In reading Sade, provocation is the red herring, the thing that wrong-foots readers because they see him abuse the old, not invent the new. Sade is an inventor because he rids his prose of social constraint in an act akin to vomiting (in counterpart, as we will see, to Fourier's "vomiting of politics"[10]). Sade purges his discourse of doxa in the way that, quite literally, his debauchees end up purging their scenes of debauchery of beauty and luxury: "there are great numbers of roses, carnations, lilies, jasmine, lilies of the valley; yet the debauchery will terminate in a sea of excrement and vomit; the flowers are inaugural; they establish the onset of a degradation that is a part of the libertine plan."[11] Reading Sade with moral condemnation means "taking for nourishment only the received word of others, the repetitious matter of common opinion."[12]

If they do not morally condemn them, readers may scorn Sade's novels for the sheer impossibility of the nature and frequency of sexual acts depicted in them. But it is not depiction that Sade is after: "the impossibilities of the referent are turned into possibilities of the discourse."[13] If read for "the performances of the discourse,"[14] Sade becomes the designer of a new paradigm, with new laws that discredit laws of referential reality. The referent becomes fabulous because the truth of realism is ruled out of court. Sade "always sides with *semiosis* rather than *mimesis*," and Barthes cheers him on for this.[15] Whereas mimesis duplicates, semiosis invents; what it invents is, by necessity, a combination of elements and therefore a system of rules according to which the new is established. Because Sade (as do Fourier and Loyola) constructs combinations that are without history or priors, he flaunts his artificiality and courts the sort of bewilderment Malevich noticed in his public and critics, "Everything we loved is lost."[16]

Sade writes about bodies, classifies their sites of erotic pleasure, and stages them in postures, operations, and scenes that allow, lead to, facilitate, intensify, increase, and multiply discharge. "Discharge" is a charged word, one that "makes sperm the substitute for speech . . . : 'Saint-Fond's discharge was brilliant, audacious, passionate.'"[17] Sadian flesh is word: the erotic principle is

> the saturation of every area of the body: one tries to employ (to occupy) every separate part. This is the same problem the sentence faces (. . . there being no distinction between the structure of ejaculation and that of language): the (literary, written) sentence is also a body to be catalyzed by filling all its principal sites

(subject-verb-complement) with expansions, incidental clauses, subordinates, determinators.[18]

Barthes means by the verb "to catalyze" ("catalyser" in Barthes's French), I think, something like "to break up into separate parts." Because the erotic body can be broken up into "the principal sites of pleasure (mouth, sexual organs, anus)"[19] just like a sentence can be broken up in "subject-verb-complement," Sade can turn the body into language, dissolve flesh into discourse.

Barthes's Fourier deals in impossibility just as much as does his Sade, and he just as enthusiastically breaks things up into parts in order to recombine them. The object of Fourier's breaking up is sensual pleasure conceived as residing in a surfeit, the *"overmuch"*[20] of material things so that happiness won't require the Freudian "sublimating transformation of a lack, but on the contrary the panic effusion of an acme of satiety."[21] But how to reconcile that acme of satiety with a continual renewal of appetite? Fourier's answers are wide ranging, pleasure inducing, and absolutely radical in admitting only "the absolutely new, that about which nothing has yet been said."[22] So, all that exists already, and is organized already according to already-developed principles, will have to be broken up so that a counterreality can be invented, one liberated from the real, from the weight of the world. Instead of Civilization, Fourier's new society of Harmony; instead of the contrast between work and leisure, a practice that transforms work into pleasure; instead of the denigration of money (and exactly because philosophers, be they Christian, Marxist, Freudian, or anything else all denigrate it for one reason or another), the exaltation of money; instead of science and politics, "Domestics," the overall name of Fourier's new system. Domestics is the getting rid of politics, and "the vomiting of politics is what Fourier calls Invention."[23] Domestics is the organizational principle of Harmony, a society carefully delineated in a paradigm of pleasures, one that omits everything that already so dolefully exists—asceticism, philosophy, libraries, need, neurosis, marriage, and bad food.[24]

Fourier's paradigm of pleasure is just such a runaway affair as Sade's paradigm of vice. Fourier's pleasure hits Barthes quicker, more directly, than Sade's pleasure in crime and evil does: Fourier is a happy writer whose pleasure "does not include vexation, in the Sadian manner, but on the contrary dissipates it."[25] The radical pleasure in Fourier's paradigm renders one innocent because Harmony strips Civilization of hypocrisy, earnestness, and all judgmental sizing up. "Harmony will decongest the passions, sadism will be reabsorbed" by pairing the sadist with someone who can relieve the sadist from sadism.[26] In Harmony, evil is transformed into sensual pleasure by balancing classifications of passions (of which there are precisely 810 per sex, so 1,620 in total). Fourier's classifications bring such pleasure because they induce a "logical vertigo"[27] that will dismiss all gravity from classifications and render them light with added absurdity. In Harmony, for instance, of fish there "will remain only the useful strains, like the whiting, the herring, the mackerel, sole, tuna, tortoise, in short, all those that do not attack swimmers."[28] This enumeration delights Barthes because of the surrealist rebound it causes in his imagination: that of entirely beneficent fish like the whiting or mackerel attacking a swimmer.

Classifications in Fourier are as endless as they are in Sade and Loyola, but Fourier's specific endlessness lies in his mania for calculation mixed with craziness. Fourier announces the height of men in Harmony to be 7 feet. He does not say what gives him this certainty, but he does justify his use of the foot as measuring unit, and it is "the foot of the King of Paris" to boot. That foot is the natural measurement "because it is equal to the 32nd part of the water level in suction pumps." Nonplussed, Barthes delights in the anacoluthon: "in the space of a few words, we have suction pumps mingled with the height of societary man."[29] There is an arbitrary connection between suction pumps, the king's foot, and the use of it as unit of measurement; arbitrariness is also the characteristic of language: nothing inherent in the signifier /pear tree/ dictates its correspondence with the signified "pear tree." But Fourier's arbitrariness arbitrates differently, and that makes him an inventor of language. Standard linguistics imagines the world as consisting of individual elements outside of language that are designated by corresponding signs of language. Differences in the world, say between pear trees and apple trees, are indicated by substitution of one sign by another, /pear/ by /apple/. Fourier's theory of language shifts away from the principle of substitution to that of addition: it is based, rather, on ratios between difference and sameness. So, different fruits, apples and pears, share the sameness of both hanging from the boughs of quite similar fruit trees. For Fourier's new-made society, this means that he puts groups of people together who can coexist based on contrasting tastes in a shared affinity. Flower lovers both, a group of lovers of small, varied flowers will coexist with the lovers of roses, and joined in this way they form a "syntagmatized paradigm,"[30] a group of elements necessarily unequal in order to assure harmonious cohabitation in the way a sentence can only be grammatical if composed from unlike elements. Haters of rancid couscous (such as Barthes declares himself to be in the opening of his essay on Fourier) would find themselves in Harmony sent to the Anti-Rancid group where they would find fresh couscous ready to be eaten.[31] In this way, Fourier would create a society so infinitely shaded into varieties of taste and passion that not a single member of the phalanstery would ever have to be excluded. In Harmony, "the wound of denial" is abolished.[32]

Happiness is guaranteed in Harmony because in his taxonomies Fourier provides for exceptions that fall outside of classification, exceptions that smooth out the edges of classificatory differences. In fact, it is always exactly one-eighth of every classification that falls outside of it, and that is the portion "of Transitions or Neuters ... this sort of buffer, damper, whose role is to muffle, to soften, to fluidify the semantic *tick-tock* ... the paradigmatic alternative obsessively produces: *yes/no, yes/no, yes/no,* etc.)."[33] The one-eighth error, which contains everything that Civilization rejects ("the sensitive, the bat, the flying fish, the amphibians, the zoophytes, sapphism, pederasty, incest, Chinese society")[34] because it is mixed and ambiguous, is what makes Harmony benevolent because it *is* mixed and ambivalent and "*confuses* meaning, the norm, normality."[35] Besides, as he invents language, Fourier creates impossibilities even more spectacular than Sade's. The saltiness of seawater is turned into lemonade; the climate is improved; Calvary is turned from a place of mournful prayer into a fertile agricultural mountain; continents are rearranged; human bodies, 7 feet tall, will reach a lifespan of 144 vigorous years.[36]

More than Sade's or Loyola's, the spirit of Fourier, though muted, was still alive in Barthes's twentieth century. John Cage, for instance, whom Barthes often mentions approvingly, can sound like Fourier. In interviews with Cage collected in *For the Birds* he, mushroom connoisseur, speaks of how "mushrooms defy our efforts at classification";[37] he declares that the "economy must be eliminated, and politics, too."[38] Following ideas of Buckminster Fuller, Cage believes that "we must put all the resources of the world into a fluid, fluctuating, mobile state so that nothing exists that we have to try to get rid of." A practical example he gives is that we should have magazines "that we could eat after reading" them.[39] Edible paper: a solution so much superior to putting newspapers online! Fourier would have liked the idea, provided the paper he ate for breakfast tasted something like "*mirlitons* (little Parisian spice cakes)."[40]

For Sade, the second language formulates the body: the erotic body and its inlets of pleasure yield to the words of a second language; for Fourier, the second language formulates newly specified passions as bases of pleasure and happiness. Loyola stays closer to home but has further to go: it is out of language (devotional Spanish and Latin) that a new language (just as devotional) must be fashioned that can prompt divine attention. And where Fourier smooths out the "semantic *tick-tock*" of the yes/no by creating potentially endlessly nuanced transitions between the yes and the no, Loyola's language of prayer and devotion aims at teaching retreatants a series of increasingly pointed yes/no questions that will abut that final question that only God may answer. The scene in Loyola's *Exercises* is that of a second-language class in which an instructor (the director of the retreat, instructed himself by the historical author Ignatius) teaches exercitants that second language intended for a pointed address of the divinity. In Loyola's text, there are two linguistic competencies at work: the spiritual instructor, an ascetic, has emptied himself of the weight of the world and knows a language that does not refer to *a priory* reality. He then teaches his pupils to empty themselves of that ballast of objectivity, a process of learning that implies ignorance of every next step: the drama for exercitants is that of not knowing how a sentence they have begun will end.

This process for exercitants of achieving unworldly objectlessness that allows full devotion to the learning of the second language involves the full ascetic discipline of Ignatius's system. Instructions include isolation, specific lighting conditions, positions ("kneeling, prostrate, standing, sitting, gazing upward"), and a very precise organization of time, from waking to sleeping, with every daily activity precisely prescribed and the slightest gap of unoccupied time filled with the thought of what is to be done next.[41] No room is left in the exercitant's mind for any word outside of the language he is concentrating on learning. All these instructions covering every moment of the retreatant's day have the function *not* of being turned into language (in the way Sade turns the body into language, and Fourier the passions) but into creating in him "a kind of linguistic vacuum necessary for the elaboration and for the triumph of the new language."[42]

The main thing to learn about Loyola's new language is that it runs counter to the natural, assertive nature of language; instead, the new language is interrogative, a language of question and answer, that is, a language of emptiness begging to be filled.

God's will is not known, so it must be asked for—and it is God who must be asked, because only He can tell. But He will only tell (if at all) if the questioner has prepared so much ground toward an answer that he is worthy of an answer. A question like "*What to do?*" gives no proof of deep contemplation by the exercitant; the question "*To do this or to do that?*" does, because, binary, it is a paradigmatic question with the paradigm worked out by the questioner.[43]

The working out of the paradigm is prepared for by earlier binary divisions. In the *Exercises*, "everything is immediately divided, subdivided, classified, numbered off in annotations, meditations, Weeks, points, exercises, mysteries, etc."[44] Ignatius's language is one of exhaustive articulation that ends by outstripping human language to the point where a divine word can take over: Barthes's Ignatius is not a mystic seeking theophany (the visible manifestation of the Deity) but a seeker of semiophany (the audible sign of Him).

Sade, Fourier, and Loyola are logothetes not so much because they are but because Barthes wants them to be. Reading them, Barthes infuses his own desire for the absolutely new into what becomes a joint project. Barthes writes himself into *Sade, Fourier, Loyola*; the secret title of the book is *Sade, Fourier, Loyola, Barthes*.

A text, Barthes writes in the Preface to his book, really only satisfies when it "transmigrates into our life, whenever . . . a *coexistence* occurs" enabling us "to live with Fourier, with Sade."[45] It is so "depressing . . . to imagine the Text as an intellectual object (for reflection, analysis, comparison, mirroring, etc.)."[46] In order to live with Fourier, Sade, and Loyola, Barthes needs to lift himself out of the depression of a purely intellectual engagement with them, and open himself up to another appeal, that of their "discontinuous chant of amiabilities."[47] Barthes wants to *like* the authors he loves, like them for their charm and personalities, and refers to this second appeal as the "amicable return" of the author.[48] It is in characteristic turns of phrase as well as in little "biographemes"[49]—Fourier's liking of little spice cakes called *mirlitons*, Loyola's "beautiful eyes," Sade's provincialism in saying "milli" for "mademoiselle"—that this return occurs. *Sade, Fourier, Loyola* ends with a short section, "Lives," in which Barthes collects biographemes that endear the logothetes to him, twenty-two for Sade and twelve for Fourier (and none for Loyola because "we know nothing of the life of Ignatius Loyola").[50] This is how Barthes, "were I a writer,"[51] would also want to be remembered.

The arresting insignificance of these biographemes (Fourier, for instance, surrounded himself with cats and flowers in old age; his parents ran a spice store; he hated old cities; he had read Sade)[52] in fact betokens intimacy. Commenting on Barthes's biographemes, Seán Burke writes:

> Those who have lost their nearest and dearest do not recall their departed in the manner of the monumental biographer, but through discrete images, a love of cats and flowers, a liking for particular cakes, watery eyes like Ignatius of Loyola. . . . For Barthes . . . the biographeme reverberates with the pathos of lost time, and yet participates in its recovery.[53]

The three logothetes (or at least two of them) clearly are near and dear to Barthes, and the biographemes he collects truly are of the kind of domestic intimacy Barthes shares with his reader in his own amicable return as an author in such later works as *Camera Lucida, Roland Barthes by Roland Barthes*, and *A Lover's Discourse*, works that mark a turn toward "*a touch of sentimentality.*"[54] In these works, Barthes discloses biographemes of his own about, for instance, his daily routines (he is a morning person),[55] preferences in pens, ink, and paper (he feels absolutely no affinity with Bics),[56] and favorite fruits (pears, peaches, and cherries; not strawberries).[57]

It is not hard to see that in *Sade, Fourier, Loyola* Barthes relies just as heavily on reflection, analysis, comparison, mirroring, etc. as his logothetes do. The prose of neither of the four is "bearable," "respirable" as Barthes's French has it: aerated, breathable.[58] Barthes's prose is dense, for instance, with neologisms ("logothete," "biographeme," "paragrammatics," "semiophany") that descend from a semiological macrocosm and impede the quick mapping of meaning onto existing categories. Barthes's new words belong to his new language, but it is an unbearable language, a desert that does not flower if we try to respond to only its intellectual appeal. If we want to live with Barthes as a logothete in the way he lives with his three logothetes, we must break up the solidity of his prose and find pockets in it that delight us, make us like him, make us hear that discontinuous chant of amiabilities.

Barthes explains how to break up unyielding prose: it is a matter of reading differently. In the section "Watered Silk" of "Sade II," Barthes introduces his new way of reading and gives us permission, so to speak, of reading him in that same way too. Complex, "polychromatic" texts—those of the three logothetes qualify—one can read "according to one's mood . . . , by 'skipping,' according to the moment." So, one day one can read "the Sadian dissertation and not the erotic scene" but another day it may be an erotic scene one skips to.[59] If a text is true to its etymology it is a fabric, a manifold of "fluctuating and glittering surface of styles, a watered silk of languages" that allows such mood-based partiality in traversing it.[60]

"Skipping" is an innocuous term for what Barthes, fifteen pages further into "Sade II," calls "cruising." Asked about this term in an interview, Barthes explains:

Cruising is the voyage of desire. The body is in a state of alert, on the lookout for its own desire. And, then, cruising implies a temporality that accentuates the meeting, the "first time." . . . Cruising is an act that repeats itself, but its catch is absolutely fresh.

That's why cruising is a notion I can easily move from the order of the erotic quest, which is its origin, to the quest of texts, for example. . . . What offers itself is the surprise of the "first time."[61]

Barthes is a cruising reader, seeking first encounters, the pleasures of the new infinitely repeated. With "cruising" referring to an element in the repertoire of homosexual practices, it is allied (in Barthes's mind) to the notion of perversion, "the search for a pleasure that is not made profitable by a social end, a benefit to the species."[62] This disinterested pleasure gives cruisers a finer sensibility, a darting awareness of everything around them, an attentiveness unavailable to noncruising readers who, bereft of that "unheard-of privilege" of "being withdrawn from all repetition,"[63] are stuck in the depressing practice of reading for "reflection, analysis, comparison, mirroring, etc." Cruising is a kind of reading that discounts context, cohesion, and ultimate sense for excitement and surprise.

What would it mean to cruise *Sade, Fourier, Loyola*? It would be to allow ourselves, according to our mood, to dilute the intellectual appeal of the book by that other appeal of charms and amiabilities, in this way making its dense solidity fragile, and thereby new.[64] We would have to recognize Barthes as a cruising writer and enter that spirit of perversion by a corresponding practice of reading, not made profitable by a final summation. This is the kind of reading British novelist Adam Thirlwell does in his 2012 foreword to a reissue of the English translation of Barthes's first full-length book, *Writing Degree Zero* of 1953. Thirlwell notes Barthes's "dandyism," his "melancholy skepticism,"[65] the echo of a "disillusioned, desperate avant-garde" that characterizes the "spiked gravity"[66] of that slender book. Thirlwell mentions, but with great tenderness for it, how this "little book is reckless, careless, snobbish, misinformed, underread. It is often obscure. It is always provincial"[67]—in the typical way of Parisian intellectuals. As Thirlwell falls for Barthes's charms, a forbidding author makes an amicable return.

Sade, Fourier, Loyola was published in 1971, but only the Preface, the essay "Sade II," and the "Lives" were written in that year; "Sade I," "Fourier," and "Loyola" were written earlier, and published as journal articles between 1967 and 1970. Andy Stafford has commented on the difference between "Sade II" and the earlier Sade essay: "Sade I" aims to reflect a reader's attention away from debauchery to the elegance of the prose; "Sade II" is an act of *theft* on Barthes's part, with pastiche and parody replacing the shock of presenting morality as irrelevant—rewriting Sade rather than writing about him.[68] Another way of contrasting "Sade I" and "Sade II" is to link them to the two ways of reading Barthes practices: reading in bed at night for pleasure (irresponsible reading); reading at the worktable in the morning (responsible reading).[69] *Sade, Fourier, Loyola* takes us from table to bed.

"Sade II" establishes the shift to a more ironic and disillusioned Barthes, "late Barthes," who deals in stolen goods where "early Barthes" dealt in pulling off the masks of bourgeois doxa. In the Preface to *Sade, Fourier, Loyola*, dated June 1971 and written last, Barthes clarifies the need for theft. There is no language site left outside of bourgeois ideology anymore; confrontation or destruction are no longer possible, "only theft: fragment the old text of culture, science, literature, and change its features according to formulae of disguise, as one disguises stolen goods."[70] Turning "late" plays havoc with many of early Barthes's binary distinctions and coveted aims. *Sade, Fourier, Loyola* celebrates the new, but ends up (at the beginning, in the Preface) with the paradox that the new is the old in broken-up disguise. But that compromised way of being new still achieves what is most important to Barthes. Barthes is particularly concerned with how language is subject to erosion and how, worn out, it licenses one's speech and thought only within narrowed confines of expression. The adamant pursuit of the new in language (and thus in its dependents: literature, culture, thought) counters this erosion. Breaking up the worn-out language into a rhapsody of bits and pieces, the way Barthes does and sees Sade do in "Sade II," "frustrates the paradigmatic structure of the narrative . . . and thereby . . . it constitutes an outrage of meaning: the rhapsodic (Sadian) novel has no *meaning* or *direction*, nothing compels it to progress, develop, end."[71] It is reading as cruising that makes us see Sade write like this; it is writing as cruising that allows us to read Barthes like this.

Barthes's *Sade, Fourier, Loyola* is about how these writers experience and impart pleasure in paradigm. The book moves from pleasure in the paradigm of an absolutely new language by way of invention to pleasure in leading the old astray by way of theft and cruising. This idea of cruising applies not only to how Barthes reads individual novels or (as in *Sade, Fourier, Loyola*) the oeuvre of specific authors but also to how he regards the canon of French literature as a whole. No respecter of chronology (Barthes prefers rhapsody); no believer in schools and movements (how could a follower be new?); no admirer, usually, of "style" (it tethers an author to codified language), Barthes, cruising for first encounters, finds those first encounters both within and without "Modernism." Early Barthes certainly was a champion of authors of the *nouveau roman*, Alain Robbe-Grillet prime among them. A recent article by Sara Kippur shows Robbe-Grillet programmatically cavalier about referentiality in a way that aligns him with the antireferentiality of Barthes. For the benefit of American learners of French, to afford them pleasure in paradigm, Robbe-Grillet turned his novel *Le rendez-vous* into a grammar manual put out by an American textbook publisher.[72] By turning his novel into a grammar book (with each chapter demonstrating a particular grammatical issue), Robbe-Grillet invalidates impulses to read his book with reference to any other reality than that of words and their rule-based combinations.

But apart from "modernists" Robbe-Grillet, Mallarmé, Bataille, and Sollers, there is in Barthes's personal canon of favorite texts also room for "premodern" writers Racine, La Bruyère, Michelet, Chateaubriand, Zola, Flaubert, and Verne. Most of all, there is room for Proust. He likes them all—not upon what traditional literary critics would call "their own terms," but for how "modern" they are, that is, how they allow Barthes to enjoy them in his cruising, skipping way, for openness, airiness, and freedom from referentiality. In a 1974 interview, Barthes declares that "avant-gardism" can be found in writers of the past because it is not a question of form "but of impulse: whenever it's the body which writes, and not ideology, there's a chance the text will join us in our modernity."[73]

Late Barthes is more comfortable with the inescapability of bourgeois ideology, or at least with the culture it has produced, than he lets on in most of *Sade, Fourier, Loyola*, the place where he emerges as "late." Complete "containment of representation" is simply not possible, and Barthes ends up not really desiring it.[74] In *The Pleasure of the Text* of 1973, he writes that the "text needs its shadow: this shadow is *a bit* of ideology, *a bit* of representation, *a bit* of subject."[75] This shadow is the counterpart of that one-eighth error that Fourier designs into his classificatory obsession: that idea of making space for nuance, for the unclassifiable. Nuances are what late Barthes is all about as well: they muffle the earlier binaries that they still maintain. The one-eighth error is the space for (linguistic) charms and (authorial) amiabilities.

In his "amicable return" as an author, Barthes's one-eighth error of amiabilities comes, for me, from his "touch of sentimentality." The charm of his prose: I cannot name a particular rhetorical figure for Barthes's prose, counterpart to chiasmus, anacoluthon, and proairesis, the tokens of the three logothetes' charms of elegance, comic absurdity, and linguistic humility. On a single page, page 9, of the Preface (stylistically the most attractive section of *Sade, Fourier, Loyola*), there is aphorism ("The pleasure of a reading guarantees its truth"); melancholy irrealis ("were I a writer, and dead"); straight melancholy (the subject dispersed "like the ashes we strew into the wind after death"); and Barthes's image of himself at work on his book as a hobbyist bending over a balsa wood project ("I unglue the text from its purpose"). On a wider scale, that of the structure of Barthes's entire undertaking, it is easier to characterize its specific feature. Barthes's sign is the paradox,[76] the inevitable product of his thought proceeding in a spiral.[77] The spiral makes Barthes's slipperiness a form of consistency. "Style," "Text," "Writing," "Author," "Method": these notions crop up again and again in Barthes, but their valences spiral from work to work. There is a direction in the spiraling, though: from desk to bed.

Notes

1 Kasimir Malevich, *The Non-Objective World*, trans. Howard Dearstyne, intro. L. Hilberseimer (Chicago: Paul Theobald and Co. 1959), 68. The print history of this book is very complicated, with an initial publication in German (*Die Gegenstandslosen Welt* 1927), and new translations into English and German based on galley proofs of Malevich's original Russian. The new English title, closely following Malevich's Russian (and rendering his first name with a "z" rather than "s"), became *The World as Objectlessness* (Basel: Kunstmuseum Basel/Hatje Cantz, 2014). I will use the term "objectlessness" occasionally on the authority of the Basel translation.
2 Charlotte Douglas, "Suprematism: The Sensible Dimension," *The Russian Review* 34.3 (July 1975): 277. Douglas here cites Malevich's *Essays*, Vol. 1, 19. The phrase "ballast of objectivity" is a close translation of "Ballast des Gegenständlichen" (66) in the original German version of Malevich's manifesto. I have not been able to find the originator of the "dead weight of the world" rendition. The Basel translation is as ungainly as Malevich's Russian apparently was: "liberated from objectness as being aware of the world" (188).
3 In this global overview of what Barthes does in *Sade, Fourier, Loyola*, I rely in part on what Barthes says about his book in an interview with Gilles Lapouge, "Voyage autour de Roland Barthes," *La Quinzaine littéraire*, December 1–15, 1971, OC III 1045–50.
4 Roland Barthes, *Sade, Fourier, Loyola*, trans. Richard Miller (Baltimore: Johns Hopkins University Press, 1976), 104.
5 Ibid., 160.

6   Ibid., 8.
7   Ibid., 48.
8   Ibid., 126.
9   Ibid.
10 Ibid., 88.
11 Ibid., 141.
12 Ibid., 126.
13 Ibid., 36.
14 Ibid.
15 Ibid., 37.
16 Malevich, *The Non-Objective World*, 68.
17 Barthes, *Sade, Fourier, Loyola*, 32.
18 Ibid., 129.
19 Ibid.
20 Ibid., 83.
21 Ibid.
22 Ibid., 88.
23 Ibid.
24 Fourier, like Sade, singles out bread as bad food. Fourier is against bread because, in Civilization, bread is "the symbol of labor and bitterness," and Harmony is to be sweet, so "sugar is an *anti-bread*" (Barthes, *Sade, Fourier, Loyola*, 116). Sade is against bread for political reasons: it is "the emblem of virtue, religion . . . and must be despised as a *moral* object" and it is at the same time an immoral food: tyrants blackmail their subjects by threatening to take away their bread. And then there is the practical reason that, in the body, it produces "digestions unfitting for coprophagy" (Barthes, *Sade, Fourier, Loyola*, 126–7).
25 Barthes, *Sade, Fourier, Loyola*, 82.
26 Ibid.
27 Ibid., 91.
28 Ibid., 92.
29 Ibid., 103–4.
30 Ibid., 98.
31 Ibid., 77–8.
32 Ibid., 114.
33 Ibid., 107.
34 Ibid., 108. Chinese society is "half barbaric, half civilized, with harems and courts of laws and etiquette."
35 Ibid., 109.
36 Ibid., 117–19.
37 John Cage, *For the Birds: John Cage in Conversation with Daniel Charles* [1976] (London: Marion Boyars, 2009), 188.
38 Ibid., 205.
39 Ibid., 61.
40 Barthes, *Sade, Fourier, Loyola*, 8.
41 Ibid., 48–9.
42 Ibid., 49.
43 Ibid., 48.
44 Ibid., 52.

45 Ibid., 7.
46 Ibid.
47 Ibid., 8.
48 Ibid.
49 Ibid., 9.
50 Ibid., 12.
51 Ibid., 9.
52 Ibid., 182–4.
53 Seán Burke, *The Death and Return of the Author: Criticism and Subjectivity in Barthes, Foucault and Derrida* (Edinburgh: Edinburgh University Press, 1992), 39.
54 Barthes, *Roland Barthes by Roland Barthes* [1975], trans. Richard Howard (New York: Hill and Wang, 2010), 66.
55 Roland Barthes, *The Preparation of the Novel: Lecture Courses and Seminars at the Collège de France (1978–1979 and 1979–1980)*, ed. Nathalie Léger, 2003, trans. Kate Briggs (New York: Columbia University Press, 2011), 232.
56 Roland Barthes, "An Almost Obsessive Relation to Writing Instruments," in *The Grain of the Voice: Interviews 1962–1980*, trans. Linda Coverdale (Berkeley, CA: University of California Press, 1991), 178.
57 Barthes, *Roland Barthes by Roland Barthes*, 116.
58 Barthes, *Sade, Fourier, Loyola*, 3.
59 Ibid., 135.
60 Ibid.
61 Roland Barthes, "Twenty Key Words for Roland Barthes," in *The Grain of the Voice: Interviews 1962–1980*, trans. Linda Coverdale (Berkeley, CA: University of California Press, 1991), 231.
62 Ibid., 232.
63 Ibid., 231.
64 The connection between the new and the fragile is also on Barthes's mind in his final Collège de France lecture, *The Preparation of the Novel*. See my "'What's Fragile is Always New': The Truth of Literature in Barthes's *The Preparation of the Novel*," *symplokē* 28.1/2 (2020): 202–3.
65 Adam Thirlwell, "Foreword," in Roland Barthes, *Writing Degree Zero* [1953], trans. Annette Lavers and Colin Smith (New York: Hill and Wang, 1967, 2012), viii.
66 Ibid., ix.
67 Ibid.
68 Andy Stafford, *Roland Barthes, Phenomenon and Myth: An Intellectual Biography* (Edinburgh: Edinburgh University Press, 1998), 174–5.
69 Barthes, "An Almost Obsessive Relation to Writing Instruments," 181.
70 Barthes, *Sade, Fourier, Loyola*, 10.
71 Ibid., 140.
72 Sara Kippur, "Robbe-Grillet in America: The *Nouveau Roman* Meets the Language Textbook," *PMLA* 135.3 (May 2020): 492–510.
73 Roland Barthes, "Roland Barthes versus Received Ideas," in *The Grain of the Voice: Interviews 1962–1980*, trans. Linda Coverdale (Berkeley, CA: University of California Press), 191.
74 The phrase "containment of representation" is part of the subtitle of a book by Susan Stewart, *Crimes of Writing: Problems in the Containment of Representation* (New York: Oxford University Press, 1991). One of the book's chapters deals with

pornography in Sade's *The 120 Days of Sodom* and in the 1986 Meese Commission *Report*. Barthes's *Sade, Fourier, Loyola* makes a brief appearance in it.
75 Roland Barthes, *The Pleasure of the Text*, trans. Richard Miller (New York: Hill and Wang, 1975), 32.
76 One of the most likable books on Roland Barthes, one that does not lack a "touch of sentimentality" itself and that works out Barthes paradoxicality, is Patrizia Lombardo's *The Three Paradoxes of Roland Barthes* (Athens: University of Georgia Press, 1989).
77 In an interview, Barthes invokes Vico and his image of history proceeding in a spiral: "things of the past return, but obviously not in the same place." Roland Barthes, "A Lover's Discourse," Interview with Jacques Henric, *Art Press*, May 1977, *The Grain of the Voice: Interviews 1962-1980*, trans. Linda Coverdale (Berkeley, CA: University of California Press, 1991), 282.

Bibliography

Barthes, Roland. "A Lover's Discourse." Interview with Jacques Henric. *Art Press*, May 1977. *The Grain of the Voice: Interviews 1962-1980*. Trans. Linda Coverdale. Berkeley, CA: University of California Press, 1991. 282-9.

Barthes, Roland. "An Almost Obsessive Relation to Writing Instruments." Interview with Jean-Louis de Rambures. *Le Monde*, 27 September 1973. *The Grain of the Voice: Interviews 1962-1980*. Trans. Linda Coverdale. Berkeley, CA: University of California Press, 1991. 177-82.

Barthes, Roland. *The Pleasure of the Text*. Trans. Richard Miller. New York: Hill and Wang, 1975.

Barthes, Roland. *The Preparation of the Novel: Lecture Courses and Seminars at the Collège de France (1978-1979 and 1979-1980)*. Ed. Nathalie Léger. Trans. Kate Briggs. New York: Columbia University Press, 2011.

Barthes, Roland. "Réponses." Interview with Jean Thibaudeau. *Tel Quel*, Autumn 1971. *Œuvres complètes*. 5 vols. Ed. Éric Marty. Paris: Seuil, 2002. III, 1023-44.

Barthes, Roland. *Roland Barthes by Roland Barthes*. 1975. Trans. Richard Howard. New York: Hill and Wang, 2010.

Barthes, Roland. "Roland Barthes versus Received Ideas." Interview with Claude Jannoud. *Le Figaro*, 27 July 1974. *The Grain of the Voice: Interviews 1962-1980*. Trans. Linda Coverdale, Berkeley, CA: University of California Press. 188-95.

Barthes, Roland. *Sade, Fourier, Loyola*. Trans. Richard Miller. Baltimore: Johns Hopkins University Press, 1976.

Barthes, Roland. *Sade Fourier, Loyola*. *Œuvres complètes*. 5 vols. Ed. Éric Marty. Paris: Seuil, 2002. III, 699-868.

Barthes, Roland. "Twenty Key Words for Roland Barthes." Interview with Jean-Jacques Brochier. *Le Magazine littéraire*, February 1975. *The Grain of the Voice: Interviews 1962-1980*. Trans. Linda Coverdale, Berkeley, CA: University of California Press. 205-32.

Barthes, Roland. "Voyage autour de Roland Barthes." Interview with Gilles Lapouge. *La Quinzaine littéraire*, 1-15 December 1971. *Œuvres complètes*. 5 vols. Ed. Éric Marty. Paris: Seuil, 2002. III, 1045-50.

Burke, Seán. *The Death and Return of the Author: Criticism and Subjectivity in Barthes, Foucault and Derrida*. Edinburgh, Edinburgh University Press, 1992.

Cage, John. *For the Birds: John Cage in Conversation with Daniel Charles*. 1976. London: Marion Boyars, 2009.

Douglas, Charlotte. "Suprematism: The Sensible Dimension." *The Russian Review* 34.3 (July 1975): 266–81.

Kippur, Sara. "Robbe-Grillet in America: The *Nouveau Roman* Meets the Language Textbook." *PMLA* 135.3 (May 2020): 492–510.

Lombardo, Patrizia. *The Three Paradoxes of Roland Barthes*. Athens: University of Georgia Press, 1989.

Malevich, Kasimir. *Die Gegenstandslosen Welt*. Trans. A. von Riesen. Munich: Albert Langen Verlag, 1927. Bauhaus Bücher 11.

Malevich, Kasimir. *The Non-Objective World*. Trans. Howard Dearstyne. Intro. L. Hilberseimer. Chicago: Paul Theobald and Co, 1959.

Malevich, Kazimir. *The World as Objectlessness*. With essays by Simon Baier and Britta Tanja Dümpelmann. Trans. Antonina W. Bouis. Basel: Kunstmuseum Basel/Hatje Cantz, 2014. Exhibition catalogue.

Stafford, Andy. *Roland Barthes, Phenomenon and Myth: An Intellectual Biography*. Edinburgh: Edinburgh University Press, 1998.

Stewart, Susan. *Crimes of Writing: Problems in the Containment of Representation*. New York: Oxford University Press, 1991.

Teeuwen, Rudolphus. "'What's Fragile is Always New': The Truth of Literature in Barthes's *The Preparation of the Novel*." *symplokē* 28.1-2 (2020): 202–23.

Thirlwell, Adam. "Foreword." In Roland Barthes, *Writing Degree Zero* [1953]. Trans. Annette Lavers and Colin Smith. New York: Hill and Wang, 1967, 2012.

5

Understanding Barthes, Understanding Proust

Thomas Baldwin

In "Pré-romans," published one year after *Le Degré zéro de l'écriture* (1953), Roland Barthes heralds Marcel Proust's *À la recherche du temps perdu* (1913–27) as the first example of a work in which literature flees, refuses, and kills itself:

> throughout his immense work, Proust is always on the point of writing. He has the traditional literary act in his sights, but constantly puts it off. It is at the end of this *never-fulfilled* wait that the work is constructed in spite of itself: it is the waiting that has made up the thickness of a work whose *suspended* character was enough to serve as a basis for the writer's expression.[1]

While Proust is presented here as a first, as a unique event in the history of writing (one that paves the way for the work of Jean Cayrol, Jean Duvignaud, and Alain Robbe-Grillet, e.g.), Barthes does not make him abscond from all literary convention—from the reassuringly ordered forms of "la Littérature."[2] Instead, he argues that Proust's novel is formed out of borders and thresholds: the suspension of tradition, a "miraculous stasis"[3] on the edge of classical convention, is the very stuff of which, for Barthes, *À la recherche* itself is made. Barthes thus describes Proust's literary monument as something like a hinge. While it is the impossibility of writing a novel (or being the preparation of a future novel)[4] that makes up the density of Proust's work, and while this may be a necessary condition for the development—or even the possibility—of the modern novel (of the *nouveau roman*),[5] *À la recherche* is not fully detached from the nineteenth-century novel's stable regimes of signification.

Barthes does not always take this nuanced view, however. In fact, on a number of occasions in the 1950s (and at other times), he draws a line between *À la recherche* and the modern novel. He also presents Proust's text as something relatively homogeneous. For example, in "Littérature objective" (1954), he compares Proust and Robbe-Grillet:

> In order to grasp the temporal nature of the object in Robbe-Grillet, we must observe the mutations he makes it undergo, and here again contrast the revolutionary nature of his attempt with the norms of classical description. The latter, certainly, has managed to submit its objects to forces of decay. But precisely, it was as if the object, long since constituted in its space or substance, thereafter

encountered a Necessity descended from the empyrean; classical time has no other figure than that of a destroyer of perfection (Chronos and his scythe). In Balzac, in Flaubert, in Baudelaire, even in Proust (but in an inverted mode), the object is the vehicle of melodrama; it decays, vanishes, or recovers a final glory, participates in short in a veritable eschatology of matter. One might say that the classical object is never anything but the archetype of its own ruin, which means setting against the object's spatial essence a subsequent (hence external) time that functions as a destiny and not as an internal dimension. Classical time never encounters the object except as its catastrophe or deliquescence.[6]

Even though Proust's eschatology of matter inverts Balzac's, Flaubert's, and Baudelaire's,[7] he (or rather even he) also fails to escape from a classical melodrama in which objects encounter time as an external, destructive force: as their destiny. Proust thus effects an inversion of the temporal nature of the object as it appears in the work of his nineteenth-century predecessors, but he cannot be said to have abandoned it altogether. While classical time has been twisted or manipulated, it is not entirely out of joint. In contrast, for Barthes, Robbe-Grillet's treatment of material objects—his *chosisme*—constitutes a definitive rejection of classical norms:

> Robbe-Grillet gives his objects an entirely different type of mutability. It is a mutability whose process is invisible: an object, first described at a moment of novelistic continuity, reappears later on, endowed with a scarcely perceptible difference. This difference is of a spatial, situational order (for instance, what was on the right is now on the left). Time dislocates space and constitutes the object as a series of slices that almost completely overlap each other: in that spatial "almost" lies the object's temporal dimension. This is a type of variation that we find in a cruder version in the movement of magic lantern slides or of animated comic strips.[8]

The minute spatial mutations in Robbe-Grillet's revolutionary fictional worlds conspire, then, to produce an image of the object as an aggregate of superimposed layers. The gaps and edges formed by these overlappings are the spaces in which the operations of time become visible. Moreover, according to Barthes, the restitution of objects in Robbe-Grillet's work occurs at a purely optical level, and their mutations are a function of dislocation rather than—as is the case in classical (nineteenth-century) novels and poetry—decomposition: sight, he says, is the only sense in which "the continuous is an addition of tiny but integral fields; space can only tolerate *completed* variations: man never participates visually in the internal process of decay."[9]

Barthes draws different distinctions between modern and classical art in "Jean Cayrol et ses romans" (1952), where he argues that "l'art classique" reduces the world to a "structure of relations."[10] Things, he says, do not matter:

> If we consider a great novel of the eighteenth century, *Les Liaisons dangereuses*, for example, we see that there are no objects to be found in it: its characters circulate

in a space without matter; their gaze only ever rests upon meanings; it would appear that this gaze is not short enough to reach objects.[11]

As is the classical novel, so is eighteenth-century painting: objects that appear in Chardin's still lifes, for example, have been submitted to a compositional law, and composition, according to Barthes, implies a movement away, a suppression of real and threatening space in favor of an "ideally human distance."[12] In what Barthes calls "le complexe classico-romantique,"[13] the material stuff of the world is experienced as a distant spectacle rather than as part of a human environment, and humanity (or at least a good amount of Western humanity) is blind to objects until they are organized within a composition, their matter concealed "behind an order."[14] The matter of objects, of *tangibilia*, is thus kept at a safe distance:

> every effort is made to remove man from direct conflict with space, in order to place a salutary delay between man and his milieu, during which space is constructed, matter moves away and loses the unusual and bothersome character of objects that do not keep their distance.[15]

Things are very different in Cayrol's "modern" novels, where matter misbehaves and overcomes a classical, ideal distance. Human subjects now inhabit a world of objects that they see and touch—that have acquired "the necessary form of a familiarity."[16] The human participates directly, with the entire surface of his or her body, in the "pressure" ("pression") and "movement"[17] of things, and he or she feels space as a "worrying juxtaposition of surfaces"[18] rather than as a series of neatly ordered depths. The modern object, Barthes says elsewhere, is "either suffocation (Ionesco) or nausea (Sartre)."[19] Furthermore, whereas objects are represented in the plates of the *Encyclopédie*—at least in their vignettes—as things that are subjected to a human gaze (and are to that extent "*signed* by man"),[20] the ontological tables are turned in the modern novel: humanity becomes spectacle as it is beset by the stubborn gaze of the objects—the surfaces—that surround it.

Barthes does not refer to Proust in the articles on Cayrol or on the plates of the *Enyclopédie*. Nevertheless, given his alignment of Proust elsewhere with both classical and modern authors (including Cayrol),[21] we might enquire if the distinctions he draws in these articles can nevertheless be made to bear upon Proust's work. To what extent does the material substance of objects matter to Proust's narrator? Is he more "modern" than he is "classical"? In other words, does Marcel perceive the world as a milieu or as a distant spectacle? What role does the surface of his body (and that of the objects he encounters) play in his experience of the world? How short or long is his gaze? Does he touch what he sees?

On several occasions, the narrator of Proust's novel is uncomfortably aware of a distance between himself and the objects (including people and places) under his gaze. His first sight of Balbec, for example, is a source of bitter disappointment for him: Swann's and Legrandin's descriptions of the town have led to the formation of a particular image of it in his mind, and the reality does not live up to it. Everything that is realized, he says, is "sterilizing."²² This painful deflation is nothing, however, compared to the paroxysms of fear he feels at the sight of his new room in Balbec's Grand-Hotel, where he is to spend the holidays with his grandmother. This enormous Pandora's box ("boîte de Pandore"²³) contains several faces and things with which he is not familiar:

> There was no space for me in my bedroom (mine in name only) at Balbec; it was full of things that did not know me, that shot back at me the distrustful glance I shot at them, and, without taking any notice of my existence, showed that I was interrupting the humdrum course of theirs. . . . I was tormented by the presence of some little bookcases with glass fronts that ran along the walls, but especially by a large cheval glass that stood across one corner and before the departure of which I felt there could be no possibility of rest for me there.²⁴

Why should such mundane objects, the surfaces of which are often shiny or reflective, hold such a terror for him? One answer seems to lie in their being different from the things in his room in Paris (they are not his). His feeling of comfort and relaxation in the company of the latter is also expressed in terms of their relative connectedness to—we could even say oneness with—his eyes and body. They trouble him as little as his own pupils, he says, "for they were merely extensions of my organs, an enlargement of myself."²⁵ While the objects in Paris are almost proprioceptively his own, and are to that extent invisible to him, those he encounters in Balbec are entirely visible yet radically apart from his cowering body. The Parisian objects are part of a milieu in which Marcel feels secure; those in Balbec make an unhomely spectacle.

In his hotel room in Balbec, the narrator undergoes what Barthes, in *Comment vivre ensemble*, and without direct reference to Proust, calls "proxemic ordeals": "At the hotel: bad bedside lamp, no desktop lamp, darkness without familiarity ≠ artificial and sophisticated reconstitution of a proxemy."²⁶ For Marcel, Paris is relatively proxemic: it is a "space of the familiar gaze," of "sleep, rest, sedentary work at home: the sphere of the 'automatic gesture.'"²⁷ By contrast, the world of Balbec—the narrator's experience of the objects and people he sees there—can be understood as a series of distressing proxemic experiments in which objects look back. The unfamiliar objects in Balbec dismiss Marcel by returning, in the form of a reflection, the suspicious glance he directs toward them. This is a mirrored glance that does not acknowledge his existence and is not "signé par l'homme":²⁸ it is a glance that excludes him. The most troubling thing, the large cheval glass, supplies nothing more than what is to him a frightening surface in or through which he can view his body—a mirror image that is in danger of returning his gaze.

While Marcel persists in the conviction that his fear of this object is somehow due to its distinctness in relation to his body, a radical sense of otherness is also expressed here not in terms of absolute proprioceptive loss, but in terms of the self-visibility that its untouchably reflective surface affords him. The distrustful glance of the cheval glass is a reflection of the uncomfortable gaze he directs toward it (rather than something generated by or within the object itself). Why should the sight of oneself—a making-visible of oneself to oneself—be so threatening? In Marcel's case, the sight of himself seeing himself in the surface of this object produces a sense of absolute alterity—a sterilizing *Unheimlichkeit*—in relation to his surroundings. A sense of otherness thus arises out of feelings of (or a desire for) self-identity (albeit superficial) rather than of difference. The flat, reflective object suppresses any sense of being-at-home. Coupled with his desire to be fully part of its world, it presents an image that, insofar as it reflects his body, is always-already distant from it (there is a genetic relation between the two, but the reflected image of the body is necessarily detached from the object it reflects and by which it is seen). It is for this reason, perhaps, that Marcel cannot view the glass-fronted bookcase and the mirror as an annex of his own organs: what he sees is the annexation—a taking away and a distancing—by the glassy surfaces of his bodily organs only to be *seen*, and while they are emphatically recognizable as his own, he is denied by them the power of proprioceptive or proxemic feeling (his own power of annexation). While, for Barthes, Aunt Léonie's proxemic bed is a site of "fantasmatic expansion,"[29] the reflective proxemy of an inhabitual, mirrored surface promises no such self-enlargement to the petrified narrator.[30]

Balbec does have its proxemic pleasures, though. Marcel encounters another set of irradiant objects on the promenade outside his hotel, in the form of a young cyclist's eyes. On this occasion, he is a voyeur of eyeballs:

> If we thought that the eyes of a girl like that were merely two glittering sequins of mica, we should not be eager to know her and to unite her life to ours. But we feel that what shines in those reflecting discs is not due solely to their material composition; that it is, unknown to us, the dark shadows of the ideas that this being is conceiving, relative to the people and places that she knows. . . . I knew that I would never possess this young cyclist if I did not possess also what was in her eyes. And it was consequently her whole life that filled me with desire; a painful desire because I felt that it was not to be realised, but exhilarating, because what had hitherto been my life, having ceased suddenly to be my whole life, being no more now than a little part of the space stretching out before me, which I was burning to cover and which was composed of the lives of these girls, offered me that prolongation, that possible multiplication of oneself which is happiness.[31]

In seeing Albertine's eyes (he seems, in fact, to see something "beyond" the mere surface of these organs), Marcel could be said to apprehend what Jean-Paul Sartre calls the "gaze" ("le regard"). For Sartre, the gaze of the "Other" engenders a making-visible to the subject of his or her own body and of his or her desire in relation to the "Other." The subject is stripped of a "presence without distance" to his or her own world and is afflicted by a "distance from others."[32] In Proust's text, the distance created by the gaze is figured in the space that stretches out before Marcel as he looks at Albertine's eyes and over which he longs to travel. The flat surfaces of the mirror and bookcase fronts in his room reveal that he is other—that he does not belong in the room (or to himself). Here, the stretched-out "space that was made of the life of Albertine"[33] is a further sign of his exile—a reminder that he can only wander across its surface and may never penetrate its depths. He is a tiny speck in the corner of her brilliant, shining eye. In spite of the sense of exclusion they both produce, there is an important difference between the two experiences in Balbec: the objects in Marcel's hotel room may reflect his body, but they do not permit a fantasmatic self-expansion; while Albertine's eyes of mica are not felt as something attached to his own organs, they nevertheless bring about a happy multiplication of the self as they promise a secret, untouched futurity.

There are further proxemic ordeals beyond Balbec, of course. Marcel frequently expresses his sense of exclusion in relation to objects and people in terms that describe resistant surfaces. In *A l'ombre des jeunes filles en fleurs*, for example, the Swanns's home is surrounded by a kind of carapace—"a cool and pink glaze."[34] This is the expression of social and psychological limits. The narrator has long desired to enter the Swann household but has been able to observe this strangely glazed place only at its edges. This is partly a result of the snooty disapproval of his family. The *couches sociales* of Combray are not easily penetrated. Moreover, in referring to objects or scenes as paintings, as mediated spectacles, Proust's narrator makes a distinction between the worlds inhabited by the spectator (the narrator himself) and by the objects he perceives.[35] Here we encounter a further complication, or rather neutralization, of Barthes's classical/modern paradigm. In *S/Z*, he says that

> realism (badly named, at any rate often badly interpreted) consists not in copying the real but in copying a (depicted) copy of the real: this famous real, as though suffering from a fearfulness which keeps it from being touched directly, *is set further away*, postponed, or at least captured through the pictorial matrix in which it has been steeped before being put into words.[36]

The world is left untouched in Laclos and Balzac: in the work of the former, it is already composed as a spectacle; in Balzac's, it is to be organized within a "tableau" before it is described in words.[37] For Barthes, writers' "dream of painting"[38] has been dead for some time—at least since Mallarmé. Nevertheless, the "model of painting"[39] lives on in *À la recherche*, but in modified—literalized—form: Marcel does not, unlike his "classical" predecessors, de-depict the real (remove it from its picture) before putting it into words. The model of painting is thus allowed to show itself within the virtual world of the text. On several occasions, Proust's narrator crosses and recrosses the boundaries between mimetic description and ekphrasis so that the artificial effects of pictures and picturing fall upon the natural effects of observation.[40] There is occasionally an edge that separates the one from the other (usually, one has to look hard for tiny flashes reflecting such things), but in *À la recherche* we are forced to occupy, or to multiply, a threshold between the two. Marcel's experience of objects is thus one that oscillates dramatically between the modern tactility (vision) and eighteenth-century or realist distance (blindness) that Barthes describes.[41]

Marcel reflects on the mediated insecurities of our encounters with objects (which may include the surfaces of human bodies as well as things like boots and spoons) and the matter of which they are made. His sense of alienation is expressed most explicitly in *Du côté de chez Swann*: "When I saw any external object, my consciousness that I was seeing it would remain between me and it, enclosing it in a slender, incorporeal outline that prevented me from ever coming directly in contact with its matter."[42] In spite (or perhaps even because) of this avowed phenomenological limitation, Marcel occasionally feels very close to the stuff of things, and this is experienced as a sense of fullness. For example, in *Le Côté de Guermantes*, he has some time to kill before he meets Robert de Saint-Loup for dinner, and he decides to return to his lodgings to read for a couple of hours. Later, once he has returned to his lodgings, he observes:

> I kept, when I was in my room, the same fullness of sensation that I had felt outside. It gave such an apparent convexity of surface to things that as a rule seem flat and empty, to the yellow flame of the fire, the coarse blue paper on the ceiling, on which the setting sun had scribbled corkscrews and whirligigs, like a schoolboy with a piece of red chalk, the curiously patterned cloth on the round table, on which a ream of essay paper and an inkpot lay in readiness for me, with one of Bergotte's novels, that ever since then these things have continued to seem to me to be enriched with a wholly special kind of existence.[43]

The menace of this transformation is both sexual and spatial. It is also framed by pleasure. The flat and unreflective surfaces of these everyday things have acquired a swollen convexity ("bombait"). The carpet, table, and block of paper are inflated by the intensity of feeling in Marcel's gaze. This is not a hapticity born merely of physical closeness, but from fullness of feeling. The surfaces of these objects have expanded into the form of the lens that is directed at them. The flat surface-now-become-lens-become-eye of the object swells and looks back into the narrator's eye. The expansion is certainly cartoonlike (recalling Tex Avery, e.g.), and it approaches schizophrenia as it is described by Deleuze and Guattari: Marcel is approaching "that unbearable point at which the mind touches matter and lives each intensity, consumes it."[44] His Dionysian fullness of feeling engenders a near contiguity of otherwise separate, albeit asymptotic surfaces.[45] What the object presents to the eye, then, is the sensation of touch as much as sight. Can we conclude from this that the distance between subject and object has been overcome, or does it create a new possibility of distance?

Proust's description also suggests an augmentation of Keplerean optics. The object is not only inscribed onto the surface of the retina, the inner surface at the back of the eye, but threatens to press itself against the external (frontal) surface of the eyeball.[46] If we look carefully at the language of the bedtime drama in Combray, we see something similar. Marcel's gaze, like his mind, becomes distended and reaches out to touch the surface of his mother ("my mind . . . rendered convex like the look which I shot at my mother"[47]). In both cases, the distance between subject and object certainly seems to have been eliminated, or substantially reduced.

In another passage, however, the narrator feels so good (having seen Albertine's naked neck and pink cheeks) that the surface of his eye grows to such an extent that it hardly feels the weight of a world that is not vast enough to fill it:

> The sea, which was visible through the window as well as the valley, the swelling breasts of the first of the Maineville cliffs, the sky in which the moon had not yet climbed to the zenith—all this seemed less than a featherweight on my eyeballs, which between their lids I could feel dilated, resistant, ready to bear far greater burdens, all the mountains of the world, upon their fragile surface. Their orb no longer found even the sphere of the horizon adequate to fill it.[48]

The breasts of the Maineville cliffs seen through the hotel window may be swollen (like the surfaces of the contents of the narrator's room in Paris) and pressed onto the surface of the eyeball, but this surface is so immense a frame that areas of it remain unmarked, empty, or unused. This is not to say that Proust has forever forsworn a conventional view of visual causality. The role of the retina in vision is not denied. It is rather that fullness of feeling concentrates the world on the surface of the eye where it is framed and where it is also the recipient of an ocular touch. Marcel's Nietzschean fullness of feeling is such that while he seems to set aside the Keplerean connection between retina and external objects, confining his impression to the surface of the eye as both bearer of their weight—what Barthes, as we saw earlier, might call their "pression"[49]—and containing frame, his ocular surface tissue has grown so vast that those objects cannot reach out and touch every part of it. It might seem, then, that the paradox of touch and vision has been obliquely resolved. At the same time, we must be cautious in assuming that the touch of the eye represents an overcoming or resolution of Marcel's sense of alienation: frightening distance as much as haptic joy may be aspects bestowed on sight by the very things that vision itself constructs and comprehends.

Returning to Barthes's observations about distance and proximity in Cayrol, we might say that, at times, "matter moves away"[50] in *À la recherche*. At others, however, it is intoxicatingly close. Marcel can thus be said to experience the matter of objects both at a classical distance and within a pleasurable version of Cayrol's modern closeness. However, things are stranger—more varied—than this. The distancing of matter in Proust does not imply, as it seems to in "classical" art (at least for Barthes), a view of "spatiality" as "a series of depths."[51] While it might be conventional to assume that perception, experience, and consciousness are not fully separable, Marcel describes consciousness as if it were somehow a hindrance to perception, that is to say, as the condition of a distance between subject and object (narrator and world). Objects acquire an impenetrable surface—a spiritual outline or edging (a "mince liséré"). Marcel's world is full of objects, but he is not a (simple) describer of objects that happen to be quite complex things. His is a world that includes the describer as well as the external objects he describes. He uses a range of devices and masks that seem to hide the external world behind teasing phenomenological thresholds. The text conjures glimpses or flashes of pictorial surfaces, for example, to show that consciousness is limited and oblique.

Classical distance is thus combined with a "worrying juxtaposition of surfaces,"[52] that is, for Barthes, unique to the modern novel. Similarly, the narrator's fullness of feeling and sense of closeness to objects is infected at its edges with contradiction: while eye and object are brought closer together in spatial terms, to have the eye reach out to touch the surface of another object is to have it do what is categorically alien to it. In Proust's dialectic, vision and touch are synthesized as the same, but the surface of a table (e.g.) also expands to touch the eye and, in doing so, threatens to blind it. The narrator's fullness of feeling and sense of closeness to objects is thus always at risk of loss. The modern gaze that is short enough to reach objects ("assez court pour atteindre des objets"[53]) is almost no gaze at all—or is at least a seriously handicapped one. The (classical) distance of objects figures prominently in Proust's work, then, but it does so, paradoxically, as a consequence of extreme perceptual proximity.

Proust's treatment of objects thus makes Barthes's classical/modern distinction a bit problematic. In the following well-known passage, we encounter further difficulties as Marcel compares the effects of recent photographic innovations and his experience in approaching and kissing Albertine's cheek:

> Apart from the most recent applications of the art of photography—which set crouching at the foot of a cathedral all the houses which, time and again, when we stood near them, have appeared to us to reach almost to the height of the towers, drill and deploy like a regiment, in file, in open order, in mass, the same famous and familiar structures, bring into actual contact the two columns on the Piazzetta which a moment ago were so far apart, thrust away the adjoining dome of the Salute, and in a pale and toneless background manage to include a whole immense horizon within the span of a bridge, in the embrasure of a window, among the leaves of a tree that stands in the foreground and is portrayed in a more vigorous tone, give successively as setting to the same church the arched walls of all the others—I can think of nothing that can so effectively as a kiss evoke from what we believe to be a thing with one definite aspect, the hundred other things which it may equally well be since each is related to a view of it that is no less legitimate.[54]

In *Proust et les signes*, Deleuze heralds the disparate shifting fragments of Albertine's face as a sign of the "final blur in which the face is released and undone."[55] Moving closer to an object, either with Marcel's puckered lips or with Cayrol's outstretched arm,[56] brings about a "worrying juxtaposition of surfaces" by virtue of which a thing with one definite aspect, in this case Albertine, is no longer visible: she has exploded into "ten Albertines."[57] The object (or face) that is close does not possess, as it does in Cayrol, the "necessary form of a familiarity."[58] For Marcel, the fascination of the photograph stems from its capacity simultaneously to represent real objects and—like kissing—to disrupt our sense that this is a reality in which we feel at home.[59] Its effect is uncanny. The familiar things and places that are known to us may be reconfigured as places and things known only to—or within—the entity of the image. In the aforementioned passage, the columns of the Piazzetta come together in an image that seems both to emanate from the real and to set real objects in new relations with each other; the latter retain their identity while taking on new aspects. In reflecting on the visible mutability of objects in this way, Proust moves away from Cayrol and, in doing so, comes closer to Robbe-Grillet.

Given Proust's domination of the French literary scene of the twentieth century (and arguably of the twenty-first), we might expect his treatment of objects to sit comfortably alongside that of "modern" writers such as Cayrol (and others). As Barthes understands such creatures, however, Proust is neither an "homme moderne" nor an "homme classique"—at least not fully. This is not to say that Proust's way with objects is simply different from Cayrol's (that Proust is more classical than the modern Cayrol, e.g.), but rather that his descriptions of objects allow us to add phenomenological complexity to rigid distinctions between classical art and modernity—that Marcel's encounters with objects, his proxemic ordeals, can be understood as a convoluted negotiation between the extremes that Barthes identifies. In the currency of Barthes, then, Proust's novel is not quite between two centuries,[60] but rather an unstable middle ground, a shifting mediation (a "mitoyenneté") between literary phenomenologies which, for Barthes, are fundamentally opposed.[61] À la recherche, then, is a work in which what we might dare to call influence,[62] understood as a circulation of languages or as contact between them, is played out.

Notes

1 Roland Barthes, "Pré-romans," in *Œuvres complètes* [*OC*], ed. Éric Marty, 5 vols. (Paris: Seuil, 2002), I, 500–2. All emphasis in original. Unless otherwise indicated, all references to Barthes's works are to this edition and take the form (*OC* I, 234), that is, volume number, followed by page reference. Where I have used a published English translation of Barthes's work, this is indicated in a note; all other translations of his work are my own. Barthes confuses author and narrator here. As Anne Simon suggests, "[u]nlike the narrator of the *Recherche*, Proust, who devoted fifteen years of his life to the writing of his work, is absolutely not bound by a Blanchovian procrastination or rhetoric of the 'book to come'" (Anne Simon, *Trafics de Proust* (Paris: Hermann, 2016), 178; my translation).
2 Barthes, *Le Degré zéro de l'écriture*, *OC* I, 190.
3 Ibid.
4 As Barthes puts it in *La Préparation du roman*: "the Novel remains at the level of . . . its Preparation" (Roland Barthes, *La Préparation du roman I et II. Cours et séminaires au Collège de France 1978–1979 et 1979–1980*, ed. Nathalie Léger [Paris: Seuil/IMEC, 2003], 49). All subsequent references to this work are to this edition.
5 See Barthes, "Pré-romans," *OC* I, 500: "The most conscious forms of novel-writing today are all part of this Proustian movement by which the writer sets his novel going before our eyes and then consigns it to silence at a point when, a hundred years earlier, he would have barely begun to speak."
6 Barthes, *OC* II, 299. I have taken—and occasionally modified—translations of this work from the following edition: Roland Barthes, "Objective Literature," in *Critical Essays*, trans. Richard Howard (Evanston: Northwestern University Press, 1972), 13–24.

7 It is not entirely clear why this should be the case. Is it because *À la recherche* begins, more or less, with the glory of the madeleine episode? Or, could it be because the destructive effects of time on the object are somehow redeemed in involuntary memory and its "translation" into writing?
8 Barthes, *OC* II, 299.
9 Ibid., 300.
10 Barthes, *OC* I, 151.
11 Ibid. Barthes makes similar claims elsewhere. In "Les Planches de l' 'Encyclopédie'" (1964), for example, he observes that "[t]he object . . . humanly, is a very ambiguous thing; we have noted that for a long time our literature did not acknowledge it" (*OC* IV, 44), and in *La Préparation du roman*, he discusses the rarity of tangible objects in "classical" texts such as Laclos's (94).
12 Barthes, *OC* I, 151.
13 Ibid., 152.
14 Ibid.
15 Ibid.
16 Ibid.
17 Ibid.
18 Ibid., 153.
19 Barthes, "Les Planches de l' 'Encyclopédie,'" *OC* IV, 44.
20 Barthes, *OC* IV, 45. As far as the plates of the *Encyclopédie* are concerned, the "vignette" is the name given to the "large-scale *tableau-vivant*" (*OC* IV, 41–2) in which objects are represented in a human context.
21 See Barthes, *Le Degré zéro de l'écriture*, *OC* I, 194, for example.
22 Marcel Proust, *À la recherche du temps perdu*, ed. Jean-Yves Tadié, 4 vols. (Paris: Gallimard, Bibliothèque de la Pléiade, 1987–9), II, 26. All references to Proust's work are to this edition and are given in the form (*ALR* IV, 321). Translations of Proust's novel are taken from the six-volume Vintage Classics edition of *In Search of Lost Time*, translated by C. K. Scott Moncrieff (except for *Time Regained*, translated by Andreas Mayor and Terence Kilmartin), revised by Terence Kilmartin and D. J. Enright (London: Vintage, 2000–2). I have occasionally tweaked passages quoted from the latter.
23 Proust, *ALR* II, 27.
24 Ibid.
25 Ibid.
26 Roland Barthes, *Comment vivre ensemble: Simulations romanesques de quelques espaces quotidiens. Cours et séminaires au Collège de France 1976–1977*, ed. Claude Coste (Paris: Seuil/IMEC, 2002), 157. All subsequent references are to this edition and are given after quotations in the text. I have taken—and occasionally modified—translations of this work from the following edition: Roland Barthes, *How to Live Together: Novelistic Simulations of Some Everyday Spaces—Notes for a Lecture Course*, trans. Kate Briggs (New York: Columbia University Press, 2013). Marcel's tormentors are not a lousy bedside lamp or an unhomely darkness, of course, but an unfamiliar clock, curtains, bookcases, and mirror. For Barthes, the ill person's bed is marked by "the most powerful proxemy," and the prime example of a proxemic bed is Aunt Léonie's (see *Comment vivre ensemble*, 157). Just like the objects of habit in Marcel's Parisian nest, his aunt's bed "is, as it were, part of the body; bodily prosthesis, like a fifth limb" (157). A number of Barthes's examples of proxemy have

a distinctly Proustian ring to them. Indeed, the first reads like a truncated rewrite of the descriptions of sleep and habit in the opening pages of "Combray": "Evening: I go to bed, I turn out the light, I disappear beneath the covers to sleep. But I need to blow my nose. I stretch out my arm in the darkness and, without fail, I locate the top drawer of the bedside table, and in this drawer, no less infallibly, I find a handkerchief that is on the right. I put it back and close the drawer again just as infallibly" (155).

27 Barthes, *Comment vivre ensemble*, 157.
28 See Barthes, "Les Planches de l' 'Encyclopédie,'" *OC* IV, 45.
29 Barthes, *Comment vivre ensemble*, 158.
30 Barthes discusses the proxemy of his own bed (in a sanatorium) in *La Préparation du roman* (see 307).
31 Proust, *ALR*, II, 152.
32 Jean-Paul Sartre, *L'Etre et le néant* (Paris: Gallimard, 1943), 309. According to Sartre, my fundamental relation to others is always tinged with anxiety. A necessary condition of "Being" is vulnerability. I must constantly come to terms with the possibility of being seen by the "Other." When the "Other" looks at me, I am immediately objectified. It is "in and through the revelation of my being-as-object for the Other that I must be able to grasp the presence of his or her being-as-subject" (296). I thus experience the Other's gaze as an intrusion, a hemorrhage within the "center" of my world (294).
33 Proust, *ALR*, II, 152.
34 Proust, *ALR*, I, 517.
35 For a discussion of the role of pictures and picturing in Proust's novel, see Thomas Baldwin, *The Picture as Spectre in Diderot, Proust and Deleuze* (Oxford: Legenda, 2011).
36 Barthes, *OC* III, 164.
37 In 1971, Barthes expresses the same view about Eugène Fromentin's *Dominique* of 1862: "'This pure subject who lives in a world untouched by triviality: everyday objects only exist for him if they are part of a painting, a 'composition'" ["Fromentin: 'Dominique,'" *OC* IV, 96]).
38 Barthes, *OC* III, 164.
39 Ibid., 163.
40 I discuss boundary crossing of this kind in Chapter Two of *The Picture as Spectre in Diderot, Proust and Deleuze* (67–96).
41 For further analysis of the "model of painting" as it pertains to Balzac's artist stories (including *Sarrasine*), see Diana Knight, *Balzac and the Model of Painting: Artist Stories in* La Comédie humaine (Oxford: Legenda, 2007).
42 Proust, *ALR*, I, 83.
43 Proust, *ALR*, II, 394.
44 Gilles Deleuze and Félix Guattari, *Capitalisme et schizophrénie I. L'Anti-Œdipe* (Paris: Minuit, 1972–3), 26.
45 It is likely that, some years before he came to write of swelling things, Proust read the following passage from *Twilight of the Idols* (1889), in which Nietzsche describes a state of Dionysian ecstasy in terms that look very much like Proust's: "In this state [of 'intoxication'] we enrich everything out of our own *plenitude*: whatever we see, whatever we want, we see swollen, crammed, strong, supercharged with energy. Man in this state transforms things until they reflect his power—until they are reflections of his perfection" (Friedrich Nietzsche, *Twilight of the Idols*, trans. Duncan Large

[Oxford: Oxford University Press, 1998], 47). Significantly, Proust contributed an article entitled "L'Irréligion d'état" to the May 1892 edition of *Le Banquet*, which also contained an article by Dreyfus on *Twilight of the Idols* entitled "La Philosophie du marteau" (see Duncan Large, *Nietzsche and Proust* [Oxford: Oxford University Press, 2001], 66n12). In *Nietzsche and Proust*, Duncan Large suggests that "[w]hether or not Proust intended it to be the case ... his 'débuts littéraires' were closely bound up with the fate of the foremost Nietzschean journal of his time. When *Le Banquet* folded in 1893, Proust, Dreyfus and Halévy all moved over to *La Revue blanche*, each to continue publishing in a similar vein to before. Moreover, Proust also contributed to other journals and newspapers which carried pieces on Nietzsche over the same period" (66–7).

46 For a discussion of Keplerean optics, see Svetlana Alpers, *The Art of Describing: Dutch Art in the Seventeenth Century* (Chicago, IL: University of Chicago Press, 1983). It should be noted that while Proust is talking about a convexity of surface, Kepler refers to the image that is formed on the concave surface of the retina.
47 Proust, *ALR*, I, 24.
48 Proust, *ALR*, II, 285.
49 Barthes, "Jean Cayrol et ses romans," *OC* I, 152.
50 Ibid., 152.
51 Ibid., 153.
52 Ibid.
53 Ibid., 151.
54 Proust, *ALR*, II, 660.
55 Gilles Deleuze, *Proust et les signes* (Paris: Quadrige/PUF, 2007), 212.
56 See Barthes, *OC* I, 153: "as soon as an author extends his arm in the direction of an object."
57 Proust, *ALR*, II, 660.
58 Barthes, *OC* I, 152.
59 Áine Larkin examines the role of photographs and photography in *À la recherche* in *Proust Writing Photography: Fixing the Fugitive in "À la recherche du temps perdu"* (Oxford: Legenda, 2011), and both Éric Marty and Kathrin Yacavone have discussed the relationship between Proust and photography as Barthes understands it. See Éric Marty, "Marcel Proust dans 'la chambre Claire,'" *Proust en devenir*, ed. Luc Fraisse, *L'Esprit Créateur* 46.4 (2006); and Kathrin Yacavone, "Reading Through Photography: Roland Barthes's Last Seminar 'Proust et la photographie,'" *French Forum* 34.1 (2009); and "Barthes et Proust: *La Recherche* comme aventure photographique," *L'Écrivain préféré*, Fabula LHT (Littérature, histoire, théorie), March 4, 2008, http://www.fabula.org/lht/4/Yacavone.html. Accessed October 7, 2021.
60 See Antoine Compagnon, *Proust entre deux siècles* (Paris: Seuil, 1989).
61 See Barthes *S/Z*, *OC* III, 141: "mediation upsets the rhetorical—or paradigmatic—harmony of Antithesis."
62 Barthes himself was not keen on "influence." In a tetchy interview with Renaud Matignon published in *France Observateur* in 1964, he says that he does not believe in influences (the interview was, in fact, published under this very title: "Je ne crois pas aux influences" [see *OC* II, 615–19]). Rather than ideas, Barthes declares, it is languages, understood as formal containers that we can "fill differently" [*OC* II, 616]), that are transmitted between texts. Consequently, and since books are more

like "currencies" than "forces," the notion of circulation, he argues, is more accurate than that of "influence" (*OC* II, 616).

Bibliography

Alpers, Svetlana. *The Art of Describing: Dutch Art in the Seventeenth Century*. Chicago, IL: University of Chicago Press, 1983.

Baldwin, Thomas. *The Picture as Spectre in Diderot, Proust and Deleuze*. Oxford: Legenda, 2011.

Barthes, Roland. *Œuvres complètes*. 5 vols. Ed. Éric Marty. Paris: Seuil, 2002.

Barthes, Roland. *Comment vivre ensemble: simulations romanesques de quelques espaces quotidiens. Cours et séminaires au Collège de France 1976-1977*. Ed. Claude Coste. Paris: Seuil/IMEC, 2002.

Barthes, Roland. *La Préparation du roman I et II. Cours et séminaires au Collège de France 1978-1979 et 1979-1980*. Ed. Nathalie Léger. Paris: Seuil/IMEC, 2003.

Compagnon, Antoine. *Proust entre deux siècles*. Paris: Seuil, 1989.

Deleuze, Gilles. *Proust et les signes*. Paris: Quadrige/PUF, 2007.

Deleuze, Gilles, and Félix Guattari. *Capitalisme et schizophrénie I. L'Anti-Œdipe*. Paris: Minuit, 1972-1973.

Knight, Diana. *Balzac and the Model of Painting: Artist Stories in* La Comédie humaine. Oxford: Legenda, 2007.

Large, Duncan. *Nietzsche and Proust*. Oxford: Oxford University Press, 2001.

Larkin, Áine. *Proust Writing Photography: Fixing the Fugitive in* À la recherche du temps perdu. Oxford: Legenda, 2011.

Marty, Éric. "Marcel Proust dans 'la chambre Claire.'" *Proust en devenir*. Ed. Luc Fraisse. *L'Esprit Créateur* 46.4 (2006): 125-33.

Nietzsche, Friedrich. *Twilight of the Idols*. Trans. Duncan Large. Oxford: Oxford University Press, 1998.

Proust, Marcel. *À la recherche du temps perdu*. 4 vols. Ed. Jean-Yves Tadié. Paris: Gallimard, Bibliothèque de la Pléiade, 1987-1989.

Sartre, Jean-Paul. *L'Etre et le néant*. Paris: Gallimard, 1943.

Simon, Anne. *Trafics de Proust*. Paris: Hermann, 2016.

Yacavone, Kathrin. "Barthes et Proust: *La Recherche* comme aventure photographique." *L'Écrivain préféré, Fabula LHT (Littérature, histoire, théorie)*, 4 March 2008. http://www.fabula.org/lht/4/Yacavone.html. Accessed 7 October 2021.

Yacavone, Kathrin. "Reading Through Photography: Roland Barthes's Last Seminar 'Proust et la photographie.'" *French Forum* 34.1 (2009): 97-112.

6

Take Two

Barthes and Film in the Age of *Mythologies*

Steven Ungar

Much remains to be said about Roland Barthes's film writings up through the 1957 publication of his third book, *Mythologies*. Not only what Barthes wrote about film up through *Mythologies*, but also why what he wrote matters to understanding his place as a critical thinker whose well-documented resistance to film did not prevent him from composing a sizeable corpus of writings on film and spectatorship. Four decades ago in the aftermath of Barthes's March 1980 death, I explored his predilection for theater and dramatic performance in conjunction with what I referred to at the time as his resistance to film. This predilection, present already in his mid-1950s writings on Bertolt Brecht and on the Berliner Ensemble's Paris productions of his plays, prioritized dramatic performance.[1] Only in retrospect have I come to see the extent to which my focus on Barthes's resistance to film prevented me from addressing the full complexity of his relations with film that were "intermittent, ambivalent, and variable."[2] More work to be done. What follows is an essay in three parts. First, I look at ten short texts Barthes wrote from 1943 to 1957 on film-related topics. In a second part, I conduct a close reading of "Un Ouvrier sympathique" (A Sympathetic Worker), a March 1955 piece Barthes devoted to Elia Kazan's 1954 feature, *On the Waterfront*. In conclusion, I compare Barthes's remarks on Kazan's film with concurrent reviews by Chris Marker and André Bazin. My intention throughout is to clarify the role of film among the media Barthes recast as case studies of a postwar France increasingly under the sway of mass media and consumerism. Recent books by Philip Watts and Patrick ffrench provide sustained readings that supplement and correct earlier accounts.[3] Rather than recapitulate how these and related studies have challenged critical assumptions (including my own) related to Barthes and film, I address a discrete set of 1950s texts, culminating with *Mythologies*.

Barthes wrote roughly thirty texts on film-related topics between 1943 and 1980. Some addressed individual films, while others were devoted to film culture—or even "cinema"—as art and industry. Yet others addressed theoretical issues related to semiology and narrative. Ten of the thirty appeared between 1943 and 1956. Six of these ten—numbers two and six through ten listed below—appeared in *Mythologies* and, starting in 1972, in English translations by Annette Lavers and Richard Howard. Deborah Glassman's English translations of the remaining four—numbers one and three through five—appeared in 2016 in Philip Watts's *Roland Barthes's Cinema*. Noa Steimatsky usefully groups the last four among "a special cluster" of vignettes whose intensified connotative method and aphoristic mode generate a redemptive dismantling of social rituals.[4]

Roland Barthes, Film-Based Articles (1943–57)

Abbreviations: *M* = *Mythologies* (French); *ME* = *Mythologies*, eds. & trans. Richard Howard & Annette Lavers (New York: Hill and Wang, 2013); *LN* = *Les Lettres Nouvelles*; *RBC* = *Roland Barthes's Cinema* (eds., Dudley Andrew, Yves Citton, Vincent Debaene, and Sam Di Iorio (New York: Oxford University Press, 2016).

1. "Les Anges du péché," *Existences* 30 (August 1943) & trans. By D. Glassman in *RBC* as "Angels of Sin."
2. "Jules César au cinéma," *LN* 11 (January 1954), in *M* as "Les Romains au cinéma" & trans. in *ME* as "The Romans in Film."
3. "Au Cinémascope," *LN* 12 (February 1954) & trans. in *RBC* as "On Cinemascope."
4. "Versailles et ses comptes," *LN* 15 (May 1954) & trans. in *RBC* as "Versailles and its Accounts."
5. "Le Pauvre et le prolétaire," *LN* 21 (November 1954) & trans. in *RBC* as "The Poor and the Proletariat."
6. "Un Ouvrier sympathique," *LN* 25 (March 1955), same title in *M* & trans. in *ME* as *"A Sympathetic Worker."*
7. "Le Visage de Garbo," *LN* 26 (April 1955), same title in *M* & trans. in *ME* as "The Face of Garbo."
8. "Puissance et désinvolture," *LN* (April 1955), same title in *M &* trans. in *ME* as "Power and Cool."
9. "*Continent perdu,*" *LN* 35 (February 1956), same title in *M* & trans. in *ME* as "*Lost Continent.*"
10. "L'Acteur d'Harcourt," *M*, in trans. in *ME as* "The Harcourt Actor."

Barthes's first film-based text was a review of Robert Bresson's *Les Anges du péché* (*Angels of Sin*, 1943). The piece appeared in *Existences*, an in-house publication produced at a sanatorium in Saint-Hilaire-du-Touvet where Barthes was under treatment for the recurring tuberculosis that had prevented him from completing the advanced degrees required for career appointment in France's secondary (*lycée*) and university systems. The piece begins with a brief plot overview before Barthes notes how Bresson's collaboration with screenwriter Father Raymond-Léopold Bruckberger, dialogist Jean Giraudoux, and set designer René Renoux had skirted elements of setting and script that might otherwise have made the film unbearable. A passing reference to Léon Poirier's 1936 *L'Appel du silence* (*The Call of Silence*) about the Catholic priest, hermit, and martyr Father Charles Eugène Foucauld (1858–1916) displays a degree of film history knowledge, especially when Barthes imagines the viewer of Poirier's film squirming in discomfort and embarrassment. Barthes ends the review with praise for the film's screenplay and dialogue:

> Listening to this film is tremendously pleasurable for the mind and the heart. Not a single sentimental sentence or pedantic remark; no catechism, no emotional outbursts; the dialogue is humane and full of grandeur and goodness; it grabs and holds the soul without any of the artifices of religious eloquence; occasionally it even gives us a glimpse of the more exquisite nourishments of mischievousness and tenderness.[5]

Barthes's attention to sound and his singling out of dialogue express a sensitivity based in rhetoric and dramatic declamation. The result marks an auspicious debut whose emphasis on detail anticipates the sensation-based and affectively charged readings of photographs he was to undertake nearly forty years later in his final book, *La Chambre Claire* (*Camera Lucida*).[6]

A decade and a half later, the mix of reportage and exposition displayed in Barthes's text on Bresson had evolved into a critical voice that wavered between breezy sophistication and social critique. This voice pervaded Barthes's 1957 book, *Mythologies*, which featured fifty-three *petites mythologies du mois* (little mythologies of the month), most of which appeared between 1954 and 1956. Primary among the venues for these short pieces was *Lettres nouvelles*, a literary monthly founded in 1953 by Maurice Nadeau and Maurice Saillet.[7] Part exercise and part critique, these one- to three-page texts fulfilled what Barthes would describe a decade later as two complementary gestures: "On the one hand, an ideological critique of the language of so-called mass culture; on the other, an initial semiological dismantling of that language."[8] Indeed, the 1970 edition of *Mythologies* featured a new foreword whose call to arms—no semiology without its attendant semioclastics—exuded the tone and energy of the May–June 1968 student-worker movement.[9] A decade after *Mythologies* first appeared, it was as though Barthes wanted to recast it as a militant tract.

As a set, Barthes's *petites mythologies* on film recast cinematic spectacle as a circulation of signs (semiosis), in which objects, gestures, and actor/agents consistently transmit and receive meaningful messages. Barthes illustrates the point in the first sentence of his *petite mythologie* on Joseph Mankiewicz's 1954 film, *Julius Caesar*, when he writes that all the male characters sport bangs. The concision of the English term, with its monosyllabic punch, departs from the French original, *tous les personnages portent une frange de cheveux sur le front*, which translates more literally as "all the characters sport a fringe of hair on their forehead."[10] The effect identifies the narrative function of this capillary sign within the display of cinematic spectacle, thereby transforming the bang into a costume detail, replete with a range of styles—curly, straight, pomaded, combed—subsumed within a broad notion of Romanity, an invented term whose sonic elegance is at odds with its artificial nature.

Barthes builds on the complexity of capillary significations by referring to sub-signs in the flowing locks of a recently awakened Portia and to Calpurnia's braid that winds around her neck and hangs over her right shoulder. He likewise identifies a complementary instance of Romanity in the sweat visible not merely among the primary characters Mark Antony, Brutus, and Cassius, but also among the dozens of extras who portray workers and soldiers. All of whom, Barthes asserts, bathe their austere and tense features in an abundant perspiration provided by applying Vaseline: "Like the Roman bangs or the midnight braid, sweat too is a sign."[11] Of course, Barthes adds, Julius Caesar, the primary victim or *object* of the crime, remains dry (*sec*), a condition that suggests a moral virtue to which the film's other characters can only aspire (perspire?).

Barthes considers Marlon Brando's Mark Antony the exception that proves the rule (see Figure 6.1). His fringe is convincing (*nous en impose*) without being laughable because it integrates Roman capillarity within the general morphology of the character he plays.[12] In conclusion, Barthes's two examples—the bangs of Romanity and the sweat of conspiracy and plotting—allow the attentive spectator to perceive an illegitimate sign within a degraded spectacle Barthes associates with the failure of bourgeois art to pass off its artifices in the name of a pompous nature. As much as Barthes singles out the aptness of Marlon Brando's bangs on his Roman forehead, listening to this native son of Omaha, Nebraska declaim his lines as Mark Antony exemplifies artifice, especially when contrasted to the working-class New Jersey accent he would soon adopt in *On the Waterfront*.

Barthes changes tone and perspective in a brief *Lettres nouvelles* piece on the emergent technology of Cinemascope, whose effects he likens to a transformation of

Figure 6.1 Marlon Brando in *Julius Caesar*, directed by Joseph L. Mankiewicz © Turner Entertainment Co. and Warner Bros Entertainment Inc. 2006. All rights reserved.

the spectator's gaze from a filiform thread of flickers within a darkened and tomblike movie theater toward an immersive experience of spectacle: "For I am no longer beneath the image but before it, in the midst of it."[13] Barthes claims no technical expertise, yet he displays an acute sensitivity to the spatial effects that offer new ways to fill this large-screen expanse. The result, he notes, may be that the close-up may not survive, because kisses and drops of sweat may merge with shadows and the background. Barthes' remark recalls the moment in Jean-Luc Godard's *Le Mépris* (*Contempt*. 1963) when Fritz Lang (playing a character named Fritz Lang) quips that Cinemascope is suitable only for filming snakes and funerals.[14] Barthes provides a striking example when he asks his reader to imagine watching *Battleship Potemkin* (see Figures 6.2 and 6.3):

> No longer positioned behind a spyglass but pressed up against the very air, the stone, the crowd: this ideal *Potemkin*, where your hand can finally reach out to the insurgents, where you can share in the light and receive the blow of the tragic Odessa Steps right to your chest as it were—that is now to become possible; the balcony of History is ready.[15]

Showing an awareness of film as art and commodity, Barthes concludes with a challenge when he asks what will be shown using this new technology, *Potemkin* or *The Robe*, Odessa or Saint-Sulpice, History or Mythology? Despite its brevity, the piece displays Barthes's understanding of technology's integral role in making film a key instance of postwar mythologies.

Barthes extends his critical take on the tensions between history and mythology in a scathing critique of *Si Versailles m'était conté . . .* (*Royal Affairs in Versailles*), in which he dismisses director Sacha Guitry's production as flabby (*mou*). By parading

Figure 6.2 *Battleship Potemkin*, directed by Sergei M. Eisenstein © Sovexport Film 1976. All rights reserved.

Figure 6.3 *Battleship Potemkin*, directed by Sergei M. Eisenstein © Sovexport Film 1976. All rights reserved.

one celebrity after another, the film's overreliance on star power in place of historical amounts to an extended insult: "In a word, the film aims to humiliate: humiliate Versailles, France, History, the history of France, cinema, humanity, men, everything really."[16] Since Barthes sees the film as hardly worth the 400 francs [equivalent to less than US$1], an alternate title for Deborah Glassman's translation might replace "Versailles and its Accounts" with "Versailles and its Accountants." A practical measure of Barthes's disappointment with Guitry's film is the fact that the May 1954 *Les Lettres Nouvelles* piece was not among the *petites mythologies du mois* reprinted in *Mythologies*.

In "Le Pauvre et le prolétaire" ("The Poor and the Proletariat"), Barthes addresses *Modern Times* (1936) in which, he argues, director Charlie Chaplin approaches the proletarian theme without assuming it politically (see Figures 6.4 and 6.5). In so doing, Chaplin allows spectators to see what the proletarian does not (yet?) see, namely the nature of his needs in the immediate form of hunger. And this even while he remains blind to and mystified by his alienation at the hands of his masters (bosses and policemen): "Now Chaplin, in accord with Brecht's idea, presents a man's blindness so that the public can see both the blind man and what is in front of his eyes."[17] Chaplin-Man *(l'homme-Charlot)* triumphs because his anarchic refusal of everything and everyone, Barthes concludes, represents the most efficacious form of revolution artistically.

Where stills of and posters for *Modern Times* famously pictured the worker literally caught up in the cogs of Taylorist assembly lines, Barthes describes Chaplin lounging in his cell below a portrait of Abraham Lincoln and seemingly unaware of the new alienation his incarceration imposes. The breezy tone of Barthes's remarks adds to the critique of unenlightened workers Barthes was to develop the following year in his review of Marlon Brando in *On the Waterfront*. It is thus to Barthes's credit that his portrait of Chaplin-Man as sympathetic figure-type—a variant of Chaplin's

Figure 6.4 Charlie Chapin in *Modern Times*, directed by Charlie Chaplin © The Roy Export Company Establishment 2003. All rights reserved.

Figure 6.5 Charlie Chapin in *Modern Times*, directed by Charlie Chaplin © The Roy Export Company Establishment 2003. All rights reserved.

tramp persona—anticipates his subsequent critique of director Elia Kazan's efforts in *On the Waterfront* to portray Terry Malloy (Marlon Brando) as a sympathetic worker.

Concerning Chaplin in *Modern Times*, Barthes notes that perhaps only Brecht had seen the need to show man always "on the eve of Revolution," which is to say, man alone, still blind, on the point of being accessible to revolutionary light by the "natural" excess of his miseries.[18] More on Brecht to follow.

"The Face of Garbo" is deservedly the most frequently cited of Barthes's *petites mythologies*.[19] And not in the least because its insistence on the Platonic perfection of the face-as-mask straddling photography and film opens onto a three-dimensional sculptural effect the regal face assumes in Rouben Mamoulian's classic feature, *Queen Christina* (1933). Indeed, this sculptural effect recalls the opening verse of Charles Baudelaire's "La Beauté": *Je suis belle, ô mortels! comme un rêve de pierre*, [I am lovely, O mortals! like a dream carved in stone]. The piece is also memorable for its ending in which Barthes characterizes Garbo's face of icy perfection as marking a transition from an iconographic age associated with terror to one of charm, as seen in Audrey Hepburn's face: "As a language, Garbo's singularity was of a conceptual order, Hepburn's of a substantial order. Garbo's face is an Idea, Hepburn's an event."[20]

Barthes contrasts Garbo's regal face in *Queen Christina* to those assumed by Audrey Hepburn in any number of her films (see Figure 6.6). The move anticipates his adaptation of Ferdinand de Saussure's assertion that meaning is best understood as a product of difference. Thus, not simply the face of Garbo in itself, but instead in its difference from that of Hepburn. To which one might complicate matters in conjunction with the animated ("warmer") face Garbo assumed as female lead opposite Melvyn Douglas in Ernst Lubitsch's 1939 comedy, *Ninotchka* (see Figure 6.7). The aforementioned photo in which she sports a fashionable ("decadent") hat she cannot restrain herself from wanting and acquiring provides evidence that, much like Hepburn (see Figure 6.8) some fifteen to thirty years later, Garbo was able to pull off the transition from icy royalty and dour Bolshevik comrade to indulgent consumer. The total mask Garbo sports in *Queen Christina* thus yields to the softer features of the persona that emerges midway through *Ninotchka*.[21] Barthes's silence suggests that perhaps he did not know the latter film.

Though ostensibly a brief meditation on the aura of cool in gangster films such as Jacques Becker's 1954, *Touchez pas au grisbi* (Hands Off the Loot), Barthes's "Power

Figure 6.6 Greta Garbo in *Queen Christina*, directed by Rouben Mamoulian © Warner Bros Entertainment Inc. 2005. All rights reserved.

Figure 6.7 Greta Garbo in *Ninotchka*, directed by Ernst Lubitsch © Warner Bros Entertainment Inc. 2005. All rights reserved.

Figure 6.8 Aubrey Hepburn in *Sabrina*, directed by Billy Wilder © Paramount Pictures 1954. All rights reserved.

and Cool'" explores slippages across two languages and two cultures. Barthes mentions Becker's film only in passing. Moreover, he does so in abbreviated reference to the key term *grisbi*, which weakens the import of his remarks by failing to mention the three leading players: Jean Gabin as an aging crime boss, Lino Ventura as his upstart nemesis, and, between them, 26-year-old Jeanne Moreau as Josy, a young moll on the make in this male-centered environment. Barthes is on target ("on the money") when he describes the shady world these three crime film types inhabit as "a universe of litotes" (classical trope of understatement) in which restraint expresses symbolic and physical power. Even so, he fails to recognize the extent to which the pulp fiction origins of US film noir take on a decidedly Gallic expression whose measure appears in the semantic fact that the French term *désinvolture* translated as off-handedness fails to denote the flat affect of the US term "cool." French gangster films generate their own aura of fashionable understatement. *Grisbi*'s "cool" may anticipate the quintessential understatement in later French gangster films, from Jean-Pierre Melville's *Bob le flambeur* (*Bob, the Gambler*, 1956) and Louis Malle's *Ascenseur pour l'échafaud* (*Elevator to the Gallows*, 1958) to François Truffaut's *Tirez sur le pianiste* (*Shoot the Piano Player*, 1960) and Melville's *Le Samouraï* (*The Samuraï*, 1967). The mournful soundtrack that Miles Davis contributed to Malle's 1958 film goes a long way toward bridging this cultural gap between US and French expressions of cool associated with film noir.[22]

The feature-length documentary *Lost Continent* (*Continente perduto*, 1954) was reputed to be the first Italian production shot in Cinemascope. Yet this distinction failed to detract from Barthes's scathing dissection of the film's efforts to cast itself as a romanticized encounter between the Occident and Orient, that is, relations personified by "studio ethnologists."[23] To the contrary, Barthes hones in on the syncretic relations involving exotic Orientals whose Buddhism, the film suggests, is a variant of the Catholic Church's predisposition toward ecumenicity. "It is this very 'all things are alike' which our ethnologists have hinted at: Orient and Occident, it is all the same, there are only differences in color."[24] When Barthes concludes that it is in the nature of the East to produce refugees, he suggests that the diasporic dispersion of indigenous peoples links the Catholic Church and French state policies that exploited human resources in the cause of colonial occupation: "We see that 'the beautiful images' of *Lost Continent* cannot be innocent."[25] In sum, Barthes recasts *Lost Continent*'s visual beauty as a lure intended to cover its failed efforts to elide history in the name of a mythic and colonial-based exoticism he does not abide.

In its emphasis on the transformation of the flesh-and-blood actor into a timeless godlike essence, "The Harcourt Actor" reads as a test-run for "The Face of Garbo." The transformation results from the portrait photo's capacity to reduce the actor's or actress' body to face, shoulders, and hair, thus rendering the headshot photo an "initiation rite, a guild diploma, his [or her] true professional *carte d'identité*."[26] What Barthes calls the Harcourt Studios glow aerating the subject of the headshot photo seemingly caught "*in repose*" off-stage is an effect of studio lighting and an aberrant camera angle that takes up position in improbable zones of a rarified space: "As if this countenance, floating between the stage's crude earth and the town's radiant sky, could be only momentarily ravished from its intemporal nature and then devoutly abandoned to its solitary and regal course."[27] As in "Garbo's Face," Barthes concludes by setting the divine and timeless glow of the Harcourt Studios photo portraits against avant-garde practices he ascribes to Thérèse Leprat and Agnès Varda, both of whom bequeathed to the actor his fleshy face enclosed within a social function to represent. In contrast to a myth as alienated as that of actors' faces in the Harcourt photo portrait, Barthes concludes, this choice on the part of Leprat and Varda is quite revolutionary.[28]

Setting aside Barthes's 1943 review of Bresson's *The Angels of Sin* as a stand-alone effort, his film-based *petites mythologies* divide into overlapping subsets. "Romans in the Cinema," "The Harcourt Actor," and "The Face of Garbo" break down the power of the face as mask associated with the larger-than-life projections. This analysis extends implicitly to "On Cinemascope," to the extent that it threatens the close-up and to "Power and Cool," in which the absence of visible affect links up with the icy mask Garbo wears in *Queen Christina*. In retrospect, Barthes's attention to production details including hairstyles, sweat, camera angles, and lighting are prototypes of what he would analyze a quarter century later in *La Chambre Claire* as the *punctum* emanating from the screen projection to solicit ("prick") the viewer's attention. A second subset centered on sociology and ideology includes "The Poor and the Proletariat" and "A Sympathetic Worker." "Lost Continent" can be added to this subset in its indictment of an insidious Orientalism badly disguised in the film's array of beautifully manufactured settings. Alternate approaches subsume all the mid-1950s *petites mythologies* under the twofold critical model of semiology and semioclastics to which Barthes alludes in his introduction to the 1970 reprint of *Mythologies* cited above.

Nowhere does Barthes deploy this twofold analysis with as much verve as in his *petite mythologie*, "Un Ouvrier sympathique" (A Sympathetic Worker), on Elia Kazan's 1954 black-and-white feature, *On the Waterfront*. To be sure, the technique of demystification Barthes mobilizes in this instance derives as much from the writings of Bertolt Brecht as from the analyses inspired by Saussurean semiology. The Brecht connection is present in Barthes's choice of title, in which the French adjective, *sympathique*, translates into English less as "sympathetic" than as the more colloquial "likeable," "friendly," or even "nice." Yet for Brecht, the term exudes a stronger semantic valence in conjunction with the identification the audience is made to direct toward the film's central protagonist. As Barthes puts it, the fusion of Terry Malloy and Marlon Brando results from concerted efforts throughout the film to elevate this "likeable worker" to the dramatic status of positive hero to whom, "despite his faults, the public gives its heart."[29]

Barthes rebukes Kazan for resorting to audience identification in a "leftist" film whose revelation of a workers' problem is very much a matter of social and economic class beyond the individual worker. The apparent resolution at the film's end is nothing more than a short-term reprieve that falls short of the permanent and revolutionary change:

> What is orchestrated for us here, despite all the caricatures, is the restoration of order; with Brando, with the longshoremen, with all the workers of America, we put ourselves, with a sense of victory and relief, back in the boss's hands which it

serves no further purpose to portray as tainted: we have long since been snared in a fatal communion with the longshoreman who discovers a sense of social justice only to bestow it as a homage to American capital.[30]

The final shot of a steel door lowering much like a stage curtain conveys narrative closure, if not also resolution. Yet the closure staged when Terry Malloy's fellow longshoremen follow him into the dockside warehouse for a day's work is superficial and temporary, nothing more than a change from one boss to another.

Brando's performance as the likeable worker who speaks out against corruption is enhanced by the moral superiority over his predecessor he obtains in the final segment when he calls out union boss Johnny Friendly (Lee J. Cobb) during a physical confrontation that exudes the drama of a Hollywood Western gunfight. Even so, the promise of a new order Terry embodies is undermined by the prospect of the day-to-day continuity in the material conditions affecting salary, collective bargaining, and occupational safety for the dockworkers. In the end, the film fails to question the causes of the workers' exploitation under capitalism. Barthes concludes roundly, "There is much more to expect from the rebellion of victims than from the caricature of their executioners."[31]

Patrick ffrench argues that Barthes played a decisive role in a shift from a sociology to a semiology of film associated with the Institute of Filmology established in 1947–8 by Gilbert Cohen-Séat, Etienne Souriau, and Henri Roques. Even so, ffrench continues, "key continuities or areas of resonance" centered on sociology sought to understand how film simultaneously reflected and informed the psychology of audiences.[32] "A Sympathetic Worker" provides evidence that Barthes's place in this transition is less one of a progression than of variable interplay. The same is true of "The Brechtian Revolution," an editorial in the January–February 1955 issue of *Théâtre populaire*, in which Barthes champions a man whose work and thought radically challenged a 24-century-old theatrical credo according to which the more the public is moved (*ému*), the more it identifies with the hero.[33] Barthes cites Brecht as breaking with this credo when he prescribes that spectators should be only half-committed in order to know what they are seeing rather than merely submitting to it. As a result, Barthes assumes the bold tone of a tract or manifesto when he writes that the theater must cease to be magical in order to become critical. And this most of all by intervening in history: "We must have an art of explanation and no longer merely an art of expression. . . . The theater must participate in history by revealing its movement."[34]

Barthes further aligned his position with regard to Brecht in "The Tasks of Brechtian Criticism," a 1956 pierce in *Arguments* in which he located semiology among a critical program whose other levels of analysis include sociology, ideology, and morality. The semiology Barthes had in mind inscribes Saussure's notions of the arbitrary sign within a dramaturgy of alienation or distancing. Barthes invokes the German term *Episierung* in place of the better-known *Verfremdungseffekt*:

> Brecht's formalism is a radical protest against the confusions of the bourgeois and the *petit-bourgeois* false Nature: in a still alienated society, art must be critical, it

must cut off all illusions, even that of "Nature": the sign must be partially arbitrary, otherwise we fall back on an art of expression, an art of essentialist illusion.[35]

The critical tasks Barthes sets forth for Brecht echo the major points he makes against Kazan and Boris Kaufman. From theater to film, Barthes attacks *On the Waterfront* as an instance of bourgeois art removed from the revolutionary program for which he turns to Brecht's theater for guidance.

"A Sympathetic Worker" stands out among Barthes's film writings through the mid-1950s by mobilizing sociological, semiological, ideological, and moral critiques whose model Barthes identifies in the revolutionary theater of Bertolt Brecht. It also holds up when compared to other reviews of the film published in France following its release. I am thinking here especially of "On the Waterfront," Chris Marker's March 1955 review of Kazan's film in the Parisian monthly *Esprit*. Much like Barthes, Marker wastes no time. His opening sentence—"Cinema has more talent than filmmakers do, that's well known"—gives immediate notice of the ambivalent position he pursues as a mix of praise and critique.[36]

Even as Marker lauds the film's formal perfection on which American cinema retains a monopoly, he characterizes its themes of corruption, betrayal, and redemption as a marvelous game of hide-and-seek setting all kinds of traps for the spectator. Even when Marker acknowledges the film's masterful display of technical elements and form, he questions the effects of this display on the message it conveys, about which, he asserts, there is much to question. He likewise offers backhanded praise when he attributes the film's singular plasticity—that is, its blend of form and narrative—to the conjunction of a photographic aesthetic and a dramaturgy that asserts within the filmed event "the possibility of obliqueness, of escape, of strangeness or the unexplained."[37]

Much like Barthes, Marker notes the productive tensions between director Kazan and cinematographer Boris Kaufman in *On the Waterfront*'s striking moments, including Terry's and Edie's walk in the urban park, the trial at which Terry denounces corrupt union boss Johnny Friendly, and the climactic fight during which Friendly and his goons pummel Terry behind the union's dockside headquarters, the inoffensively named Hoboken Yacht Club. Singled out among these are the sequences filmed on *the roof* (Marker's emphasis), with its pigeons, its TV antennas, and the Hudson in the distance, each of which creates "one of those moments as a result of which we think of *the roof* in *Waterfront* in the same way we think of *the mud* in *Shane* or of *the studio* in *Sunset Boulevard*."[38] Much as he had done seven years earlier when he contrasted Robert Montgomery's *Lady in the Lake* with Edward Dmytryk's *Murder My Sweet*, Marker's invocations of films directed by George Stevens and Billy Wilder display his familiarity with major US releases of the period. In this, Marker echoes the *Cahiers du cinéma*'s Young Turks—aka Hitchcocko-Hawksians—whose support of Howard Hawks had begun as early as 1951–2. Writing in September 1952, Godard had described Hawks as "the greatest American artist." Richard Brody has noted that in the first episode of his *Histoires du cinema*, Godard made pointed reference to Stevens's *A Duel in the Sun*. A decade later, Godard included Brooks and Wilder in his "Dictionnaire des cinéastes américains" (Dictionary of American Filmmakers).[39]

Figure 6.9 Marlon Brando and Eva Marie Saint in *On the Waterfront*, directed by Elia Kazan © Columbia Pictures 1954. All rights reserved.

As direct as Marker is in his praise *On the Waterfront*'s visual style, he does not shrink from what he finds bothersome (*ennuyeux*) in the film (see Figure 6.9). To this end, he openly addresses those moments when the scriptwriter and director reveal their true natures, the former (Budd Schulberg) through his hypocrisy and guilty conscience, the latter (Kazan) through his excessive fondness for the theater. This is when, Marker writes, the film takes a turn for the worse. It is also the point when his remarks turn increasingly *ad hominem*. Evoking the film's climactic sequence during which the badly beaten Terry leads his fellow dockworkers to their day's work, Marker finds the use of a hand-held camera to convey Brando's stumbling gait nothing less than unbearable: "This is theater, theater at its worst, in spite of all the technique."[40]

The fact that Marker refers twice in the same paragraph to the actor Brando rather than to the character Terry Malloy suggests that his reservations concerning the film's depiction of Terry's awakening of conscience, motivated by his guilt for abetting Joey's death as well as his attraction to Edie, draw on the persona of Brando's role enhanced by the appeal of his movie star status. This status, in turn, transposes the social problem depicted by the film to the function of allegory or fable supporting a sense of the film as a thinly disguised justification of Kazan's and Schulberg's respective naming of names before the House Un-American Activities Committee during its hearings on Communists in Hollywood:

> Let's not be fooled, however, and let this situation involving priests, gangsters, and dockworkers prevent us from seeing that this film is the story of a denunciation, that it pits the code of silence, friendship even, against a state policy based on snitching (*mouchardage*). As such, it is infinitely more about McCarthyism than the sanctimonious working-class moral lesson it supposedly imparts.[41]

Marker refuses to be taken in by the twofold swindle (*double escroquerie*) concerning the film's depiction of a social and religious awakening of conscience. To which, Marker adds, nothing in the film supports Terry Malloy's awakening as one associated with social/economic class. In fact, Marker continues, the only awakening of conscience (*prise de conscience*) hidden behind crude and convenient screens is that of a woman, that is, the awakening on the part of the female lead Eva Marie Saint's Edie Doyle. Edie is both agent and subject of the awakening because she precipitates Terry's break with the hypermasculine (*viril*) milieu of the union leadership and boxing club. As Marker puts it, "Ultimately, the entire story of Brando is one of escape from this milieu in the direction of the woman. Ultimately, it is for her and through her that he *betrays*."[42]

Published two months before Marker's review in *Esprit*, André Bazin's January 1955 review of *On the Waterfront* focused on Brando's star presence and the broader topic of unionization in the United States before adding that French spectators might find the latter topic hard to appreciate because of its relative paucity compared to France's substantive unionist tradition. Returning to Marlon Brando, Bazin noted the actor's physical appeal as a mix of Greek features and the primitive mystery of a figure one might find in a Gauguin painting. Even so, Bazin continued, it sufficed to consider that by the time he appeared in *On the Waterfront*, this young screen god had already embodied with equal force of conviction the genial cunning of Mark Antony in Joseph Mankiewicz's *Julius Caesar*, the generous and simple anger of a revolutionary leader in Kazan's *Viva Zapata*, and the spectacular imbecility of the rowdy motorcycle gang leader Johnny Strabler in László Benedek's *The Wild One*.[43] Not since Gary Cooper, Bazin concluded, had a young male lead displayed dramatic resources with such promise.

My goal in singling out "A Sympathetic Worker" has been to make a case for the key role of Barthes's mid-1950s writings on film within *Mythologies*. And this as a means of reassessing the critical model he adapted from Bertolt Brecht in the cause of a revolutionary theater. In so doing, I also mean to support claims for Barthes as a social critic whose sense of *On the Waterfront* suggested affinities with the nonpartisan left exemplified by the *Arguments* group and its eponymous journal to which he contributed "The Tasks of Brechtian Criticism." Where I might once have associated this debt to Brecht with a resistance to film, I hope to have shown the extent to which Barthes's *petites mythologies* on film-based topics approximate what Daniel Mendelsohn has recently explored as practices of philology attuned to the full meaning of a literary text, that is, not merely its specific language and formal qualities but also "the history, religion, sociology, and politics of the civilization that produced it."[44]

Barthes was never primarily an ideological critic, even if his remarks on Brecht form a background or model for what he says concerning Marlon Brando's performances in *Julius Caesar* and *On the Waterfront*. Philippe Roger makes a strong case for seeing Barthes's writings of the 1950s, especially those on theater and Brecht, as a double accompaniment—Marx with Barthes and Barthes with Marx—endorsing what Edgar Morin once called a Marxist vulgate typical among intellectuals who had perhaps read only a few pages of Marx and Sartre.[45] In sum, I hope to have begun a reassessment of the *petites mythologies* Barthes devoted to film with a view toward reassessing his later pieces at a remove from a resistance to film whose limitations I have come to recognize.

Notes

1. See Steven Ungar, "Persistence of the Image: Barthes, Photography, and the Resistance to Film," in *Signs in Culture: Roland Barthes Today*, eds. Steven Ungar and Betty R, McGraw (Iowa City: University of Iowa Press, 1989), 139–56.
2. Dudley Andrew, Yves Citton, Vincent Debaene, and Sam Di Iorio, "Editors' Preface," in Philip Watts, *Roland Barthes's Cinema* (New York: Oxford University Press, 2016), ix.
3. See Watts, *Barthes's Cinema*, and Patrick ffrench, *Roland Barthes and Film: Myth, Eroticism and Poetics* (London: Bloomsbury Academic, 2020).
4. Noa Steimatsky, *The Face on Film* (New York: Oxford University Press, 2017), 82–3.
5. Roland Barthes, "The Angels of Sin (*Les Anges du péché*, 1943)," in Watts, *Barthes's Cinema*, 115.
6. Watts, *Barthes's Cinema*, 12.
7. Watts notes that this print venue specializing in postwar modernity featured writers including Samuel Beckett, Henri Michaux, Richard Wright, Heinrich Böll, Kateb Yacine, Michel Leiris, and Édouard Glissant (Watts, *Barthes's Cinema*, 12).
8. Barthes, *Mythologies*, trans. Richard Howard and Annette Lavers (New York: Hill and Wang, 2013). See Steven Ungar, "From Event to Memory Site: Thoughts on Rereading *Mythologies*," *Nottingham French Studies* 36.1 (1997): 24–33.
9. Barthes, "Preface to the 1970 Edition," in *Mythologies* (2013), x. Neither version includes some fifteen texts classified as mythologies in the 1993 and 2002 editions of Barthes's *oeuvres complètes* Éric Marty oversaw at the Editions du Seuil. Nine of the fifteen appeared in 1959, two years after the first edition of *Mythologies*. I consider Barthes's 1964 illustrated book, *La Tour Eiffel* (*The Eiffel Tower*), a *grande mythologie* in keeping with the large-scale object to which it is devoted. Barthes evolved beyond the demystification model he eventually came to see as arrogant and outmoded. Yet its insights persist in his writings on still and moving images through *La Chambre Claire*; his final book was published weeks before his March 1980 death.
10. Barthes, "Romans in the Movies," in *Mythologies* (2013), 19.
11. Ibid., 20.
12. *The Shorter Oxford English Dictionary* lists the primary meaning of the word "capillarity" in conjunction with tension on a liquid surface, with no mention of Barthes's usage in conjunction with the adjective "capillary." "Capillarity" is thus an invented term (neologism), similar to "Romanity." Both express Barthes's love of words (logophilia).
13. Barthes, "On Cinemascope," in Watts, *Barthes's Cinema*, 116.
14. Jonathan Rosenbaum notes that *Le Mépris* was shot in scope format and that Lang's *Moonfleet* (1955) was shot in MGM's Cinemascope variant, Metroscope. See Jonathan Rosenbaum, "On Cinemascope, Snakes, Funerals, Lang, and Welles," https://www.jonathanrosenbaum.net/2019/01/49899/. Accessed November 25, 2020.
15. Barthes, "On Cinemascope," 116–17.
16. "Versailles and its Accounts," in Watts, *Barthes's Cinema*, 117.

17 Barthes, "The Poor and the Proletariat," *Mythologies*, 36.
18 Ibid., 36.
19 I favor this formulation used by Annette Lavers in place of Richard Howard's "Garbo's Face" because the former catches the priority of the face-as-object over the proprietary sense of the latter.
20 Barthes, "Garbo's Face," 75.
21 Steimatsky astutely adds another film, George Cukor's *Two-Faced Woman* (1941), to chart Barthes's remarks concerning Garbo's transition from archaic divinity and a secularized individuality (see Steimatsky, *The Face on Film*, 127).
22 For further reading, see Ginette Vincendeau, "Noir Is also a French Word," in Ian Cameron, ed. *The Movie Book of Film Noir* (London: Studio Vista, 1992), Robin Buss, *French Film Noir* (London: Marion Boyars, 1994), and *European Precursors of Film Noir, Iris*, no. 21 (Institute for Cinema and Culture, University of Iowa, 1996).
23 Watts notes that Barthes's reference to ethnologists aligns with his turn to anthropology and to the writings of Claude Lévi-Strauss as a new, scientific way to engage film in ways that diverge from those of André Bazin (Watts, *Barthes's Cinema*, 39).
24 Barthes, "Lost Continent," in *Mythologies* (2013), 185.
25 Ibid., 186.
26 Barthes, "The Harcourt Actor," in *Mythologies* (2013), 17.
27 Ibid., 16.
28 By the mid-1950s, Varda (1928–2019) was official photographer at the Théâtre National Populaire as well as a free-lance photojournalist whose work appeared in mass-circulation venues *Prestige-France*, *Marie-Claire*, and *Réalités*. She often noted with pride that she had obtained a Certificat d'Aptitude Professionnelle (Certificate of Professional Aptitude). Thérèse Leprat (née Cahen, 1895–1966) was best known for her photo portraits and for collaborations with theatrical, literary, and film figures Jean-Louis Barrault, Jean Cocteau, and Jean Marais.
29 Barthes, "A Sympathetic Worker," in *Mythologies* (2013), 71.
30 Ibid., 71–2.
31 Ibid., 72. Barthes elaborates on programmatic impact of Brecht's strategy of alienation to counter audience identification by creating a spectator whose reluctance to identify forms the basis of the transition from a magical to a critical theater. See Barthes, "The Brechtian Revolution [1955]," in *Critical Essays*, trans R. Howard (New York: Hill and Wang, 1972), 37–9.
32 ffrench, *Roland Barthes and Film*, 63–4.
33 Barthes, "The Brechtian Revolution," 37.
34 Ibid., 38.
35 Barthes, "The Tasks of Brechtian Criticism," in *Critical Essays*, 75.
36 "On the Waterfront," trans. Jennifer Cazenave, *Cinéaste* 43.3 (Summer 2018): 15. The French original, which appeared as "On the Waterfront," *Esprit* 224 (Mar 55): 440-3, cites the film title in English, rather than the standard title in French, *Sur les Quais*.
37 Ibid., 15.
38 Ibid.
39 Godard, "Défense et illustration du découpage classique," *Cahiers du cinéma* 15 (September 1952). Reprinted in *Jean-Luc Godard par Jean-Luc Godard, vol. I (1950–1984)* (Paris: Cahiers du cinéma, 1998), 84; Richard Brody, *Everything Is Cinema: The Working Life of Jean-Luc Godard* (New York: Metropolitan Books, 2008), 527.

Godard's listings of Brooks and Wilder appear in "Dictionnaire des cinéastes américains," *Cahiers du cinéma* 150-1 (December 1963–January 1964), reprinted in *Godard par Godard*, 249–51.
40 Marker, "On the Waterfront," 16.
41 Ibid., 16.
42 Ibid., 17.
43 André Bazin, "*Sur les quais*; avec le plus grand acteur du monde [1955]," in *Écrits complets*, Vol. II, ed. Hervé Joubert-Laurencin (Paris: Éditions Macula, 2018): 1621.
44 Daniel Mendelsohn, *Three Rings: A Tale of Exile, Narrative, and Fate* (Charlottesville: University of Virginia Press, 2020), 33.
45 Philippe Roger, "Barthes with Marx," *Writing the Images After Roland Barthes*, ed. Jean-Michel Rabaté (Philadelphia: University of Pennsylvania Press, 1997), 175.

Bibliography

Barthes, Roland. "Angels of Sin." In Philip Watts, *Roland Barthes's Cinema*. Eds. Dudley Andrew, Yves Citton, Vincent Debaene, and Sam Di Iorio. New York: Oxford University Press, 2016. 113–15.
Barthes, Roland. "The Brechtian Revolution." In *Critical Essays*. Trans Richard Howard. Evanston: Northwestern University Press, 1972. 37–9.
Barthes, Roland. "On Cinemascope." In Watts, *Barthes's Cinema*, 116–17.
Barthes, Roland. "The Face of Garbo." In *Mythologies* (2013), 73–5.
Barthes, Roland. "Lost Continent." In *Mythologies* (2013), 184–6.
Barthes, Roland. *Mythologies* [1957]. Rev. ed. Paris: Seuil, 1970.
Barthes, Roland. *Mythologies*. Trans. Richard Howard and Annette Lavers. New York: Hill and Wang, 2013.
Barthes, Roland. "The Poor and the Proletariat." In *Mythologies* (2013), 35–7.
Barthes, Roland. "Power and 'Cool.'" In *Mythologies* (2013), 76–8.
Barthes, Roland. "The Romans in Movies." In *Mythologies* (2013), 19–21.
Barthes, Roland. "A Sympathetic Worker." In *Mythologies* (2013), 70–2.
Barthes, Roland. "The Tasks of Brechtian Criticism." In *Critical Essays*, 70–6.
Barthes, Roland. "On Versailles and its Accounts." In Watts, *Barthes's Cinema*, 117–21.
Bazin, André. "*Sur les quais*; avec le plus grand acteur du monde." In *Écrits complets*, Vol. II. Ed. Hervé Joubert-Laurencin. Paris: Éditions Macula, 2018. 1620–1.
Brody, Richard. *Everything Is Cinema: The Working Life of Jean-Luc Godard*. New York: Metropolitan Books, 2008.
Buss, Robin. *French Film Noir*. London: Marion Boyars, 1994.
European Precursors of Film Noir. Iris, no. 21. Institute for Cinema and Culture, University of Iowa, 1996.
ffrench, Patrick. *Roland Barthes and Film: Myth, Eroticism and Poetics*. London: Bloomsbury Academic, 2020.
Godard, Jean-Luc. "Défense et illustration du découpage classique." In *Jean-Luc Godard par Jean-Luc Godard, vol. I (1950–1984)*. Paris: Cahiers du cinéma, 1998. 84.
Marker, Chris. "On the Waterfront." Trans. Jennifer Cazenave. *Cinéaste* 43.3 (Summer 2018): 15–17.

Mendelsohn, Daniel. *Three Rings: A Tale of Exile, Narrative, and Fate.* Charlottesville: University of Virginia Press, 2020.

Roger, Philippe. "Barthes with Marx." In *Writing the Images After Roland Barthes.* Ed. Jean-Michel Rabaté. Philadelphia: University of Pennsylvania Press, 1997. 174–86.

Rosenbaum, Jonathan. "On Cinemascope, Snakes, Funerals, Lang, and Welles." https://www.jonathanrosenbaum.net/2019/01/49899/. Accessed 20 February 2021.

Steimatsky, Noa. *The Face on Film.* New York: Oxford University Press, 2017.

Ungar, Steven. "Persistence of the Image: Barthes, Photography, and the Resistance to Film." In *Signs in Culture: Roland Barthes Today.* Eds. Steven Ungar and Betty R. McGraw. Iowa City: University of Iowa Press, 1989, 139–56.

Ungar, Steven. "From Event to Memory Site: Thoughts on Rereading *Mythologies*." *Nottingham French Studies* 36.1 (1997): 24–33.

Vincendeau, Ginette. "Noir Is also a French Word." In *The Movie Book of Film Noir.* Ed. Ian Cameron. London: Studio Vista, 1992. 49–58.

Watts, Philip. *Roland Barthes's Cinema.* Eds. Dudley Andrew, Yves Citton, Vincent Debaene, Sam Di Iorio. New York: Oxford University Press, 2016.

7

Barthes, Bazin, and Écriture

Dudley Andrew

Among the many uncanny histories you can stumble upon over in the tangled fields of film writing, I am quickly drawn to the proximity, in that field, of two colorful wildflowers whose roots just may intertwine, Roland Barthes and André Bazin. Everyone finds them attractive, I should think. But only in the last couple of years has their proximity urged us to take them together, as nourished by the same culture, some of the same questions, and perhaps nourished by each other. In 2016, I was honored to coedit Philip Watts's posthumous monograph which we entitled *The Cinema of Roland Barthes*. Watts dedicated a chapter to the rapport between these two men, inspiring me to look even closer, something made far simpler by the publication of Bazin's *Ecrits complets*. These two volumes start with his earliest writings on film, in 1942, which corresponds to the well-known collection of Roland Barthes's *Oeuvres Complets* in three volumes also beginning in 1942. One of Barthes's very first articles (published August 1943) was on Bresson's *Les Anges du péché*, a film Bazin mentions three months later in his fourth article, then reviews at more length in his eleventh piece. Thus, their paths crossed at the outset of their critical careers over Bresson's first feature.

When these two names come up, usually it is to upgrade Bazin's status. Barthes is the prestigious intellectual whose late book *La Chambre Claire* mentions Bazin and should have been dedicated to him, given its recital of the catechism of "The Ontology of the Photographic Image." Instead, *La Chambre Claire* is dedicated, memorably, not to any person but to a book: "*L'Imaginaire* de Sartre." Yet this only further links the two critics, since Sartre's book was crucial to Bazin, whose personal copy I own, and within which I discovered marginalia and a page of Bazin's typed notes.[1] He bought the third edition, which probably came out in 1941 the year when his aspirations for a career as an academic literary scholar were shattered. Barthes, doubtless reading the same book, perhaps in its first edition the year before, likewise saw his aspirations for a professorship in literature crumble, due to tuberculosis. From 1941 to 1946, he was sequestered in sanitoria, while Bazin advanced faster, climbing from articles in student bulletins and small cultural reviews during the Occupation to a position where he was well-enough known to be able to publish an article in Sartre's *Les temps modernes*, and to occasion a personal response from Andre Malraux for his review of *Espoir* in *Poésie*. He had also moved into the inner circle at *Esprit*, where he could be found with his assistant Chris Marker and alongside Claude-Edmonde Magny, Jean Cayrol, and other literary figures who would become crucial to Barthes.

Three years older than Bazin, Barthes was slower to make his way. Before he had published anything substantial, he likely had encountered Bazin's "Ontology" essay in *Problèmes de la peinture*, or "Le Mythe du cinema total," published as it was in Bataille's journal *Critique*. James Tweedie and Philip Watts both imply that Barthes could well have discovered the template for his *Mythologies* in Bazin's cultural pieces, such as the 1946 "Entomologie de la pin-up." It's a perfect "Mythologie," quite similar to Barthes's first one, "Le monde où l'on catche (The World of Wrestling)," published in *Esprit* in 1952. This was actually Barthes's fourth article for *Esprit*, and Bazin surely encountered Barthes's writings there, if not the man himself. Bazin, by the way, was just then writing an essay for *Esprit* called "L'Enfance sans <u>mythe</u>: les Jeux interdits." "Myth" was on the minds of both men. And both men also wrote for *L'Observateur*, on occasion on the same topics (Cinemascope, *On the Waterfront*).² Both would begin to interact quite closely with Edgar Morin, the sociologist who had professional views about "mythe," and who turned both these classically trained literary scholars toward questions of media and communications.

Bazin died at forty, which is about the age Barthes was when he could be said to have caught up to him in recognition. He would of course quickly surpass him, for Barthes kept writing for a quarter century, while Bazin was gone in 1958, leaving 2,600 pieces compared to Barthes's fewer than fifty at that date.

With their *Oeuvres* and *Ecrits complets* before us, several exciting crossover passages and ideas stand out and can now be readily compared. For instance, Barthes's famous and wonderful "Visage de Garbo" came out two months after he would have read Bazin's essay on *Queen Christina* in the February 1955 *France Observateur* (where he was film critic while Barthes was in charge of theater). Bazin writes,

> Ici, en une seule image—digne des plus grandes traditions de la statuaire ou de la peinture de la femme—le metteur en scène résout naturellement l'expression du maximum d'audace par le maximum de pudeur. C'est le couple de la litote érotique et, pourtant, de l'efficacité. Voilà, un Bonheur qu'aucun cinéma du monde (sauf peut-être le japonais ne saurait plus ou, plus exactement, ne pourrait plus trouver).³

Two months later, on April 26, 1955, in *Les Lettres Nouvelles*, Barthes wrote that Garbo's "is not a painted face but one in plaster protected by the surface of its shadows and not by its lineaments. . . . Even in its extreme beauty, this face is not drawn but instead sculptured in something smooth and friable, which is to say both perfect and ephemeral."

An even better example, noted by Hervé Joubert-Laurencin, occurred the year before. Reviewing *Le Rouge et le Noir* in *Cahiers du cinéma*, Bazin wrote of an adaptation so bad that "Je peux même assurer que dans le cas d'un spectateur déjà peu enclin à aimer Stendhal, il aggravait l'allergie, à la manière de cette publicité de margarine [Astra] qu'on dirait payée par le syndicat des laiteries coopératives."⁴ Three weeks later, Barthes analyzed the paradox of the same margarine ad in "Opération Astra," though for him the shortcomings of margarine shown in the ad worked in its favor. By the way, in the supplemental Christmas issue of *Cahiers du cinéma*, published at the very same moment, Bazin wrote one of his essays most in the mode that Barthes made famous and which I enjoyed translating and publishing in English: "A Contribution to an *érotologie* of Television."[5]

That these two great essayists occasionally glanced at each other seems clear; but what of substance might this have affected? This is where I turn to Barthes's first significant concept, the one that gave its name to the title of his first book in 1953: *Le Degré zéro de l'écriture*. This term, it turns out, he introduced six years earlier in an article published in *Combat*, on August 2, 1947. As I suggest in *What Cinema Is!*, these are the very years when Bazin's attention shifted from realism to adaptation and the cultural function of cinema.[6] This shift, quite evident if you scan his writings in 1948, came under pressure of this term from Barthes or from notions that he and Barthes adopted at the same time.

Literature, Cinema, and the Neutral Style

Bazin's career was propelled by the certainty that he was witnessing a significant evolutionary development in cinema from its classic era to its modern one. While Renoir, Welles, and the neorealists formed the cutting edge of this evolution, he also detected a drift to the modern in the main current of films, in adaptations, generally a conservative mode. Several of his first twenty articles mention adaptation as he anticipates the mass of Hollywood films to follow the GIs onto the beaches of Normandy. Alerted by his friend Roger Leenhardt, he believed that Hollywood had entered a writers' era, with Steinbeck, Dos Passos, Hemingway, Caldwell, and Faulkner in privileged positions, sometimes writing scripts. Like his colleague at *Esprit*, Claude-Edmonde Magny, Bazin was certain that these writers had learned many literary techniques from cinema, and now were rewarding Hollywood with a maturity in subject matter and a suppleness of style that should create a more discriminating American public, and ultimately a more sensitive and reflective citizenry everywhere. The stakes were high.

This optimism is on full display in his first real discussion of adaptation, appearing in the serious literary journal, *Poésie*, just before the German surrender. And the pretext couldn't have been more perfect for it came in a review of *The Human Comedy*, written by that most optimistic of American authors, William Saroyan. Saroyan had published this novel in 1943 from his screenplay, a loosely plotted sequence of touching anecdotes about daily life in a small town during wartime; an immediate bestseller, Clarence Brown managed to get it onto the screen that very year with Mickey Rooney in the lead. You can feel Saroyan himself in the voice-over that Ray Collins narrates from beyond the grave, for that voice hovers benevolently above the town, dominating the limited perspectives of the camera, and making this an unquestionably literary film, a sort of gift of cinema to literature, rather than a usurpation. Neither the novel nor (especially) the film may be exceptional; but that didn't diminish the surprise Bazin felt in realizing that *The Human Comedy* exemplifies a new cultural economy: the near-simultaneous appearance of book and film, and the participation of the novelist:

> Until now, the fidelity of an adaptation (when one bothered to think about it) was generally confined to the story and to the psychology of the characters. At most, it went as far as covering what is conventionally called "atmosphere." Now, it seems, fidelity aspires to go further, to the point of giving us a complete equivalent of the written novel, in form and content. . . . To take a further step, cinematic technique had to attain the prodigious <u>impersonal</u> flexibility toward which the Americans seem to strive. Only this *a priori* absence of style could have made possible a total openness to the spirit and the *form* of the novel.[7]

These breakthrough ideas about adaptation were provoked because the literary source was contemporary, not classic. Brand new novels, often featuring innovative narrative techniques like *The Human Comedy*, required flexibility in scripting and direction. Bazin's review of Billy Wilder's *The Lost Weekend* notes that this time it was a film that made a book famous, resulting in a lightning-fast 1946 French translation that the publisher astutely brought out two weeks before the film's Paris premiere.[8] Bazin came to that premiere just having read this translation and so could appreciate Wilder's achievement in turning an "anti-cinematic novel of interior monologue" into a film that he believed should forever dispel doubts about cinema's capacity for subtlety. From the verbal flow of the novel, Wilder ingeniously produced the hallucinatory objectivity that characterizes the experience of an advanced alcoholic, an experience that may not be far from that of the film viewer! Wilder achieves this through a neutral style, devoid of the contortions of expressionist lighting and camera angle.

Now what Bazin called "neutral style" is a "form" right in line with the "zero degree writing" that Barthes introduced in 1947, form being Bazin's equivalent of *écriture*, a material shape that interacts with its culture. Scarcely a month after Barthes's piece, Bazin reviewed Autant-Lara's scandalous 1947 *Le Diable au corps* from Raymond Radiguet's even more scandalous 1923 novel. To compare works separated by over a quarter century, Bazin diminishes the issue of textual fidelity (Aurenche and Bost are true to the novel's topic and spirit, but utterly betray Radiguet's style); instead, Bazin considers aesthetic choices as a function of the different societies addressed (post–First World War and post–Second World War) and by the different relations that the art forms, novel and cinema, maintain with those societies. The cinema had not caught up with the way literature written in 1923 could provoke the middle class through its insouciance. "I suffered when I saw *Le Diable au corps*," he says, for the novel's blazing style had been transformed. Bazin then deepens the term "transformation," not just by letting us hear "form" within "transform," but by turning to physics, more precisely to electrical engineering:

> The work of the screenwriters Aurenche and Bost consisted, so to speak, in "transforming" (in the sense that an electric transformer does) the voltage of the novel. The aesthetic energy is almost all there but it is distributed—or, perhaps

better, dissipated—differently according to the demands of the cinematic optic. . . . Aurenche and Bost have succeeded in transforming the absolute amoralism of the original into an almost too obvious morality.⁹

This is a wonderfully fertile analogy. Aurenche and Bost literally change the "form" in which the subject matter (the characters and situations) appear, "trans-forming" it from prose to moving pictures and recorded sound. The adaptation is a genuine apparatus, a "transformer" that takes the electrical current flowing at full power in one system (220 volts) and reduces it to whatever voltage best functions for what is technically called, in the parlance of engineers, an "equivalent circuit." Radiguet's high-voltage novel, in other words, required a "step-down process" to drive a film that, less intemperate than the novel, needs to operate at cooler temperature. What would have happened, he asks, had Jean Vigo adapted Radiguet? The overlap in temperament between writer and director would have resulted in so little transformation, or step-down, that the movie "would have been impossible to show to the public because the reality of the book would have ignited the screen." The cultural circuits would have been overtaxed by dangerously high voltage.

You can see Bazin alluding to Sartre here, just as Barthes does, by conceiving style as what is utterly personal, biological, ahistorical. At the end of "Cinéma comme digeste," Bazin insists that Malraux's single style—absolutely the same in the novel and film *Espoir*—appears under two different *forms*; this amounts to two distinct instances of *écriture* which the artist chooses but which exist beyond his style. The form or *écriture* affects the diffusion of the works, and how they are categorized and consumed. Bazin even leapfrogs over Barthes by predicting, two decades before Barthes's famous 1968 manifesto, a future in which "the very notion of the author himself would be destroyed," as would the unity or integrity of the work of art, since "the standard differentiation among the arts in the 19th century and the relatively recent subjectivist notion of the author as identified with the work no longer fit in with the aesthetic sociology of the masses, in which the cinema runs a relay race with drama and the novel and doesn't eliminate them but reinforces them."¹⁰

Barthes had similarly argued for the historically variable category, *écriture*, as existing in culture beyond the artist's style; but artists can choose their *écriture*, their publics, since literature has become fragmented. The avant-garde writing Barthes analyzes in this first piece of criticism are Camus's *écriture blanche* and Queneau's *écriture parlé*, both of which abandon the flourishes that the public associates with Literature. Barthes would go on to champion Robbe-Grillet, Borges, and other writers whose apparently neutral and transparent prose does not satisfy the bourgeois reader wanting to see his world reinforced. Now this is analogous to Bazin's "defense d'une nouvelle avant-garde," that group of contemporary filmmakers who have missed a rendezvous with their audience (Vigo, Bresson, the Renoir of *La Règle du jeu*, the Welles of *The Magnificent Ambersons*). In the only article Bazin wrote for *Combat*, "Nous autres chevaliers de l'avant-garde," he hails these filmmakers for not following the ostentatious avant-garde of the 1920s into rarified poetic expression; they have chosen a narrative form of *écriture* that nevertheless is at odds with the classical model that dominates the theaters. These films are doubly "maudits," neither poetry nor "good prose."

Bazin was hardly alone in promoting this new "form" of cinema. Alexandre Astruc, who had been a regular critic at *Combat*, publishing an essay there just before Barthes's piece, seems equally affected by it. In March 1948, his famous "Caméra-Stylo" article uses phrases like these: "le cinéma s'arrachera peu à peu à cette tyrannie du visuel, de l'image pour l'image, de l'anecdote immédiate, du concret, pour devenir un moyen d'écriture aussi souple et aussi subtil que celui du langage écrit." He goes on, "La mise en scène n'est plus un moyen d'illustrer ou de présenter une scène, mais une véritable écriture."

Bazin and Astruc undoubtedly were in frequent contact as both used the same examples again and again to promote "La Nouvelle Avant-garde." Two months before Astruc's "Caméra-Stylo," Bazin penned a review of *Les Dernières Vacances* astutely titled, "Roger Leenhardt a fait un film qu'il n'a pas écrit," [Roger Leenhardt has made a film from a novel he didn't write] where he puts Leenhardt alongside Bresson, who had adapted Diderot, and Malraux, who had adapted himself, in order to get beyond adaptation toward something more fundamental, style.[11] In a longer review of the same film, he elaborated: "L'écriture cinématographiques retrouve en quelque sorte ici et par ses moyens propres, cette syntaxe de la lucidité qui caractérise tout un classicisme romanesque français, de *La Princesse de Clèves* à *L'Etranger*."[12] Now *L'Etranger* was precisely Barthes's chief example of "le degré zéro de l'écriture." Bazin follows him in this: "Considéré comme descriptif, le découpage des *Dernières Vacances* pourrait en effet souvent paraître élémentaire, mais il est d'abord le mouvement d'une pensée où se retrouvent précisément résolues esthétiquement les contradictions les plus frappantes de la personalité de Roger Leenhardt."[13] Découpage becomes the site of a cinematographic *écriture* which embodies the "movement of thought." In the most advanced postwar cinema, this movement flows through judiciously neutral styles. For this, Bazin praised Leenhardt, calling him "un écrivain du cinéma."[14]

Leenhardt, Astruc, and Bazin, all men with literary experience, became the architects of a way of thinking about cinema through the categories of literature while avoiding the trap set by the word "adaptation." These three joined Jean Cocteau to form Objectif 49, a ciné-club committed to unfurling examples of the process Bazin announced in his homage to Leenhardt: "tout ce qui depuis dix ans compte réellement dans la production mondiale, de *La Règle du jeu* à *Citizen Kane* et à *Paisà*, n'est-ce pas précisément des romans (ou des nouvelles) qui ont préféré être des films?"[15] I would add, invoking Barthes, the following: the auteurs of these films had chosen their form; it is called *l'écriture cinématographiqe*.

René Clément: The Debate over Style

After more than a half-century of semiotics and structuralism, one can debate the naked terms Bazin uses to discuss adaptation: "contenu," "style," "forme" (sometimes "mythe"). You can do the same with Barthes's terms, which are nearly identical:

"langage," "style," "écriture." Both men are explicit and precise in their definitions. Bazin writes: "One should not confuse prose style with grammatical idiosyncrasies or, more generally still, with formal constants. Such confusion is widespread—and unfortunately not merely among French teachers. 'Form' is at most a sign, a visible manifestation, of style."[16]

A couple of years later, and after his own internment in a sanitorium for tuberculosis, where he too read and thought a great deal away from the turmoil of a war, a cold one, Bazin added an historical dimension to these analytic categories, just as Barthes had done. Where Barthes saw the unity of classical literature breaking up into numerous options that a writer like Flaubert could choose (modernism being a spectrum of such choices), so Bazin found cinema to be going through the same maturation, as the Classical became the Modern:

> Sound cinema, having reached the end of, or at least a plateau in, its formal evolution, is reflecting—perhaps for the first time—on its true formal problems. Such a cinema cannot evade any longer the decisive importance of style: that is, the fundamental state of the art where every technique is completely responsible for what it expresses, or every form is a sign, and where nothing is really said without its being couched in the necessary form.... To speak of "form" in this new sense is the very opposite of an analysis of subject matter, and we wouldn't any longer be able to confine ourselves to noting that this or that particular stylistic aspect has not been introduced. We'd have to make sure that it has been *conquered*, for the filmmakers as well as for ourselves the critics: that it has become "of the cinema" even as Stendhal's characters, Gide's moral views, or Victor Hugo's political convictions have become "of literature."[17]

In bringing up the writer's "responsibility," Bazin comes very close to Barthes, who also talks about authors "reconquering" language by taking responsibility for their *écriture*. Both critics twist Sartre's ethics of choice against their master thanks to this third term, *écriture* (forme) set between language (entirely public) and style (purely individual, even biological). What Sontag wrote in her preface to the English translation of *Le Degré zéro de l'écriture* applies to cinema's auteurs: "Sartre has suppressed the fact that the choices made by writers always face in *two* directions: toward society and toward the nature of literature itself.... The writer's choice—which amounts to 'a way of conceiving literature'—is a matter of 'conscience, not of efficacy.'"[18] Barthes and Bazin, unlike Sartre, were sensitive to literature and cinema as institutions that could change. They championed artists (Robbe-Grillet and Queneau, or Bresson and Varda) who could be avant-garde and usher in something new in the history of literature.

Bazin kept this notion of evolution in mind as he wrote about the spectrum of filmmakers for his columns. Let me conclude on a controversial example, René Clément, because Bazin had such hopes for him as a "responsible" auteur, while the young Turks at *Cahiers du cinéma* found him hopelessly conventional, a reliable metteur en scène ready to compromise to command bigger budgets. Already in 1947, Bazin had declared: "Clément est de ceux chez qui le style s'identifie avec la volonté créatrice. Il voit ce qu'il veut: on le sent partout dans le jeu des acteurs, dans le décor, le montage" [Clément is one of those for whom style can be identified as creative will. He sees just what he wants: you can feel this everywhere, in the acting, in the décor, in the montge]. Such willful intentionality is what marks modern *écriture* in Barthes's sense.

Bazin hoped Clément might turn out to be a popular avatar of Bresson. Clément had both the instinct and the technique to produce starkly realist images (France's only candidate for its own neorealism), yet after 1950 he took on a succession of literary adaptations capable of pushing cinema beyond its usual conventions. Bazin applauded as he went from *Les Jeux interdits* to *M. Ripois*, to *Gervaise*, and then to *Barrage contre le Pacifique*, the first adaptation of a work by Marguerite Duras.

The adaptation of *Les Jeux interdits* was scripted by Aurenche et Bost, which sunk it in Truffaut's eyes. Bazin, however, compared it to a novel by Erskine Caldwell, direct and objective. Without flourishes, it offered further proof that cinema had matured thanks to literature. Indeed, this film didn't need to represent a novel since in effect it was itself a new kind of novel, one appearing in images on screen.[19]

He and Truffaut would hotly disagree about Clément's next film, *M. Ripois*, where Bazin felt more was at stake for *écriture cinématographique*. Reviewing it from Cannes, where it took the Special Jury Prize, Truffaut pressed the point he had made just three months before in his tirade "A Certain Tendency in French Cinema."[20] French cinema was cynical and condescending even to literary masterpieces like this recently resurrected best seller by Louis Hemond which Truffaut adored. Bazin also reviewed *Monsieur Ripois* from Cannes, and the two must have sparred over drinks later on, for in Bazin's long article in *Esprit*, a few months later, clear echoes of Truffaut's review are audible. Both mention Bresson's *Journal d'un curé de campagne* as a touchstone of cinematic ambition in going beyond fidelity to writing, but only Bazin believes Clément to have reached "beyond the spectacle, [to] interest us less through the representation of events than through our comprehension of them." For that is what strong novels do. They organically move from perceptions and actions, including dialogue, to reflection and assessment. The myriad ways they accomplish this alchemy we classify as authorial style. This is Bazin's theme.

Truffaut is gratified that at least Clément had sense enough to fire Aurenche from a project that got off the ground when a genuine novelist with a real style, Raymond Queneau, brought *M. Ripois ou la Nemesis* to his attention. Since Queneau went on to compose the dialogue, the director apparently started with some ambition; but Truffaut accuses Clément of lowering his sights and producing a fashionably cynical study of a mediocre Don Juan, even denigrating his main character and the women he gets involved with. "*M. Ripois*, like its chief character, has no soul. . . . When he suppressed everything that was moving in Hémon's book, Clément behaved like the pseudo-intellectuals with which French cinema is overpopulated."[21] In yet another review, he wrote: "L'infidélité à la lettre s'accompagne donc ici d'une infidélité à l'esprit: M.Ripois n'a pas d'âme, mais le livre en possède une; or, il semble que René Clément, établissant une confusion entre la 'cruauté' et le 'cynisme' ait réalisé 'un film sans âme.'"[22] Truffaut is a tremendously insightful, pithy critic. And he remembered what he wrote, so that when he came to make *Jules et Jim*, a novel that has much in common with *M. Ripois*, he strove to avoid pitfalls into which he was sure Clément had stepped.

Bazin saw the pitfalls too, but he thought *M. Ripois* "Clément's most important film," even if "not the masterpiece some people would like to see in it."[23] Echoing Truffaut, he continued: "My major criticism is that it is too intellectual and calculated a creation and therefore insufficiently suffused with sensibility." But where the young firebrand stopped as usual with a summary judgment—that, having no feeling for Hémon as novelist, "the filmmaker was tinkering with a masterpiece"[24]—Bazin took the occasion of this ambitious work gone awry to interrogate Clément's "calculated" mise en scène, as a cinematic "writing" (he underlines the term) parallel to, if less successful than, Hémon's. Thus, in this case as often, Truffaut was the sharper critic, perhaps helping Bazin to recognize his reactions to the film, and then use those reactions to come to general principles about the art form. Bazin was ultimately a theorist, here a theorist of adaptation.

It was in this role that he identified what he believes to be the classical novel's most distinguished and important property, the copresence of objectivity and subjectivity. Through the alchemy of prose, novels slip from description to comprehension and vice versa, sometimes undetected, sometimes brazenly. From the silent era on, films have attempted to represent this mingling of perception and reflection, but in delivering scenes set in the world and then representing consciousness or response to the world, they tend to become awkward. Bazin thought that modern cinema was evolving toward solutions that suppressed special effects so as to render consciousness through perception. This is what he had admired in Billy Wilder's *Lost Weekend*. And this is where he believed Clément had made genuine gains. "The dramatic or objective action, if I may call it that, as defined by the protagonists' behaviors and their words, indeed takes place on the screen before our very eyes. However, the cuts (the shifting of the frame and the movement of the camera) are built not on this apparent reality but rather on the thoughts of Ripois," on what he and the camera notice. "Obviously, the goal may not be especially original—other examples could date back even to silent cinema—but the novelty lies in the fact that the duplicity of both points of view, the objective and subjective, is throughout expressed simultaneously in the mise en scène, without any editing effects, close ups, or superimpositions." Bazin then dares to conclude: "This way of no longer *describing*, but, I want to say, *writing*' the scene is what delivers its hidden meaning, that which it has in the characters' minds."[25]

Here we have an early formulation of what Pasolini would call the filmic equivalent of "free indirect discourse,"[26] where it is difficult to discern exactly when perception edges into reflection, or if the author's vision is distinct from that of his character. Of course, most novels do draw this distinction through punctuation, chapter headings, italics, and changes in the mood and tense of verbs. They display their written nature. To be faithful to this "literary reality"—Bazin's phrase—films can turn to voice-overs that literally comment or reflect on the image that is projected simultaneously on the screen. Jean-Pierre Melville and Bresson had pioneered setting an authorial voice across an entire film so as to stress its status as a verbal object, as had Alexandre Astruc, author of the essay "la caméra-stylo" in his maiden film, the 1953 *Le Rideau Crimoisie*.

In *M. Ripois*, the author Louis Hémon deployed internal monologue intermittently, and quite naturally or realistically, at points when his character's thoughts come into focus; Bazin admired the way Clément followed him here by employing "voice-over commentary which he combines brilliantly with real dialogue and direct sound ... with the soundtrack constantly interlacing these two literary levels."[27] Now the monologues that Raymond Queneau came up with haven't the nearly hieratic register heard in Melville, Bresson, or Astruc's films, but they are literary all the same, and therefore abstract in relation to the images that play alongside them. The real gain Bazin attributes to Clément has to do with his film's realism. Those other films lifted their images to a literary level not just through their literary voice-over but also via enclosed decors and studied gestures. Clément took the other tack, dropping the literary commentary like rain, so to speak, onto images taken directly from the streets of London. "The moral isolation of the poor man in the city is no longer just a plausible-enough statement of the writer or the screenwriter: representing it coincides with putting it to the test. To express it is to experience it."[28] The voice-over achieves even more in film than introspective monologues do in the novel, for it operates via "an actor inserted into a reality that pays him no heed."[29] And we sense this directly.

André Bazin would have talked about these issues constantly in the office at *Cahiers du cinéma*, where his most attentive listener was Eric Rohmer, the professor of literature, the former novelist who had turned to cinema as a new way to write his novels. The core of Rohmer's aesthetic is summarized here in Bazin's reading of the achievement of *M. Ripois*, where a scripted plot and literary reflection come into contact with genuine weather conditions, with oblivious buses and cars, and with real passers-by, some of whom are visibly amused by the production of a movie taking place right then and there as an event. Take a look at the Prologue from Rohmer's *L'Amour l'après-midi* and compare it to Gerard Philipe's wandering the London streets as he plays the character M. Ripois, who sizes up the truly unknown women who pass him by. This is cinematic *écriture*.

Where Truffaut had lamented that Clément didn't use enough of Raymond Queneau's script and dialogue, Bazin faults Queneau's penchant for brilliant wordplay: "We can be allowed to regret this shift to comedy, for it is far more difficult for a work to succeed when its heartless hero doesn't require a heart even of the public."[30] Did Clément respect his scriptwriter more than the novelist he adapted? Queneau, one of Barthes's heroes in *Le Degré zéro de l'écriture*, appealed to the least-admirable qualities of the director. As Bazin says, once again echoing Truffuat: "Clément's most vulnerable spot is not around the heart; his temptation is the exercise of style."[31] *L'exercise du style*, Queneau's most famous book, here works against his own adaptation of a novel in which he saw such rich possibilities. Where Truffaut, the absolutist, dismissed this film, Bazin, the dialectician, found that in this exercise in adaptation, one could feel the cinema progress. More important, one could sense that cinema and prose fiction share a project of *écriture*, as writers and filmmakers were moving back and forth between these forms to bring contemporary reality to urgent expression.

Notes

1. Dudley Andrew, "The Ontology of a Fetish," *Film Quarterly* 61.4 (Summer 2008): 62–7.
2. Philip Watts, *Roland Barthes' Cinema* (New York: Oxford University Press, 2016), 36.
3. André Bazin, "La Reine Christine," in *France Observateur* 249 (February 17, 1955), reprinted in André Bazin, *Écrits complets* [*EC*], ed. Hervé Joubert-Laurencin (Paris: Éditions Macula, 2018), II, 1650. My translation of the relevant passage: "in a single image—worthy of the grand tradition of statuary or painting of female subjects—the director resolves in a natural way the expression of the highest possible audacity with the greatest modesty. We have here the satisfaction provided by a litotes that is at once erotic and efficacious. Here is a happy fullness that no other cinema in the world (except perhaps the Japanese) knows how or, more precisely, is able anymore to find."
4. André Bazin, "Des caractères; *Le Rouge et le Noir*," *Cahiers du cinéma* 41 (December 1954); *EC* II, 1601–3. Joubert-Laurencin glosses Bazin's reference to "Astra" in *EC* II, note 19, 1602. My translation: "I can even state that for a viewer already disinclined to like Stendhal, he made the aversion worse, like that [Astra] margarine commercial that seemed to have been paid for by the union of cooperative dairies."
5. André Bazin, "Pour contribuer à une érotologie de la télévision," *Cahiers du cinéma* 42 (December 1954); *EC* II, 1603–6; "A Contribution to an *Erotologie* of Television," in *André Bazin's New Media*, ed. and trans. Dudley Andrew (Berkeley, CA: University of California Press, 2014), 105–15.
6. Dudley Andrew, *What Cinema Is!* (Chichester: Wiley-Blackwell, 2010), 110–12.
7. André Bazin, "A Propos de *Human Comedy*," *Poésie* 45.23 (February–March 1945); *EC* I, 113–15.
8. André Bazin, "*The Lost Weekend (Le Poison)*; Le drame de l'alcool," *L'Écran Français* 86 (February 18, 1947): 6, 18; *EC* I, 246–7.
9. André Bazin, "L'adaptation ou le cinéma comme Digeste," *Esprit* 146 (July 1948), 39; *EC* I, 445. Translation in *Bazin on Adaptation: Cinema's Literary Imagination* (Oakland: University of California Press, 2022), ch 3.
10. Ibid.
11. André Bazin, "Roger Leenhardt a filmé le roman qu'il n'a pas écrit," *Ecran Français* (January 27, 1948); *EC* I, 370. Translation in *Bazin on Adaptation: Cinema's Literary Imagination*, ch. 9.
12. André Bazin, "Le style, c'est l'homme même; *Les Dernières Vacances*," *La Revue du cinéma* 14 (June 1948); *EC* I, 423. My translation: "Here cinematographic writing in a certain manner recovers via its own means that syntax of lucidity that characterizes the full novelistic classicism of France, from *The Princesse of Cleves* to *The Stranger*."
13. Ibid. My translation: "Taken as a description, the découpage of *The Last Vacation* could in effect often seem to appear simple, but it comprises first of all the movement of a thought where the most striking contradictions of the personality of Roger Leenhardt find themselves aesthetically resolved."
14. André Bazin, "Roger Leenhardt a filmé le roman qu'il n'a pas écrit," *EC* I, 370.
15. Bazin, "Le style, c'est l'homme même," *EC* I 423. My translation: "Everything that in the past ten years has really counted in film production in the world, from *The Rules*

of the Game to Citizen Kane and Paisa, aren't these precisely novels (or short stories) that actually wanted to be films?"
16 André Bazin, "L'adaptation ou le cinéma comme digeste," *Esprit* 146 (July 1948): 33; *EC* I, 442. Translation in *Bazin on Adaptation: Cinema's Literary Imagination*, ch. 3.
17 André Bazin, "De la forme et du fond ou la 'crise' du cinéma," in *Almanach du théâtre et du cinéma*, ed. J. Vagne (Paris: Éditions de Flore/La Gazette des Lettres, 1951); *EC* I, 687.
18 Susan Sontag, "Preface," in Roland Barthes, *Writing Degree Zero and Elements of Semiology* (Boston: Beacon Press, 1968), xv–xvi.
19 Bazin may have responded to the film's odd genesis, for it was originally written as a failed screenplay by François Boyer, a student of Clément's at IDHEC just after the war, and only came back to him five years later after getting a second life as a novel translated into English. Clément, in short, could circumvent the embellishments of Aurenche and Bost, and apply his more neutral style to something that did have the smell of the Occupation about it.
20 François Truffaut, "A Certain Tendency in French Cinema," in *Cahiers du Cinéma the 1950s* (Cambridge, MA: Harvard University Press, 1986).
21 François Truffaut, "Monsieur Ripois," in *The Films in My Life*, trans. Leonard Mayhew (New York: Simon and Schuster, 1985), 199.
22 François Truffaut, "*Monsieur Ripois et la Némésis*; Un grand metteur en scène au service d'un scénario inégal," *Arts* 465 (May 26, 1954), in Truffaut, *Chronique d'Arts Spectacles 1954–1958*, ed. Bernard Bastide (Paris: Gallimard, 2019), 72. My translation: "Infidelity to the letter thus brings with it here infidelity to the spirit: M. Ripois may have no soul, but the book definitely has one; and so it seems that René Clément establishing a confusion between 'cruelty' and 'cynicism' has made a film without a soul."
23 André Bazin, "Des romans et des films: *M. Ripois* avec ou sans Némésis," *Esprit* 217–18 (August/September 1954); *EC* II, 1545. English translation, "Of Novels and Films: M. Ripois with or without Nemesis," in *Bazin on Adaptation*, Chap. 13.
24 Truffaut, "Monsieur Ripois," 200.
25 Bazin, "M. Ripois with or without Nemesis," The homophonic pun Bazin uses here is "pas décrit mais écrit." P 136.
26 Pier Paolo Pasolini, "Le cinéma de poésie," *Cahiers du cinéma* 171 (October 1965).
27 Bazin, "M. Ripois with or without Nemesis," 136.
28 Ibid., 139.
29 Ibid.
30 Ibid., 144.
31 Ibid., 141.

Works Cited

Andrew, Dudley. "The Ontology of a Fetish." *Film Quarterly* 61.4 (Summer 2008): 62–7.
Andrew, Dudley. *What Cinema Is!* Chichester: Wiley-Blackwell, 2010.
Barthes, Roland. *Œuvres complètes*. 5 vols. Ed. Éric Marty. Paris: Seuil, 2002.
Barthes, Roland. *Writing Degree Zero and Elements of Semiology*. Preface by Susan Sontag. Boson: Beacon Press, 1968.

Bazin, André. *André Bazin's New Media*. Ed. Dudley Andrew. Berkeley, CA: University of California Press, 2013.

Bazin, André. *André Bazin on Adaptation: Cinema's Literary Imagination*. Oakland: University of California Press, 2022.

Bazin, André. *Écrits complets*. Ed. Hervé Joubert-Laurencin. Paris: Editions Macula. 2018.

Pasolini, Pier-Paolo. "Le cinéma de poésie." *Cahiers du cinéma* 171 (October 1965).

Sontag, Susan. "Preface." In Roland Barthes. *Writing Degree Zero and Elements of Semiology*. Boston: Beacon Press, 1968. xv–xvi.

Truffaut, François. "A Certain Tendency in French Cinema." *Cahiers du Cinéma the 1950s*. Ed. Jim Hillier. Cambridge: Harvard University Press, 1986.

Truffaut, François. *Chroniques d'Arts Spectacles 1954–1958*. Ed. Bernard Bastide. Paris: Gallimard, 2019.

Truffaut, François. *The Films in My Life*. New York: Simon and Schuster, 1985.

Watts, Philip. *Roland Barthes' Cinema*. Eds. Dudley Andrew, Yves Citton, Vincent Debaene, and Sam Di Iorio. Oxford: Oxford University Press, 2016.

8

Barthes's Hedonism

Jeffrey R. Di Leo

One of the more significant philosophical achievements of Roland Barthes was the revival of the hedonic tradition. His prolegomenon on this topic is *The Pleasure of the Text*, where he effectively and innovatively introduces hedonism into literary criticism and theory. He does this by uniting notions about textual generation with then current work in literary theory and psycholinguistics. In broad terms, Barthes proposes and explores three distinct kinds of pleasure: the first is the pleasure and comfort that comes from Readerly textual fulfillment, which he terms "plaisir"; the second is the rapture and ecstasy that comes from Writerly textual unsettlement and discomfort, which he terms "jouissance"; and the third is the textual pleasure that comes from finding ecstatic moments in Readerly texts.[1] In *The Pleasure of the Text*, he writes:

> Text of pleasure [*plaisir*]: the text that contents, fills, grants euphoria; the text comes from culture and does not break with it, is linked to a *comfortable* practice of reading. Text of bliss [*jouissance*]: the text that imposes a state of loss, the text that discomforts (perhaps to the point of a certain boredom), unsettles the reader's historical, cultural, psychological assumptions, the consistency of tastes, values, memories, brings to a crisis his relation with language.[2]

But when compared to the passage that follows this one, we see Barthes the *textualist* under the intertext of Philippe Sollers, Julia Kristeva, Jacques Derrida, and Jacques Lacan (a point he acknowledges) transforming into Barthes the *moralist* under the intertext of hedonists spanning from Aristippus and Epictetus to Sade and Schopenhauer (a point he does not acknowledge, which we will come back to later).[3] And, perhaps more significantly, Barthes transforming his attention from the concerns of literary theory and cultural criticism (which, for purposes of parallelism, might be termed, *art de textualité*) to philosophy in its broadest and most ancient sense, namely one concerned with the art of living (*art de vivre*), the knowledge of how to enjoy life. Continues Barthes:

> Now the subject who keeps the two texts in his field and in his hands the reins of pleasure [*plaisir*] and bliss [*jouissance*] is an anachronistic subject, for he simultaneously and contradictorily participates in the profound hedonism of all

culture (which permeates him quietly under cover of an *art de vivre* shared by the old books) and in the destruction of that culture: he enjoys the consistency of his selfhood (that is his pleasure [*plaisir*]) and seeks its loss (that is his bliss [*jouissance*]). He is a subject split twice over, doubly perverse.[4]

The stage is now set for his full entry into the hedonic tradition in *Roland Barthes by Roland Barthes*, a philosophical treatise on hedonism in the guise of a postmodern autobiography.

"Being a hedonist (since he regards himself as one)," confesses Barthes in *Roland Barthes by Roland Barthes*, "he seeks a state which is, really, comfort."[5] His adoption here of hedonism was done with a full awareness that he stood alone among the literary theorists and philosophers of his time (and now ours) in his explicit engagement with the hedonic tradition. In a parenthetical comment in *The Pleasure of the Text*, Barthes asks, "[W]ho today would call himself a hedonist with a straight face?"[6] "[I]t can embarrass the text's return to morality, to truth: it is an oblique, a drag anchor, so to speak, without which the theory of the text would revert to a centered system, a philosophy of meaning."[7]

If *The Pleasure of the Text* is a hedonics of the art of reading, then *Roland Barthes by Roland Barthes* is a hedonics of the art of *living* (*art de vivre*). Writes Barthes in the latter book:

> the art of living has no history: it does not evolve: the pleasure which vanishes vanishes for good, there is no substitute for it. Other pleasures come, which replace nothing. *No progress in pleasures*, nothing but mutations.[8]

Consequently, the comfort that Barthes's hedonic *art de vivre* seeks is

> more complicated than the household kind whose elements are determined by our society; it is a comfort he arranges for himself (the way my grandfather B., at the end of his life, had arranged a little platform inside his window, so as to obtain a better view of the garden while he was working). This personal comfort might be called: *ease*.[9]

The hedonic project of *Roland Barthes by Roland Barthes* is to provide both a "theoretical dignity" and "an ethical force" to ease.[10] Barthes notes that "the exact antonym" of ease is "embarrassment."[11] In personal terms, his own desire for ease stemmed from the various embarrassments he endured in pursuit of a "bourgeois *art de vivre*"[12] as a child.

> This art subsisted, incorruptible, amid every financial crisis; not misery, as a family experience, but embarrassment; i.e., a terror of certain terms, the problems of vacations, of shoes, of schoolbooks, and even food. This *endurable* privation (as embarrassment always is) may account for a little philosophy of free compensation, of the *overdetermination* of pleasures, of *ease*. . . . His formative problem was doubtless money, not sex.[13]

This passage reveals several important aspects of Barthes's hedonism: (1) *Money* is a source of pleasure; (2) *Sex* is a source of pleasure; and (3) Pleasure is *overdetermined*—that is to say, pleasure has many sources. Let's now look briefly at each of these in turn.

Money

Barthes rejects the approach to money of three of the most dominant "moralisms" of his milieu: Marxism (which links money to the origins of class privilege and oppression), Christianity (which advocates poverty, arguing that money is the root of all evil), and Freudianism (which assimilates it with feces).[14] Instead, he follows the position of Fourier on money: money creates happiness. However, "what is defended is not money saved, hoarded, blocked; it is money spent, wasted, swept away by the very moment of loss, made brilliant by the luxury of a production; thus money metaphorically becomes gold: the Gold of the Signifier."[15] This position on the "the Gold of the Signifier" echoes his general view of realist literature that he offered in his reading of "Sarrasine" in *S/Z*: the view that literature has no real content that guarantees its authenticity in the same way that the gold standard in banking guarantees or backs the value of currency. Barthes is saying here that the value of currency or money is derived by the conventions of its circulation not by a reserve of gold bars in a bank vault. In the same way that the circulation of the signifier comes to establish the credibility of the content and characters of literature, so too does the circulation of money establish its "Gold-reserve-like" credibility.[16]

One of Barthes's biographers notes that "the more [money] he had, the more he needed."[17] Later in life, when "the penury of his early years was far behind him," maintains Tiphaine Samoyault, "he adopted his tastes and expenditure to what he had, leading a more luxurious life and proving very generous to his friends, thereby ensuring that he was preoccupied by money and worried about not having enough."[18]

In *Sade/Fourier/Loyola*, a book published a couple of years before *The Pleasure of the Text*, Barthes says that, for Fourier, "Money participates in the brilliance of pleasure ('The senses cannot have their full indirect scope without the invention of money'): money is desirable, as in the best days of civilized corruption, beyond which it perpetuates itself by virtue of a splendid and 'incorruptible' fantasy."[19] Money then takes the same position of hedonism in the philosophical tradition as something that is repressed:[20]

> it is because all (civilized) Philosophy has condemned money that Fourier, destroyer of Philosophy and critic of Civilization, rehabilitates it: *the love of wealth* being a pejorative *topos* (at the price of a constant hypocrisy: Seneca, the man who possessed 80 million sesterces, declared that one must rid oneself of wealth), Fourier turns contempt into praise: marriage, for example, is a ridiculous ceremony, save "when a man marries a very rich woman; then there is occasion for rejoicing"; everything, where money is concerned, seems to be conceived in view of this counter-discourse, frankly scandalous in relation to the literary constraints

of the admonition: "Search out the tangible wealth, gold, silver, precious metals, jewels, and objects of luxury despised by philosophers."[21]

As such, Fourier's claims are the "basis for the major transgression against which *everyone*—Christians, Marxists, Freudians—for whom money continues to be an accursed matter, fetish, excrement, has spoken out: who would dare defend money?"[22] This "dare" echoes the implied dare Barthes would later make regarding hedonism: "[W]ho today would [dare] call himself a hedonist with a straight face?"[23]

Sex

The Pleasure of the Text is an erotics of reading, whose deployment of *plaisir* and *jouissance* deal with a state (*plaisir*) and an action (*jouissance*), both of which, comments Richard Howard, "in our culture [English], are held to be unspeakable, beyond words."[24] What Barthes calls *jouissance*, the Bible translates as "knowing," the Stuarts called "dying," and we call "coming," that is, the orgasm.[25] In light of these alternatives, Richard Miller's translation of *jouissance* as "bliss," is, well, a bit sexually deflating. "The pleasure of the text is like that untenable, impossible, purely *novelistic* instant so relished by Sade's libertine when he manages to be hanged and then to cut the rope at the very moment of his orgasm, his bliss," writes Barthes.[26]

At the center of Barthes's hedonism is the erotic body which experiences pleasure. Asks Barthes:

> Does the text have human form, is it a figure, an anagram of the body? Yes, but of our erotic body. The pleasure of the text is irreducible to physiological need. The pleasure of the text is that moment when my body pursues its own ideas—for my body does not have the same ideas I do.[27]

Like the rationalist René Descartes, who through self-examination arrives with certainty at his existence as *res cogitans*, a thinking thing,[28] Barthes goes through a parallel process, albeit to establish his own material existence as an "individual" erotic body:

> Whenever I attempt to "analyze" a text which has given me pleasure, it is not my "subjectivity" I encounter but my "individuality," the given which makes my body separate from other bodies and appropriates its suffering or its pleasure: it is my body of bliss I encounter.[29]

This body is less the *res extensa* of Descartes than the body that Jeremy Bentham says Nature has provided to govern us through "two sovereign masters, *pain* and *pleasure*."[30] "My body exists," writes Barthes, "for myself only in two general forms: migraine and sensuality."[31] For him, "[m]igraine is merely the very first degree of physical pain, and sensuality is for the most part considered only as a kind of reject-version of active pleasure. In other words, my body is not a hero."[32]

Through this process of establishing the existence of the erotic body, namely the body subject to pain [*migraine*] and pleasure [*sensuality*], the subject appears to return, "not as illusion, but as *fiction*."[33] Continues Barthes:

> A certain pleasure is derived from a way of imagining oneself as *individual*, of inventing a final, rarest fiction: the fictive identity. This fiction is no longer the illusion of unity; on the contrary, it is the theater of society in which we stage our plural: our pleasure is *individual*—but not personal.[34]

The last clause here emphasizes difference between the "individual," which for him is the erotic body which has returned as a fiction, and the "personal," which for him is akin to the Gold described earlier, namely that which guarantees the "individual" in the same way that the gold standard in banking guarantees the value of currency.

Barthes believes that his erotics of the text reveals a radical materialism which connects his work to an older philosophical tradition. "Have not the rare materialists of the past, each in his way, Epicurus, Diderot, Sade, Fourier, all been overt eudaemonists?"[35] Still, each of these materialists composed a discourse very different from Barthes. "What shall we call such discourse?" wonders Barthes? "[E]rotic, no doubt, for it has to do with pleasure; or even perhaps: *aesthetic*, if we foresee subjecting this old category to a gradual torsion which will alienate it from its regressive, idealist background and bring it closer to the body, to the *drift*"—and ultimately, to materialism.[36]

In *Sade/Fourier/Loyola*, these themes are brought back into the context of *the art of living*, noted earlier:

> whenever the "literary" Text (the Book) transmigrates into our life, whenever another writing (the Other's writing) succeeds in writing fragments of our own daily lives, in short, whenever *co-existence* occurs. The index of the pleasure of the Text, then, is when we are able to live with Fourier, with Sade. To live with an author does not necessarily mean to achieve in our life the program that the author traced in his books (this conjunction is not, however, insignificant, since it forms the argument of *Don Quixote*; true, Don Quixote is still a character in a book); it is not a matter of making operative what has been represented, not a matter of becoming sadistic or orgiastic with Sade, a phalansterian with Fourier, of praying with Loyola; it is a matter of bringing into our daily life the fragments of the unintelligible ("formulae") that emanate from a text we admire.[37]

The problem of sex in Barthes's hedonism thus amounts to being able "to live with Sade"—but not necessarily becoming sadistic or orgiastic. His erotics of reading finds a full role for sex and sexuality in his writing without him ever having to explicitly make reference to his own sexual life or sexuality. Indeed, in all of the writing he published during his life, including his "autobiography," his sexual life is not addressed. The posthumous publication of *Incidents* in 1987 is the first published book where he directly puts his sexual life to writing.[38] Jonathan Culler notes that *Incidents* is "Loosely influenced by André Gide's journal, which had narrated homosexual encounters in North Africa." Culler says that it "avoids narrative and presupposes rather than describes homosexual encounters in laconic fragments."[39] Nevertheless, as we shall see, the connection between Barthes and Gide regarding hedonism goes much deeper than just style.

Overdetermination of Pleasure

Money and sex are sources of pleasure in Barthes's hedonism. However, they are just the beginning of the long queue of potential sources of pleasure. In *Roland Barthes by Roland Barthes*, he discusses the pleasure of kissing,[40] embracing,[41] inserting ("Is there not a kind of voluptuous pleasure in inserting"[42]), the endoxal products of mass culture,[43] writing beginnings/fragments ("he tends to multiply this pleasure: that is why he writes fragments"[44]), the Political ("I believe I understand that the Political pleases me as a *Sadean* text and displeases me as a *Sadistic* text"[45]), Haiku,[46] sexy sentences,[47] ideology,[48] contrary opinions of whether he is a Sorbonne professor,[49] calculation,[50] writing,[51] etymology,[52] piano playing,[53] perversion ("in this case, that of the two H.'s: homosexuality and hashish"[54]), friends,[55] fantasizing[56]—and his displeasure of translation, foreign literature, and foreign languages ("little taste for foreign literature, constant pessimism with regard to translation"[57]) and dreaming ("Dreaming (whether nicely or nastily) is insipid"[58]). At one point, he even explicitly confronts and lists, without explanations, many of the things he likes and dislikes:

> *I like:* salad, cinnamon, cheese, pimento, marzipan, the smell of new-cut hay (why doesn't someone with a "nose" make such a perfume), roses, peonies, lavender, champagne, loosely held political convictions, Glenn Gould, too-cold beer, flat pillows, toast, Havana cigars, Handel, slow walks, pears, white peaches, cherries, colors, watches, all kinds of writing pens, desserts, unrefined salt, realistic novels, the piano, coffee, Pollock, Twombly, all romantic music, Sartre, Brecht, Verne, Fourier, Eisenstein, trains, Médoc wine, having change, *Bouvard and Pécuchet*, walking in sandals on the lanes of southwest France, the bend of the Adour seen from Doctor L.'s house, the Marx Brothers, the mountains at seven in the morning leaving Salamanca, etc.
>
> *I don't like:* white Pomeranians, women in slacks, geraniums, strawberries, the harpsichord, Miró, tautologies, animated cartoons, Arthur Rubinstein, villas, the afternoon, Satie, Bartók, Vivaldi, telephoning, children's choruses, Chopin's concertos, Burgundian branles and Renaissance dances, the organ, Marc-Antoine Charpentier, his trumpets and kettledrums, the politico-sexual, scenes, initiatives, fidelity, spontaneity, evenings with people I don't know, etc.[59]

The field of pleasure established by Barthes in *Roland Barthes by Roland Barthes* is vast, diverse, and idiosyncratic. These are not things that every hedonist *should* like (or dislike); rather, they represent the likes (and dislikes) of one (and only one) hedonist: Roland Barthes. "The important thing," writes Barthes, "is to equalize the field of pleasure, to abolish the false opposition of practical life and contemplative life."[60] The listing here and the various pleasures (and displeasures) described throughout the book establish both the relativity (likes and dislikes are individual) and the flatness of pleasure in Barthes's hedonism: there are no higher and lower pleasures here[61]—the pleasures of the body are the same level as the pleasures of the mind. Still, pleasures can and should be regarded differently. For example, "[w]riting is a dry, ascetic pleasure, anything but effusive."[62] Thus, the paradox of pleasure in Barthes: all pleasures are equal but not the same.

For many philosophers, a paradox like this at the center of their philosophy might be regarded as a problem. But not for Barthes. His pluralistic approach to pleasure in particular is grounded on a pluralistic (or "patchwork" or "plural") approach to philosophy in general: "He [Barthes] often resorts to a kind of philosophy vaguely labeled *pluralism*."[63] "Philosophically, it seems you are a materialist (if the word doesn't sound too old-fashioned); ethically, you divide yourself: as for the body, you are a hedonist; as for violence, you would rather be something of a Buddhist!"[64] In short, Barthes believes that his work "sum[s] up all the decadent philosophies: Epicureanism, eudaemonism, Asianism, Manicheaism, Pyrrhonism."[65]

The ultimate statement of his philosophical pluralism perhaps comes in relation to sex:

> Who knows if this insistence on the plural is not a way of denying sexual duality. The opposition of the sexes must not be a law of Nature; therefore, the confrontations and paradigms must be dissolved, both the meanings and the sexes be pluralized: meaning will tend toward its multiplication, its dispersion (in the theory of the Text), and sex will be taken into no typology (there will be, for example, only *homosexualities*, whose plural will baffle any constituted, centered discourse, to the point where it seems to him virtually pointless to talk about it).[66]

Pluralism (or, the *plural*) provides Barthes the opportunity not only to embrace all pleasure equally but also to erase sexual duality, and thereby embrace only *homosexualities*.

A Life of Boredom

On September 17, 1979, less than a year before his untimely death on March 26, 1980, Barthes speaks of his boredom:

> A sort of despair came over me, I wanted to cry. I realized that I would have to give up boys, because they had no desire for me, and because I am either too scrupulous or too clumsy to impose mine on them; that this was an inescapable fact, proven by

all my attempts at flirting, that this makes my life sad, that, ultimately, I'm bored, and that I must remove that interest, or that hope, from my life.[67]

A few nights before, he speaks of being bored by some of the Pleynet painters at the opening of a museum ("the ones that bore me are the ones I know, the theoreticians, the sad ones [Devade, Cane, Dezeuze]").[68] But boredom though is not just something that occupied him in later life.

In a letter to Philippe Rebeyrol on August 31, 1932, a sixteen-year-old Barthes describes himself as a "decidedly boring fellow," who fears that he will "bore" his friend.[69] This youthful boredom is again noted in *Roland Barthes by Roland Barthes*, where he says it goes back to his early youth:

> As a child, I was often and intensely bored. This evidently began very early, it has continued my whole life, in gusts (increasingly rare, it is true, thanks to work and to friends), and it has always been noticeable to others. A panic boredom, to the point of distress: like the kind I feel in panel discussions, lectures, parties among strangers, group amusements: wherever boredom can be seen. Might boredom be my form of hysteria?[70]

Throughout *Roland Barthes by Roland Barthes*, he discusses boredom in a variety of disparate contexts: avant-garde texts,[71] Michelet,[72] cruising ("Crazy, the power of distraction of a man who is bored, intimidated, or embarrassed by his work"[73]), dreaming ("(nothing so boring as the account of a dream!)"[74]), migraines,[75] self-commentary ("What a bore!"[76]), foreseeable discourse,[77] scholarship "apropos of Bataille,"[78] and postponement of books to be written.[79] Even the process of "rereading" himself in *Roland Barthes by Roland Barthes* is found by Barthes to be boring.[80]

The presence of all of this boredom in the life of a self-professed hedonist should not be a major surprise, particularly to a writer who frequently places himself within the context of this "very old tradition."[81] Boredom may philosophically be either seen as part of the life condition of the hedonist (a la Schopenhauer's *ennui*) or used as a criticism of hedonism as a way of life: an art of living. The fact that Barthes realizes both that "the art of living has no history" and that when pleasure vanishes it "vanishes for good"[82] should be a clue that the life of the Barthesian hedonist is a life *replete with boredom*. In short, the continual presence of boredom in the life of a person devoted to the pursuit of pleasure is almost proof of Barthes's lifelong commitment to hedonism—even if it was only later in life that he theorized—or dare we say, "came out"—regarding this hedonism.

But why then, given all of the boredom in the life of this self-professed hedonist, does Barthes seem to be disappointed to hear that hedonism is regarded as a pessimism by Nietzsche ("for Nietzsche, hedonism is a pessimism"[83])? Nietzsche surely derived this position from Schopenhauer, the great early influence in his philosophical life—and antagonist for the wide-ranging interest and debate about it in nineteenth-century Germany—and beyond.[84] And, Schopenhauer's pessimism regards the hedonistic life as one *characterized by* restlessness, boredom (*ennui*), and, ultimately, suffering.[85] Does

Barthes really expect us to embrace hedonism as an *optimism*? I believe so. However, he establishes this by taking a somewhat indirect route.

Instead of following one or more of the usual hedonist suspects, such as Epicurus, Diderot, Sade, or Fourier (figures he discusses in *The Pleasure of the Text* and *Roland Barthes by Roland Barthes*) or in the footsteps of the decadent philosophies he mentions (though rarely discusses), that is, Epicureanism, eudaemonism, Asianism, Manicheaism, and Pyrrhonism, the intertext for Barthes's hedonism goes in a very different direction: the moral philosophy of André Gide. Barthes provides an indication of this by curiously citing the intertext of the genre of "morality" as "(Nietzsche)," rather than more obvious hedonists such as those noted earlier. In addition, he iconically associates Nietzsche with Gide by also placing the latter's name in parentheses. This makes Gide the only other intertext in his Phases chart cited in parentheses, whose genre—"(desire to write)"—is also the only one cited parenthetically. Thus, the parenthetical citations of "Nietzsche," "Gide," and the "desire to write" serve to connect them all to the genre of "morality"—or, more specifically, *Gidean* morality.[86]

The Gidean *Abgrund*

André Gide sparked in Roland Barthes the desire both to write—and to become a hedonist, that is to say, a moral philosopher. Gide also influenced Barthes's fragmentary writing style (which could mistakenly also be associated with Nietzsche's fragmentary writing style):

> His first, or nearly first text (1942) consists of fragments; this choice is then justified in the Gidean manner "because incoherence is preferable to a distorting order." Since then, as a matter of fact, he has never stopped writing in brief bursts: the brief scenes of *Mythologies*, the articles and prefaces of *Critical Essays*, the lexias of *S/Z*, the fragments of the second essay on Sade in *Sade, Fourier, Loyola* and of *The Pleasure of the Text*.[87]

But Gide represents more than just a style of writing for Barthes—he is literally his *Abgrund*:

> One of his first articles (1942) concerned Gide's *Journal*; the writing of another ("*En Grèce*," 1944) was evidently imitated from *Les Nourritures terrestres*. And Gide occupied a great place in his early reading: a diagonal cross-breed of Alsace and Gascony, as Gide was of Normandy and Languedoc, Protestant, having a taste for "letters" and fond of playing the piano, without counting the rest—how could he have failed to recognize himself, to desire himself in this writer? The Gidean *Abgrund*, the Gidean core, unchanging, still forms in my head a stubborn swarm. Gide is my original language, my *Ursuppe*, my literary soup.[88]

Going back to his 1942 essay on Gide, "On Gide and His Journal," we learn a bit more about Barthes's early attraction to Gide. Here he calls Gide "another Montaigne,"[89] presumably because both are skeptics who question all values, and both revel in their uncertainties and inconsistencies. He also places Gide and Nietzsche (along with another thinker) together in rarified company: "In the last hundred years, there have been three men who have had the most intense, the most intimate, and even what I call the most fraternal attraction to Christ's person—outside of dogmatic or mystical knowledge: Nietzsche (as a *frère ennemi*), Rozanov, and Gide."[90] In the case of Gide, this fraternal attraction to Christ's person leads to the somewhat odd combination of evangelical spirit coupled with hedonism.[91] Both Gide and Nietzsche are also linked by their break from conventional morality in their work. For Gide, a trip to North Africa in 1893 and 1894 brought him into contact with the radically different moral standards of the Arab world that helped liberate him from Victorian conventions.[92] This intellectual revolt also brought Gide to a growing awareness of his homosexuality, where he was aided by a famous literary mentor, Oscar Wilde.

In 1897, Gide published *The Fruits of the Earth* (*Les nourritures terrestres*), a book-length prose poem, where he established a sophisticated hedonism, which both glorifies pleasure and apologies for detachment. However, for Gide, the most important thing in life was "not satisfying hunger or slaking thirst, but sustaining a mood of exhilaration."[93] Moreover, according to Pascal Bruckner, Gide believed that the "noble desire of desiring is always to be preferred to a grim satisfaction: 'Possession seemed to me less valuable than pursuit, and I came more and more to prefer thirst to quenching it, the promise of pleasure to pleasure itself.'"[94] As such, Gidean hedonism, which places a higher value on the pursuit of pleasure, differs greatly from Barthes's hedonism, where quenching pleasure—albeit a wide spectrum of pleasures—is clearly preferable.

The next major step in Gide's revolt from his puritan, moralistic upbringing was his first novel (or as he termed it, *récit*), *The Immoralist* (*L'immoraliste*), which was written in 1901 and published in 1902. In *The Immoralist*, Michel marries a family friend, Marceline, to cheer up his dying father and to provide for his own needs. While recovering from tuberculosis in North Africa, Michel finds himself drawn sexually to young Arab boys. He is encouraged by a friend in France to ignore moral convention and to pursue his desires. However, as he is pursuing his desires, he is also ignoring the needs of his pregnant wife who has contracted tuberculosis. She has a miscarriage and later dies in the presence of Michel. The work is a moral examination of hedonism as well as a critique of *The Fruits of the Earth* in that it explores the point where pursuit of individual pleasure (*hedonism*) must be superseded by altruistic concerns, that is, care for others (or, *altruistic hedonism*).[95]

In his essay, Barthes connects the self-examination of Gide's journal to his novels and *récits*. "It is because at a certain moment he [Gide] wanted to be someone that he summoned up . . . Michel," comments Barthes, "that he wrote *Fruits of the Earth*, *The Immoralist*, and *The Counterfeiters*."[96] This is then followed by a quote from a Gide journal entry from 1924: "The desire to portray characters one has encountered is, I believe, quite common. But the creation of new characters becomes a natural need only in those tormented by an imperious complexity and whom their own gesture does not exhaust."[97] In short, Barthes views works such as *Fruits of the Earth* and *The Immoralist* as Gide "should be":

> If we admit that the work is an expression of Gide's will (Lafcadio's life, Michel's, Edouard's), the *Journal* is actually the converse of the work, its contrary complement. The work: Gide as he should (would) be. The *Journal*: Gide as he is, or more exactly: as Edouard, Michel, and Lafcadio have made him.[98]

Barthes views récits such as *The Immoralist* as "fictionalizations—if that—of a case, of a theme, of a pathology."[99] They are also "myths" wherein

> Each hero engages the reader, promulgates example or iconoclasm. Mythology, as in these récits of Gide's, proves nothing: it is a fine work of art in which a great deal of faith circulates; a fine fiction in which one agrees to believe because it explains life and at the same time is a little stronger, a little larger than life (it affords the image of an ideal; every mythology is a dream). And these récits of Gide's, like every myth, are an equivalence between an abstract reality and a concrete fiction. All of these books are Christian works.[100]

Gide's work can be described as grounded in "never resolved tensions between a strict artistic discipline, a puritanical moralism, and the desire for unlimited sensual indulgence and abandonment of life."[101] These are the words the Nobel Prize organization used in 1947 when it announced his award for literature. He wrote many plays, novels, journals, letters, poems, and critiques, as well as did translations. Barthes writes that it comprises "a net of which no mesh can be dropped," and that it is futile to try to divide it up chronologically or methodologically.[102] "It almost requires to be read in the fashion of certain Bibles," comments Barthes.[103] Is it much of a jump then to regard Gide as Barthes's "Bible" on hedonism, rather than say Sade or Fourier, the two writers he refers to most frequently in reference to hedonism?

Barthes says that Gide possesses "a conscience which ordinary morality has the odd habit of calling sickly." Indeed, Gide's moral philosophy meets with a mixed reception which alternately calls him a liberator, a corrupter of youth, an immoral man, and a literary moralist—or, more recently, a "homosexual moralist."[104] But Barthes defends Gide's moral consciousness, because he "explains himself, surrenders himself, delicately retracts or asserts himself bravely enough, but never abuses the reader as to his mutations."[105] For him, Gide puts "everything in the *movement* of his thought and not in its brutal profession."[106] Might not the same be said of Barthes? Particularly of his final movement and mutation to hedonist?

Gide does these things, according to Barthes, out of authenticity ("the impulses of a soul are the mark of its authenticity"), aesthetic pleasure, the scrupulous search for truth, and, "lastly, the moral importance accorded to states of conflict, perhaps because they are warrants of humility."[107] As the moral philosophy of Gide is where Barthes started his journey as a writer, what prevents us now explaining his late turn to hedonism, or, alternately, to the genre of morality, as a return to his beginnings?[108] After all, as we saw, Barthes adores "beginnings." Culler comments that "Barthes's revival of hedonism may be his most difficult project to assess, for it seems to indulge in some of the mystifications he had effectively exposed, yet it continues to challenge intellectual orthodoxy."[109] I would wager that reading Barthes's revival through his formative and lasting affection for the work of Gide makes this process a whole lot easier to assess.

Conclusion

Barthes's revival of hedonism was not an exercise in academic philosophy even if he seeks to place himself within the context of its "repressed" traditions.[110] Rather, it was in practice a journey back to how he came to be a writer concerned with not just the art of writing but also the art of living. Gide appears to have been his constant companion in this journey from his earliest days as a writer to his final assessments of his career in *Roland Barthes by Roland Barthes*. When Barthes speaks of "actually" seeing Gide eating a pear and reading a book,[111] it is in contradistinction to the way he "imagined" him.[112] The major difference between Barthes's "actual" Gide and his "imagined" one comes down to a pear. The same fruit that Augustine of Hippo stole, which has come down through intellectual history to be a symbol of moral guilt and disobedience.[113]

For me, this is the most revealing moment in Barthes's account of his hedonism. And it comes in the context of a fragment entitled "The writer as fantasy" (*L'écrivain comme fantasme*). "Surely," writes Barthes, "there is no longer a single adolescent who has this fantasy: *to be a writer!*"[114] "Imagine," he continues, "wanting to copy not the works but the practices of any contemporary—his way of strolling through the world, a notebook in his pocket and a phrase in his head."[115] Barthes is speaking here not about the "art of writing," namely copying works, but rather the "art of life," namely copying *life practices*. This line is then followed by his picture of the two Gides: one imagined and one actual. The fragment then concludes as follows: "For what the fantasy imposes is the writer as we can see him in his private diary, *the writer minus his work*: supreme form of the sacred: the mark and the void."[116] Who was the Gide we see in his journal? For that matter, who was the Barthes we see in *his* private diary? We got a glimpse of this Barthes (of his private diary) earlier in the selection from *Incidents*; for Gide, his journal was the place where he could "revel in his contradictions," where "I am never," rather "I become"[117]—the place where Gide is the *existential* hedonist.

Unlike Gide, who started publishing selections of his journals during his lifetime (in 1932, to be specific[118]), making him the first author to do this, Barthes's private writing remained private until after his death, when some of it started to be released.[119] Still, writes Barthes, "Am I not justified in considering everything I have written as a clandestine and stubborn effort to bring to light again, someday, quite freely, the theme of the Gidean 'journal'?"—given that "the (autobiographical) 'journal' is, nowadays, discredited."[120] The spectacle though of a young person fantasizing about revealing their private writings to the world is a peculiar one to resist, that is, to use as the basis of rejecting the fantasy of becoming a writer. Perhaps it is because in such journals and diaries the art of living is revealed in ways that an author's work cannot match in terms of authenticity. Or, more specifically, in the case of a philosopher such as Barthes, in terms of *parresia*, the ability it gives him to speak the truth freely. The full scope of Barthes's hedonism is not possible without *parrēsia*.[121] So too is his ability to pursue the art of living in the spirit of his ancient Greek philosophical predecessors, the hedonists who he at times seems to be so interested in associating with in his work. Nevertheless, based on his fragment, "The writer as fantasy," the prospect of being seen in his private diary makes the potential young writer tremble with the prospect of this as a career. Hence, Gide's pear, or, a hedonism with extreme existential guilt. If, for Nietzsche, hedonism is a pessimism, then, for Barthes, hedonism without boredom is only a fantasy—that one can live out in a private diary.

Notes

1   Barthes's distinction between "plaisir" and "jouissance" draws on the psychoanalytic work of Jacques Lacan, who on March 5, 1958, told his students that he wanted to show them what was meant by "a notion . . . that has always been implied in our reflections on desire but that deserves to be distinguished from it, and which can only be articulated after one is sufficiently imbued in the complexity that constitutes desire" (Jacques Lacan, *Le Séminaire V. Les Formations de l'inconscient, 1957-8* [Paris: Seuil, 1998], 251). Lacan would spend the next twenty years unraveling and deepening our understanding of what is meant by the notion "jouissance." Writes Néstor Braunstein, in Lacan, "with jouissance we have a double polarity; first in respect to desire, as advanced in 1958, and then in respect to pleasure, according to conventional use" (Néstor Braunstein, "Desire and Jouissance in the Teachings of Lacan," *The Cambridge Companion to Lacan*, ed. Jean-Michel Rabaté [Cambridge: Cambridge University Press, 2003], 104). "Jouissance," continues Braunstein, "is the dimension discovered by the analytic experience that confronts desire at its opposite pole. If desire is fundamentally lack, lack in being, jouissance is positivity, it is a 'something' lived by a body when pleasure stops being pleasure. It is a plus, a sensation that is beyond pleasure" (104).
2   Roland Barthes, *The Pleasure of the Text*, trans. Richard Howard (New York: Hill and Wang, 1975), 14. Originally appeared as Roland Barthes, *Le Plaisir du texte* (Paris: Éditions du Seuil, 1973). All references to Barthes's works in this chapter are to the English translation unless otherwise stated.
3   In *Roland Barthes by Roland Barthes*, trans. Richard Howard (New York: Hill and Wang, 1977), 145, Barthes cites the five "Phases" to date of his life distinguished by "Intertext," "Genre," and "Works." The fourth phase he labels by Genre as "textuality," by Intertext as "Sollers, Kristeva, Derrida, Lacan," and by Works as "*S/Z* [1970], *Sade, Fourier, Loyola* [1971], *L'Empire des signes* [1970]." The fifth phase he labels by Genre as "morality," by Intertext as "(Nietzsche)," and by Works as "*The Pleasure of the Text* [1973], *Roland Barthes by Roland Barthes* [1975]." *Roland Barthes by Roland Barthes* (1977) originally appeared as Roland Barthes, *Roland Barthes par Roland Barthes* (Paris: Éditions du Seuil, 1975).
4   Barthes, *The Pleasure of the Text*, 14.

5 Barthes, *Roland Barthes by Roland Barthes*, 43.
6 Barthes, *The Pleasure of the Text*, 64.
7 Ibid., 64–5.
8 Barthes, *Roland Barthes by Roland Barthes*, 50.
9 Ibid., 43.
10 Ibid., 43–4.
11 Ibid., 45.
12 Ibid.
13 Ibid.
14 Ibid., 45–6. See, also, Roland Barthes, *Sade/Fourier/Loyola*, trans. Richard Miller (New York: Hill and Wang, 1976), 86. Originally appeared as Roland Barthes, *Sade, Fourier, Loyola* (Paris: Éditions du Seuil, 1971).
15 Ibid., 46.
16 Philip Thody, *Roland Barthes: A Conservative Estimate* (London and Basingstoke: The Macmillan Press LTD, 1977), 115.
17 Tiphaine Samoyault, *Barthes: A Biography* [2015], trans. Andrew Brown (Malden, MA: Polity Press, 2017), 391.
18 Ibid., 391.
19 Barthes, *Sade/Fourier/Loyola*, 85.
20 "An old, a very old tradition: hedonism has been repressed by nearly every philosophy" (Barthes, *The Pleasure of the Text*, 57).
21 Barthes, *Sade/Fourier/Loyola*, 85–6.
22 Ibid., 86.
23 Barthes, *The Pleasure of the Text*, 64.
24 Richard Howard, "A Note on the Text," in Roland Barthes, *The Pleasure of the Text*, vi.
25 Ibid.
26 Barthes, *The Pleasure of the Text*, 7.
27 Ibid., 17.
28 René Descartes, *Meditations on the First Philosophy* [1641], in *The Philosophical Works of Descartes*, two vols., trans. Elizabeth Haldane and G. R. T. Ross (Cambridge: Cambridge University Press, 1967), I: 132–99.
29 Barthes, *The Pleasure of the Text*, 62.
30 Jeremy Bentham, *An Introduction to the Principles of Morals and Legislation* [1789/1823], in *Selected Writings*, ed. Stephen G. Engelmann (New Haven, CT and London: Yale University Press, 2011), 111.
31 Barthes, *Roland Barthes by Roland Barthes*, 60.
32 Ibid, 60.
33 Barthes, *The Pleasure of the Text*, 62.
34 Ibid.
35 Ibid., 64.
36 Barthes, *Roland Barthes by Roland Barthes*, 84.
37 Barthes, *Sade/Fourier/Loyola*, 7.
38 Roland Barthes, *Incidents*, trans. Teresa Lavender Fagen (London and New York: Seagull Books, 2010). Originally appeared as *Incidents* (Paris: Éditions du Seuil, 1987).
39 Jonathan Culler, *Barthes: A Very Short Introduction* (Oxford: Oxford University Press, 1983/2002), 110.
40 Barthes, *Roland Barthes by Roland Barthes*, 141.

41 Ibid., 141.
42 Ibid., 135.
43 Ibid., 122.
44 Ibid., 94.
45 Ibid., 147.
46 Ibid., 94.
47 Ibid., 164.
48 Ibid., 104.
49 Ibid., 61.
50 Ibid., 100.
51 Ibid., 86.
52 Ibid., 85.
53 Ibid., 70.
54 Ibid., 63.
55 Ibid., 65.
56 Ibid., 88.
57 Ibid., 115.
58 Ibid., 87.
59 Ibid., 116–17.
60 Barthes, *The Pleasure of the Text*, 59.
61 Compare this, for example, to John Stuart Mill, who makes a distinction between "higher pleasures," which are of more value, and "lower pleasures," which are of lesser value (*Utilitarianism*, third edition [London: Longmans, Green, Reader, and Dyer, 1867], 14).
62 Barthes, *Roland Barthes by Roland Barthes*, 86.
63 Ibid., 69.
64 Ibid., 143.
65 Ibid., 144.
66 Ibid., 69.
67 Barthes, *Incidents*, 171.
68 Ibid., 167; September 14, 1979.
69 Roland Barthes, *Album: Unpublished Correspondence and Texts*, trans. Jody Gladding, ed. Éric Marty (New York: Columbia University Press, 2018), 2. Originally appeared as *Album: Inédits, correspondances et varia* (Paris: Éditions du Seuil, 2015).
70 Barthes, *Roland Barthes by Roland Barthes*, 24.
71 Ibid., 54.
72 Ibid., 55.
73 Ibid., 71–2.
74 Ibid., 87.
75 Ibid., 124.
76 Ibid., 142.
77 Ibid., 149.
78 Ibid., 159.
79 Ibid., 174.
80 Ibid., 71. For an excellent introduction to boredom in Barthes, see Neil Badmington, "Bored with Barthes: Ennui in China," in *The Afterlives of Roland Barthes* (New York and London: Bloomsbury, 2016), 83–108.
81 Barthes, *The Pleasure of the Text*, 57.

82 Barthes, *Roland Barthes by Roland Barthes*, 50.
83 Barthes, *The Pleasure of the Text*, 57.
84 See, Frederick C. Beiser, *Weltschmerz: Pessimism in German Philosophy, 1860–1900* (Oxford: Oxford University Press, 2016).
85 This commentary on hedonism was most famously established by Arthur Schopenhauer, who argued that the irrational striving of the will and the fact that for him the satisfaction of the will is a contradiction in terms makes his pessimism totalizing. For Schopenhauer, "life swings like a pendulum backwards and forwards between pain and ennui" (Arthur Schopenhauer, *The World as Will and Idea* [1819, 1st ed.; 2nd ed. 1844], 3 vols., trans. R. B. Haldane and J. Kemp [London: Routledge & Kegan Paul Ltd., 1883, 1957], vol. 1, 402). When the will "lacks objects of desire, because it is at once deprived of them by a too easy satisfaction, a terrible void and ennui comes over it"; but when the will is in the throes of its unquenchable thirsts, "the nature of brutes and man is subject to pain originally and through its very being" (ibid.). In short, Schopenhauer's pessimism regards the hedonistic life as one characterizing by restlessness, boredom (*ennui*), and, ultimately, suffering. But, for Schopenhauer this *is* life. Our hedonism necessarily entails suffering.
86 Barthes, *Roland Barthes by Roland Barthes*, 145.
87 Ibid., 93.
88 Ibid., 99.
89 Roland Barthes, "On Gide and His Journal [1942]," trans. Richard Howard, in *A Barthes Reader*, ed. Susan Sontag (New York: Hill and Wang, 1982), 3.
90 Ibid., 9–10.
91 Pascal Bruckner, "Happiness," in *The Columbia History of Twentieth-Century French Thought*, ed. Lawrence D. Kritzman (New York: Columbia University Press, 2006), 243.
92 Barthes refers to these different standards in *Roland Barthes by Roland Barthes*: "Consider the Arab countries. Here certain rules of 'good' sexuality are readily transgressed by an open practice of homosexuality" (133).
93 Bruckner, "Happiness," 243.
94 Ibid.
95 The English Utilitarians, John Stuart Mill and Jeremy Bentham, are often referred to as *altruistic utilitarians*, because their hedonism involves a concern for the pleasure of others. See, for example, Bentham, *An Introduction to the Principles of Morals and Legislation*, and Mill, *Utilitarianism*.
96 Barthes, "On Gide," 12.
97 Ibid.
98 Ibid.
99 Ibid., 12–13.
100 Ibid., 13.
101 "André Gide, Literature 1947," in *Nobel Lectures, Literature 1901–1967*, ed. Horst Frenz (Amsterdam: Elsevier Publishing Company, 1969), 428.
102 Barthes, "On Gide," 11.
103 Ibid.
104 See, Vivian Kogan, "André Gide," in *The Columbia History of Twentieth-Century French Thought*, ed. Lawrence D. Kritzman (New York: Columbia University Press, 2006), 537–9, and Patrick Pollard, *Gide: Homosexual Moralist* (New Haven, CT: Yale University Press, 1991).

105 Barthes, "On Gide," 8.
106 Ibid.
107 Ibid.
108 Barthes notes "*morality* should be understood [as a Genre] as the precise opposite of ethics (it is the thinking of the body in a state of language)" (*Roland Barthes by Roland Barthes*, 145).
109 Culler, *Barthes*, 84.
110 Barthes, *The Pleasure of the Text*, 57.
111 "(actually saw him [Gide], one day in 1939, in the gloom of the Brasserie Lutétia, eating a pear and reading a book)" (Barthes, *Roland Barthes by Roland Barthes*, 77–8).
112 "(the way I imagined Gide travelling from Russia to the Congo, reading his classics and writing his notebooks in the dining car, waiting for the meals to be served)" (Barthes, *Roland Barthes by Roland Barthes*, 77).
113 "The evil in me was foul, but I loved it," wrote Augustine of the pear theft. "I loved my own perdition and my own faults, not the things for which I committed wrong, but the wrong itself" (Saint Augustine, *Confessions*, trans. R. S. Pine-Coffin [New York: Penguin Books, 1961], 47; Book II, Section 4).
114 Barthes, *Roland Barthes by Roland Barthes*, 77.
115 Ibid.
116 Ibid., 79.
117 Kogan, "André Gide," 537.
118 The first pages from the journal, from 1929, were published by Gide as "Pages de journal," *La Nouvelle Revue Française* 225 (June 1, 1932): 985–1004, with other pages following thereafter in NRF. The complete journal was first published in 1939 (*Journal 1889–1939* [Paris: Gallimard, 1939]), and appeared in English several years later (*The Journals of André Gide*, volume 1: *1889–1913*; volume 2: *1914–1927*; and volume 3: *1928–1939*, trans. Justin O'Brien (New York: Knopf, 1947–1949). Volume 4: *1939–49*, also translated by O'Brien, appeared in English in 1951 (Knopf).
119 For a sense of the private Barthes, see, in addition to *Incidents*, his *Album* and *Mourning Diary: October 26, 1977–September 15, 1979*, ed. Nathalie Léger, trans. Richard Howard (New York: Hill and Wang, 2010). See also, Sam Ferguson, *Diaries Real and Fictional in Twentieth-Century French Writing* (Oxford: Oxford University Press, 2018), for an excellent account and comparison of Gide and Barthes's journal writing.
120 Barthes, *Roland Barthes by Roland Barthes*, 95.
121 For Aristippus, widely credited as the first philosopher of hedonism, the value of philosophy is the ability it gives him to speak the truth freely (*parrēsia*). Michel Foucault famously examines this sense of *parrēsia* in *The Government of the Self and Others: Lectures at the Collège de France, 1982–1983*, trans. Graham Burchell, ed. Frédéric Gros (New York: Palgrave Macmillan, 2010), 342–3. However, in the Loeb edition of Diogenes Laertius, *The Lives and Opinions of Eminent Philosophers*, the same thought by Aristippus is expressed as follows: "Being asked what he had gained from philosophy, he replied, 'The ability to feel at ease in any society'" (*Diogenes Laertius I: Lives of the Eminent Philosophers*, Book II, Section 67 [Cambridge, MA: Loeb Classical Library/Harvard University Press, 1925], 197). Both of these senses of *parrēsia*—feeling at ease and truth speaking—comport well with Barthes's hedonism.

Bibliography

Augustine, Saint. *Confessions*. Trans. R. S. Pine-Coffin. New York: Penguin Books, 1961.
Badmington, Neil. "Bored with Barthes: Ennui in China." In *The Afterlives of Roland Barthes*. New York and London: Bloomsbury, 2016. 83–108.
Barthes, Roland. *Album: Inédits: correspondances et varia*. Paris: Éditions du Seuil, 2015.
Barthes, Roland. *Album: Unpublished Correspondence and Texts*. Trans. Jody Gladding. Ed. Éric Marty. New York: Columbia University Press, 2018.
Barthes, Roland. *Incidents*. Paris: Éditions du Seuil, 1987.
Barthes, Roland. *Incidents*. Trans. Teresa Lavender Fagen. London and New York: Seagull Books, 2010.
Barthes, Roland. *Mourning Diary: October 26, 1977–September 15, 1979*. Ed. Nathalie Léger. Trans. Richard Howard. New York: Hill and Wang, 2010.
Barthes, Roland. "On Gide and His Journal [1942]." Trans. Richard Howard. In *A Barthes Reader*. Ed. Susan Sontag. New York: Hill and Wang, 1982. 3–17.
Barthes, Roland. *Le Plaisir du texte*. Paris: Éditions du Seuil, 1973.
Barthes, Roland. *The Pleasure of the Text*. Trans. Richard Howard. New York: Hill and Wang, 1975.
Barthes, Roland. *Roland Barthes par Roland Barthes*. Paris: Éditions du Seuil, 1975.
Barthes, Roland. *Roland Barthes by Roland Barthes*. Trans. Richard Howard. New York: Hill and Wang, 1977.
Barthes, Roland. *Sade, Fourier, Loyola*. Paris: Éditions du Seuil, 1971.
Barthes, Roland. *Sade/Fourier/Loyola*. Trans. Richard Miller. New York: Hill and Wang, 1976.
Barthes, Roland. *S/Z: An Essay* [1970]. Trans. Richard Miller. New York: Hill and Wang, 1974.
Beiser, Frederick C. *Weltschmerz: Pessimism in German Philosophy, 1860–1900*. Oxford: Oxford University Press, 2016.
Bentham, Jeremy. *An Introduction to the Principles of Morals and Legislation* [1789/1823]. In *Selected Writings*. Ed. Stephen G. Engelmann. New Haven and London: Yale University Press, 2011. 103–51. Preface and Chapters 1-5.
Braunstein, Néstor. "Desire and Jouissance in the Teachings of Lacan." In *The Cambridge Companion to Lacan*. Ed. Jean-Michel Rabaté. Cambridge: Cambridge University Press, 2003. 102–15.
Bruckner, Pascal. "Happiness." In *The Columbia History of Twentieth-Century French Thought*. Ed. Lawrence D. Kritzman. New York: Columbia University Press, 2006. 242–5.
Culler, Jonathan. *Barthes: A Very Short Introduction*. Oxford: Oxford University Press, 1983/2002.
Descartes, René. *Meditations on the First Philosophy* [1641]. In *The Philosophical Works of Descartes*. 2 vols. Trans. Elizabeth Haldane and G. R. T. Ross. Cambridge: Cambridge University Press, 1967. I: 132–99.
Ferguson, Sam. *Diaries Real and Fictional in Twentieth-Century French Writing*. Oxford: Oxford University Press, 2018.
Foucault, Michel. *The Government of the Self and Others: Lectures at the Collège de France, 1982–1983*. Trans. Graham Burchell. Ed. Frédéric Gros. New York: Palgrave Macmillan, 2010.
Frenz, Horst, ed. "André Gide, Literature 1947." In Nobel Lectures, *Literature 1901–1967*. Amsterdam: Elsevier Publishing Company, 1969. 421–9.

Gide, André. *The Fruits of the Earth* [1897]. Trans. Dorothy Bussy. New York: Alfred A. Knopf, 1952.

Gide, André. *The Immoralist* [1902]. Trans. Richard Howard. New York: Alfred A. Knopf, 1970.

Gide, André. *Journal 1889–1939*. Paris: Gallimard, 1939.

Gide, André. *The Journals of André Gide: 1889–1949*. 4 vols. Trans. Justin O'Brien. New York: Knopf, 1947–1951.

Gide, André. "Pages de journal." *La Nouvelle Revue Française* 225 (1 June 1932): 985–1004.

Kogan, Vivian. "André Gide." In *The Columbia History of Twentieth-Century French Thought*. Ed. Lawrence D. Kritzman. New York: Columbia University Press, 2006. 537–9.

Lacan, Jacques. *Le Séminaire V. Les Formations de l'inconscient, 1957–1958*. Paris: Seuil, 1998.

Laertius, Diogenes. "Life of Aristippus." In *The Lives and Opinions of Eminent Philosophers, Books 1–5*. Trans. R. D. Hicks. Loeb Classical Library. Cambridge, MA: Harvard University Press, 1925. 194–233.

Mill, John Stuart. *Utilitarianism*, 3rd ed. London: Longmans, Green, Reader, and Dyer, 1867.

Pollard, Patrick. *Gide: Homosexual Moralist*. New Haven, CT: Yale University Press, 1991.

Samoyault, Tiphaine. *Barthes: A Biography* [2015]. Trans. Andrew Brown. Malden, MA: Polity Press, 2017.

Schopenhauer, Arthur. *The World as Will and Idea* [1819/1844]. 3 vols. Trans. R. B. Haldane and J. Kemp. London: Routledge & Kegan Paul Ltd., 1883, 1957.

Thody, Philip. *Roland Barthes: A Conservative Estimate*. London and Basingstoke: The Macmillan Press LTD, 1977.

Part II

Legacies and Afterlives

9

Point Counterpoint

Derrida's "The Deaths of Roland Barthes"

Brian O'Keeffe

We know, from *Roland Barthes by Roland Barthes*, that Barthes felt caged by the stolid consistencies of narrative, imprisoned by conventional autobiography. For, in response to the bland curiosities of the "Who are you?" question (bland but vaguely threatening), autobiography requires the self to braid a tightly raveled *trame narrative* that masters the rawness of lived life by imposing the reassuring fiction that life resembles a Novel. Yet autobiography supposes an "I," precludes any reference to "he" or "him." In "Myself, I," Barthes complains that "I am forever enclosed within the pronominal lists."[1] So Barthes tries *"I am He."*[2] But when Barthes adopts *He*, it's like eavesdropping on himself. *He* imagines that one Barthes is talking (or gossiping) behind another Barthes's back—*he* becomes paranoid. "*I am speaking about myself as though I were more or less dead*, caught up in a faint mist of paranoiac rhetoric."[3] Consider those italics: *more or less*. Did these third-person self-estrangements and the paranoia of being-spoken-about amount to an experiment in writing to and about himself as a specter—more dead than living, but less than definitively dead?

Let's be haunted by that question. Certainly, he/him impersonalities liberate Barthes from the restriction of the autobiographical essay which forbids the *fantaisie* of a made-up, even novelistic self (that's the good side of the Novel). In "Fatigue and freshness," Barthes contemplates the "doom of the essay, compared to the novel: doomed to *authenticity*—to the preclusion of quotation marks."[4] Imagine a series of novelistic aliases—sundry "Roland Barthes"—where quotation marks prevent the conflation of such avatars into one real Barthes. This would be "a text with uncertain quotation marks, with floating parentheses."[5] Yet Barthes's alertness to discourse commits him to persistent quotation from our linguistic Babel. That can overwhelm the writer, and so he dreams of respite from the indigestible glut of discursive palaver. He dreams of retirement while meanwhile suffering the affliction of a disease: "I *see* language."[6] Barthes continues,

> [I]t is the discourse of others, *insofar as I see it* (I put it between quotation marks). Then I turn the scopia on myself: I see my language *insofar as it is seen*: I see it

> *naked* (without quotation marks): this is the disgraced, pained phase of the image-repertoire. A third vision then appears: that of infinitely spread-out languages, of parentheses never to be closed: a utopian vision in that it supposes a mobile, plural reader, who nimbly inserts and removes the quotation marks: who begins to write *with me*.[7]

Quotation marks put language at a safe distance, but, once removed, language appears in close-up, zooms into such intolerable proximity to Barthes that he feels *seen* as if in a mirror—Barthes shamed by the intimacy he now has to acknowledge between himself and his linguistic self-image. Third vision, however: the fantasy of unclosed parentheses. I think of Virginia Woolf's *Orlando*: a mobile and plural reader of her (and his) identity, nimbly cowriting the text as it's being written, sliding in and out of quotation marks, evading such marks especially when they would "cite" him/her as tokens of types—type "woman," type "man." Barthes would have enjoyed *Orlando* (or *Orlando by Orlando*), I think.

But is anyone nimble enough to write with Barthes? *With him*, but now *after* his death? A nimble writer would know what Barthes didn't want. Unwanted are adjectives that describe what Barthes is (or was) *like*. Adjectives doom him to changelessness—last words pronounced, parentheses closed, epitaphs already affixed. "The adjective is funereal."[8] The more solemnly adjectives adhere to the man, the less he can resist his own qualification. *While living* it's possible to experience death: these adjectives already garland millstones around his neck. It's like he attends his own funeral, eavesdrops on the adjectives duly assigned, sees already what's made of him while living and foresees, by the same token, what will be made of him once dead. Worse still are autobiographies or biographies that rivet the self, word by word, onto a boilerplate page. Such texts are dead, each word an epitaph: "*Text of the Dead*: a litaneutical text, in which no word can be changed."[9]

How to write about Barthes's death and heed many of the things—premonitory things concerned with death and the more or less dead—he alerts us to? Derrida's "The Deaths of Roland Barthes" risks an answer. Consider what Derrida wanted to avoid when writing of Barthes's death(s): an excessive fidelity, namely excessive quotation from Barthes himself. "But this excess of fidelity would end up saying and exchanging nothing. It returns to death. It points to death, sending death back to death."[10] Quotations point to the texts from which they're excerpted, but since all texts are divorced from the "dead" author—Barthes *dixit*—then only death, via quotation, circulates here. Excessive quotations might add up to the entire text but they only add "more" death to the author's death in respect of his own text. Quotation feeds the text back to itself. It *returns* to itself, citation by citation, such that the text is summarized or summated not by Derrida but by itself, *as* itself.

Derrida writes:

> When I say Roland Barthes, it is certainly him whom I name, him beyond his name. But since he himself is now inaccessible to this appellation, since this nomination cannot become a vocation, address, or apostrophe (supposing that this possibility

revoked today could ever have been pure), it is him in me that I name, toward him in me, in you, in us that I pass through his name.[11]

Rhetorical performances cannot resuscitate the dead. To invoke *him* in order to convoke him is a sad impossibility. Such exercises in vocation must be revoked: an option rescinded, to be sure, but the impurity of "revoke" also affords the possibility of revoking Barthes—revoicing his voice, as if it were he speaking through Derrida, as at a séance, with Derrida as the *medium*. As if Derrida lets that voice speak in and as himself—a haunting or possession, "him in me." But Derrida passes "through his name," seeking "him beyond his name." Barthes cannot, surely, be reduced to the barebones of his name. But how to write about, or speak to people without naming them? For then the reference refers to nobody or to an anonymity. *He* might hide behind such masks, but one cannot then address the person designated as "you." Speaking *of* Barthes must involve speaking *to* Barthes. A dialogue therefore—alas permanently interrupted—rather than an exercise in indirection: one must *tutoyer* (him) lest one compound Barthes's paranoia. *On dit de Barthes que* . . .

Derrida writes: "I would have wanted to avoid, and thus spare him, the double wound of speaking of him, here and now, as one speaks of one of the living *or* of one of the dead."[12] Spare him that: his inclusion into the two "sets" all mortals belong to—being one of the living, or else one of the dead. Death will have his day, and that "day" terminates the days of our lives. That's that—death's scythe makes its cut into lifetime, and Barthes never escaped what all flesh is heir to. Spare him the double wound of ontology's decisions upon Being/non-Being, life/death. Still, we can live on in the memory of those who survive us (if so, we must, *while living*, leave something for them to remember). Derrida resists philosophy's binary oppositions between *être* and *néant*, life and death. Can Barthes not enjoy the unborn time of living-on? Or are such supplementary times—living-on, survival—unphilosophical, as if Derrida ignores the difference between persons alive and dead? Does Derrida believe in ghosts that are *more or less* dead? Did Derrida believe all this for Barthes?

Specters of Barthes? But even ghosts ask to be remembered, as Hamlet knew. "Adieu, adieu, adieu, remember me,"[13] says the ghost in Act 1, Scene 5. Hamlet wipes from the table of his memory "all trivial fond records, all saws of books,"[14] the better to fix that commandment within the book and volume of his brain. *He writes.* "So, uncle, there you are. Now to my word. It is 'adieu, adieu, remember me.' I have sworn't."[15] Ghosts occult the precincts of the living long enough to call them to the duty of remembrance. *He writes.* I fancy Derrida putting aside all trivial fond records (Derrida's essay isn't sentimental) and all saws of books (no glib recourse to the *Roland-Barthes sans peine*), bending the book and volume of his brain to finding an appropriate written response to Barthes's commandment to remember him.

A response inspired by *Hamlet*, but also, perhaps, by Barthes's "The person divided?": for classical metaphysics, a person would exemplify "a good paradigm (*high/low, flesh/spirit, heaven/earth*)."[16] Nowadays, however, we might declare "I am not contradictory, I am dispersed."[17] That declaration might liberate us from binary classifications but it casts us toward the borderlines of Being. You say: "you are no longer classifiable, not out of an excess of personality, but on the contrary because you pass through all the fringes of the phantom, the specter."[18] To "disperse" oneself is to verge upon spectral "fringes" beyond ontology's purview. Barthes embraces these hauntologies of the self, as does Derrida—"hauntology" is central to *Specters of Marx*. So Derrida tries to respond to him who says "remember me." That response would perforce begin "Ay, thou poor ghost."[19]

Death and the Name

Derrida reads *Writing Degree Zero* and *Camera Lucida* on an island: "I have just read two of his books I had never read before. I thus secluded myself on this island as if to convince myself that nothing had been finalized or had come to an end."[20] As if. Perhaps Derrida smuggled *Roland Barthes by Roland Barthes* onto his island and read "From writing to the work": "Snare of infatuation: to suggest that he is willing to consider what he writes as a work, an '*oeuvre*'—to move from the contingency of writings to the transcendence of a unitary, sacred product."[21] Was Derrida ensnared into arresting the dissemination of "écriture" in favor of a unitary product—Barthes's *oeuvres complètes*? (Islands abet fantasies concerning unities since they're geographical unities themselves.) Derrida: "I read the first and last Barthes with the welcome naiveté of a desire, *as if* by reading the first and last without stopping, back to back, as a single volume with which I would have secluded myself on an island, I were finally going to see and know everything."[22] Nonstop reading distends reading time into a *present* without past or future. Hence a volume, not a book. Books are subject to the vicissitudes of historical time—paper corrodes, crumbles, biodegrades. Books rely on less corruptible digital formats in order to *last*, but a volume lives on in the meanwhile-time of ceaseless reading—solitary on his island, Derrida can't be *interrupted*.

But Derrida's desire to see and hence know Barthes is forlorn. Derrida's desire for the seamless volume, for the *oeuvre*, is delusory. So he returns from his island, and begins with his title. Why deaths? "The plural seems to follow. . . . It follows an order, that's it, and it even obeys; it lets itself be dictated. It asks (for) itself. . . . At the very moment I allowed myself to order a plural for these deaths, I too had to give myself over to the law of the name."[23] Plurals follow and thereby heed a singular "law"—*it*. What does *it* ask (for) itself? The law asks to be obeyed in the singular. *It* is the "law of the name." *It* says: a name mustn't be transferable since otherwise the name isn't *proper* to that one person. Furthermore, that person should bear the name in life and especially in death.

So what's in a name? *Death* is in a name: "The proper name . . . alone and by itself says death. . . . It says death even while the name's bearer is still alive."[24] My proper name accompanies me throughout my finite life—that name announces my finitude and hence "by itself says death." Moreover, "the proper name alone and by itself forcefully declares the unique disappearance of the unique—I mean the singularity of an unqualifiable death."[25] There is nothing, Shakespeare said, we can call our own but death. But what also dies with the death we each, singly, must own, is the name. What died with Barthes was the unique property of his proper name: it was as unique to him as was the dying of his own death. A man can die but once, wrote Shakespeare (him again), and the proper name dies only once as well. Nonetheless, "Death inscribes itself right in the name, but *so as* immediately to disperse itself there, so as to insinuate a strange syntax—in the name of only one to answer as many, to answer to several names in just one name."[26] Let's not invoke the biblical "My name is Legion, for we are many." Let's contemplate, instead, the idea that once a name is slotted into a sentence, suborned therefore by syntax, then autobiographical narrative begins: sentences add detail to the chronicle that the proper name always foretells—the chronicle of a death foretold by the name, the story of individual finitude. Fleshed out, that chronicle becomes a life-story; death diversifies itself as stories are recounted concerning the deaths of others. Death thereby disperses into the texture of an autobiography which, presumably, is authored by someone who hasn't died all at once, before even the first chapter (all autobiographies resemble Balzac's *La Peau de chagrin*).

Ghostly Presences

How to mourn Roland Barthes? Derrida writes:

> I was searching, *like him*, as him, for in the situation in which I have been writing since his death, a certain mimetism is at once a duty (to take him into oneself, to identify with him in order to let him speak within oneself, to make him present and faithfully to represent him) and the worst of temptations, the most indecent and most murderous.[27]

Like or as him? "*Comme lui, comme lui*": Derrida's original French equivocates the matter since "comme" means both "as" and "like." Imagine Derrida taking Barthes into himself: complete identification, he *as* him, would accomplish such perfect mimetism that *likeness* wouldn't be the benchmark for assessing Derrida's representation of Barthes. Representation: the bringing-back-to-presence of a man accomplished by his reembodiment as Derrida. Imagine Derrida as the perfect host, wholly parasited by Barthes. Imagine Derrida haunted (or possessed) by Barthes. Imagine Derrida performing the Eucharistic sacrament: "Take this and eat it, do this in memory of me." Such eating ritually enacts Christ's miraculous transubstantiation. Could the doctrine of Real Presence apply to Barthes and enable his reincarnation or transubstantiation (*and* solve the problem of mimesis)? Fancy or fidelity? Or does all this surrender to the most murderous and indecent of temptations? Why? Perhaps fantasies of perfect representation imply the perfection of reanimation. If so, what is to be reanimated must firstly be dead. The order of mimesis, to adapt Christopher Prendergast's formulation, hence orders death for presentation in order that representation be measured by the Lazarus criterion.

Real Presence? The Eucharist? Does mourning imply symbolic eating? Where, in the body, is he who, or that which one mourns, relocated to? If mourning involves remembrance, what's the organ of memory? How is that organ, if it be one, stimulated to remembrance? Is it pricked by a punctum and furthermore stung by a ghost's commandment—"remember me"? Punctum: the "point" opposed to the studium in *Camera Lucida*. A pointy hedgehog now scuffles into view via "Che cos'è la poesia?" What is poetry? Poems belong to the genus *poiesis*. But *a* poem might desire its own identity, and resist such "belonging." Derrida lends a helping hand: a poem is a hedgehog, he says. But Derrida's poem-hedgehog is stranded on an *autostrada*, about to be run down by a truck—a poem about to be "killed" by genericity. The imperiled *hérisson* rolls into a prickly ball. Like Shakespeare's porpentine shooting its quills, the *hérisson* casts its spines, pricking and prodding Derrida into acts of rescue. The hedgehog implores: "Eat, drink, swallow my letter, carry it, transport it in you, like the law of a writing become your body: *writing in (it)self*."²⁸ In fact, the ingested letter writes its edict on Derrida's heart. Naturally: the heart is the organ of memory. Perfect memorization implies learning something, like a poem, by heart. Thus the body must be pricked, the spine must penetrate within, turn into a pen's nib, and write its plaintive commandment "remember me!" on the heart. It takes only a prick—a *punctum*—to spear open the body and let the other in.

Derrida's heartfelt whimsy invites us to imagine poems dying and possibly living on. Derrida writes: "I am *a* dictation, pronounces poetry, learn me by heart, copy me down, guard and keep me, look out for me, look at me, dictated dictation, right before your eyes: soundtrack, *wake*, trail of light, photograph of the feast in mourning."²⁹ A poem's identity is an identity dictated to it by *poiesis*. Yet that singular poem dictates on its own behalf and for the sake of its saving: "Learn me by heart!" Death is upon it. Genericities and generalities always deal death to singularities. *Poiesis* will deal this death to *a* poem. Knowing this, it leaves a *wake*, a trail, something of itself for Derrida to take inside himself, keep, and learn. It prepares thereby for its own *wake*, its mourning feast, in hopes of living-on. Perhaps human hearts are too fallible, however. Technology is better: soundtracks recorded on tape, and *photographs*. Are we that far from *Camera Lucida*?

Pricked to the quick, Derrida receives the commandment conveyed by those arrow-like quills: take responsibility for me! Responsibility singularizes Derrida—the ethical burden is as singular to Derrida as is the saving he must perform—the saving of *a* poem. So for a poem-hedgehog pointing at Derrida, so for the punctum shooting out of a photograph: it singularizes. The punctum is

> a point of singularity that punctures the surface of the reproduction—and even the production—of analogies, likenesses, and codes. It pierces, strikes me, wounds me, bruises me, and, first of all, seems to concern only me. Its very definition is that it addresses itself to me. The absolute singularity of the other addresses itself to me, the Referent that, in its very image, I can no longer suspend, even though its "presence" forever escapes me, having already receded into the past.³⁰

That point "seems to concern only me." He cannot seemingly evade what finds only him. Consider deixis, ostensive definition, and the Referent. All that tensile pointing toward the always-reached Referent—bulls eye! Of photographic pointing, Derrida says that "it would appear that the *punctum* aims at *me* at the instant and place where I aim at it."[31] Apparently so. If the punctum aims at him, and he at it, can we imagine two points, point and counterpoint, meeting at the time of *appointment*? Perhaps. Derrida cites Barthes: "For *punctum* is also: sting, speck, cut, little hole—and also a cast of the dice. A photograph's *punctum* is that accident that pricks me, points me."[32] Die-cast and accident: always a chance for chance. Despite the fore-destined fortunes of the Referent, *un coup de dès n'abolira jamais le hasard*. Reference is a *journey*, suffers therefore the vicissitudes of "ference"—trans-ference, inter-ference. Deixis and ostension can fail, despite all tensions and intentions to the contrary. Perhaps the punctum won't prick Derrida, therefore. The prick might reach the heart. Then again, it might only *bruise* the body's surface.

"*Punctum* seems to say . . . the point of singularity, the traversal of discourse toward the unique, the 'referent' as (*comme*) the irreplaceable other, the one who was and will no longer be, who returns like (*comme*) that which will not come back, who marks the return of the dead right on (*à même*) the reproductive image."[33] *Like* implies mimetology—assessments of adequate resemblances. But imagine a return of the dead *as* the return of "one who was and who will no longer be." *A même*: the problematic of mimesis might depend on identifying the slightest gap between original and copy. Slight, but almost indiscernible if the copy lies, like a plaque, on the original's very surface. *A même* also asserts the "same" (*même*): if a reproduction asserted that sameness, then the scene of the mimetological crisis of decision (real or simulacrum?) shifts away from the theatrical *skena* otherwise preferred by philosophers of mimesis and ends up *right on* the photographic subjectile.

Derrida writes of the referent's *revenance* in terms of the photograph and the punctum thus:

> Though it is no longer *there* (present, living, real), its *having-been-there* presently a part of the referential or intentional structure of my relationship to the photograph, the return of the referent indeed takes the form of a haunting. This is a "return of the dead," whose spectral arrival in the very space of the photogram indeed resembles that of an emission or emanation. Already a sort of hallucinating metonymy: it is something else, a piece come from the other (from the referent) that finds itself in me.[34]

Images capture *having-been-there*: what the photographer photographed, the photographer herself (and the camera). All were there. All now gone. But photographs (or photograms) can transmit, or even *emit*, a *piece* of the foregone present. What is a "hallucinating metonymy"? Perhaps the punctum penetrates Derrida, thereby rendering him porous to the "death" that all pastness figures. Perhaps he feels *more or less* dead, like a ghost suspended in time and for a time. But what, then, of the studium's interaction with the punctum?

They compose together, the one *with* the other, and we will later recognize in this a *metonymic* operation; the "subtle beyond" of the *punctum*, the uncoded beyond, composes with the "always coded" of the *studium*. It belongs to it without belonging to it and is unlocatable within it; it is never inscribed in the homogenous objectivity of the framed space, but instead inhabits it, or, rather, haunts it.[35]

Derrida cites Barthes: "It is an addition [*supplément*]: it is what I add to the photograph and *what is nonetheless already there*."[36] Derrida adds: "We are prey to the ghostly power of the supplement; it is this unlocatable site that gives rise to the *specter*."[37]

The Studium/Punctum opposition isn't static. Rather, it modulates, almost like a musical composition. The punctum relates-without-relating to the studium. But where, within the image's framed space, is the punctum? Not entirely absent, it haunts the *parergon* that delimits-without-delimiting the homogenous space within the frame. The punctum is latent, as if awaiting confirmation of its "thereness" insofar as the punctum must still strike Derrida and prompt him, like Barthes, to "add" what, nonetheless, is always-already there. The punctum *is* there, but supplements its presence by haunting the photographic space and surface.

The punctum-as-supplement *is* and *is not yet*. Ghosts flit about the Studium/Punctum opposition because "the 'versus' of the conceptual opposition is as unsubstantial as a camera's click."[38] Derrida quotes Barthes: "*Life/Death*: the paradigm is reduced to a simple click, the one separating the initial pose from the final print."[39] Derrida adds: "Ghosts: the concept of the other in the same, the *punctum* in the *studium*, the completely other, dead, living in me. This concept of the photograph *photographs* every conceptual opposition; it captures a relationship of haunting that is perhaps constitutive of every 'logic.'"[40] Extraordinary. Can a photograph snapshot a conceptual opposition at the moment of its forming up? Binary oppositions—cliché! What to do with Derrida's challenge to logic and concept formation? Perhaps that's moving too fast: the real question is whether Derrida is even serious (does he see ghosts when looking at photographs?), and if Barthes is serious either, since apparently, as Derrida cites him, he too could say, of a photograph of himself, that "I then experience a micro-version of death (of parenthesis): I am truly becoming a specter."[41]

But these parenthetical glitches in lifetime are *feigned* experiences, surely. And Derrida's hauntology is surely a feigned philosophy—a feint and whimsical jab at ontology's seriousness. Perhaps. Time, now, to relay *Camera Lucida* to *Specters of Marx*. Hauntology supplements (and resists) ontology's decisions upon Being and non-Being, life and death. Ontology's decisions seem unarguable: for instance, it says that one cannot outlive one's own death. Yet, Derrida argues, ontology is disturbed by thoughts concerning less decidable lives and deaths, troubled sometimes by whatever is unamenable to its preferred categories and binarisms. Derrida (nick)names these undecidable existences "specters." Hauntology, Derrida claims, is "larger and more powerful than an ontology or a thinking of Being (of the 'to be,' assuming that it is a matter of Being in the 'to be or not to be,' but nothing is less certain)."[42] "To be or not to be?" Ontology's own question. But it's not certain, Derrida avers, that ontology provides a definitive answer. Nor is it the only question. For human beings (and not just they) might ask: After I am *not*, is there only Sartre's *néant*, only that undiscovered country from whose bourn no traveler returns? What's the borderline of that *bourn* anyway? Can't I live on, postmortem? This isn't about immortality. It's about wakes and mourning rituals, about being pricked by the other. All this implies vulnerability: vulnerability to hedgehogs and porpentines turning their quills into nibs so as to inscribe the writ of the commandment "remember me" right on the heart. Given this writ, and in sufferance of that pang, we must "learn to live *with* ghosts."[43] This would involve learning to address and respond responsibly to others, to care for their lives, afterlives, and aftermaths.

Points in Time

Hauntology notwithstanding, there still remains some deconstructive work to do on the Studium/Punctum distinction. The distinction, or relation, Derrida writes, "is no longer one of simple exclusion, since the punctual supplement parasites the haunted space of the *studium*."[44] Moreover, "The *punctum* irradiates and, what is most surprising, lends itself to metonymy."[45] Metonymy, fragments, and the "bit": speaking of fragments, Barthes says that "even within each fragment parataxis reigns."[46] Thus each fragment is further fissured by parataxis; fragments of fragments thereby proliferate and supply themselves to metonymy.

Barthes also says that "the fragment has its ideal: a high condensation, not of thought, or of wisdom, or of truth (as in the Maxim), but of music."[47] Condensation: the punctum's point is as sharply honed as a singular note. "Then," Barthes asks, "if you put the fragments one after the next, is no organization possible? Yes: the fragment is like the musical idea of a song cycle . . . : each piece is self-sufficient, and yet it is never anything but the interstice of its neighbors: the work consists of no more than an inset, an *hors-texte*."[48] But does "interstice" separate or hitch fragments together, or else does "interstice" imply a joining-without-joining? Such music will always be out of joint, as it were. Barthes appreciates Schumann's *intermezzi*: "Everything he produced was ultimately *intercalated*: but between what and what? What is the meaning of a pure series of interruptions?"[49] Interstices, insets, and *hors-textes* ask likewise: if I considered myself a supplement, can I be more than merely ancillary to the music of the song cycle, or the coherence of a text?

It's a question for music and texts, but also a question for time itself. What is the meaning of a pure series of interruptions? Do events occur only once? Must one protect the once-and-never-again event from repetition (or metonymy, as if the event shears off a "bit" of its own eventuality)? Or should we do the opposite, namely welcome repetition and metonymy so as to prevent the event from receding into an irrecoverable past? Would that imply maintaining the event in the *maintenant* of the "now"? We might indeed declare *Maintenant!* in defiance of time that passes and which will render all present events past and gone. And say so in order that the living inherit the past—inherit a piece of the past, at least, the part proffered by metonymy, so that there be the possibility of *bequest*. That implies something *left* for the present and future—the *wake*, *sillage*, or track without which there is no following, nothing to take up, keep, and inherit.

Save the event's irreplaceable singularity? Or destroy it for the sake of the saving achieved by repetition, representation, remembrance? But these questions cannot be answered unless we know what time is: Is it serried into points or punctums, or is time Deleuze's rhapsody of becoming, or Bergson's *durée*? Is time composed of events that interrupt the flux, or is the putative rupture of each event compromised by the ambiguities of the "inter"—inter-stice, inter-calation, inter-mezzo? Perhaps points-in-time are mere interims, scanty intervals that don't impede time's flow for that long— barely a split-second long. Seconds, like atoms, can split. Is it therefore hopeless to imagine capturing an instant's instantaneity so as to confirm its status as an *un-splittable* temporal point or an *un-fragmentable* event? Is that what cameras can do—photograph time's indivisible arrow point at the moment of the cliché? Derrida asks: "For is not Time the ultimate resource for the substitution of one absolute instant by another, for the replacement of the irreplaceable, the replacement of this unique referent by another that is yet another instant, completely other and yet still the same? Is not time the punctual form and force of all metonymy—*its last recourse*?"[50] For time to pass, it must pass on something of itself. Part of what came before, that is, but only a part, otherwise there's no past. Whence "the metonymy of the instantaneous."[51] For there's no time if a point-in-time remains adamantine in its separateness, shares nothing of itself with the following instant—that would be pure interruption. The punctum must induce the *next* punctum. Contained in Barthes's punctum, Derrida accordingly finds *dynamis*, a force which, unleashed by metonymy, *makes time*.

But the punctum shears into time and interrupts *duration*. Time therefore confronts the alternate time it "composes" with: countertime, *contretemps*. Now to Derrida's "Aphorism Countertime." At issue is the difference between aphorisms and fragments. Fragments can suffer further fragmentation, whereas aphorisms do not. Aphorism "brings to an end by separating, it separates in order to end (*finir*)—and to define (*définir*)."[52] Aphorism characterizes what points-in-time wish for themselves—finite ends, sharp edges enabling chronological definition. But when the aphoristic point-in-time is exposed to countertime, time skews out of joint, chronology is warped by anachrony, and the synchronicities imposed upon time—calendars, timetables—are interrupted.

"Aphorism Countertime" is a reading of *Romeo and Juliet*. Dwelling on that reading will not, I hope, appear a digression too far if it is granted that the themes of Shakespeare's play resemble those addressed in "The Deaths of Roland Barthes": death, survival, the name, and, withal, the anxieties of those who declare their love—there, then, and till death do them part (such parting, of course, adds further fragments to the *Discours amoureux*). Romeo and Juliet hate their names. Would Romeo but "doff" his name, he would gain all of her. Might Romeo take another human name, or even the name of a rose? Yet Romeo's name is proper to him, his to bear throughout life and unto death. As Derrida puts it, "*he is not without* his name."[53] Is that true? It's not as if the name partakes of that person's own Being. If one doffed one's name, one doesn't actually die for lack of it. Thus, Derrida writes, "one might as well say that I should be able to survive it."⁵⁴ Except that, while the man can die, the name isn't buried with him: names live on as authors' signature imprints on their books, for instance. So the name "is destined to survive me. In this way it announces my death."⁵⁵ To bear a name while living is to intimate the death that only one's name can survive. Hence "non-coincidence and contretemps between my name and me."⁵⁶ I am coextensive with my proper name, the time of my name is the time of me, *I am not without my name*. Nonetheless, my name is always-already outlasting me because while that name partners me throughout life and unto death, it also survives my death. The name announces this to me, each hour my death is died. The name says this at each "hourly" present of my life, says this all the while secure in the knowledge that such presents augur no death for it, only for me. Meanwhile present with me, my name is also in *contretemps* with me because my time ends when I am not, whereas the time of the name isn't bounded by that ending.

In *Romeo and Juliet*, there are two names, two persons, two deaths. One must die before the other, one will see the other die, one will live on, if only for seconds afterward, past the other. Impossible, surely, that each should survive the other. Yet that's what happens—on stage at least. *Romeo and Juliet* is a tragic love story, of course. What is love? Derrida: "I love because the other is the other, because his or her time will never be mine."⁵⁷ I love the fact that the other has a different being-in-time to my own. That time is the time of the other, namely *contretemps*. No love of the other, Derrida suggests, without *contretemps*: lovers "cross" each other's time and hence enjoy the *contretemps* joining them in a time now out of joint. Barthes almost expresses the same insight when, in "Jubilatory discourse," he writes of "the (improbable but ever hoped-for) case when two *I love you*'s, emitted in a single flash, would form a pure coincidence."⁵⁸ Derrida would probably replace "pure coincidence" with "*contretemps*," however. Yes, lovers hope to coincide at the same point in time, but that implies the possibility of splitting the instant of pure coincidence in two so that there be time and countertime, the point of the one and the counterpoint of the other. Hoped for is a temporal overlap, rather than a time lag, where one anxiously awaits the other's "je t'aime."

Living On: Borderlines

In "The Deaths of Roland Barthes," Derrida speaks of "contrapuntal theory."⁵⁹ It's also a theory of *contretemps*. It's moreover a theory of tragic impossibility and hopeful possibility—living-on *is* possible, but, tragically, the dramaturgy of *Romeo and Juliet* isn't available to we mortals. Only one person can survive the other. One must die before the other. Barthes suffered to see his mother die, Derrida suffered to see Barthes die, and Juliet her Romeo. The *peine de la vie* is the *peine de la mort*. That's what a camera forces the surviving person to see as a *truth*: I shall not see her like again, Barthes might have said of his mother. Then again, thanks to the Winter Garden Photograph, he can. But do we get only a bit of the deceased person (metonymy) or all of that person—a holistic, if not hologrammic or spectral semblance of the same person she was? That's the question we might put to cameras. To be or not to be? Besides Hamlet's question is the question of whether technologies of supposedly total image reproduction, like photography, give us the part, or the whole. That's the supplementary query Derrida adds to Hamlet's, and ontology's question. It is, therefore, hauntology's question.

To have been and not yet be fully gone? That's the question posed by all who wish to live on. It's the question ontology never poses. But a poem can ask this, as can a hedgehog, or any Other. *Pace* Heidegger and Sartre, who like neat answers concerning life and death, Being and non-Being, Derrida equivocates. It's not just whimsy. It's an equivocation responsive to the seriousness of the death event. Equivocation: Did Barthes's mother die? Yes, she died but once. But she lives on thanks to a photograph. What of ghosts? Dead, in the eyes of the living, they linger long enough to summon the living to remembrance. If remembrance is possible, so they live on. Did Barthes die but once? Yes, all in all he did, but he has his plural deaths nonetheless. And he too survives, thanks to his renown and his books.

Only on an island will one presume to contemplate Barthes's *oeuvres complètes* and find completion in the possibility of there being a last, readable word signed by Barthes. No. Loving friendship protests against this. Barthes protested against this too: in "The image-system," Barthes writes, "In earlier times, scholars sometimes discreetly followed a proposition with the corrective word '*incertum*.'"[60] I deliberately abuse Latin grammar in the name of the neutral: *Barthes semper incertum est*. Write that "sentence" and you beckon Barthes toward the sempiternal uncertainties of a ghostly netherworld he might have enjoyed, given his attraction to "the fringes of the phantom." In "The Deaths of Roland Barthes," Derrida, I think, discreetly follows the ontological proposition that Barthes is dead with the *corrective* word *Incertum*. Let's leave it at that.

Notes

1. Roland Barthes, *Roland Barthes by Roland Barthes*, trans. Richard Howard (Berkeley, CA: University of California Press, 1994), 168.
2. Ibid., 168.
3. Ibid.
4. Ibid., 89.
5. Ibid., 106.
6. Ibid., 161.
7. Ibid.
8. Ibid., 68.
9. Ibid., 149.
10. Jacques Derrida, "The Deaths of Roland Barthes," *Psyche: Inventions of the Other, Volume 1*, ed. Peggy Kamuf and Elizabeth G. Rottenberg (Stanford: Stanford University Press, 2007), 275.
11. Ibid., 277.
12. Ibid., 274.
13. William Shakespeare, *Hamlet*, ed. Ann Thompson and Neil Taylor (London: Thomson Learning, 2007), 220.

14 Ibid., 219.
15 Ibid., 220.
16 Barthes, *Roland Barthes by Roland Barthes*, 143.
17 Ibid.
18 Ibid., 144.
19 Shakespeare, *Hamlet*, 219.
20 Derrida, "The Deaths of Roland Barthes," 266.
21 Barthes, *Roland Barthes by Roland Barthes*, 136.
22 Derrida, "The Deaths of Roland Barthes," 267.
23 Ibid., 264.
24 Ibid.
25 Ibid.
26 Ibid.
27 Ibid., 268.
28 Jacques Derrida, "Che cos'è la poesia?" *Points: Interviews, 1974–1994*, ed. Elisabeth Weber (Stanford: Stanford University Press, 1995), 293.
29 Ibid., 289.
30 Derrida, "The Deaths of Roland Barthes," 269.
31 Ibid.
32 Ibid., 270.
33 Ibid., 287.
34 Ibid., 285.
35 Ibid., 271.
36 Ibid.
37 Ibid.
38 Ibid.
39 Ibid., 272.
40 Ibid.
41 Ibid., 285.
42 Jacques Derrida, *Specters of Marx*, trans. Peggy Kamuf (New York: Routledge, 2006), 10.
43 Ibid., xviii.
44 Derrida, "The Deaths of Roland Barthes," 272.
45 Ibid., 288.
46 Barthes, *Roland Barthes by Roland Barthes*, 93.
47 Ibid., 94.
48 Ibid.
49 Ibid.
50 Derrida, "The Deaths of Roland Barthes," 291.
51 Ibid., 292.
52 Jacques Derrida, "Aphorism Countertime," *Psyche: Inventions of the Other, Volume 2*, ed. Peggy Kamuf and Elizabeth G. Rottenberg (Stanford: Stanford University Press, 2008), 127.
53 Ibid., 139.
54 Ibid., 140.
55 Ibid.
56 Ibid.
57 Ibid., 131.

58 Barthes, *Roland Barthes by Roland Barthes*, 112.
59 Derrida, "The Deaths of Roland Barthes," 297.
60 Barthes, *Roland Barthes by Roland Barthes*, 105.

Bibliography

Barthes, Roland. *Roland Barthes by Roland Barthes*. Trans. Richard Howard. Berkeley, CA: University of California Press, 1994.

Derrida, Jacques. "Aphorism Countertime." In *Psyche: Inventions of the Other, Volume 2*. Ed. Peggy Kamuf and Elizabeth G. Rottenberg. Stanford: Stanford University Press, 2008. 127–42.

Derrida, Jacques. "Che cos'è la poesia?" *Points: Interviews, 1974–1994*. Ed. Elisabeth Weber. Stanford: Stanford University Press, 1995. 288–99.

Derrida, Jacques. "The Deaths of Roland Barthes." In *Psyche: Inventions of the Other, Volume 1*. Ed. Peggy Kamuf and Elizabeth G. Rottenberg. Stanford: Stanford University Press, 2007. 264–97.

Derrida, Jacques. *Specters of Marx*. Trans. Peggy Kamuf. New York: Routledge, 2006.

Prendergast, Christopher. *The Order of Mimesis*. Cambridge: Cambridge University Press, 1988.

Shakespeare, William. *Hamlet*. Ed. Ann Thompson and Neil Taylor. London: Thomson Learning, 2007.

10

Objects of Desire

Chosisme after Object-Oriented Ontology

Zahi Zalloua

About a half-century before Object-Oriented Ontology (OOO) became fascinated with objects, Roland Barthes championed a *chosiste* aesthetics, whose crystallized embodiment he found in the experimental novels of Alain Robbe-Grillet. In his early essays, Barthes famously described Robbe-Grillet's art of the *nouveau roman* (the New Novel) as *chosiste*—thing-oriented, or *chose*-oriented. As a "destroyer of meaning," Robbe-Grillet eschews the narrative traps of the classical novel.[1] His novels are not to be deciphered, nor mined for deep or symbolic meanings. Barthes's *chosisme*, we might say, echoes Robbe-Grillet's own view that "the world is neither significant nor absurd. It *is*, quite simply."[2] Barthes's *chosisme* gestures to the status of literary objects when objects lose their ideological mask or assumed purpose, when "tell[ing] a story has become strictly impossible [*raconter est devenu proprement impossible*],"[3] as Robbe-Grillet would famously put it. Robbe-Grillet's inventive way of writing bewildered many readers and literary critics, striking them as lacking order or design. Declining the instrumentalization of objects, Robbe-Grillet—as theorized by Barthes—makes them appear as an "optical resistance,"[4] even attributing to objects the dignity of *Dasein* by acknowledging their primacy, their *being there* status.

Barthes's *chosisme* finds much resonance with the proponents of the contemporary and fashionable movement of OOO. Steve Connor, in fact, describes in a 2010 article this general focus on the object or thing as a "thingly turn, a *neue Sachlichkeit*, a *nouveau chosisme*."[5] And yet Barthes's *chosisme* also differs from OOO's to the extent that his *chosisme* does not so much get rid of the subject in favor of a flat ontology (the anti- or posthumanism of OOO) as foreground both the autonomy of the object *and* its entanglement with desire. Barthes's subsequent texts on the play of writing focused more and more on this entanglement and the unruly pleasures, or moments of *jouissance*, that it induces in the subject, or more specifically, in the reader of literature. In what follows, I will first explore *chosisme* as a modern precursor to OOO. Then I will give an account of OOO's tenets and its penchant for a "weird realism" as a "pro-object" literary genre. Finally, I will argue for Barthes's divergence from OOO and his anticipatory critique of the movement through a reading of Robbe-

Grillet's novel *La jalousie* (*Jealousy*), which stages the (anti)hermeneutic and affective perplexities of relationality. Here I will be drawing on Barthes as a theorist of both *chosisme* and *jouissance*, reading *chosisme* with *jouissance* to show how the former is supplemented—but not replaced—by the latter. Unlike that of OOO enthusiasts, Barthes's object-oriented aesthetics is imbued with human desire, endlessly marked, rather than disavowed, by the subject/reader's practices and predilections.

Chosisme

For Barthes, *chosisme* is an aesthetic attitude—an anti-hermeneutics of a sort—functioning, first and foremost, as counter to anthropomorphism. A pure *chosisme* frames the object as bereft of meaning, devoid of humanistic investment. Indeed, human meaning is the enemy of a *chosiste* aesthetics. For Barthes, literature—epitomized by Robbe-Grillet's *nouveau roman*—works to remove meaning from its production, declining any concern with plot or human feelings. Barthes claims that "Robbe-Grillet's intention is to accord objects a narrative privilege hitherto granted only to human objects," creating thus an "'objective' universe" in which "substance is presented no longer as a function of the human heart (memory, instrumentality), but as an implacable space which man can frequent only by movement, never by use or subjection."[6] As Johnathan Culler points out, Robbe-Grillet's obsession with details "purges meaning and breaks the fascination of narrative."[7] His novels exist in that "very narrow zone, in that rare vertigo where literature unavailingly tries to destroy itself, and apprehends itself in that one and the same movement, destroying and destroyed."[8] Indeed, Robbe-Grillet's art attests to literature's ways, to its mode of dwelling, of paradoxically being in a "state of permanent presuicide," existing only as "the figure of its own problem, self-pursuing, self-scourging."[9]

Chosisme insists on literature's dehumanization. Robbe-Grillet's inhuman gaze—its cold, scrupulous visual descriptions—does precisely that. Robbe-Grillet's art "describes objects in order to expel man from them."[10] Objects take precedence over the subject, over the investment of meaning in them: "The author's entire art is to give the object a *Dasein*, a 'being-there,' and to strip it of a 'being-something.'"[11] *Chosisme*, understood as a neutral, demythifying descriptive technique, is thus an antidote to either the domestication or fetishization of objects, to the wild anthropomorphism of humanists and bourgeois readers alike. Robbe-Grillet concurs: "features and objects will be *there* before being *something*."[12] "Remain[ing] on the surface," Robbe-Grillet's art "'paint[s]' the object," declining to indulge in the all-too-humanist cravings for depth or interiority.[13]

Neo-Chosisme, or against Correlationism

If restoring the otherness or meaningless of (nonhuman) objects characterizes the early Barthesian *chosiste* approach to literature, inaugurating an anti-humanist-inspired "new realism," OOO's *neo-chosisme* is part of a larger project, announcing nothing short of a paradigm shift. Its *neo-chosisme* follows from a deep suspicion for anything that smells of "correlationism," a widely used term coined by Quentin Meillassoux to name the adversaries of pure ontology or realism. OOO unabashedly pleads for *ontological* realism; there is an external world that is not contingent on me. Any hermeneutic framework that qualifies its access to the external world—to the "great outdoors," as Meillassoux puts it[14]—is effectively tainted by correlationism: "The thesis of the correlationist . . . is that I can't know what reality would be *without me*."[15] Or again: "correlationism consists in disqualifying the claim that it is possible to consider the realms of subjectivity and objectivity independently of one another."[16] Objectivity is always qualified/neutralized by subjectivity. You're correlationist if you always add "for me" (the categories of the mind, consciousness, language, power, etc.) to any claim that you make about the external world. For OOO and its sympathizers, it is Immanuel Kant who committed the original sin of correlationism. He initiated the paradigmatic shift away from metaphysical inquiry to (the limits of) epistemology. According to Graham Harman, Kant's famous Copernican Revolution was in fact a "Ptolemaic Counter-Revolution."[17] Kant kept the human subject at the center of its universe. Harman and others see continuity between Kant and the '68 generation of philosophers. The "linguistic turn," along with what it spawned (postmodernism, Lacanian psychoanalysis, deconstruction), shares this Kantian lineage, which has plagued and hamstrung contemporary continental philosophy. OOO points to an exit and purports to be a remedy for this prison house of '68 theory. It calls for a return to ontology. What fuels this philosophical rebellion against the subject is a "passion for the real," a passion for authenticity, something beyond mediation, unaffected by constructionist concerns and the categories of subjectivity and representation. This desire for exteriority—more reality and less humanity—takes the form of an irresistible passion for objects, a reenchantment of the world, ignited by a "posthumanist reversion to a pre modern ontology."[18]

OOO contests the undeserved importance attributed to the human subject, to its monopolization concern, determining unevenly the relation between itself and the external world: "The human remains 50 per cent of every philosophical situation, receiving a full half of reality, while all of the many atoms, frogs, schools, puppies, comets, supernovae, tectonic plates and black holes in the universe are packed like sardines into the other half."[19] Fellow OOO practitioner Levi Bryant concurs: "humans occupy no privileged place within being . . . between the human/object relation and any other object/object relation there is only a difference in degree, not kind."[20] Harman laments philosophy's obsession with itself—with the subject and the vagaries of thoughts—neglecting to care about the nonhuman all around it, failing "to think . . . the interaction of two non-human entities"[21] without referring back to human surveillance. The ontology of the human explains it all. No speculation about these other worlds is necessary.

Literature holds some promise in countering philosophy's narcissistic ways. Harman is keen to praise the "weird realism" of H. P. Lovecraft: "no other writer is so perplexed by the gap between objects and the powers of language to describe them."[22] Harman appreciates Lovecraft's aesthetics; his passion for the real, we might say, is "violently anti-idealist."[23] With his horror fiction, Lovecraft puts the metaphorical powers of language in the service of disclosing a reality that is itself "incommensurate with any attempt to represent or measure it."[24] Lovecraft's language does not master the world of objects. Far from it, Lovecraft's weird realism lies in disclosing language's impotence, gesturing to a reality that is irremediably untranslatable. What Lovecraft offers us in his stories is not an adequate representation of reality but the reminder and remainder of language's inability to seize reality as such:

> The meaning of being might even be defined as untranslatability. Language (and everything else) is obliged to become an art of allusion or indirect speech, a metaphorical bond with a reality that cannot possibly be made present. Realism does not mean that we are able to state correct propositions about the real world. Instead, it means that reality is too real to be translated without remainder into any sentence, perception, practical action, or anything else.[25]

Lovecraft's description of his famous monster Cthulhu displays what Harman admires about the author:

> If I say that my somewhat extravagant imagination yielded simultaneous pictures of an octopus, a dragon, and a human caricature, I shall not be unfaithful to the spirit of the thing. A pulpy, tentacled head surmounted a grotesque and scaly body with rudimentary wings; but it was the *general outline* of the whole which made it most shockingly frightful.[26]

As "a writer of gaps and horror," Lovecraft rejects the norms of representational realism, opting instead for more affectively disruptive scene for his readers. He makes the readerly relation with Cthulhu indirect, calling for his readers to experience the full horror of the monster by staging their encounter with Cthulhu as something that surpasses the sum of his parts:

> Lovecraft hints at an octopoidal dragon while also suspending that literal depiction in three separate ways: (1) he downplays it as merely the result of his own "extravagant imagination"; (2) he evasively terms his description "not unfaithful to the spirit of the thing" rather than as dead-on correct; (3) he asks us to ignore the surface properties of dragon and octopus mixed with human and to focus instead on the fearsome "general outline of the whole," suggesting that this outline is something over and above a literal combination of these elements.[27]

Lovecraft's art unfolds obliquely, opening an "*indirect* access" to things-in-themselves, making him an unlikely "Kantian writer of 'noumenal' horror."[28] What we get in Lovecraft is *ontological* realism but not *epistemological* realism: the belief that this external and independent world is knowable. Lovecraft's weird realism happens when he "poise[s] his creatures forever on the very brink of knowability,"[29] when he jolts readers from their correlationist bias, thwarts their humanist sensibilities, exposing them to the unsettling ontological truth of a *world-without-them*. Lovecraft's realism is weird precisely because his aesthetics produces worlds that are frighteningly not mine, that do not accommodate human concerns and desires.

Harman's Lovecraft readjusts the balance between human and nonhumans. In his literary universe, *real* objects remain enigmatic; they are not unfairly reduced to their *sensual* qualities. The ontological privilege of being human—claiming 50 percent of every philosophical scene, purview over a full half of reality—is suspended, even if momentarily, by Lovecraft's brand of realism.

Jouissance after the Death of the Author/Culture/Object

Like Barthes, Harman stresses the autonomy of the aesthetic object, freeing it from paternal control: "The literary text runs deeper than any coherent meaning, and outruns the intentions of author and reader alike."[30] In an allusion to Barthes's canonical essay, "The Death of the Author," Harman urges the field of literary studies to move even further from the humanist orbit and declare the "death of the culture," where culture stands for relationality and correlationism, for that which distorts our understanding of the life of objects (including literary works or literary characters):

> The call for "the death of the author" needs to be complemented by a new call for "the death of the culture." Rather than emphasize the social conditions that gave rise to any given work, we ought to do the contrary, and look at how works reverse or shape what might have been expected in their time and place, or at how some withstand the earthquakes of the centuries much better than others. To call someone "a product of their time and place" is never a compliment; neither should it be a compliment when aimed at a literary work.[31]

Literary critics who give primacy to culture do not respect "the autonomy and materiality of the world."[32] Their cultural analyses "disperse things into language, as if human words had sovereign power."[33] They are guilty of what Harman calls "overmining":

> Everyone wants to demolish the object, as if it were some naïve remainder that no philosopher could allow on earth unchallenged. On one side the object dissolves downward into its physical subcomponents, so that what we call a "table" is just a set of subatomic particles or an underlying mathematical structure. This strategy can be called *undermining*. On the other side the object can be dissolved upward into its effects on human consciousness, so that what we call a "table" is nothing in its own right, but only a functional table-effect for someone or a table-event for other entities. By analogy, I have called this strategy *"overmining."*[34]

The death of the culture is a precondition for appreciating not what a work of literature does (its impact on readers; its place within a given horizon of expectation) but what a work of literature *is*: for coming to terms with its presence and withdrawal.

But Harman fails to realize that Barthes already suggested this point—the call for "the death of the culture"—when he dismissed a series of analogous concepts or "hypostases" of the "Author": "society, history, psyché, liberty."³⁵ Barthes is suspicious of any master signifier deployed to contain the text, to arrest its proliferation of meanings. "To give a text an Author," he warns, "is to impose a limit on that text, to furnish it with a final signified, to close the writing."³⁶ Ending his essay with the memorable line, "the birth of the reader must be at the cost of the death of the Author,"³⁷ Barthes reminds us that this reader *à venir* must not duplicate the logic of the Author—*to give a text a Reader or a Culture is to impose a limit on that text, to furnish it with a final signified, to close the writing.*

Rather than dismissing the reader as signaling a regrettable (re)turn to correlationism, Barthes holds open the meaning of this reader *à venir*, unwilling to either fetishize or chastise readerly presence. In this respect, Barthes's attitude toward literary meaning is infinitely more subtle than Harman's OOO approach. Commenting on literature's specificity or singularity, Barthes writes: "What do things signify, what does the world signify? All literature is this question, but we must immediately add, for this is what constitutes its speciality, literature is the question minus its answer."³⁸ The gap between the question (which all readers of literature invariably repeat) and its (missing, forestalled) answers is where pleasure and *jouissance* reside, or, better yet, happen.

Enjoyment, *jouissance*, is arguably intrinsic to the experience of literature, and yet OOO seems to ignore this dimension of literature altogether—perhaps because it is too tainted with correlationism: *doesn't my textual enjoyment come at the expense of the object?* Literature pleases; it entertains us. But still, what is meant by enjoyment is not always clear. In *The Pleasure of the Text*, Barthes famously distinguishes between pleasure (*plaisir*) and enjoyment (*jouissance*). The French word carries with it a sexualized sense of pleasure, from the verb *jouir*, meaning "to come," that evokes, at once, joy and dismay. Barthes argues that *plaisir* results from a "*comfortable practice of reading*,"³⁹ a communicable knowledge about the reader's societal values, whereas *jouissance* "imposes a state of loss"⁴⁰ by jolting the reader out of docility and complacency, out of his sense of communal belonging. Barthesian reading perverts.

Yet Barthes himself refuses a dogmatic opposition between the two. He disabuses his readers of the binary opposition's (*pleasure/jouissance*) apparent stability: "terminologically, there is always a vacillation—I stumble, I err. In any case, there will always be a margin of indecision; the distinction will not be the source of absolute classifications, the paradigm will falter, the meaning will be precarious, revocable, reversible, the discourse incomplete)."⁴¹ *Jouissance* as a doctrinal idea betrays the illogical logic of the concept.⁴² Fetishized as subversive, *jouissance* becomes deployable as a concept denoting *a priori* unsettlement. Opposing *jouissance* casts you—in the eyes of its "faithful" practitioners—in the position of the reactionary, the bourgeois, the ego-loving subject. But Barthes constantly warns against such a static logic, against the instrumentalization of *jouissance* that would turn it into a rigid principle of subversion. *Jouissance* in the service of hermeneutic power is no longer *jouissance*. Or, as Jane Gallop puts it, "if *jouissance* is celebrated as something that unsettles assumptions, it becomes ineffective when it itself settles into an assumption. If *jouissance* is 'beyond the pleasure principle,' it is not because it is beyond pleasure but because it is beyond principle."[43] There isn't a proper of *jouissance*; any reader/critic who seeks to contain and harness its destructive force ends up ironically diffusing its affective force.

In introducing the idea of *jouissance*, Barthes also stressed its proximity with *plaisir*, complicating the distinction itself: "French has no word that simultaneously covers *plaisir* (contentment) and *jouissance* (rapture)."[44] Simply hierarchizing their values will not do. *Jouissance* is not predicated on the overcoming of *plaisir* as such. Barthes maintains that the text of pleasure holds the potential for unruliness and inventiveness. Why? Because the idea of pleasure itself—or rather the insistence on pleasure—"can embarrass the text's return to morality, to truth: to the morality of truth: it is an oblique, a drag anchor, so to speak, without which the theory of the text would revert to a centered system, a philosophy of meaning."[45] The reader's taste for pleasure, then, produces cognitive friction, blocking the most blatant forms of instrumentalization and commodification: or, in Harman's terms, literature's affective surplus eludes a work's reduction to either scientific-like knowledge ("undermining") or pure didacticism ("overmining"). At the same time, however, pleasure itself is not immune from co-optation; pleasure and the processes of normalization are not, strictly speaking, mutually exclusive. The subject of enjoyment solicited by the text can be motivated by either pleasure or *jouissance*:

> Now the subject who keeps the two texts in his field and in his hands the reins of pleasure and bliss is an anachronic subject, for he simultaneously and contradictorily participates in the profound hedonism of all culture . . . and in the destruction of that culture: he enjoys the consistency of his selfhood (that is his pleasure) and seeks its loss (that is his bliss). He is a subject split twice over, doubly perverse.[46]

The hedonist subject is necessarily split, since "a particular text is neither wholly a 'text of pleasure' nor a 'text of bliss [*jouissance*]': it is always already both." The textual object is undecidable, announcing contradictory pleasures, which, in turn, result either in the fortification of selfhood or in its demise. Moreover, ecstatic moments can happen when least expected; *jouissance* can erupt in a realist novel, in any "text of pleasure." The same follows for explicitly anti-realist, postmodern texts, for texts that flaunt their unreadability: "textual pleasure and textual effects depend upon the possibility of finding ecstatic moments in the comfortable texts of pleasure or of making ecstatic post-modern writing sufficiently readable that its disruptive, violent, orgasmic effects can be generated."[47] *How* we read matters as much as *what* we read. *Jouissance* is not tied to the essence of the object, but to the reader's *relation* to it (precisely to the kind of "relationism" that OOO chastises).

The reproduction—or death—of culture lies, then, in the question of enjoyment. The stakes of reading could not be higher: *How do you enjoy a literary object?* Surely a foreign question for OOO, but an inevitable one for Barthes. Moreover, this is a question that *Jealousy*'s own "weird realism" itself allegorizes or stages in several key scenes, most notably with the following three objects: the centipede, the native song, and the African novel embedded in the narrative of *Jealousy*.

Jealousy's Realisms

Published in 1957, as the *nouveau roman* was rising on the Parisian literary scene, Robbe-Grillet's novel *Jealousy* induced in its first readers a reaction of puzzlement and consternation.[48] It is not an exaggeration to say that *Jealousy* was initially perceived by literary critics as an object like no other. One critic from the newspaper *Le Monde* thought "that he had surely received a copy whose pages had been mixed up by the printer, that it was a jumbled mess."[49] The novel's explicit challenge to hermeneutic containment and cognitive mastery posed a problem: How does a reader enjoy or respond to a work that stubbornly insists on its refractory otherness?

Confronted with *Jealousy*'s alien and alienating unruliness, some critics have sought to tame the novel's appeal to *jouissance*, fixing its promiscuous slippage of meaning by resorting to well-established modes of inquiry. In *The Novels of Robbe-Grillet*, Bruce Morrissette treats *Jealousy* as a text of pleasure, offering the first systematic and explanatory study of the novel, basing his reading in part on the authority of its jacket blurb, which he faithfully paraphrased as follows:

> The story with its three characters—the husband, the wife, the presumed lover— is "narrated" by the husband, a tropical planter who, from the vantage points in his banana plantation house, surrounded on three sides by its wide veranda, suspiciously keeps watch over his wife.[50]

According to Morrissette, two chronologies control the novel's action: an external chronology (which is impossible to determine) and a chronology of the husband's psychological states. The novel's disconcerting chronological impasses can be explained as symptoms of the inner psychic unity governing the order of the novel's events. This psychic unity ultimately refers us to a stable, coherent subject, to a readable subject/work, one situated in the tradition of the psychological novel. *Jealousy*'s initial disturbing effects—the stuff of *jouissance*—are thus eliminated through a critical but faithful rereading (faithful, that is, to a hermeneutics of comprehension, where the critic's duty is first and foremost to meaning), one that restores the comforting sense of interpretive mastery.

In his 1973 *Lecture politique du roman* (*Political Reading of the Novel*), Jacques Leenhardt does not question the referential interpretation of *Jealousy*. But whereas Morrissette's referential approach led him to a psychological reading, Leenhardt insists instead on the sociological relevance of the novel. For Leenhardt, *Jealousy* is decidedly not about the psychic reality of a jealous husband. Leenhardt's Marxist reading of *Jealousy* purports to make visible what Fredric Jameson describes as the novel's language or, to be more precise, its signifier's "material and referential *preconditions*."[51] Privileging the social, in turn, enables the reader to escape the all-too-common psychologization of the husband in order to better attest to his ideological subject position. Leenhardt reads the novel allegorically as a textual site of tension between two competing colonial models: the husband, who stands for the old racist French empire, and the new, more utilitarian, neocolonial model, allegorized in the figure of Franck.[52]

On Leenhardt's account, the motor of the story is not erotic jealousy per se, but the husband's fear of losing his material possessions and patriarchal privilege. The narrator's obsessive, depersonalized gaze, for instance, is not merely an index of the husband's isolated pathology; rather, it reflects the anxieties of late French colonialism on the eve of the 1960 accessions to independence in West Africa. Leenhardt historicizes the Cartesian subject and its desire for control, situating this subject (embodied here by the husband) in the early moments of decolonization, an era that confirmed the death of a traditional French imperialism based on territorial conquest and control, while also witnessing a rise in neocolonial capitalist systems of domination.[53] On this reading, the narrator-husband's obsessive gaze is symptomatic of his uneasiness and loss of footing in the changing field of power. It is exemplified in his geometrical descriptions of his banana plantation:

> The bulge of the bank also begins to take effect starting from the fifth row: this row, as a matter of fact, also possesses only twenty-one trees, whereas it should have twenty-two for a true trapezoid and twenty-three for a rectangle (uneven row).[54]

As Leenhardt keenly observes, "Looking and being looked at . . . places jealousy at the center of the plantation problem, which is a microcosm of the colonial problem."[55] For Leenhardt, neither *Jealousy*'s textual self-reflexivity nor its psychological realism should blind the reader to the novel's historical frame of reference or its ideological content. From this vantage point, *Jealousy*'s realism, its epistemological claims about the referential world, lie not so much in the evocation of the narrator's psychic reality but in the novel's representation of a colonial mentality, or, more precisely, in its staging of the ideological tension inherent in the devolution and devaluation of Western colonialism.

Already in 1959, however, literary critic and novelist Maurice Blanchot was warning against any referential reading of the novel at all; that is, a reading in which the primary goal is to explicate and domesticate Robbe-Grillet's unruly narration by imposing a hermeneutic order. In *The Book to Come*, Blanchot not only questions the primacy of the husband's jealousy but also problematizes the very existence of such a central character. Taking objection, in particular, to the jacket blurb's characterization of the narrator as a jealous husband,[56] Blanchot underscores the novel's radical alterity, its irreducibility to a thematic analysis, and its departure from preexisting literary models. More importantly, noting the "powerful absence [at] the center of the plot and of the narration," he reminds the reader that no character is ever in fact named as the narrator:

> According to the critics, we are to understand that what is speaking in this absence is the very character of the jealous one, the husband who watches over his wife. I think this misunderstands the authentic reality of this narrative as the reader is

invited to approach it. The reader indeed feels that something is missing; he has the premonition that it is this lack that allows everything to be said and everything to be seen—but how could this lack be identified with someone? How could there still be a name and an identity there? It is nameless, faceless; it is pure anonymous presence.[57]

For Blanchot, the anonymity of the narrative voice reflects the demands of writing and crystallizes the singular experience of literature, that is, literature's resistance to readerly cognitive demands: "The essence of literature is precisely to escape any essential determination, any assertion that stabilizes it or even realizes it: it is never already there, it always has to be rediscovered or reinvented."[58]

During a conference on the status of the *nouveau roman* in the fall of 1982 at New York University, Robbe-Grillet responded directly to Blanchot's concerns about the jacket blurb, as well as the type of readings that it authorizes:

Blanchot was right. I wrote to him that he was right, but that it was I who had written this blurb and that, in fact, it was not intended for him, but for those hurried critics who do not have time to read the books they have to write about in papers. The blurb was, of course, not addressed to Maurice Blanchot who, in the cell of his tower, *actually reads books*.[59]

Are those who actually read the book also said to enjoy them? Can we further link *jouissance* to hermeneutics? And is deciding on *Jealousy*'s irrecuperability or retrievability central to the determination of the kind of enjoyment that the novel solicits?

Enjoying the Literary Object

Barthes's approach resonates with Blanchot's quite a bit. They both reject an image of the novel as a meaning generating machine, which in turn solicits an expert or specialist reader searching for secrets. Barthes writes:

The Robbe Grillet novel is . . . [an object] full of secrets; criticism must then begin scrutinizing what is behind this object and around it: it seeks "keys" (and usually finds them).[60]

And Blanchot puts the point thus:

[The specialist] interrogates the work in order to know how it was fashioned. He asks it the secrets and the conditions of its creation, and examines it closely to see whether it answers adequately to these conditions, etc. The reader, having become the specialist, becomes an author in reverse.[61]

What Barthes and Blanchot ask of the reader is to stay alert to *Jealousy*'s fundamental resistance to comprehension, to its defiance of hermeneutic commentary or symbolic mastery. But whereas a Blanchotian approach adopts a purist stance vis-à-vis the literary object, an indefatigable reverence for the text, a Barthesian one is more inclined to entertain interpretations—what does *Jealousy*'s objects signify? what does its world mean?—as long as the reader remains attentive to literature's ways: *literature is the question about the signification of the world and its objects minus the answer*. This is why Barthes's *chosiste* approach is not simply an anti-humanist one. Barthes muses, "Must we choose between the two Robbe-Grillets—the 'thing-oriented' [*chosiste*] Robbe-Grillet number 1 and the humanist Robbe-Grillet number 2, between the Robbe-Grillet of the early criticism and the Robbe-Grillet of Bruce Morrissette?"[62]

If one interpretive current reads the novel mimetically or referentially (e.g., as a story about a jealous husband or as an allegory of political struggle), Blanchot denies *Jealousy*'s mimetic intent altogether, interpreting the narrative voice as a figure for the anonymity of language itself. Blanchot's paradoxical (non)reading preserves the irreducible distance between the reader and Robbe-Grillet's novel; it "does not comprehend (strictly speaking)," but "attends,"[63] as he writes in *The Infinite Conversation*. Reading *as such* is prior to or beyond comprehension and meaning. In *The Writing of the Disaster*, Blanchot formulates his perplexing mode of reading as an act of testimony: "There is the reading that is no longer passive, but is passivity's reading. It is without pleasure, without joy; it escapes both comprehension and desire. It is like the nocturnal vigil, that 'inspiring' insomnia when, all having been said, 'Saying' [*le Dire*] is heard, and the testimony of the last witness is pronounced."[64]

There is much in Blanchot to please a OOO enthusiast. Reading here bears witness to the real object. OOO would translate "without pleasure, without joy" as without correlationist bias. The "Saying" is heard in the acknowledgment of the work/object's irresistible withdrawal. A Barthesian approach, however, declines this Blanchotian temptation—the urge to remain silent or simply affirm the unsayability of the work—and favors instead a more compromised form of relationality with the literary object. As Barthes points out, "neither culture nor its destruction is erotic, it is the gap between them that becomes so."[65] And again: "the text needs its shadow, a *bit* of ideology, a *bit* of representation, a *bit* of subject: ghosts, pockets, traces, necessary clouds: subversion must produce its own chiaroscuro."[66] The reader revels in being the thrall of *plaisir* and *jouissance*, in sustaining "the consistency of his selfhood" and in pursuing "its loss." Interpretive *jouissance* is thus not to be aligned exclusively with agrammaticality itself. On the question of agrammaticality, Jacques Derrida is very suggestive: "There is no pure a-grammaticality; or rather, there *is* pure a-grammaticality but as soon as it appears as such, or as it enters a text or a situation, it starts to become grammatical."[67] Barthesian *jouissance* emerges from within a preexisting grammar—the *bits* of ideology, representation, and subject (the stuff of realisms). But the happening of *jouissance*, of course, always comes with a risk. *Jouissance* can be converted back into *plaisir*, its "other" grammar reinscribed within the economy of the same, eclipsing the eventness of the novel and reinstituting a digestive logic (à la Morrissette and Leenhardt).

The *bits* of ideology, representation, and subject are what a OOO-inspired literary criticism tries to excise or at least downplay in its appreciation of a literary object, since all three smuggle culture back into the pristine object, diluting its essence. For Barthes, this smuggling is far less straightforward than OOO would hold, pointing to what makes literature messy and enthralling in the first place. Enjoyment returns us to the singularity of literature: the question of meaning minus its answer.

The Centipede, the Native Song, the African Novel

Jealousy gives rise to enjoyment through its staging of these *bits* of ideology, representation, and subject: through the way the novel both evokes and troubles a grammar of meaning. Robbe-Grillet once referred to his novel as an "engine of war against order."[68] Order stands for the reign of grammar/meaning. As an engine of war, *Jealousy* sabotages meaning, enacts its agrammaticality, through its interpretive irresolution, an irresolution that requires a continual, if not obsessive, return to the work itself, to its self-reflexive figures—of which the centipede, the native song, and the African novel bear special mention (this is Robbe-Grillet's own litany of objects *of desire*[69]).

The unruly affect of jealousy is enlisted in *Jealousy*'s war against order. It registers subjective dispossession, a weak sovereignty, a compromised and compromising consciousness. Jealousy robs the narrator's gaze of its habitual sense of power; it is what makes the narrator's objectivizing consciousness fail to contain the objects that *should* fall within its horizon of intelligibility. The novel records this alienation in what is perhaps *Jealousy*'s most famous scene: the crushing of the centipede by Franck, a neighbor and fellow plantation owner, who is suspected of having an adulterous affair with the wife, A. . . . This "primal" scene—the one that the reader is implicitly asked to reconstruct from the numerous fragmented descriptions—takes place in the dining room. When Franck "bravely" kills the centipede upsetting A . . ., he boldly usurps the husband's power, undermining his position as dutiful protector of his wife/possession. The overtly sexual description of A . . .'s hand clenching a knife handle, a phallic symbol, further highlights the husband's emasculation and displacement. The image of the centipede (and the stain that it leaves on the wall) haunts the narrator, who constantly revisits and reimagines the scene. His most dramatic fantasy emerges after A . . . accompanies Franck on a shopping trip for a new truck. Left alone on his plantation, the narrator becomes obsessed by the image of the centipede. The image's unruly plasticity reaches its apogee when the centipede—said earlier to be "of average size" (64)—becomes transmuted into a monstrous insect: "It is enormous: one of the largest to be found in this climate. With its long antennae and its huge legs spread on each side of its body, it covers the area of an ordinary plate" (112). It is as if the image becomes imbued with agency, just as the narrator becomes devoid of his. In this Kafkaesque rendering of the scene, not only the centipede but also the location of the event, have undergone a radical transformation: as if caught *in flagrante delecto*,

A... and Franck have been transported to a hotel room, in a scene that the narrator-husband appears to be *imagining*, and not, strictly speaking, perceiving.

How would OOO judge the centipede scene? Does the centipede suggest a mind-independent reality? Is the novel's depiction of the insect's "liveliness"—its status as undead—a break with the correlationist circle? Is *Jealousy* staging this as a conflict between a *real* object (the centipede) and its *sensual* qualities (the husband's imperfect account)? Yes and no. In favor of a positive OOO reading, we might say that the narrator's geometric style, his theoretical understanding of objects around him, does not exhaust the being of the centipede nor does it reduce it to erotic jealousy or colonial displacement. The example of the centipede is arguably at odds with Barthes's *chosisme* or Robbe-Grillet's own manifesto, where perception—this "cleansing power of the sense of sight"—should enable the subject to describe things as they are ("neither significant nor absurd") and leave things "in their respective place."[70] If perception truly had a cleansing function, however, the narrator's representation of the centipede should remain constant in each retelling of the episode instead of falling prey to the husband's distorting, anthropomorphic hallucinations. The centipede should have simply been, in the words of the *chosiste* Barthes, "an optical resistance."[71] But here OOO would distinguish between the anthropomorphic hallucinations (the appearances of the centipede to a pathological mind) and the real object. The narrator obsesses over the sensual centipede, while the OOO reader witnesses the object's withdrawal to a dark subterranean reality. The centipede—as real object—withdraws; its caricatures (psychological and postcolonial readings) are destroyed and recreated throughout the novel. A OOO reading would surely insist on the difference between the sensual centipede and the real centipede. According to this line of thought, the novel serves as a warning against the translation or representations of the "real" centipede: the jealous mind of the narrator (or that of the contaminated reader/critic) always distorts its objects.

But is this really the point of *Jealousy*? A Barthesian sensibility reorients us back to the pleasures of objects, to objects that are encountered as first and foremost objects *of desire*. As a locus of dispossession, desire attenuates, if not ruins, correlationalist comfort, placing its subject at the mercy of objects. But this is not a recycling of anthropocentrism; what we have is the *anthropos* without anthropocentrism, the subject without the sovereignty of the subject. If OOO decouples meaning and (real) objects, Barthes entangles the two, complicating the subject's hegemonic control over objects. *Jouissance* is only possible because meaning and objects can never fully coincide, because desire does not function in the service of the readerly ego. Moreover, the reality of objects is not some inaccessible noumena. No, as Robbe-Grillet puts it, "reality begins at the precise moment when meaning becomes uncertain,"[72] when agrammaticality enters and disrupts the hermeneutic scene.

The type of interpretive irresolution produced by the centipede disruption is further accentuated in the novel's two memorable mise en abyme: the native song and the African novel that both A... and Franck have been reading. Juxtaposing competing models of interpretation in these episodes, *Jealousy* throws into question the viability and completeness of either. In the first example, the native song challenges comprehension completely, possessing no identifiable meaning; it is described as a "native tune, with incomprehensible words, or even without words" (83).[73] The song sparks the narrator's curiosity; he wonders about its internal logic, while recognizing the melody's intrinsic opacity ("it is difficult to determine if the song is interrupted for some fortuitous reason . . . or whether the tune has come to its natural conclusion" [83]). The narrator also suggests that his experience of its opacity is due, at least in part, to his own cultural horizon of expectation:

> The poem is at moments so little like what is ordinarily called a song, a complaint, a refrain, that the western listener is justified in wondering if something quite different is involved. The sounds, despite apparent repetitions, do not seem related by any musical law. There is no tune, really, no melody, no rhythm. It is as if the man were content to utter unconnected fragments as an accompaniment to his work. (127, translation modified)

From the perspective of the Westerner, the song appears enigmatic, unintelligible, beyond interpretation, as if the song's saying and literariness are intimately tied to its agrammaticality—its lack of conformity to "musical law." In fact, the song-poem appears profoundly anti-representational, devoid of any constative utterances (utterances of which the truth or falsity can be determined), since it does not describe nor communicate anything about the world. If the reader's subject position parallels that of the narrator, then any reading of the novel (realist or anti-realist) would effectively be ruled out: the reader confronts an artwork that is wholly other, utterly inaccessible.

In the second example, the African novel also draws attention to the interpretive act—the event of reading. Thematically analogous to *Jealousy*, the novel tells the story of an adulterous wife and her negligent husband. Like *Jealousy*, it also displays a lack of verisimilitude and a potential to generate multiple readings. Interpretive differences between Franck and A . . . emerge for example with respect to female sexuality. Franck finds one female character's sexual escapades shocking, while A . . . does not:

> "After all," he says, "sleeping with Negroes . . ." A . . . turns toward him, raises her chin, and asks smilingly: "Well, why not?" (126)

In contending that women can sleep with whomever they choose (in this case, Blacks, the colonized and racialized others), A . . ., in her playful rebuke, sets herself apart from Franck, implicitly refusing to conform to his masculinist desire to control or possess her fully—leaving him quite speechless ("Franck smiles in his turn, but answers nothing" [126]] and awkwardly grimacing: "The movement of his mouth ends in a sort of grimace" (126). At other points, however, she and Franck delight in the novel's ability to outrage and spark imagination:

> They . . . sometimes deplore the coincidences of the plot, saying that "things don't happen that way," and then they construct a different probable outcome starting

from a new supposition, "if it weren't for that." Other possibilities are offered, during the course of the book, which lead to different endings. . . . They seem to enjoy multiplying these choices, exchanging smiles, carried away by their enthusiasm, probably a little intoxicated by this proliferation. (75)

This interpretive play is short-lived: Franck reestablishes hermeneutic order, putting an end to textual enjoyment and interpretive "intoxication," converting this "text of *jouissance*" into one of pleasure: "Franck sweeps away in a single gesture all the suppositions they had just constructed together. It's no use making up contrary possibilities, since things are the way they are: reality stays the same" (75). Unlike the native song, then, the African novel both produces and resolves interpretive anxieties—at least for Franck.

What is the reader to make of these two models of reading? Each one serves to illustrate the two extreme poles of interpretation: the native song is unreadable (the stuff of *jouissance*), whereas the African novel is all too hermeneutically containable (the stuff of *plaisir*). At which end of the interpretive pole do we situate *Jealousy*? Or, is the question itself misplaced? Some critics, wanting to underscore the poetics of *Jealousy* against its thematics or psychological preoccupations (which others use to recuperate the novel under the label of realism), have understandably stressed its proximity to the native song-poem. As Ann Jefferson writes, for example, "In reading the narrative as the expression of the husband's jealousy, we are making it impossible to read it as a 'poem,' as literature."[74] Yet this type of reading also restricts *Jealousy*'s "literariness," defining it too narrowly as poetry—a reified, self-enclosed, timeless, and autonomous aesthetic object—impenetrable to the reader's interpretive and appropriating gaze. As Fredric Jameson notes, "the very concept of the work of art qua aesthetic object is itself a fetishization and an abstraction."[75] To situate *Jealousy* beyond any cognitive horizon—a consequence of identifying the novel purely with the poem-song—is to mystify the agrammaticality of Robbe-Grillet's novel. Such a move essentializes the (non)meaning of *Jealousy* (this is a move that OOO duplicates), making it appear immune to the vicissitudes of desire, to correlationist encroachments. The native song is safeguarded from anthropocentric contamination—but at what cost? It treats the novel as an aesthetic object, but not an object *of desire*.

Reading the native song along *with*, rather than simply *against*, the African novel gives a fuller account of the ways that the novel allegorizes, and/or rather stages its own allegorization of irresolution. If we shift focus from the intrinsic properties of the song-poem to its horizon of intelligibility, then a *rapprochement* can be made with the African novel. The two models are not mutually exclusive, for both highlight the relational quality of otherness. That is to say, the alterity of the song-poem and the African novel is not affirmed in abstraction, but experienced as an interruption of otherness, a rupture, a textual disturbance, *relative to* listener-readers' understanding and expectations. The native song is perceived as agrammatical, as other, mainly because it disrupts the husband-narrator's grammar, his familiarity with music; similarly, the excitement that the African novel initially provokes stems from its ability to unsettle A . . . and Franck's expectations ("things don't happen that way"). When

Franck strips the African novel of its potential for inventiveness, excising meanings that cannot now be imagined or anticipated, denying its reception "as an other that opens up new possibilities,"[76] he effectively displaces and destroys the experience of the novel's alterity, along with its transformative and *dis*organizing potential, returning it to the logic of the same and reinscribing the work of art within the established norms of readability, preventing any *plaisir* slippage into *jouissance*.

If Franck serves as an example to avoid, the desiring reader of *Jealousy* cannot simply negate this mode of reading or posit the work outside the realm of interpretation, fetishizing, as it were, the text's inaccessibility and ungraspability. As Robbe-Grillet himself put it, a literary work that could theoretically "escape from this system of recuperation . . . would not be an interesting text, because it would be an angelical text, that is, a text which is in and for itself. One cannot be outside of ideology."[77] A text of *jouissance* is not outside of ideology. Rather, it strives and excites in the undoing of ideology. Again, how we should understand Barthesian *jouissance* is key here. There is a danger in simply aligning it with the experience of aesthetic alterity or cognitive resistance. An "angelic text" is incontrovertibly free of meaning but also free of *jouissance*. The reader of an "angelic text" possesses, strictly speaking, no relation to the pristine text. There is precisely no experience of the gap, what renders *jouissance* as such possible. We can compare Barthes's emphasis on this gap ("neither culture nor its destruction is erotic, it is the gap between them that becomes so") with Harman's "no other writer [Lovecraft] is so perplexed by the gap between objects and the powers of language to describe them." Harman praises Lovecraft for his powers to make his readers taste the existence/inaccessibility of the noumena, by thematizing the gap between *res* and *verba*, disabusing them of their epistemic penchants. Barthes's gap follows from a rejection of *purity*—the presence of culture (ideology = naturalized meaning) or its absolute negation (the destruction of meaning; the ideology of thinking one has transcended ideology—the "angelic text"). Like Harman, Barthes rejects relationism but the solution is not to affirm the essence of the object. Rather, *jouissance* emerges at the moment when relationism's armor begins to falter, when irresolution overwhelms the reader, when *chosisme* not only names optical resistance but hermeneutic defiance as well.

A Barthesian hermeneutics thrives on this gap—the stuff of *jouissance* and endless invention. It embraces an open-ended dialectics—a dialectics without synthesis, if you will—whereby the readerly impulses for culture and its destruction, for "order and disorder," as Robbe-Grillet puts it, interact playfully to create a productive tension, "a sort of mutual recuperation."[78] Such a reading practice is *not* inimical to realist, or anti-realist, interpretations of *Jealousy*; indeed, it fosters a parallactic sensibility, attracting and defying the reader's will to interpret by urging him or her to join and disjoin incongruous positions and incommensurable meanings: *chosisme* with *jouissance*, for instance. And it is in this spirit that we can (re)read the novel *Jealousy* as an irresistible object of desire, alternating between mastery over and reverence for the work as object—and for the work and its objects. Preserving the irresolution at the heart of novel does not require the reader to retreat into a paralyzing, skeptical void, remaining silent or simply affirming the unsayability of the work—from the

Blanchotian temptation to OOO's cult of withdrawnness. On the contrary, readers must engage with the unruly work; they are compelled (by the literary object itself) to desire it, to give it particular shape and meaning, and, yes, this reading will inevitably betray the novel's opacity and enigmaticity.

OOO's *neo-chosiste* response to hermeneutic betrayal is to ontologically recuperate the text/object, to affirm that no readings exhaust the essence of the novel. OOO's real literal object is an "angelic object," whose mystical withdrawnness renders it immune to anthropocentric overreach. Humans can produce readings of literary objects yet they are but caricatures of real objects—to be praised paradoxically only when they succeed in enacting their failure, in discrediting themselves in the name of real objects. In contradistinction to OOO, Barthes's response amount to a doubling down on this betrayal, refusing to fetishize or naturalize the text, to imagine it in a state of phantasmatic purity, unsullied by human desires. Again, the specificity of literature—or we might say the "real" of literature—is the question of meaning minus its answer. To put it differently, the enigmaticity of the literary object does not reside exclusively with the real object (what the text *is*) but comes into being dialectically in its encounter with readers. The real object is not prior or beyond its readings or the so-called caricatures but is its readings (not all caricatures are alike after all). Whereas OOO would lament this conclusion—seeing it as yet another anthropocentric capitulation, denigrating the ontology of objects—a Barthesian rejoinder would insist that without readerly desires, with the pure withdrawnness of objects, no actual reading would ever be possible. *Pace* OOO, the agrammaticallity of the real object, for Barthes, is not to be ethically fetishized but hermeneutically engaged.

Notes

1. Roland Barthes, "The Last Word on Robbe-Grillet?," in *Critical Essays*, trans. Richard Howard (Evanston: Northwestern University Press, 1972), 198.
2. Alain Robbe-Grillet, *For a New Novel: Essays on Fiction*, trans. Richard Howard (Evanston: Northwestern University Press, 1996), 19.
3. Ibid., 33.
4. Roland Barthes, "Objective Literature," in *Critical Essays*, trans. Richard Howard (Evanston: Northwestern University Press, 1972), 14.
5. Steven Connor, "Thinking Things," *Textual Practice* 24.1 (2010): 1.
6. Roland Barthes, "Literal Literature," in *Critical Essays*, trans. Richard Howard (Evanston: Northwestern University Press, 1972), 51–2.
7. Jonathan D. Culler, "Barthes, Theorist," *The Yale Journal of Criticism* 14.2 (2001): 441.
8. Barthes, "Literal Literature," 58.
9. Ibid., 58.
10. Roland Barthes, "There is No Robbe-Grillet School," in *Critical Essays*, trans. Richard Howard (Evanston: Northwestern University Press, 1972), 94.
11. Barthes, "Objective Literature," 15.
12. Robbe-Grillet, *For a New Novel*, 21.
13. Barthes, "Objective Literature," 14.

14 Quentin Meillassoux, *After Finitude: An Essay on the Necessity of Contingency*, trans. Ray Brassier (New York: Continuum, 2008), 7.
15 Quentin Meillassoux, *Time Without Becoming*, ed. Anna Longo (Haverton: Mimesis International, 2014), 23, emphasis added.
16 Meillassoux, *After Finitude*, 5.
17 Graham Harman, *Quentin Meillassoux: Philosophy in the Making* (Edinburgh: Edinburgh University Press, 2011), 51.
18 Russel Sbriglia and Slavoj Žižek, "Introduction: Subject Matters," in *Subject Lessons: Hegel, Lacan, and the Future of Materialism*, ed. Russel Sbriglia and Slavoj Žižek (Evanston: Northwestern University Press, 2020), 9.
19 Graham Harman, "Object-Oriented Ontology," in *The Palgrave Handbook of Posthumanism in Film and Television*, ed. Michael Hauskeller, Curtis D. Carbonell, and Thomas D. Philbeck (Basingstoke: Palgrave Macmillan, 2015), 405.
20 Levi R. Bryant, *The Democracy of Objects* (Ann Arbor: Open Humanities Press, 2011), 32.
21 Graham Harman, "The Battle of Objects and Subjects: Concerning Sbriglia and Žižek's *Subject Lessons* Anthology," *Open Philosophy* 3 (2020): 317.
22 Graham Harman, *Weird Realism: Lovecraft and Philosophy* (Winchester: Zero Books, 2012), 3.
23 Ibid.
24 Ibid., 51.
25 Ibid., 16.
26 H. P. Lovecraft, "The Call of Cthulhu," *Weird Tales* (1928), H. P. Lovecraft Archive. http://www.hplovecraft.com/writings/texts/fiction/cc.aspx. Accessed April 21, 2020.
27 Harman, *Weird Realism*, 24.
28 Ibid., 17, 27.
29 Ibid., 148. Harman acknowledges that Lovecraft at times fails to live up to his own ideal, deviating from "the proper path of H. P. Lovecraft" (Harman, *Weird Realism*, 148).
30 Graham Harman, "The Well-Wrought Broken Hammer: Object-Oriented Literary Criticism," *New Literary History* 43.2 (2012): 200.
31 Ibid., 201.
32 Jeffrey Jerome Cohen, *Stone: An Ecology of the Inhuman* (Minneapolis, MN: University of Minnesota Press, 2015), 45.
33 Ibid., 45.
34 Harman, "The Well-Wrought Broken Hammer," 199.
35 Roland Barthes, "The Death of the Author," in *Image-Music-Text*, trans. Stephen Heath (New York: Hill and Wang, 1977), 147.
36 Ibid.
37 Ibid., 148.
38 Barthes, "The Last Word on Robbe-Grillet?" 202. In "The Death of the Author," Barthes also remarks: "writing ceaselessly posits meaning ceaselessly to evaporate it, carrying out a systematic exemption of meaning" (147). And in *The Pleasure of the Text*, he writes, "What is significance? It is meaning, *insofar as it is sensually produced*" (Roland Barthes, *The Pleasure of the Text*, trans. Richard Miller [New York: The Noonday Press, 1975], 61).
39 Barthes, *The Pleasure of the Text*, 14.
40 Ibid.

41 Ibid., 4.
42 Ibid., 44.
43 Jane Gallop, "Beyond the *Jouissance* Principle," *Representations* 7 (1984): 113.
44 Barthes, *The Pleasure of the Text*, 19, translation modified.
45 Ibid., 64–5.
46 Ibid., 14.
47 Jonathan D. Culler, *Barthes: A Very Short Introduction* (Oxford: Oxford University Press, 1983), 83.
48 The discussion here builds on my reading of Robbe-Grillet's novel in *Reading Unruly: Interpretation and Its Ethical Demands* (Lincoln: University of Nebraska Press, 2014).
49 Quoted in Alain Robbe-Grillet's "Order and Disorder in Film and Fiction," trans. Bruce Morrissette, *Critical Inquiry* 4.1 (1977): 3.
50 Bruce Morrissette, *The Novels of Robbe-Grillet* (Ithaca: Cornell University Press, 1975), 112–13.
51 Fredric Jameson, "Modernism and Its Repressed; or, Robbe-Grillet as Anti-Colonist," *The Ideologies of Theory: Essays 1971–1986*, vol. 1 (Minneapolis, MN: University of Minnesota Press, 1988), 169.
52 Jacques Leenhardt, *Lecture politique du roman. La Jalousie d'Alain Robbe-Grillet* (Paris: Les Editions de Minuit, 1973), 25–6.
53 While the novel's geographical location is never stated, it is reasonable to assume from the description of the climate and vegetation that it most likely takes place in the Caribbean or Africa.
54 Alain Robbe-Grillet, *Jealousy*, trans. Richard Howard (New York: Grove Press, 1965), 52. Henceforth all references to these editions will be stated parenthetically in the text.
55 Leenhardt, *Lecture politique du roman*, 55, my translation.
56 Robbe-Grillet has also encouraged the identification between the narrator and the jealous husband in interviews: "In *La Jalousie* we see a narrator, an adult, Caucasian male who tries to maintain order. Moreover, he's a colonial plantation owner, that is, he belongs to the colonial system. Against him, limiting and destroying his power, we have the blacks, tropical vegetation, and his own wife, whose is suspected of maintaining a questionable relationship with the subversive world" (Leenhardt Robbe-Grillet, "Images and Texts: A Dialogue," trans. Karlis Racevskis, *Generative Literature and Generative Art*, ed. David Leach [Fredericton: York Press, 1983], 43).
57 Maurice Blanchot, *The Book to Come*, trans. Charlotte Mandell (Stanford: Stanford University Press, 2003), 261n1.
58 Ibid., 201.
59 Quoted in Lois Oppenheim, ed., *Three Decades of the French New Novel* (Chicago, IL: University of Illinois Press, 1986), 26, emphasis added.
60 Barthes, "The Last World on Robbe-Grillet?" 202.
61 Maurice Blanchot, *Space of Literature*, trans. Ann Smock (Lincoln: University of Nebraska Press, 1982), 203.
62 Barthes, "The Last Word on Robbe-Grillet?" 202.
63 Maurice Blanchot, *The Infinite Conversation*, trans. Susan Hanson (Minneapolis, MN: University of Minnesota Press, 1993), 320.
64 Maurice Blanchot, *The Writing of Disaster*, trans. Ann Smock (Lincoln: University of Nebraska Press, 1986), 101. Compare the Blanchotian reading to the Barthesian text of *jouissance*: "the text that imposes a state of loss, the text that discomforts

(perhaps to the point of a certain boredom), unsettles the reader's historical, cultural, psychological assumptions, the consistency of his tastes, values, memories, brings to a crisis his relation with language" (Barthes, *The Pleasure of the Text*, 14). Is a Blanchotian reading "without *jouissance*" as well? By associating jouissance with boredom, Barthes seems at once to repeat Blanchot and exceed him. *Jouissance* is not in the business of nurturing the readerly ego; boredom points to the failure to instrumentalize the affect of *jouissance*—to the persistence of an overwhelming enjoyment.

65   Barthes, *The Pleasure of the Text*, 7.
66   Ibid., 32.
67   Jacques Derrida, "Following Theory," in *Life.After.Theory*, ed. Michael Payne and John Schad (New York: Continuum, 2003), 13–14.
68   Robbe-Grillet's "Order and Disorder in Film and Fiction," 12.
69   Compare with Harman's own list: "diamonds, rope, neutrons . . . armies, monsters, square circles, and leagues of real and fictitious armies" (Graham Harman, *The Quadruple Object* [Ropley: Zero Books, 2011], 5).
70   Robbe-Grillet, *For a New Novel*, 73.
71   Barthes, "Objective Literature," 14.
72   Leenhardt Robbe-Grillet, *Ghosts in the Mirror*, trans. Jo Levy (London: John Calder, 1988), 149.
73   The novel establishes a certain proximity between A . . . and the colonized other: "A . . . is humming a dance tune whose words remain unintelligible" (49). On the relation between A . . . and the world of the colonized, see Leenhardt, *Lecture politique du roman*, 99.
74   Ann Jefferson, *The Nouveau Roman and the Poetics of Fiction* (Cambridge: Cambridge University Press, 1980), 139.
75   Jameson, "Modernism and Its Repressed," 177.
76   Attridge, *The Singularity of Literature* (New York: Routledge, 2004), 49.
77   Robbe-Grillet, "Order and Disorder in Film and Fiction," 18–19.
78   Ibid., 11.

Bibliography

Attridge, Derek. *The Singularity of Literature*. New York: Routledge, 2004.
Barthes, Roland. "The Death of the Author." In *Image, Text, Music*. Trans. Stephen Heath. New York: Hill and Wang, 1977. 142–8.
Barthes, Roland. "The Last Word on Robbe-Grillet?" In *Critical Essays*. Trans. Richard Howard. Evanston: Northwestern University Press, 1972. 197–204.
Barthes, Roland. "Literal Literature." In *Critical Essays*. Trans. Richard Howard. Evanston: Northwestern University Press, 1972. 51–8.
Barthes, Roland. "Objective Literature." In *Critical Essays*. Trans. Richard Howard. Evanston: Northwestern University Press, 1972. 13–24.
Barthes, Roland. *The Pleasure of the Text*. Trans. Richard Miller. New York: The Noonday Press, 1975.
Barthes, Roland. "There Is No Robbe-Grillet School." In *Critical Essays*. Trans. Richard Howard. Evanston: Northwestern University Press, 1972. 91–5.

Blanchot, Maurice. *The Book to Come*. Trans. Charlotte Mandell. Stanford: Stanford University Press, 2003.
Blanchot, Maurice. *The Infinite Conversation*. Trans. Susan Hanson. Minneapolis, MN: University of Minnesota Press, 1993.
Blanchot, Maurice. *The Space of Literature*. Trans. Ann Smock. Lincoln: University of Nebraska Press, 1982.
Blanchot, Maurice. *The Writing of the Disaster*. Trans. Ann Smock. Lincoln: University of Nebraska Press, 1995.
Bryant, Levi R. *The Democracy of Objects*. Ann Arbor: Open Humanities Press, 2011.
Cohen, Jeffrey Jerome. *Stone: An Ecology of the Inhuman*. Minneapolis, MN: University of Minnesota Press, 2015.
Connor, Steven. "Thinking Things." *Textual Practice* 24.1 (2010): 1–20.
Culler, Jonathan D. *Barthes: A Very Short Introduction*. Oxford: Oxford University Press, 1983.
Culler, Jonathan D. "Barthes, Theorist." *The Yale Journal of Criticism* 14.2 (2001): 439–44.
Derrida, Jacques. "Following Theory." In *Life.After.Theory*. Ed. Michael Payne and John Schad. New York: Continuum, 2003. 1–51.
Gallop, Jane. "Beyond the *Jouissance* Principle." *Representations* 7 (1984): 110–15.
Harman, Graham. "The Battle of Objects and Subjects: Concerning Sbriglia and Žižek's *Subject Lessons* Anthology." *Open Philosophy* 3 (2020): 314–34.
Harman, Graham. *Guerrilla Metaphysics: Phenomenology and the Carpentry of Things*. Chicago: Open Court, 2005.
Harman, Graham. "Object-Oriented Ontology." In *The Palgrave Handbook of Posthumanism in Film and Television*. Ed. Michael Hauskeller, Curtis D. Carbonell, and Thomas D. Philbeck. Basingstoke: Palgrave Macmillan, 2015. 401–9.
Harman, Graham. *The Quadruple Object*. Ropley: Zero Books, 2011.
Harman, Graham. *Quentin Meillassoux: Philosophy in the Making*. Edinburgh: Edinburgh University Press, 2011.
Harman, Graham. *Weird Realism: Lovecraft and Philosophy*. Winchester: Zero Books, 2012.
Harman, Graham. "The Well-Wrought Broken Hammer: Object-Oriented Literary Criticism." *New Literary History* 43.2 (2012): 183–203.
Jameson, Fredric. "Modernism and Its Repressed; or, Robbe-Grillet as Anti-Colonist." In *The Ideologies of Theory: Essays, 1971–1986, volume 1*. Minneapolis, MN: University of Minnesota Press, 1988. 167–80.
Jefferson, Ann. *The Nouveau Roman and the Poetics of Fiction*. Cambridge: Cambridge University Press, 1980.
Leenhardt, Jacques. *Lecture politique du roman. La Jalousie d'Alain Robbe-Grillet*. Paris: Les Editions de Minuit, 1973.
Lovecraft, H. P. "The Call of Cthulhu." *Weird Tales* (1928). H. P. Lovecraft Archive. http://www.hplovecraft.com/writings/texts/fiction/cc.aspx.
Meillassoux, Quentin. *After Finitude: An Essay on the Necessity of Contingency*. Trans. Ray Brassier. New York: Continuum, 2008.
Meillassoux, Quentin. *Time Without Becoming*. Ed. Anna Longo. Haverton: Mimesis International, 2014.
Morrissette, Bruce. *The Novels of Robbe-Grillet*. Ithaca: Cornell University Press, 1975.
Robbe-Grillet, Alain. *For a New Novel: Essays on Fiction*. Trans. Richard Howard. Evanston: Northwestern University Press, 1996. 15–24.

Robbe-Grillet, Alain. *Ghosts in the Mirror*. Trans. Jo Levy. London: John Calder, 1988.
Robbe-Grillet, Alain. "Images and Texts: A Dialogue." Trans. Karlis Racevskis. In *Generative Literature and Generative Art*. Ed. David Leach. Fredericton NB: York Press, 1983. 38–47.
Robbe-Grillet, Alain. *Jealousy*. Trans. Richard Howard. New York: Grove Press, 1965.
Robbe-Grillet, Alain. "Order and Disorder in Film and Fiction." Trans. Bruce Morrissette. *Critical Inquiry* 4.1 (1977): 1–20.
Sbriglia, Russel and Slavoj Žižek. "Introduction: Subject Matters." In *Subject Lessons: Hegel, Lacan, and the Future of Materialism*. Ed. Russel Sbriglia and Slavoj Žižek. Evanston: Northwestern University Press, 2020. 3–28.
Zalloua, Zahi. *Reading Unruly: Interpretation and Its Ethical Demands*. Lincoln: University of Nebraska Press, 2014.

11

Orpheus Turning

The Reader to Come in *Camera Lucida*

Daniel T. O'Hara

Orpheus' music and grief so moved Hades, king of the underworld, that he was allowed to take Eurydice with him back to the world of life and light. Hades set one condition, however: upon leaving the land of death, both Orpheus and Eurydice were forbidden to look back.[1]

Harold Bloom, before he died on October 14, 2019, ends the first, hundred page-plus chapter of the final book he saw through the press, *Take Arms Against a Sea of Troubles*, with the following sentence, separated off as its own paragraph: "Ancient theurgy was a praxis by which a god or gods could be summoned, maintained, and even created."[2] We see this praxis at work at the conclusion of W. B. Yeats's "Ego Dominus Tuus" ("I Your Lord"), a 1915 poem first published as part of his occult avatar of Dante's *Vita Nuova*, *Per Amica Silentia Lunae*, also a mixture of verse and prose, celebrating and lamenting the fate of love and its haunting remainder:

> Hic. Why should you leave the lamp
> Burning alone beside an open book,
> And trace these characters upon the sands?
> A style is found by sedentary toil
> And by the imitation of great masters.
> Ille. Because I seek an image, not a book.
> Those men that in their writings are most wise,
> Own nothing but their blind, stupefied hearts.
> I call to the mysterious one who yet
> Shall walk the wet sands by the edge of the stream
> And look most like me, being indeed my double,
> And prove of all imaginable things
> The most unlike, being my anti-self,
> And, standing by these characters, disclose

> All that I seek; and whisper it as though
> He were afraid the birds, who cry aloud
> Their momentary cries before it is dawn,
> Would carry it away to blasphemous men.³

Yeats practices what I would call "occult modernism."⁴ This is the form of modernism that, lacking a transcendental spiritual horizon of traditional Christian faith, cobbles together from many contemporary and ancient sources of ancient wisdom to guide one through the travails of life made worse by secular modernity and science. In this last stanza, the visionary part of Yeats, christened *Ille* (Latin for "That There"), explains for his more modern half *Hic* (Latin for "This Here") as to why he is practicing the ancient art of theurgy, of summoning the Daimon, as Yeats calls it, to clarify and unify—in a more encompassing reading of the poet and his world than is available to him at the time of the poem—all the broken pieces of life. Such an Image or Mask—terms Yeats also uses—is of all things not impossible the most difficult to envision and conjure into existence,

> the mysterious one who yet
> Shall walk the wet sands by the edge of the stream
> And look most like me, being indeed my double,
> And prove of all imaginable things
> The most unlike, being my anti-self⁵

I begin with this excursion mostly into Yeats (and a bit of Bloom) because what I call occult modernism continues broadly across modernity and persistently up to the present day precisely as a rhetorical/psychological practice whereby a modern writer may discover what he or she needs most to continue writing. More amateurish than professional, more motiveless flailing at times, this practice of vision best encompasses and clarifies the core passages of Roland Barthes's last text, *Camera Lucida*, such as, most centrally and memorably, "in her very illness, I had engendered my mother."⁶ Certainly, this is a visionary emanation, not bodily engendering, about which I will speak more later.

Another way to conceive this psycho-rhetorical-magical practice is to recall the broken dialectic of German Romanticism, in literature and philosophy. This means entertaining for experiment's sake the idea that Hegel may be right about the German Romantics, that time and time again they divide a subject into opposites and then use the paradigm of opposition to blow up all possible realistic reconciliations, instead dreaming up a vision of phantasmic or utopian resolution to become available in the future, personal or social, that they are prophesizing, with tragically arrogant or despairingly absurd consequences.⁷ This interrupted dialectic pervades explicitly Roland Barthes's own thinking and writing, as he derives it from the linguistic paradigm of ever-imposed binary oppositions, from signifier/signified onwards to *Studium/Punctum* of *Camera Lucida*.⁸ For Barthes, as we will see, the linguistic paradigm of binarism inspires his constructive and deconstructive moves.

Another brief example of this ironic dialectic at work is the anecdote on the French edition's back cover, which I discuss later in more detail. The gist is that a Tibetan Sage responds to a disciple who, noticing his Master's grief over his son's death, reminds his Teacher that he has taught repeatedly that all Reality is Illusion. The Master's response to his doubting Thomas of a disciple is to reaffirm his teaching before adding that his son's death is "Super-Illusion." Here, the opposition of Reality and Illusion is metonymically displaced rather than metaphorically resolved by a concrete synthesis found in some existing institution, a la Hegel's resolution of freedom and authority in the Prussian state. The metonymic displacement is here the trope of "Super-Illusion." Such a trope or image holds open the space of resolution for whatever utopian alternative may arise as chance and imagination determine. We will see this particular trope when discussing the differences between the French and English versions of the text.

Barthes begins, in *Camera Lucida*, as any modern French thinker might, by dismissing all previous authorities, artists, or scholars, or cultural historians, and declaring from his own assumed position of apparently innocent neutrality that he is not sure "that Photography existed," by which he means he has had "a genius of its own."[9] This is the Cartesian gesture par excellence, the quintessential modern gesture. Unlike his predecessors, Barthes also declares his "uneasiness."[10] Although he wants to be "a primitive without culture,"[11] innocent of all opposing complicities in the modern history of arguments about Photography (Barthes capitalizes the allegorical personae in his quest-romance), Barthes confesses that he cannot help but be a subject "torn between two languages: one expressive, the other critical."[12] The critical language, he goes on to say (and will demonstrate), is composed by the three discourses he is uneasily haunted by, "sociology, semiology, and psychoanalysis,"[13] almost from the beginning of his career, even as semiology is the discourse he has famously contributed to the most. This is why he says then he can only "bear witness" to his own responses as he adopts "a desperate resistance to any reductive system."[14] Barthes claims, after Nietzsche, the figure he will also basically conclude with, "the ego's 'ancient sovereignty.'"[15] Rather than I think therefore I am, I am therefore I feel. In this manner, he promises "to take only himself as mediator" in quest to discover "a mathesis singularis," which he admits is a bizarre notion.[16] While the *Studium* is the cultural archive, the *Punctum* is the individual imaginary of the photograph.

Barthes then divides Photography into three kinds of action: "to do, to undergo, and to look,"[17] and assigns the personae or roles to be played, accordingly: Operator, Spectrum, and Spectator. Rather than call the object in the photograph the Subject, he prefers Spectrum because the photographer shoots the target of the photograph because of the original action of light. He wants repeatedly to underscore the material basis of photography, its basis in the operation of light as a carnal medium upon chemicals (silver nitrates) to produce and carry the emanations from the Referent at the scene of the shoot to the future spectator of the picture, who is thus literally touched. The spectrum of the light waves, a material phantasm, really comes from the past, impacting the spectator of the future in this cosmic and atomic "alchemy" or "magic."[18] Barthes will recur to this dimension of photography again and again.

Turning to himself as Spectrum, Barthes notes the importance of the photograph, in its very temporal movement, as a sharp reminder of death, a "microcosm" of death.[19] Each snapshot is "a little death," for real. Whatever pleasure the photograph may bring, its certain pastness previews the subject's ultimate immobility, its passing to come. The click of the camera may no longer be heard by the Spectrum, in Barthes's vision, save in memory, even as the light, as from a distant star (he cites Sontag's then recent book), still strikes the Spectator's eye, but especially when they are one and the same as both Spectrum and Operator, as in Mapplethorpe's self-portraits. In short, Death's selfie.

Barthes always invents as part of his technique of analysis grand opposing opposites or binaries, following the semiological paradigm of language with its division of the sign into signifier/signified. For Photography, Barthes draws upon his Latin imaginative usage for the *Studium* and the *Punctum*. As deconstruction teaches, all binaries are weighted in their opposition, with one of them being favored over the other in the pair. Any analysis is rigged from the start, unless the critic immediately searches for a third element, which usually gives rise to another pair, and so on. Such reflexiveness pervades Barthes. Nonetheless, in terms of the plot of *Camera Lucida*, especially in Part 1, the *Punctum* outweighs for him the *Studium* the way Godzilla would Bambi. The forty-eight sections, arranged in 24 (Part 1)/24 (Part 2) in the original French edition, mark the number of days spent composting the text, even as Part 2 would deconstruct Part 1 step by step in reverse, a movement Barthes reiterates when he reverses the chronological order of his mother's photographs.

The *Studium/Punctum* pair are like ironic versions of Gestalt psychology's elementary figure/ground opposition with an important revision. The figure/ground analytic scheme is itself a version of the part/whole one; in fact, it is most like the center and circumference variant. The *Studium/Punctum* division is less strict, blurring the lines, as Barthes often does. The former is best thought of as the cultural context the spectator brings to the viewing of a photograph, the cultural capital, thanks to the spectator's educational training. The latter, the *Punctum*, breaks (or punctuate) the *Studium*.

> This time it is not I who seek out [the *Punctum*] (as I invent the field of the *Studium* with my sovereign consciousness) it is the element which rises from the scene, shoots out an arrow, and pierces me. A Latin word exists to designate this wound, this prick, this mark made by a pointed instrument: points, *Punctum*: sting, speck, cut, little hole—and also cast of the dice. A photograph's *Punctum* is that accident which pricks me (but also bruises me, is poignant to me).[20]

This binary in photography, for Barthes, can make for "a kind of primitive theater, a kind of Tableau Vivant," a contest of opposite drives in one thing, "a [phantasmatic] figuration of the motionless and the made-up face beneath which we see the dead,"[21] as if in the photographic portrait especially we are seeing the actor from a Noh drama, much as Yeats does in his most famous plays, such as *At the Hawk's Well*.

In relating Barthes to Yeats, I note the analogies, not necessarily the direct operation of influence. For the Noh drama provides Barthes with the imagery on the basis of which he reads his favorite photos, finding in them interesting, if often finally boring, instances of the *Studium*, a recognition scene in which he learns nothing new about the world or himself. In a few of them, however, he finds, as if it were given to him in an act of secular grace, a miracle, the wounding of his soul by a chance partial object of the photograph in question. Neither the intentional invention of the photographer's art, nor the already known detail from the cultural archive, the suddenly revealed epiphanic *Punctum* pierces him to the point of what he terms "the photographic ecstasy."[22] "The Photographer's 'second sight' does not consist in 'seeing' but in being there. And above all, in imitating Orpheus, he must not turn back to look at what he is leading—what he is giving to me."[23] Depending on how we envision this scene, Barthes is playing the role of Apollo, Orpheus's father, in one mythic variant, or that of Hades, or Death. Given the imperative injunction, one would automatically assume the former alternative; however, as the text continues, this reader must wonder. Here is the French: "Le yoyance du Photograph ne consiste pas a 'voir' mais a se trouver la. Et surtout, imitating Orpheus, qu'il ne retourne pas sur ce qu' il conduit et me donne."[24]

I have quoted this passage in the original French because it clearly but quietly shows why Barthes's last investigation, as he calls it, later needs a new English translation. Generally speaking, Richard Howard's translations of Barthes, while never judged perfect—what translation can be—have been found to be correct, fluent, and even eloquent. In this last one, however, there are many problems, too many to detail here. In this passage, *voyance* means being able to see what is not physically sensible, perceivable as in the spiritualist or occult mind reading. "Second Sight" is a colloquial or slang expression for such clairvoyance that downplays the romantic visionary dimension, but there is no indication that Barthes wants such an emphasis. What Howard does here is what he does throughout: he softens all sharpness, colloquializes all formalities. As with the publisher's removal of the anecdote from *Pratique de la voie tibetaine*, the back cover, as well as the only color photograph from the first page, Howard's translation seeks to make Barthes more palatable for an even larger popular audience than that which made *A Lover's Discourse* a big hit. In the aforementioned passage, clairvoyance, rather than second sight, registers the seriousness of the occult penumbra, rather than makes it easier to absorb it into the background noise of pop culture. To clarify about the missing anecdote, it presents the Tibetan Sage Marpa's response to one of his disciples who, seeing his master apparently grieving his son's death, asks, since you always have told us all is illusion, is not the death of your son also an illusion? Marpa responds, saying certainly, but the death of my son is a super-illusion.[25] We will return to this anecdote later.

A good, brief example of the *Punctum* at work (before turning to the Winter Garden Photograph's powerful effects on Barthes) is Lewis H. Hine's 1924 portrait of "two retarded children at an institution in New Jersey." Barthes remarks:

> hardly see the monstrous heads and pathetic profiles (which belong to the *Studium*); what I see . . . [as the *Punctum*] is the off-center detail, the little boy's huge Danton collar, the girl's finger bandage; I am a primitive, a child or a maniac; I dismiss all culture, I refuse to inherit anything from another eye than my own.[26]

The *Punctum* is this piercing off-center detail—Mapplethorpe's open left hand at the edge of the photograph, his young man's hirsute face and partially clothed body all the way to the other edge, half-hidden by the picture's limit. Barthes is pierced, wounded by "the right degree of openness" here in the hand, "the right density of abandonment." Similarly, with every *Punctum*. Unlike pornography, say, which shows all but does not generously give anything away, any part of itself, the *Punctum* of the open hand, the overlarge collar, the bandaged finger, embodies Eros itself, "the Kairos of desire." Even as they trigger deeply piercing affect, such details are real features of the photographs whose poignant resonance arrive after the snap.

Barthes finishes off Part 1, twenty-four sections with titles on the contents page only, making what he calls his palinode. This reflexive ironic move is typical of him, as of modernism generally. He always calls critical attention to his structures, his designs or deliberate lack of them, as in his final lectures where alphabetical order replaces any other or haiku fragments dominate. Barthes aims to disabuse his readers of their assumptions about both the things he is investigating and his relationship to his findings. All analytic objects and results are provisional, improvised, open to revision, not natural but could have been otherwise. Part 2 in the original French edition also has twenty-four sections, the mirror image of the first, only devoted, apparently to revoking what he has said in Part 1, or at least presenting a parallel image of it. For some reason, though, Howard removes the last number from Part 2, instead opting for a blank space and what then appears as a coda, an afterthought. This change misses the point of the palinode terminology Barthes is at pains to present in the last section of Part 1. For a palinode is a recantation, a singing again, intended to take back, revoke, section by section, what he has elaborated under the aegis of a casual phenomenology of pleasure (despite his dedication: "In homage to *L'Imaginaire* by Jean-Paul Sartre"), which is too much a hedonic project for him now. Instead, in recanting what came before, Part 2, less point by point than in an equally casual manner, will demonstrate the affective play of love and death in ethical and self-creative terms, what he says are "the pangs of love,"[27] his original suffering, not pleasure of any sort occasioned by his mother's actual and his own foreseen death.

One evening in November, not so long after his mother's death, "engulfing"[28] himself in her photographs, he finds neither the right photographic performance of her essence nor the "livening resurrection of the beloved face."[29] Barthes then turns over the forgotten Winter Garden Photograph. It shows his mother as a five-year-old, in 1898, standing next to her seven-year-old brother. They are posed within the glassed-in garden, standing before and leaning against, respectively, a fence rail, his mother holding the finger of one hand in the other, urged a bit forward of her brother, Barthes imagines, by the photographer to show his shoot at its best.

Barthes goes on to claim that he sees "the genius of the beloved face"[30] in this previously overlooked photograph he has never previously studied. Its "discretion" of regard for him is the highest "civil value" beyond common mores or aesthetic concerns.[31] "A figure of sovereign innocence," in the original etymological sense of doing no harm, his mother does not "suppose herself," embodying instead the paradox of "the assertion of a gentleness."[32] At five, and for all the later years Barthes knows her, she possesses, he repeats, "this sovereign innocence,"³³ an "out-of-play" exemption, a neutrality that he feels and receives from this photograph as a virtual act of secular grace.

These are extraordinary visionary, even occult-tinged claims. Why make them? Here are more such claims, which may offer a clue:

> For once, photography (in the Winter Garden Photograph) gave me a sentiment as certain as a remembrance, just as Proust experiences it one day when, leaning over to take off his boots, there suddenly came to him his grandmother's "true face," "whose living reality I was experiencing for the first time, in an involuntary and complete memory."³⁴

The blending of Barthes's and Proust's languages tells a lot, even as knowing that Proust uses the grandmother in the novel often as a substitute for his own actual mother. Although or perhaps precisely because Barthes claims that his vision of photography's essence (as revealed by the Winter Garden Photograph) inspires his "photographic ecstasy," this experience is not at all Proustian because it need not depend, as herein, upon on actual remembrance. Barthes would thereby reinvent photography as an antithetical remembrance. It is also, and I would stress, primarily a belated failed revision of Proust, whose evocation Barthes would use so as to transume his favorite precursor, even as Barthes risks being in turn undone by Proust's grander troping in his monumental novel. Proust continues in his own distinctive voice:

> [I was] imperiously required to seek out the cause of this happiness . . . and certainty [of involuntary memory] . . . . I began to divine this cause as I compared these varied impressions . . . all of which, the sound of the spoon on the plate, the uneven flagstones, the taste of the madeleine, had something in common, I was experiencing in the present moment and *at the same time in a moment far away*, so that the past was made to encroach upon the present and make one uncertain about which of the two [moments] I was in; the truth was that the being within me, this impression was enjoying it because of something shared between a day in the past and the present moment, something extratemporal, and this being appeared only when, through one of these moments of identity between the present and the past, it was able to find itself in the only milieu in which it could live and enjoy the essence of things, that is to say, outside of time.³⁵

This passage from Proust allows Barthes to confirm in his mind that the snapshots of involuntary memory in his predecessor's "culture of redemption" (as Leo Bersani christens it)³⁶ are not the same as the photographic punctum as summed up in the Winter Garden Photograph. Ironically, however, Barthes's reader cannot even consult memory, willingly or not, to match the poignant details with the actual photograph for Barthes suppresses it, excusing such action as preserving the punctum effects for himself alone and protecting them from the profanation of strange eyes that cannot experience the wound of the punctum. Although there is nothing actually prohibiting someone who never knew Barthes's mother from experiencing a punctum of his or her own, only being unable to experience the same one as Barthes, who clearly hopes his writing will best convey otherwise. "The Winter Garden Photograph was indeed essential, it achieved for me, utopically, the impossible science of the unique being."[37] With this utopic trope of his Barthes would trump Proust's grand trope of "the being within." Reprojecting this Proustian trope of involuntary memory, Barthes would push to the forefront the invisible perfection—to anyone's but his eyes—of the Winter Garden Photograph. If successful, this troping upon trope with his last slender volume would mean he had subsumed, transumptively, the 3,000-plus page Proustian tome—tomb?—of a novel. Does Barthes prove successful?

Chapter 29 "The Little Girl," as I read it, returns a big, albeit heartfelt, "No!" To put it a bit gnomically, Barthes, after finding Death in each and every photograph, including his own and in the invisible Winter Garden Photograph of his own five-year-old mother-to-be, containing supposedly the essence of photography itself, would give birth to her as a child from "the pricking" he received from his chance viewing of it one night in November 1977. He thereby wittingly declares "dead" his revisionary aspiration to sacrifice all others, even himself, that she might transcend time itself. Barthes knows he has tragically failed in his quest behind the quest of discovering photography's essence. Here are the relevant snippets to this effect from an even longer passage conveniently spliced together:

> Nor could I omit from my reflection: that I had discovered this photograph by moving back through Time. . . . I stare intensely at the Sovereign Good of Childhood, of the mother, of the mother-as-child. . . . [I]t was at this moment that everything turned around and I discovered her *as into herself*. . . . During her illness, I nursed her, held the bowl of tea she had liked because it was easier to drink from than from a cup; she had become my little girl, uniting for me with that essential child she was in her first photograph. . . . Ultimately, I experienced her, strong as she had been, my inner law, as my feminine child. Which was my way of resolving Death. If as so many philosophers have said Death is the harsh victory of the race, that the particular owes for the satisfaction of the universal, if after having been reproduced as other than himself, the individual dies, having thereby denied and transcended himself, I who had not procreated, I had, in her very illness, engendered my mother. . . . My particularity could never again universalize itself (unless, utopically, by writing, whose project henceforth would become the unique goal of my life). From now on I would no more than await my total, undialectical death.[38]

The ghost of Hegel, of course, reeks throughout this passage. The final nail in his own coffin, however, is the last sentence of the section, separated off in both the English and French versions: "That is what I read in the Winter Garden Photograph."[39] That is, Death, his own death most of all.

Proust's philosophy of involuntary memory, borrowed from Bergson or not, has thus ironically trumped, after all, over Barthes's aspiration, since we (as well as

Barthes) can understand him here only if we use Proust as the ground plan of his would-be higher and farther leaps. To put it more starkly: Barthes can only triumph by envisioning the most profane vision of them all, even worse than that of Proust, as offered by Gide, who would get off in a male brothel when masturbating only at the climax of the spectacle of two half-starved rats savaging each other to the death in a cage whose floor is covered by a photographic portrait of his mother's smiling face; Barthes envisions that he engenders his mother-as-child, whose sovereign innocence is sealed off by this revisionary horror of incest in reverse, this self-begetting phantasmagoria in the extreme. Barthes's would-be triumph must be presented by reference to Proustian memory.[40] Thus, Barthes, a la Yeats in "Ego Dominus Tuus," summons his daemonic reader, Proust-Death. Rather than coming to bring knowledge of the magical rituals of self-divinization or theurgy, Barthes's daemon is the reader par excellence to come for him, Death itself.

Given the unabashedly Proustian nature of these aforementioned passages, in which the Winter Garden Photograph acts as a prothesis for the earlier moment of memory even as the near mystical, occult phantasm drawn out of Mallarmé's hymn to poetic eternity and immortality acts as surrogate for the present moment, we are left with the anterior future of Death in the person of Barthes himself—playing Hades to his own would-be Orpheus—and nursing his own sovereignly innocent and therefore repressively sinful mother as child. Instead of transuming Proust, that is, reinternalizing the returning dead precursor, eating this awful offal, Barthes produces a mish-mosh as or even more horrible, ready for any convenient cistern. Compare Barthes's clusterfuck of engendering his own mother as child/child as mother with Proust in his fluent imaginative creation of visionary proportions:

> At most I noted incidentally that the differences ... between the real impression— that difference why a uniform depiction of life cannot be a good likeness— was probably because the slightest word ... the most insignificant action was surrounded by and was a reflection of things ... in the middle of which—here the pink reflection of the evening on the flowered-covered wall of a country restaurant, a feeling of hunger, the desire for women, the pleasure of luxury—there, the blue scrolls of the morning sea enveloping the musical phrases which partially emerge from them lie the shoulders of mermaids—the gesture, the simplest action remains enclosed as within a thousand sealed vessels.[41]

Admittedly, Barthes does draw upon Mallarmé's poetic strength, citing the opening lines of "The Tomb of Edgar Poe": "Such as into Himself at last eternity changes him," omitting "Himself" for obvious reasons when referring to his five-year-old mother's piercing effect. But the previous Proust passage anticipates Barthes's late discussions of the *Punctum*'s elements of bodily gesture, musical air, and phantasmatic madness. Besides, Barthes's bizarre Poe allusion, a writer we know celebrated and was horrified by incest of all kinds, confirms him in the lineage of decadent symbolist modernism. The mystery of the self-begotten divinity makes for me the best, most appropriate mythic allusion for this volume, that of Orpheus, as if turning the mirror of the

Camera Lucida; so, wherever it points, there appears sunlight (hence the French title *La Chambre Claire* as opposed to "the dark room" of photography), and wherever he turns to look, there appears the vision of Death itself, Hades in person, receiving mother/child/son in his engulfing embrace. Barthes's ironic self-image, of course, is soon-to-be literalized for him by time's winged van.

It would be smugly satisfying to conclude on this ironic note, this fatal pratfall, but as Barthes continues to discuss the musical "air" and the "look" of the Winter Garden Photograph as the paradigm of photography's essential *Punctum*-effect, he progressively shreds more vertiginously, ever more maddeningly, phantasmatic features that are themselves disintegrating, even as they lead him from a Cartesianism into a revisionary stance displacing cognition by sentiment, on to his imitation of Rousseau's famous celebration of pity. Barthes would even transume, in the end, the master-critic of pity Nietzsche himself, as he would apparently embrace this suspect virtue with a vengeance (despite his critically framing homage to Sartre and Tibetan Sage) as the defining pathos of modernity itself and its quintessential medium of expression photography:

> I collected in a last thought the images which had "pricked" me (since this is the actions of the *Punctum*), like that of the black woman with the golden necklace and strapped pumps. In each of them, inescapably, I passed beyond the unreality of the thing represented. I entered crazily into the spectacle, into the image, taking into my arms what is dead, what is going to die, as Nietzsche did when . . . on January 3, 1889, he threw himself in tears on the neck of a beaten horse [pulling a junk van]: gone mad, for Pity's sake.[42]

What can one say? If all the associations of Nietzsche's name Roland Barthes would summon up here, only the pure obscenity of white noise can be the likely result. Unlike Barthes, who discovers his Ariadne in the photograph of his dead mother as a five-year-old amid the labyrinth of photography's essences and geniuses, his best reader, lacking a muse, is no doubt still to come—and doubling then as his anti-self: "I shall find the dark grow luminous, the void fruitful when I know I have nothing, that the ringers in the tower have appointed for the soul a passing-bell."[43]

Notes

1 The Editors of Encyclopaedia Britannica, "Orpheus: Greek Mythology," *Encyclopaedia Britannica*, February 5, 2020, https://www.britannica.com/topic/Orpheus-Greek-mythology. Accessed January 20, 2021.
2 Bloom, Harold, *Take Arms Against a Sea of Troubles: The Power of the Reader's Mind Over a Universe of Death* (New Haven, CT: Yale University Press, 2020), 123.
3 W. B. Yeats, *The Collected Works of W. B. Yeats, Vol. I: The Poems*, Revised ed., ed. Richard J. Finneran (New York: Simon & Schuster, 1989), 203.
4 "Occult modernism" is a term I am using in light of Tobias Churton, *Occult Paris: The Lost Magic of the Belle Epoque* (Rochester, VT: Inner Traditions, 2016). The

origins of modernism in this period, including Yeats but also Proust and via him upon musicians and composers and actors, clearly influenced Barthes.
5   Yeats, *The Collected Works of W. B. Yeats*, 203.
6   Barthes, Roland, *Camera Lucida: Reflections on Photography*, trans. Richard Howard (New York: Vintage Classics, 2020), 85. Originally published in French as *La Chambre Claire* by Editions du Seuil 1980. This translation was first published in the United States by Hill and Wang in 1981. As I will note, this translation is more flawed than it might appear, beginning with the title, which literally in English is "the bright room" pivoting off of "the dark room," which at the time is so much associated with photography. Although a title of one of the later sections, "camera lucida" refers to a device once used to take a picture, not develop it. Barthes was dead before Richard Howard took up the translation duties.
7   Still the best analysis of the interrupted dialectic of the German Romantics (the Schlegel brothers and their circle) remains Soren Kierkegaard, *The Concept of Irony, with Constant Reference to Socrates/Schelling Lecture Notes: Kierkegaard's Writings, II*, vol. two, ed. and trans. Howard V. Hong and Edna H. Hong (Princeton, NJ: Princeton University Press, 1992).
8   The most useful studies of Barthes and to which I am happily indebted are, in his favorite alphabetical order, the following: Thomas Baldwin, *Roland Barthes: The Proust Variations* (Liverpool: Liverpool University Press, 2019); Geoffrey Batchen, ed., *Photography Degree Zero: Reflections on Roland Barthes's Camera Lucida* (Cambridge, MA: MIT Press, 2009); Jacques Derrida, "The Deaths of Roland Barthes," In *The Work of Mourning*, trans. Pascale-Anne Brault and Michael Naas (Chicago, IL: University of Chicago Press, 2001); Jean-Michel Rabaté, ed., *Writing the Image After Roland Barthes* (Philadelphia: University of Pennsylvania Press, 1997); and Nancy Shawcross, *Roland Barthes on Photography: The Critical Tradition in Perspective* (Gainsville: University Press of Florida, 1997). I am particularly indebted for my main title to Beryl Scholassman, "The Descent of Orpheus: On Reading Barthes and Proust," in *Writing the Image after Roland Barthes*, ed. Jean-Michel Rabaté (Philadelphia: University of Pennsylvania Press, 1997), 144–62. We reach different conclusions to say the least, and I make use of the mythic variations more to highlight the ambiguity of the image of Orpheus not in his descent as in his ascent—will he turn toward Eurydice and watch her thereby dissolve into smoke, will he turn only to the Sun, Apollo, his father, will he turn in a modern variation back to Hades to confront him madly on his loss? The image of Orpheus turning may even suggest his forbidden gaze of looking back lands upon the reader.
9   Barthes, *Camera Lucida*, 3.
10   Ibid., 9.
11   Ibid.
12   Ibid.
13   Ibid.
14   Ibid.
15   Ibid.
16   Ibid, 10.
17   Ibid.
18   Ibid.
19   Ibid., 11.
20   Ibid., 33.

21 Ibid., 31.
22 Ibid., 59–61.
23 Ibid., 58.
24 Roland Barthes, *La chambre claire: note sur la photographie* (Paris: Editions du Seuil, 1980), 80.
25 Ibid., cover 4.
26 Barthes, *Camera Lucida*, 61.
27 Ibid., 77.
28 Ibid., 76.
29 Ibid.
30 Ibid., 79.
31 Ibid., 80.
32 Ibid., 82.
33 Ibid., 84.
34 Ibid., 83.
35 Marcel Proust, *Finding Time Again*, trans. and intro. Ian Patterson (London: Allen Lane/Penguin, 2002), 178. Although *Time Regained* is a more effective title, Patterson's translation *Finding Time Again* overall works better I have found. I am also much indebted to Christopher Prendergast, *Mirages and Mad Beliefs: Proust the Skeptic* (Princeton, NJ: Princeton University Press, 2013).
36 Bersani argues forcefully against what he calls "the culture of redemption." This is the artistic and critical practice of responding to the death of the God and the subsequent nihilism by aspiring, romantically even, into the postmodern age, to use art to fabricate new saving myths, particularly the myth of transforming the materials of life into visions of idealistic glories. Abrams in *Natural Supernaturalism* argues for the positive valuation of this legacy.
37 Barthes, *Camera Lucida*, 83.
38 Ibid., 85–7.
39 Ibid., 87.
40 The figurative snapshots of memory, like the reanimated mother-child of the Winter Garden Photograph, are more mirror images than self-cancelling detritus of any critiqued cultural of redemption. William C. Carter, *Proust in Love* (New Haven, CT: Yale University Press, 2006), 196, rehearses the Andre Gide anecdote summarized here.
41 Proust, *Finding Time Again*, 178.
42 Barthes, *Camera Lucida*, 142.
43 W. B. Yeats, *Per Amica Silentia Lunae* (Project Gutenberg, 2010), 29, www.gutenberg.org/ebooks/33338.

Bibliography

Abrams, M. H. *Natural Supernaturalism: Tradition and Revolution in Romantic Literature*. New York: Norton, 1971.

Baldwin, Thomas. *Roland Barthes: The Proust Variations*. Liverpool: Liverpool University Press, 2019.

Barthes, Roland. *Camera Lucida: Reflections on Photography*. Trans. Richard Howard. New York: Vintage Classics, 2020.

Barthes, Roland. *La chambre claire: Note sur la photographie*. Paris: Editions du Seuil, 1980.

Batchen, Geoffrey, ed. *Photography Degree Zero: Reflections on Roland Barthes's Camera Lucida*. Cambridge, MA: MIT Press, 2009.

Bersani, Leo. *The Culture of Redemption*. Cambridge, MA: Harvard University Press, 1990.

Bloom, Harold. *Take Arms Against a Sea of Troubles: The Power of the Reader's Mind Over a Universe of Death*. New Haven, CT: Yale University Press, 2020.

Carter, William C. *Proust in Love*. New Haven, CT: Yale University Press, 2006.

Churton, Tobias. *Occult Paris: The Lost Magic of the Belle Epoque*. Rochester, VT: Inner Traditions, 2016.

Derrida, Jacques. "The Deaths of Roland Barthes." In *The Work of Mourning*. Trans. Pascale-Anne Brault and Michael Naas. Chicago, IL: University of Chicago Press, 2001. 31–68.

The Editors of Encyclopaedia Britannica. "Orpheus: Greek Mythology." *Encyclopaedia Britannica*, 5 February 2020. https://www.britannica.com/topic/Orpheus-Greek-mythology.

Kierkegaard, Soren. *The Concept of Irony, with Constant Reference to Socrates/Schelling Lecture Notes: Kierkegaard's Writings, II*, vol. 2. Ed. and trans. Howard V. Hong and Edna H. Hong. Princeton, NJ: Princeton University Press, 1992.

Mallarmé, Stéphane. "The Tomb of Edgar Poe." Trans. by Peter Manson. The Poetry Society, 2013. https://poetrysociety.org.uk/poems/the-tomb-of-edgar-poe/.

Prendergast, Christopher. *Mirages and Mad Beliefs: Proust the Skeptic*. Princeton, NJ: Princeton University Press, 2013.

Proust, Marcel. *Finding Time Again*. Trans. and intro., Ian Patterson. Gen. Ed. Christopher Prendergast. London: Allen Lane/Penguin, 2002.

Rabaté, Jean-Michel, ed. *Writing the Image after Roland Barthes*. Philadelphia: University of Pennsylvania Press, 1997.

Scholassman, Beryl. "The Descent of Orpheus: On Reading Barthes and Proust." In *Writing the Image after Roland Barthes*. Ed. Jean-Michel Rabaté. Philadelphia: University of Pennsylvania Press, 1997. 144–62.

Shawcross, Nancy. *Roland Barthes on Photography: The Critical Tradition in Perspective*. Gainsville: University Press of Florida, 1997.

Yeats, W. B. *The Collected Works of W. B. Yeats, Vol. I: The Poems*. Revised ed. Ed. Richard J. Finneran. New York: Simon & Schuster, 1989.

Yeats, W. B. *Per Amica Silentia Lunae*. Project Gutenberg, 2010. www.gutenberg.org/ebooks/33338.

12

No Wish to "Understand" nor to "Grasp"

Opacity in the Work of Roland Barthes and Édouard Glissant

Andy Stafford

Transparence needs to be combatted everywhere.

Édouard Glissant[1]

"Understanding," isn't it a modern virus?

Roland Barthes[2]

Introduction: Opacity in the Dialectic of Language

In a reminiscence toward the end of his life about his friendship with Roland Barthes, the Moroccan sociologist Abdelkébir Khatibi described an intriguing and regular exchange: "Barthes would say to me privately, in response to a reproach frequently made to him: 'When someone tells me to *be clear*, what they really mean is *be like me.*'"[3] Revealing not so much a tetchy theorist of semiotics as an astute commentator on interpersonal relations, the retort from Barthes summarized two decades of critical—and often complex—research on language. From the 1950s to the 1970s, he had worked extensively to account for how communication between humans operated, in all its forms and media, by locating semiology within political, ideological, and social realities. However, by the mid-1970s, at the height of his career, Barthes began to theorize the self within this language nexus. The demand for his work to have "clarity" in the very language that he used to describe how language operated hid a more troubling phenomenon: how linguistic exchange seemed to *force* the self into the straitjacket held by the Other. The interpersonal skills of communication in modern life had become an illness—a virus (to reinforce our own experience of pandemics in the twenty-first century)—that made "understanding" into what Fredric Jameson called "the prison-house of language."[4]

At almost exactly the same time as Barthes moved to theorize the self, the Martinican and French poet and novelist Édouard Glissant was drafting his magnum opus on Caribbean politics and ideology, *Le Discours antillais* [Caribbean Discourse], finally published—soon after Barthes's death—in 1981. At first glance, little brings the two writers together. Barthes never visited the French Caribbean nor commented on its postcolonial paradox of being part of France though 3,000 miles away; similarly, Glissant did not join the heated debates over structuralism and the *nouvelle critique* raging through the 1960s, nor engage with Ferdinand de Saussure's semiological challenge to Western epistemologies. And yet, both writers—emerging from left-wing, anti-capitalist, even Marxian, intellectual cultures—became engaged, separately, in the critique of "clarity."[5]

Work on the postcolonial in Barthesian theory has not looked, so far, at the question of language, and even less so into anti-colonialism and, in particular, the critique of science.[6] However, it is well under way in the study of Glissantian theory benefiting currently from a surge of translation projects and critical commentary— though the extent to which his theory of opacity is purely a postcolonial critique, rather than a much wider politico-cultural strategy of resistance, is a keenly debated topic.[7] Indeed, the critique of science is a crucial area of both writers' work on opacity; and Glissant underlines the importance of Nietzsche in this "rupture of the speech of 'comprehension,'" just as Barthes does.[8]

Despite extensive translation of his work since the late 1960s, Barthes's writing on opacity has yet to be translated. Indeed, the brief fragment "Opacity/Transparence" in his celebrated "biography of the self" *Roland Barthes by Roland Barthes* (published in 1975 and translated swiftly by Richard Howard in 1977) still needs to be augmented by a translation of its longer version in the *Fragments inédits* that he wrote in 1974, not least because its thirty-four fragments were originally intended to be the organizing system of *Roland Barthes by Roland Barthes*.[9] In other words, the binary opacity/transparence—in genetic terms—is a key, if subsequently marginalized, opposition in Barthes's account of his writing career up until 1975. There is however little doubt that opacity is a fundamental element of Glissant's work and acknowledged as such in a rapidly growing body of research.[10]

In this chapter, then, we will bring together the two writers' separate work on opacity in a "staged" dialogue that looks at the ethological and political ramifications in both textualism and ideological critique. Above all, it will be Ethics—how to behave with the Other, others, other cultures—that is the meeting point in Barthes and Glissant's work on opacity, especially in its language dimensions.[11] It will be noted that playing with language is common to both writers, and especially so for the verb "comprendre" (to understand) which Glissant deftly splits into two syllables, com- and -prendre, with which to illustrate his view that "understanding" involves necessarily "prendre" (taking), and for Barthes, "saisir" (to grasp or to take), which is often a synonym for "to understand." However, as the aforementioned epigraphs suggest, both writers feel a deep suspicion toward moves and ways to understand the Other.

For one critic, Glissant's very theory of Créole language is itself a form of opacity, a "cross-cultural" language disallowed by the slave Plantocracy of the Caribbean, but used as a secret (i.e., scrambled and accelerated) form of communication beyond the ears of slave-masters; however, it is not, as Charles Forsdick points out, to be equated with the "obscure . . . instead the non-reducibility of otherness."[12] This opacity has a parallel in what is called the "second wave" of Saussureanism that developed in the 1960s, and which informs Barthes's "Death of the Author" thesis, involving a view of language as a cacophony of voices and codes without origin.[13] We will see in a moment how one critic tries to oppose the "Death of the Author" to Glissant's notion of poetic "intentionality."

Glissant's notion of intentionality, tightly linked to opacity, betrays elements of positivity.[14] Indeed, Michael R. Griffiths argues that Glissant's opacity "can only be recognized as the deliberate, intentional relation to the Other (or refusal thereof)," a "counter-poetics" that "proffers the possibility of a more robust and ethical relation in a future to come"; however, in Glissant's schema, the Créole population deliberately refuses comprehension (in both senses) and relies thereby on the complexity of orality as a form of "negative opacity."[15] In Naïma Hachad's thesis, opacity is a critique of the too-easy multiculturalism made by transparency.[16] Inscrutability of all sorts becomes then a crucial form of tactical resistance to colonial, postcolonial, and neocolonial oppression. As Adlai Murdoch puts it: "the practice of opacity becomes a form of subjective and communal recognition that abrogates the hierarchization of power at work in earlier iterations of creolization"; as Glissant puts it:

> I claim the right to *opacity* for everyone, which is not a withdrawal . . . I do not have to "understand" anyone, an individual, a community, a people, to "take them with me" at the price of stifling them, of losing them in an amorphous totality which I would manage, in order to be willing to live alongside them, to build with them, to take risks with them.[17]

We will see in a moment how this claim seems to echo the Barthes of the 1970s whose development of the "Neutral" represents, according to some critics, a highly political move toward opacity.[18]

The final link in the opacity-intentionality nexus is the crucial notion of Relation for Glissant:

> It is the opacity of the diverse animating the imagined transparency of Relation. . . .
> The thought of opacity distracts me from absolute truths whose guardian I might believe myself to be.[19]

This is an important deployment of opacity as a strategy.[20] But lacking in Glissant's account is any consideration of *social* relations, which, as we shall see, is largely synonymous in Barthes's work with Marx. Indeed, as maverick and unorthodox as Barthesian dialectics are, they are nevertheless grounded in an acute sensitivity to social relations, what Jean-Claude Milner calls Barthes's "Marxist undercurrent."[21] It might not be possible to say the same of Glissant's notion of "Relation" as a dialectical formulation, for the totality implied in the Glissantian notion of *Tout-Monde* lacks a sensitivity to *social* relations, preferring cultural, linguistic relationality, in what he calls "cultural sociology."[22] Indeed, it is not clear how Glissant's promotion of opacity might negotiate the social relations not just of class and ideological power but also of what Paul Gilroy has signaled as the central alienation of modernity for Black people, that of "double consciousness."[23] In *The Souls of Black Folk*, W. E. B. Du Bois had defined "double consciousness" thus: "It is a peculiar sensation, this double consciousness, this sense of always looking at oneself through the eyes of others, of measuring one's soul by the tape of a world that looks on in amused contempt and pity."[24] A critique of social relations may not be able to counter the powerful political, psychological, and ideological distortions operated by "double consciousness"; but we will see how Barthes's discussion of opacity begins to address the social dynamic beneath it. The discussion of opacity and transparence begins early in Barthes's career.

Text: Intention and Performance

In his very first essay in 1953, *Writing Degree Zero*, Barthes had set out the relationship, in the seventeenth century, between Literature and language as one of aristocratic "clarity," but one which began to break down at the end of the eighteenth century:

> Classical art could have no sense of being a language, for it *was* language, in other words it was transparent, it flowed and left no deposit.... [T]owards the end of the eighteenth century this transparency becomes clouded; literary form . . . acquires a weight.[25]

However, he argued, it was not so much the French Revolution of 1789 as the failed revolution of 1848 that confirms the modern appearance of literary language as a (potentially infinite) plural set of styles with which a writer signaled their relationship to the modern institution "Literature." Challenging Jean-Paul Sartre's infamous view in *What is Literature?* (1947) that all language is "transparent," Barthes would later claim, in a 1971 interview in *Tel Quel*, that in his "degree zero" theory of 1848 as the "turning-point" for the demise of "clarity," he had "marxianised" Sartre's view of literary language.[26] Though this early essay does not contain the word "opaque," Barthes was clearly invoking the transparency/opacity metaphor, and prefiguring the famous quote in *Roland Barthes by Roland Barthes* in 1975, "I have a disease, I see language."[27] In between these two suggestions that language is opaque, Barthes also proposed an opacity of the text.

In the very first paragraph of "Death of the Author," published in French in 1968, Barthes sets out his critique of authorial intentions by using the theory of the *inorigins* of textual meanings—what we might call the text's opacity—but he emphasizes also the continuity of this across ages and civilizations:

> [W]riting is the destruction of every voice, of every point of origin. Writing is that neutral space, composite, oblique space where our subject slips away, the negative where all identity is lost, starting with the very identity of the body writing.

No doubt it has always been that way.[28]

Griffiths however suggests a non-Barthesian—if not anti-Barthesian—move by Glissant in calling his 1969 collection of essays *L'intention poétique*, published only one year after Barthes's infamous critique of textual intentionalism, in "Death of the Author," had appeared.[29] Griffiths claims that, in sharp distinction to Glissant, Barthes's "diachronic emphasis on the paradoxical modernity of the author function is contrasted with the premodern"; and that this division contributes to a "relegation" of the primitive past in which, for Barthes, there was no notion of "genius" for the narrator of stories; this, for Barthes, was in contradistinction to the modern period in which the "genius" of the author is invented. For Glissant by contrast, Griffiths stresses, "the shaman, story-teller, *quimboiseur*, is sustained into the present." But Griffiths' view of a Glissant "divergent" from Barthes's textualist radicalism is misplaced.

Though he acknowledges Barthes's Marxian point about how capitalism has tried (but failed?), in textualist terms, to attach authority to author—"certain writers have long since attempted to loosen it" (Mallarmé, Valéry, Proust)—Griffiths imparts an unproblematic Hegelian progressivism to Barthes's theory. He suggests that "it is unsurprising" that Glissant's "assertion of a synchronic and cross-cultural approach to authorial intention . . . should emerge against a field in French theory" beholden to a "diachronic emphasis."[30] In fact, however, far from Barthes historicizing the primitive against the modern, there is a surprising eternalism in the text-as-theater in the following:

> in ethnographic societies the responsibility for a narrative is never assumed by a person but by a mediator, shaman or relator, whose "performance"—the mastery of the narrative code—may possibly be admired but never [their] "genius."[31]

This strikes me as a huge intervention in favor of, a justification of, oral culture. Furthermore, in the notion of the "voice-off," J. C. Carlier has pointed to the double nature of Barthes's own voice in "Death of the Author"; it is as if Barthes himself has to "perform" the "death of the author" thesis, in such a way that we both listen to the theory but do not impart (any? too many?) intentions to the essayist (Barthes) who is writing the death of the author theory. This is not so much Barthes sidestepping a performative contradiction—how can Barthes *tell* us the death of the author (intentionally, as it were)?[32] Rather, it is redolent of the "voice-off" of Barthes's essayism in "Death of the Author," in which the opacity of the self as writer is—paradoxically, for the "Death of the Author" essay—confirmed at any one moment. We are then in the rich realms of the poetic, skilled essayist whose writing can be (re-)related in/to the contemporary world, not (so much) by abandoning clarity for opacity but by their essays being a collection of "voices"—of "performances" of the essayistic code—that provocatively undermine the author's authority of any text (including Barthes's ownership of his own essay). But also, the unity of a text is in the reader; and that is multiple (in one reader) and infinite (in all of them to come). Glissantian Relation is nowhere clearer than in Barthesian textualism; and relation, as we saw earlier, needs opacity.

Griffiths rightly underlines that "intention" is a key part of both opacity and relation in Glissant's schema; and he sharply differentiates Glissant's intentionalism from Barthes's work, especially in "Death of the Author." But this discounting of Barthes's theory misses two things. First, the developments in Glissant's writing belie a much more "Barthesian" optic. The decentering of self, the complex dialectic of writing/orality, and the privileging of "partage" [sharing]—especially in the "How to live together" lectures that Barthes gave in 1976-7—are all *loci* in his work of the 1970s.³³ Second, Griffiths' sharp differentiation of Glissant from Barthes does not consider the opacity of the text. Surely, in Glissantian terms (to turn the tables), Barthes is proposing not only the *inorigins* of the plurality of voices but also an opacity of the text which relativizes intention, and thereby localizes but strengthens intention. As Neal Allar argues, Glissant's opacity not only represents an "epistemological resistance" to a radical "writing back" against colonialism and neocolonialism but also allows the reader to be on an "equal footing" with the poet, a "collective poetics," and "affirmative modality for reading, writing and interacting in the postcolonial world"; and this in turn avoids a reductive (passive) definition of opacity in favor of a globalized "*imprévisible*."³⁴ This is precisely the import of Barthes's "Death of the Author" thesis.

The later, culturalist and political, mobilization of opacity rests then on an implicit rereading by Glissant of his earlier poetic writings in the 1950s. Furthermore, as Allar argues, "rather than expressing anxiety about an inaccessible 'deeper' meaning concealed beneath the surface of the text, Glissant emphasizes the material text itself."³⁵ Indeed, with these parallels in Glissant and Barthes's emphases on a counter-poetics in mind, we might suggest that one link between Glissant's theory and poetry has a bearing on Barthes's own strategy of opacity in tactical, "Neutral," silence.³⁶ But before we look at the Neutral strategy and its role in promoting opacity, we must investigate briefly Barthes's early attitude to opacity following his Marxian critique of Sartrian transparence that we noted earlier. It is worth, first, considering the "window/countryside" bind described in *Mythologies*, because it suggests an awareness of the transparence/opacity contradiction that Barthes wanted to believe had been solved, at least in historiographical terms, by Jules Michelet.

From Barthesian "Double Grasp" to "No Grasp"

In the mid-1950s, Barthes was acutely aware of the need for a concept of mediation in a phenomenological understanding of perception, one which he applied to the human mind's susceptibility to the ideological function of myth and its attendant distortions. He underlined, in "Myth Today," the essay at the end of *Mythologies*, that the human eye—and by extension human consciousness—struggles to keep a handle on the double nature of perceived reality, such is the mediated way in which the external world appears to us:

> If I am in a car and I look at the scenery through the window, I can at will focus on the scenery or on the windowpane. At one moment I grasp the presence of the glass

and the distance of the landscape; at another, on the contrary, the transparence of the glass and the depth of the landscape; but the result of this alternation is constant: the glass is at once present and empty to me, and the landscape unreal and full.[37]

As a conclusion to the study of how myth operates under capitalist social relations, the implication is that we cannot *see* the ideology in social relations while also participating in its circulation. Barthes's (partial) solution to this—at least across the period of the 1960s known as "High" structuralism—is to invoke semiology, as the science of signs, with which to show how communication between humans (in whatever form) operates on (at least two) different levels. In a sense, the semiological demonstration of language's susceptibility to producing second-order meanings which superimpose themselves on the simple, first-order meaning generated by the signifier-signified association, is an attempt to expose the mediated—or "connotative"—manner in which we experience communication. However, it did not cover the phenomenological conundrum of *perception* set out in the window/countryside example mentioned earlier. The solution to this, at least in historiographical terms, was proposed by Jules Michelet's writing of popular history, in what we might call today *history from below*.

In opposition to the "récit" (narrative) normally associated with history writing, Michelet combines, Barthes suggested in his 1954 book on the historian, the "tableau" with the "survol" (flying over). For Barthes, this writing technique allowed the nineteenth-century historian to be also a "marcheur" (walker) with the people whose "history" he is writing. Barthes suggests that this leads to a new split: "either the malaise of the slow advance, or else the euphoria of the panorama," or a combination of the two, what he calls "this double grasp."[38] But the "double grasp" brings other benefits to Barthes's mind. By sometimes leaving behind the history in which he is "rowing," Michelet's historical prose displays moments of surprise in which the historian, the "voyageur," stops to look, and here is "a second level of history, which is completely panoramic, made of intellection."[39] In other words, Michelet's historiography is able to be both *in* the time of the history described (in which the future is perfectly, we might say, opaque to the actants described) *and*, simultaneously, viewing and describing this moment from the vantage point of much later as the historian tries to make sense of the same history (an "intellection" that makes the subsequent meaning of the events, we might then say, "transparent").[40] The "double grasp" manages then to solve (in some sense) the historian's version of the window/countryside conundrum: the "countryside" is the moment of history (the historian "walking" with the people in their making of history) and the "window," the "tableau" that the historian constructs from a time in the future which *sees* the mediated historical event.

Though Barthes never leaves behind his work on and fascination with Michelet, there is little doubt that the dramatic social and political events of May 1968 in France play their part in heavily nuancing all notions of the "double grasp." Despite the "stereographic" approach deployed in his 1970 essay *S/Z*, the creative criticism adopted by Barthes to consider how we read and rewrite Balzac's story *Sarrasine* prefers to rest at the surface of meaning construction. Furthermore, in *Empire of Signs*, published the same year after his return from Japan, Barthes ends the essay with an anodyne photograph of a domestic room, next to which he appends the following elliptical caption: "Aucun vouloir-saisir et cependant aucune oblation" (no will-to-seize and yet no offering up); and the essay ends by noticing how the Japanese house, "often deconstructed," has "no site which designates the slightest propriety . . . the center is rejected": for there is in a Japanese house, as Barthes finishes the essay, "nothing to *grasp*."[41] Somewhere then, between 1954 and the view of Michelet's "double grasp" and the "no wish to grasp" in his Japan of 1970, Barthes brackets, if not overturns, the "double grasp."[42] This stark move from a multitasking comprehensiveness in historiography (and which can be seen in the politicized reading of the double level of signification operated by myth in *Mythologies*) to a tactical and strategic respect of nongrasping is a key development in Barthesian thought and critique.

The "no-wish-to grasp"—the "nothing to *grasp*"—accompanies the deconstruction of "property" in the Japanese house, a deconstruction that has its echo in the absence of property in favor of "guardianship" that Glissant valorizes in the pre-Colombian Amerindian tribes of the Popul-Vuh and the Chilam-Bilam in South America. Guardianship is then the polar opposite of Western notions and practices of "comprendre" (as the very word in French has the notion of taking/owning in "-prendre").[43]

In the "Death of the Author," it allows Barthes to question the profound intention of an author in any literary text, to reject the author's ownership over, and, in *S/Z*, to a bracketing, if not a discounting, of the critic's traditional aim to "penetrate" (and, in some sense, own) a story's "secret" meaning. Thus, in the wake of May 1968, the structuralist attempts to account for the double dimension of the paradigmatic and the syntagmatic were now being replaced by the "symphony" of codes that the reader hears in order to act back on the text. In ways that have encouraged many to see this post-1968 Barthes as "postmodernist," the literary critic is now a creative critic whose attention to the "surface" of communications, to how literary meaning operates, is structured in the act of reading. Postmodernist or not, the radical questioning of "depth" in literary and other forms of communication is certainly part of a poststructuralist critique of a science of the text; or rather, the assertion that the "science of the text" *is* its (re-)writing by each reader as a collapsing of the binary oppositions' art/science and literature/metalanguage and which, for our purposes, suggests an opacity of the Text. It is a relatively simple move for Barthes then, in the early 1970s, to apply this opacity of the Text to the self: how to stop the Other—others, society in general—"understanding" the self, or believing that it could actually "understand" the self. The "inorigins" of the voices in a text in "Death of the Author" and the inorigins of wealth that *S/Z* finds structuring Balzac's curious tale *Sarrasine* combine in the Barthes of the 1970s to encourage him to insist on an "inorigins" of the self, an opacity that refuses to allow an oppressive social determinism of each person.

NVS (Non-Wish to Grasp)

One part of Barthes's interest in opacity comes across clearly in his critique of the adjective; and here we find a fascinating dovetailing with Caribbean Créole theory and writing in which Édouard Glissant is a key player. Already, in his two "petites mythologies du mois" in November 1955, "Lexique marocain" and "Grammaire marocaine" (which are joined together as one essay as "Grammaire africaine" in *Mythologies*), Barthes was underlining the ideological function of adjectives in France's attempts to persuade the French population to back its bloody colonial wars in North Africa.[44] Later, in 1972—as he begins to look for an opacity of the self—he describes the adjective as "the poorest of linguistic categories": "are we condemned to the adjective?," he asks (gently parodying Sartre's existentialist belief in the inevitability of "freedom"); and the only way to achieve any notion of perfection in relations with others is "to abolish—in oneself, between oneself and others—*adjectives*; a relationship which adjectivizes is on the side of the image, on the side of domination, of death," because, as he adds in "His Voice," "by its descriptive quality alone, the adjective is funereal."[45] And when the adjective is then turned into a noun—what Barthes calls an act of "enallage" (or grammatically incorrect use of a figure of speech)—the existential killing of the Other is complete. We can now see how Barthes arrives at the "fried" image of the subject and at the key anti-determinist notion of the *aclassé* (without social class), the *atopos*—without place (as opposed to *utopos*, literally "nowhere").[46] It also completes the transition from the "double grasp" to what he calls in *A Lover's Discourse* in 1977, in highly elliptical terms, "Thus": "the loved object . . . exonerated from any adjective."[47]

In this way, Barthes was questioning not just the image applied to the subject (him, as it happens—how else can we know?!), but also to the Other, especially the loved other, in his attempt to avoid what Rosi Braidotti calls the temptation of the "metaphorization of others."[48] Barthes's solution then is to develop a "neutral" form: in trademark Barthesian fashion—proposing a behavior essayistically, which is purely utopian—he devises what he calls the "no-wish-to-grasp," or "NVS."

The NVS is rhetorically negative ("no-wish") but conceptually, and even in practice, it is a positive form of action to avoid "enallage." Before we discuss this move, it is worth pausing, briefly, to find parallels in Glissant's writing. In a fascinating echo of Barthes's critique of the adjective, the Martinican creolist Raphaël Confiant asserts that the Créole language (at least the French version, and in its "natural" oral form) contains no adjectives.[49] In the same collection of essays and stories from the French Caribbean, Glissant seems to go one stage further than Confiant. In a powerful echo of the *atopos* of self as theorized by Barthes, Glissant affirms that the very structure of Créole language radically decenters the self. Instead of the standard French way to say "I have a bad back" ("J'ai mal au dos") (the example is well chosen as a bad back is a typical injury of the cane-field work that marked slavery and post-slave societies)—in which the feeling self ("je") is the Cartesian center of the sentence and of the painful feeling—Glissant counterposes the Créole way of signaling such a discomfort: "mon dos me fait mal" (my back is hurting me).[50] This example is not only a typically Barthesian way of using a basic language unit of meaning to make a profound point about consciousness and its interaction with (and influence on) human communication; making the back into a separate part of the human body also—and crucially for our discussion on opacity—brackets, if not removes, the self with respect to a simple unified and Cartesian individuality.

As Lucy O'Meara points out, the Cartesianism of the "ego isolated" is a key dimension in Barthes's belief that the "fascism of language" is its alienating imposition of individuality and the concomitant exclusion of complexity.[51] The conflictual dualism of self-and-other can be overcome in Barthes's schema by creating the NVS, aiming, as O'Meara puts it, at a "non-dualistic harmony" in which, dissolved in nature, the self is not beholden to binary conceptions; this "ethics of non-committal" involves a *délicatesse*, an "aeration" of haiku and morality. The "ultimate project," announces Barthes in his "Inaugural Lecture" in 1977, is to "inquire into the conditions and processes by which discourse can be disengaged from all will-to-possess [vouloir-saisir]."[52]

For Eric Marty, the very acronym "NVS" avoids the evil of classification and illusion that besets the Word, for the Letter, by being anterior to the Word, acts so as to neutralize its "Terror."[53] NVS invites silence, effacement, suspension, and not liquidation of the imaginary nor renouncement, and involves no oblation nor lassitude: "non" here is not negative, except that it is without adjective: thus the Neutral, "neither coloured nor deep" is what Marty calls, in a rather peremptory fashion, "alterity without others."[54] It is worth pausing on this rejection of oblation as, though not a word to be found in Glissant's notion of opacity, it hints at a rejection of slavishness.

Barthes analyzes oblation briefly in his seminars on the *Discours amoureux*, in relation to Goethe's fictional and Heine's poetic writings on love, deciding that oblation's ultimate end, suicide, is, psychoanalytically and in reality, a "failed experiment."[55] It is above all the "Bad night" of attachment to things, in distinction to the "good night" of "obscurity": the "vouloir-saisir" must end, but its opposite, the NVS, must not—unlike oblation—be seen.[56]

There is no need for us to dwell on the origins of the NVS in Taoism. But it suggests a relation of human to human outside of the (modern) Western ideology of "understanding" the other. NVS is also part of what Barthes calls in *How to Live Together* an "acceptable distance," which, as Corina Stan points out, is part of both idiorrhythmia and the excessiveness of *délicatesse* in Barthes's imagined schema.[57] Similarly, Glissant argues in *Tout-Monde* that opacity "does not suggest a renouncing of the self. It suggests distance (a distancing) driven by the fossilized shattering of Being."[58] Indeed, Glissant's shattering of being, in favor of "Relation," seems driven by the same concerns as Barthes's NVS.

Glissant defines opacity as "irreducibility of terms in a relation of difference," finding its definition first in the negative example of the error in Victor Segalen's approach to Far Eastern cultures:

> He suffered from this accursed contradiction. Unable to know that a transfer into transparency ran counter to his project and that, on the contrary, respect for mutual forms of opacity would have accomplished it, he was heroically consumed in the impossibility of being Other. Death is the outcome of the opacities, and this is why the idea of death never leaves us.[59]

However, for Glissant, "the opacity of the other" is "like a positive given and not like an obstacle."[60] Celia Britton underlines that "'La Relation'—as a central concept in Glissant's theoretical work—is a non-hierarchical, non-reductive relation to the Other."[61] As Glissant puts it, "how to be oneself without closing oneself off from the other, and how to open oneself to the other without losing oneself?"[62] Indeed, in Glissant's schema, truly human "Relation" must be based on the nonproprietorial.[63] This is a critical component of the *Discours antillais*, a refusal to own.

However, despite the critique of property in his work (especially in the *Discours antillais*), Glissant does not venture into *social* relations as such. The critique of property is well known as a key part of the theories of the young Karl Marx, and private property is often a synonym in his work for class relations. Man, writes Marx, "has become the tense essence of private property," for it is inside each person not external to them; and he relates this directly to (heterosexual) marriage and to the exclusive and communal ownership of women, but which appears to man as the most "*natural relation of human being to human being.*"[64] It is against this background that we must consider the section "Opacity and transparence" in *Roland Barthes by Roland Barthes* for the way it addresses the contradiction of social relations.

In the posthumously published, much longer version, "Argument," Barthes sets out the idea that, from the start of his writing career, the opacity and the transparence of social relations play out in a "simultaneity" of chronology and logic.[65] In short, Barthes underlines the "oscillation" in his work between seeing the opacity of social relations in the stereotypes of life, and then, ultimately (or utopically), its transparence, which is the desire for *rest* in which "social interlocution" and its thickness can be glimpsed opening up, lightening up even disappearing into invisibility. However, this merely leaves the writer in a double bind. The greater the "social division," the greater, paradoxically, the opacity of this social division—and here is the window/countryside conundrum we saw in *Mythologies* mentioned earlier—against which the "subject" struggles as best they can; at the same time, if they are themselves "the subject of language," their "battle cannot have a direct political outcome"—such is the opaque nature of language that we saw in *Writing Degree Zero* mentioned earlier—because this would mean a return to the stereotypes of opacity. Naturally, Barthes sees this contradiction as a spiral along which his writing moves—in oscillation—to the same places but always, across time and subject, arriving further down the line, in what he calls an "apocalyptic" battle. Nevertheless, he stresses, this battle is part of life, of living and breathing under capitalist social relations.

Using the Glissantian word "partage," Barthes affirms that the writer "shares excessively," breathing out heavily (exaspérait) the values of the critique of those social relations contained in the stereotype; and yet, at the same time, the writer lives "utopically," taking in air (respire), breathing in the "final transparence" of social relations. This is the life of breathing: pushing out combative air to clear opacity and taking in air with which to be able to continue the combat.[66] It leads to Barthes wanting to affirm the "right to difference," but this allows him only to recognize a further contradiction—the critique of liberalism accompanied by a defense of "freedom of expression"—which is resolved, partially only, by a sublimation into the "distance" afforded by the NVS, a "democracy of differences" which Barthes sees as redolent of Charles Fourier's utopianism.[67]

Conclusion: Opacity of Self Is Opacity of Culture?

Although Barthes's NVS cannot get beyond the contradictions of social relations (how could it be under capitalism?), it would not do justice to Glissant and to his extensive work on opacity to criticize him for not applying opacity to social relations. It may be that his emphasis on contact between cultures leaves little room for contact between humans. Indeed, we could turn the tables and suggest that Barthes's emphasis on the social relations in opacity ignores, or at least marginalizes, opacity between cultures. This too would be a slight injustice. One of Barthes's strategies for avoiding transparency of cultures is to explore the Neutral. Japan, for example, is presented as deliberately opaque in *Empire of Signs*, in which the Neutral, as one critic has underlined, becomes a less judgmental way of traveling: the Neutral in Japan "dodges," "baffles," "outplays" the contrastive machinery of meaning-production, which is otherwise "unshakeable" for Barthes.[68]

Indeed, common to both Glissant and Barthes is a positive approach to autoethnography: Barthes liked to cite Michelet's quotation "This book is myself"; just as Glissant's belief that the writer is the "Ethnologist of oneself" points to the fundamental weakness of transparency in objective ethnography.[69] For Glissant, ethnology and ethnography, like anthropology, are compromised not just by their concerted growth alongside slavery and then European colonialism in the past but also by the continued application of its incipient scientism—"comprendre"—to today's diversity of cultures.[70] Raphael Lauro notes that Glissant is sensitive to the accusation of his *own* transparency toward the West, but that Glissant does not reject this idea and only warns of "the error" in the act of "reading" the West.[71] Glissant responds in trademark, oral and theatrical style:

> And now what they tell me is, "You calmly pack your poetics into these craters of opacity and claim to rise so serenely beyond the prodigiously elucidating work that the West has accomplished, but there you go talking nonstop about this West."— And what would you rather I talk about at the beginning, if not this transparency whose aim was to reduce us? Because, if I don't begin there, you will see me consumed with the sullen jabber of childish refusal, convulsive and powerless. This is where I start. As for my identity, I'll take care of that myself. There has to be dialogue with the West, which, moreover, is contradictory in itself (usually this is the argument raised when I talk about cultures of the One); the complementary discourse of whoever wants to give-on-and-with must be added to the West. And can you not see that we are implicated in its evolution?[72]

There is little sense of opacity being, finally, positive in Barthes's work, as Griffiths argues for it to be in Glissant's work and in its prelude to a world "relation."[73] Opacity is a fact of language and social relations under capitalism; and in personal relations, the only recourse, to Barthes's mind, is an NVS strategy. By way of a tentative answer to our question as to its operability for wider cultural relations, NVS has much in common with the critique of "com(-)prendre," but it cannot reach the optimism of Glissant's

Tout-Monde. By the same token, the Tout-Monde needs to address the stereotype in social relations, to consider the Neutral as a strategy and as standing outside of claims, albeit admirably utopian, to the right to diversity. In short, opacity needs now to negotiate "double consciousness."

Notes

1. Édouard Glissant, *Le Discours antillais* (Paris: Editions du Seuil, 1981), 356 (my translation).
2. Roland Barthes, *Le Discours amoureux. Séminaire à l'École pratique des hautes études 1974–1976* (Paris: Editions du Seuil, 2007), 119 (my translation).
3. Interview in Abdelkébir Khatibi, *L'œuvre de Abdelkébir Khatibi (Préliminaire)* (Rabat: Marsam, 1997), 25 (my translation).
4. Fredric Jameson, *The Prison-House of Language: A Critical Account of Structuralism and Russian Formalism* (Princeton, NJ: Princeton University Press, 1972).
5. There is little evidence (as of yet) of Glissant and Barthes knowing each other well. They did however cross paths, in the early years of their career, on the editorial board of the radical left literary journal, *Les Lettres Nouvelles*; and in many of the two dozen numbers of the journal where Barthes's "petite mythologie du mois" appeared, Glissant also intervened on variety of literary topics.
6. On orientalism, see Diana Knight, *Barthes and Utopia: Space, Travel, Writing* (Oxford: Oxford University Press, 1997), and Marie-Paule Ha, "Another Barthes," *Figuring the East: Segalen, Malraux, Duras and Barthes* (New York: SUNY Press, 2000), 95–117; and on postcolonial theory, see Andy Stafford, "Edward Said and Roland Barthes: Criticism versus Essayism; Or, Roads and Meetings Missed," in *Edward Said and the Literary, Social and Political World*, ed. Ranjan Ghosh (London: Routledge, 2009), 19–35.
7. The impressive "Translating Glissant" project (parented by Liverpool University Press) has published so far: *Introduction to a Poetics of Diversity*, and *Treatise on the Whole-World*, both trans. Celia Britton (2020); and *The Baton Rouge Interviews with Édouard Glissant and Alexandre Leupin*, trans. Kate M. Cooper (2020).
8. Édouard Glissant, "Le chaos-monde, l'oral et l'écrit," in *Écrire la "Parole de nuit": La nouvelle littérature antillaise*, ed. Ralph Ludwig (Paris: Gallimard, 1994), 111–29 (129, my translation). In the *Discours amoureux* seminar, Barthes quotes Nietzsche's regret that science, in its hurry and "blinded by the desire to know all, at any cost," lacks the "délicatesse" to stand back: "we are scientific" concludes Barthes, "through a lack of subtlety" (389, my translation).
9. Roland Barthes, "Argument," in *Le lexique de l'auteur. Séminaire à l'École pratique des hautes études 1973–1974, suivi de Fragments inédits du "Roland Barthes par Roland Barthes*," ed. Anne Herschberg Pierrot (Paris: Seuil, 2010), 331–42; *Roland Barthes by Roland Barthes*, trans. Richard Howard (London: Macmillan, 1977), 138.
10. See the splendid Glissant website, https://www.glissantstudies.com/. Accessed January 30, 2021.
11. In his study of the Language turn, Henry Paget includes references to both Barthes and Glissant; Henry Paget, *Caliban's Reason: Introduction to Afro-Caribbean*

Philosophy (London: Routledge, 2000), the analysis is in part indebted (244) to Barthes's *Pleasure of the Text*.

12 H. Adlai Murdoch, "Édouard Glissant's Creolized World Vision: From Resistance and Relation to *Opacité*," *Callaloo* 36.4 (Fall 2013): 876–89 (879); Charles Forsdick, "L'exote mangé par les hommes," in Charles Forsdick and Susan Marson, *Reading Diversity* (Glasgow: University of Glasgow French and German Publications), 5–24 (18).

13 Though Adlai Murdoch argues that opacity in Glissant's view "worked to further the preservation and production of selfhood for the dominated subject" see "Édouard Glissant's Creolized World Vision," 880.

14 For Glissant, it is "the opacity of the other as a positive given and not as an obstacle ... sharing out [mettre en commun], not trying to be in charge [régenter] once again"; see Glissant, "Le chaos-monde," 127–8, my translation.

15 Michael R. Griffiths, "Toward Relation: Negritude, Poststructuralism, and the Specter of Intention in the Work of Édouard Glissant," *Discourse* 36.1 (2014): 31–53 (43–4). Britton argues: "understanding appears as an act of aggression because it constructs the Other as an *object* of knowledge" (cited in Murdoch, "Édouard Glissant's Creolized World Vision," 883–4).

16 See Naïma Hachad, "Corps et corpus bilingues d'Abdelkébir Khatibi et Adelfattah Killito," unpublished PhD thesis (Emory University, 2010), 215.

17 Glissant cited in Murdoch, "Édouard Glissant's Creolized World Vision," 886.

18 See "A Great Pedagogy of Nuance: Roland Barthes's The Neutral," *Theory & Event* 8.4 (2005), in which de Villiers argues that the Neutral becomes an (unmarketable) political strategy, allowing the question of sexuality to be sidestepped, an opacity which counters D. A. Miller's "bringing out" of Roland Barthes; see also Nicholas P. Greco, "'The Antithesis of Inner and Outer: Abolished': Roland Barthes and the Politics of the Closet," *Roland Barthes Studies* 6 (2020), who relates opacity to enigma in *S/Z*.

19 Édouard Glissant, *Poetics of Relation* (1992), trans. Betsy Wing (Ann Arbor, MI: University of Michigan Press, 1997), 192. Celia Britton, in *Édouard Glissant and Postcolonial Theory: Strategies of Language and Resistance* (Charlottesville: Virginia University Press, 1999), identifies Barthes as the "relation" overlap in postcolonial theory (202n18).

20 On opacity as a wider form of cultural praxis, see Patrick Crowley, "Édouard Glissant: Resistance and Opacity," *Romance Studies* 24.2 (2006): 105–15.

21 Jean-Claude Milner, *Le Pas philosophique de Roland Barthes* (Paris: Verdier, 2003), 58n7 (my translation).

22 On Glissant's departure from Marxist categories in favor of "cultural action," see Celia Britton, *Perspectives on Culture and Politics in the French Caribbean* (Cambridge: Legenda/MHRA, 2018), 9.

23 Paul Gilroy, *The Black Atlantic: Modernity and Double Consciousness* (London: Verso, 1993).

24 W. E. B. Du Bois, *The Souls of Black Folk: Essays and Sketches* [1903] (New York: Bartleby.com, 1999), 5.

25 Roland Barthes, *Writing Degree Zero* [1953], trans. Annette Lavers and Colin Smith (London: Jonathan Cape, 1967), 9.

26 See Roland Barthes, "Responses. Interview with *Tel Quel*" [1971], trans. Vérène Grieshaber, in *The "Tel Quel" Reader*, eds. Patrick ffrench and Roland-François Lack (London: Routledge, 1998), 252.

27 Barthes, *Roland Barthes by Roland Barthes*, 161.
28 Roland Barthes, "Death of the Author" [1967], in *Image, Music, Text*, trans. Stephen Heath (Glasgow: Fontana, 1977), 142. Indeed, in the introduction to *Tout-Monde*, Glissant describes how "the book is constructed so that one cannot tell who is speaking . . . . What is projected as speech encounters a multiple other who is the multiplicity of the world" (cited in Griffiths, "Toward Relation," 45).
29 Griffiths, "Toward Relation," 34–5.
30 Ibid., 35.
31 Barthes, "Death of the Author," 142.
32 J.-C. Carlier, "Roland Barthes's Resurrection of the Author and Redemption of Biography," *Cambridge Quarterly* 29:4 (2000): 388–9.
33 Glissant, "Le chaos-monde," 112–13, 114, 116.
34 Neal Allar, "The Case for Incomprehension," *Journal of French and Francophone Philosophy* XXIII.1 (2015): 43–58; Allar argues that Glissant's poetry is already "deleuzian" even before Gilles Deleuze wrote his first book, that Glissant's Hegelianism is indebted to Negritude's insistence on "dépassement" [getting past] (45–6).
35 Ibid., 55.
36 In his work on the opaque in Glissant's poetry, Arnaud Villani uses the work on Incommunication by the Palo Alto researchers (1952–61), led by Geoffrey Bateson, for whom refusing to communicate is a form of communication; Bateson's "double bind" experiment analyses someone—a person suffering a bipolar moment, for example—when they cannot process two incongruent messages of which they are not allowed to discuss the incongruence and from which they cannot escape; see Arnaud Villani, "Le poème opaque d'Édouard Glissant," *Chimères* 90 (2016): 191–200.
37 Roland Barthes, "Myth Today," in *A Barthes Reader*, ed. Susan Sontag (New York: Hill and Wang, 1982), 110. Misleadingly called today "labour essentialism," *homo faber* is the only place where for Barthes language avoids myth, as it is "functionally absorbed" in transformation of the world (Ibid., 135). Glissant's critique of Marxist categories in Martinique *Le Discours antillais* are described by one critic as rejections of categories such as "proletariat, infra- and superstructure, and even the category of labor itself"; see Nick Nesbitt, "Early Glissant. From the Destitution of the Political to Antillean Ultra-Leftism," *Callaloo* 36.4 (2013): 943; it resembles Barthes's suggestion in "Myth Today" that the proletariat/ruling class opposition has been replaced by that of the colonized versus the colonizer (*A Barthes Reader*, 137n34).
38 Roland Barthes, *Michelet*, trans. Richard Howard (Oxford: Blackwell, 1987), 20.
39 Ibid., 22.
40 For one filmmaker in the Caribbean, Tony Coco Viloin, history "has always been narrated from the outside and not from the inside." See http://africultures.com/entretien-dolivier-barlet-avec-tony-coco-viloin-guadeloupe-2508/ (my translation).
41 See Andy Stafford, "The Barthesian 'Double Grasp' in Japan: Reading as Undialectical Writing," in *The Pleasure in/of the Text About the Joys and Perversities of Reading*, eds. Fabien Arribert-Narce, Endo Fuhito, Kamila Pawlikowska (Oxford/Lausanne: Peter Lang, 2021), 129–52.
42 Playing it out possibly in *Empire of Signs* as I have argued in my forthcoming chapter "The Barthesian 'Double Grasp' in Japan: Reading as Undialectical Writing," in *Roland Barthes's* The Pleasure of the Text, eds. Endo Fuhito and Fabien Arribert-Narce (Peter Lang, 2021).

43 Glissant, "Le chaos-monde," 120–1.
44 The adjective's role in the language of colonial control is to "reinvigorate" the nouns deployed to communicate the naturalness of the brutal civil war in French Algeria; but, he writes, sooner or later, "all the adjectival designs which strive to give nothingness the qualities of being are the very signature of culpability"; see Roland Barthes, "African Grammar," in *The Eiffel Tower and Other Mythologies*, trans. Richard Howard (New York: Hill and Wang, 1979), 109.
45 Especially in evidence in writing on music in "the most facile and trivial form, that of the epithet": the adjective, by creating a musical imaginary merely tries to "reassure," "protect from [. . .] loss" the subject that is "constituted" by listening; see Roland Barthes, "The Grain of the Voice," in *Image, Music, Text*, trans. Stephen Heath (Glasgow: Fontana, 1977), 179 and *Roland Barthes by Roland Barthes* (43, 68).
46 Roland Barthes "The Image," in *The Rustle of Language*, trans. Richard Howard (Oxford: Blackwell, 1986), 350–8. On the *aclassé*, see Andy Stafford, "*Classé, surclasser, déclassé*; or, Roland Barthes, Classification without Class," in *L'Esprit Créateur* 55.4 (Winter 2015): 148–64.
47 Roland Barthes, *A Lover's Discourse: Fragments*, trans. Richard Howard (London: Jonathan Cape, 1979), 220; see also *The Neutral*, "The Adjective," 52–61.
48 Rosi Braidotti, *Metamorphoses: Towards a Materialist Theory of Becoming* (Cambridge (UK): Polity Press, 2002), 13.
49 Raphaël Confiant, "Questions pratiques d'écriture créole," in "*Ecrire la parole de nuit*," ed. Ralph Ludwig (Paris: Gallimard, 1994), 172–5.
50 Glissant, "Le chaos-monde," 117.
51 Lucy O'Meara, *Roland Barthes at the Collège de France* (Liverpool: Liverpool University Press, 2012), 126–7.
52 Roland Barthes, "Inaugural Lecture" [1978], in *A Barthes Reader*, 459; in *A Lover's Discourse*, NVS is translated into English as "non-will-to-possess [N.W.P.]" (233).
53 Éric Marty, *Roland Barthes, le métier d'écrire* (Paris: Éditions du Seuil, 2006), 333; the capitalization of "Terror" here is doubtless Marty's allusion to Barthes's early interest in ancient Greek theater, in which the word is a form of terror; see Claude Coste, "Roland Barthes: Terror in Poetry," *Barthes Studies* 2 (2016), http://sites.cardiff.ac.uk/barthes/article/roland-barthes-terror-in-poetry/. Accessed January 29, 2021.
54 Marty, *Roland Barthes*, 328–9, 324–5.
55 Barthes, *Le Discours amoureux*, 218–20.
56 Marty, *Roland Barthes*, 323; see the final section of *A Lover's Discourse*, "Sobria ebrietas" (232–4).
57 Corina Stan, "A Sociality of Distances: Roland Barthes and Iris Murdoch on How to Live with Others," *MLN* 129.5 (2014): 1170–98. Indeed, the Neutral is defined by Barthes as a "dream of a minimal sociality" (*The Neutral*, 201).
58 Cited in Murdoch, "Édouard Glissant's Creolized World Vision," 882.
59 Glissant, *Poetics of Relation*, 194.
60 Glissant, "Le chaos-monde," 127–8 (my translation).
61 Celia Britton, "Opacity and Transparence: Conceptions of History and Cultural Difference in the Work of Michel Butor and Edouard Glissant," *French Studies* 49.3 (July 1995): 315.
62 Glissant's *Introduction to A Poetics of Diversity* cited in Murdoch, "Édouard Glissant's Creolized World Vision," 885.
63 Glissant, "Le chaos-monde," 120–1.

64   Karl Marx, *Economic and Philosophical Manuscripts* (1844) in *Early Writings*, trans. Rodney Livingstone and Gregor Benton (London: Penguin, 1975), 342, 346–7.
65   The thirty-four fragments in *Le lexique de l'auteur* appear to be an intellectual's *apologie* of semiology—as Validity that critiques all "Causes"—against Marxism as Truth and "Alibi" (338) which, in its exclusion from language and from the freedom of "production," is condemned to a form of oblation (336).
66   Barthes, *Roland Barthes by Roland Barthes*, 138; "exaspéré" [exasperated] is then used in the very next figure, "Antithesis" (138).
67   Barthes, *Le lexique de l'auteur*, 334–5 (my translation).
68   Piers M. Smith, "The Neutral View: Roland Barthes's Representations of Japan and China," *IAFOR Journal of Literature and Librarianship* 5.1 (Autumn 2016): 55.
69   Cited in Tim Watson, *Culture Writing: Literature and Anthropology in the Midcentury Atlantic World* (Oxford: Oxford University Press, 2018), 128; Part II of Watson's study, on Francophone dimensions in the first chapter, called "L'Ethnologue de soi-même," then analyses anthropology in Glissant's early novels.
70   Glissant's suspicion is doubtless indebted to Aimé Césaire's; see Jason Allen-Paisant, "Unthinking Philosophy: Aimé Césaire, Poetry, and the Politics of Western Knowledge," *Atlantic Studies* (September 9, 2020), https://www.tandfonline.com/doi/abs/10.1080/14788810.2020.1816129. Accessed February 20, 2021.
71   Raphaël Lauro, "Edouard Glissant's Excursions and Detours," *Discourse* 36.1 (Winter 2014): 3–30 (note 50).
72   Glissant, *Poetics of Relation*, 190–1.
73   Though one exception to this negativity is the question of opacity in relation to "coming out" as a homosexual; on this, see Nicholas de Villiers, *Opacity and The Closet: Queer Tactics in Foucault, Barthes and Warhol* (Minneapolis, MN: University of Minnesota Press 2012), ix–xi, who points out that if sexuality is not declared, it tends to signal, in a homophobic society, homosexuality, and that Barthes uses opacity to thwart "confession," only for this opacity itself then to point to homosexuality (and presumably, so on).

Works Cited

Allar, Neal. "The Case for Incomprehension." *Journal of French and Francophone Philosophy* XXIII.1 (2015): 43–58.

Allen-Paisant, Jason. "Unthinking Philosophy: Aimé Césaire, Poetry, and the Politics of Western Knowledge." *Atlantic Studies*, September 9, 2020. https://www.tandfonline.com/doi/abs/10.1080/14788810.2020.1816129. Accessed February 20, 2021.

Barthes, Roland. "Death of the Author" [1967]. In *Image, Music, Text*. Trans. Stephen Heath. Glasgow: Fontana, 1977. 142–8.

Barthes, Roland. *Le Discours amoureux. Séminaire à l'École pratique des hautes études 1974–1976*. Paris: Editions du Seuil, 2007.

Barthes, Roland. *The Eiffel Tower and Other Mythologies*. Trans. Richard Howard. New York: Hill and Wang, 1979.

Barthes, Roland. *L'Empire des signes*. Geneva: Skira, 1970.

Barthes, Roland. *Empire of Signs*. Trans. Richard Howard. New York: Hill & Wang, 1982.

Barthes, Roland. "The Grain of the Voice." In *Image, Music, Text*. Trans. Stephen Heath. Glasgow: Fontana, 1977. 179–89.

Barthes, Roland. "Image." In *The Rustle of Language*. Trans. Richard Howard. Oxford: Blackwell, 1986. 350–8.

Barthes, Roland. "Inaugural Lecture" [1978]. In *A Barthes Reader*. Ed. Susan Sontag. New York: Hill and Wang, 1982. 457–78.

Barthes, Roland. *Le Lexique de l'auteur. Séminaire à l'École pratique des hautes études 1973-1974, suivi de Fragments inédits du "Roland Barthes par Roland Barthes."* Ed. Anne Herschberg Pierrot. Paris: Editions du Seuil, 2010.

Barthes, Roland. *A Lover's Discourse: Fragments*. Trans. Richard Howard. London: Jonathan Cape, 1979.

Barthes, Roland. "Myth Today" [1957]. In *A Barthes Reader*. Ed. Susan Sontag. New York: Hill and Wang, 1982. 93–149.

Barthes, Roland. *The Neutral. Lecture Course at the Collège de France, 1977-1978*. Trans. Rosalind Krauss and Denis Hollier. New York: Columbia University Press, 2005.

Barthes, Roland. *Œuvres complètes*. Ed. Éric Marty. 2nd ed. 5 vols. Paris: Gallimard, 2002.

Barthes, Roland. *Roland Barthes by Roland Barthes*. Trans. Richard Howard. London: Macmillan, 1977.

Barthes, Roland. *Michelet*. Trans. Richard Howard. Oxford: Blackwell, 1987.

Barthes, Roland. "Responses. Interview with Tel Quel [1971]." In *The "Tel Quel" Reader*. Eds. Patrick ffrench and Roland-François Lack. Trans. Vérène Grieshaber. London: Routledge, 1998. 249–67.

Barthes, Roland. *Writing Degree Zero* [1953]. Trans. Annette Lavers and Colin Smith. London: Jonathan Cape, 1967.

Braidotti, Rosi. *Metamorphoses: Towards a Materialist Theory of Becoming*. Cambridge: Polity Press, 2002.

Britton, Celia. "Opacity and Transparence: Conceptions of History and Cultural Difference in the Work of Michel Butor and Édouard Glissant." *French Studies* 49.3 (July 1995): 308–20.

Britton, Celia. *Édouard Glissant and Postcolonial Theory: Strategies of Language and Resistance*. Charlottesville: Virginia University Press, 1999.

Britton, Celia. *Perspectives on Culture and Politics in the French Caribbean*. Cambridge: Legenda/MHRA, 2018.

Carlier, J.-C., "Roland Barthes's Resurrection of the Author and Redemption of Biography." *Cambridge Quarterly* 29.4 (2000): 386–93.

Confiant, Raphaël. "Questions pratiques d'écriture créole." In *Écrire la "Parole de nuit." La nouvelle littérature antillaise*. Ed. Ralph Ludwig. Paris: Gallimard, 1994. 171–80.

Coste, Claude. "Roland Barthes: Terror in Poetry." *Roland Barthes Studies* 2 (2016). http://sites.cardiff.ac.uk/barthes/article/roland-barthes-terror-in-poetry/. Accessed February 20, 2021.

Crowley, Patrick. "Édouard Glissant: Resistance and Opacity." *Romance Studies* 24.2 (2006): 105–15.

Du Bois, W. E. B. *The Souls of Black Folk: Essays and Sketches* [1903]. New York: Bartleby.com, 1999.

Forsdick, Charles and Susan Marson. *Reading Diversity*. Glasgow: University of Glasgow French and German Publications, 2000.

Gilroy, Paul. *The Black Atlantic: Modernity and Double Consciousness*. London: Verso, 1993.

Glissant, Édouard. *L'intention poétique*. Paris: Editions du Seuil, 1969.
Glissant, Édouard. *Le Discours antillais*. Paris: Editions du Seuil, 1981.
Glissant, Édouard. "Le chaos-monde, l'oral et l'écrit." In *Écrire "la parole de nuit": la nouvelle littérature antillaise*. Ed. Ralph Ludwig. Paris: Gallimard, 1994. 111–29.
Glissant, Édouard. *Poetics of Relation* [1992]. Trans. Betsy Wing. Ann Arbor, MI: University of Michigan Press, 1997.
Glissant, Édouard. *Introduction to a Poetics of Diversity*. Trans. Celia Britton. Liverpool: Liverpool University Press, 2020.
Glissant, Édouard. *Treatise on the Whole-World*. Trans. Celia Britton. Liverpool: Liverpool University Press, 2020.
Glissant, Édouard. *The Baton Rouge Interviews with Édouard Glissant and Alexandre Leupin*. Trans. Kate M. Cooper. Liverpool: Liverpool University Press, 2020.
Greco, Nicholas P. "'The Antithesis of Inner and Outer: Abolished': Roland Barthes and the Politics of the Closet." *Roland Barthes Studies* 6 (2020). http://sites.cardiff.ac.uk/barthes/files/2020/11/GRECO-The-Antithesis-of-Inner-and-Outer.pdf. Accessed January 10, 2021.
Griffiths, Michael R. "Toward Relation: Negritude, Poststructuralism, and the Specter of Intention in the Work of Édouard Glissant." *Discourse* 36.1 (2014): 31–53.
Ha, Marie-Paule. *Figuring the East: Segalen, Malraux, Duras and Barthes*. New York: SUNY Press, 2000. 95–117.
Hachad, Naïma. "Corps et corpus bilingues d'Abdelkébir Khatibi et Adelfattah Killito." Unpublished PhD thesis. Emory University, 2010.
Jameson, Fredric. *The Prison-House of Language: A Critical Account of Structuralism and Russian Formalism*. Princeton, NJ: Princeton University Press, 1972.
Khatibi, Abdelkébir. *L'œuvre de Abdelkébir Khatibi (Préliminaire)*. Rabat: Marsam, 1997.
Knight, Diana. *Barthes and Utopia: Space, Travel, Writing*. Oxford: Oxford University Press, 1997.
Lauro, Raphaël. "Édouard Glissant's Excursions and Detours." *Discourse* 36.1 (Winter 2014): 3–30.
Marty, Eric. *Roland Barthes, le métier d'écrire*. Paris: Editions du Seuil, 2006.
Marx, Karl. "Economic and Philosophical Manuscripts (1844)." In *Early Writings*. Trans. Rodney Livingstone and Gregor Benton. London: Penguin, 1975. 279–400.
Milner, Jean-Claude. *Le Pas philosophique de Roland Barthes*. Paris: Verdier, 2003.
Murdoch, H. Adlai. "Édouard Glissant's Creolized World Vision: From Resistance and Relation to Opacité." *Callaloo* 36.4 (2013): 876–89.
Nesbitt, Nick. "Early Glissant: From the Destitution of the Political to Antillean Ultra-Leftism." *Callaloo* 36.4 (2013): 932–48.
O'Meara, Lucy. *Roland Barthes at the Collège de France*. Liverpool: Liverpool University Press, 2012.
Paget, Henry. *Caliban's Reason: Introduction to Afro-Caribbean Philosophy*. London: Routledge, 2000.
Smith, Piers M. "The Neutral View: Roland Barthes's Representations of Japan and China." *IAFOR Journal of Literature and Librarianship* 5.1 (Autumn 2016): 53–60.
Stafford, Andy. "Edward Said and Roland Barthes: Criticism versus Essayism; Or, Roads and Meetings Missed." In *Edward Said and the Literary, Social and Political World*. Ed. Ranjan Ghosh. London: Routledge, 2009. 19–35.
Stafford, Andy. "Classé, surclasser, déclassé; or, Roland Barthes, Classification without Class." Special number on Roland Barthes. Eds. Thomas Baldwin, Katia Haustein, and Lucy O'Meara. *L'Esprit Créateur* 55.4 (Winter 2015): 148–64.

Stafford, Andy. "The Barthesian 'Double Grasp' in Japan: Reading as Undialectical Writing." In *The Pleasure in/of the Text About the Joys and Perversities of Reading*. Eds. Fabien Arribert-Narce, Endo Fuhito, Kamila Pawlikowska. Oxford/Lausanne: Peter Lang, 2021. 129–52.

Stan, Corinna. "A Sociality of Distances: Roland Barthes and Iris Murdoch on How to Live with Others." *MLN* 129.5 (2014): 1170–98.

Villani, Arnaud. "Le poème opaque d'Édouard Glissant." *Chimères* 90 (2016): 191–200.

de Villiers, Nicholas. "A Great Pedagogy of Nuance: Roland Barthes's The Neutral." *Theory & Event* 8.4 (2005).

de Villiers, Nicholas. *Opacity and The Closet: Queer Tactics in Foucault, Barthes and Warhol*. Minneapolis, MN: University of Minnesota Press, 2012.

Watson, Tim. *Culture Writing: Literature and Anthropology in the Midcentury Atlantic World*. Oxford: Oxford University Press, 2018.

13

Roland Barthes and Don DeLillo on Living Together/Apart

Herman Rapaport

"This is me, I am shapeless," he said.
"But even when you're here, I think of you coming from a distant city on your way to another distant city and neither place has shape or form."

—Don DeLillo, *Falling Man*

This chapter situates aspects of Roland Barthes's seminar *How to Live Together* (1976–7) in the context of Don DeLillo's novel *Falling Man* (2007). In fact, the central theme of Barthes's seminar is less that of simply living together than it is about living together/apart, something that has become very acute in American society of late, both on account of how politically divided America has become and of how appeals to social distancing have characterized the Covid-19 pandemic. Because DeLillo's novel is about the immediate aftereffects of 9/11, it well postdates Barthes's seminar by some thirty years and significantly predates our current moment of 2020. As we will see, Barthes's tropological critical approach to considering issues of living together/apart is very prescient with respect to *Falling Man*, which contains many of the tropes of sociality Barthes considers, as well as tropes DeLillo posits on his own that vastly enrich our understanding of Barthes's course. That is, the seminar will explain the novel as much as the novel will explain a very attenuated seminar written as bits and pieces. A close reading of aspects of *Falling Man* will show further how Barthes and DeLillo are in an implicit interlocution that serves to validate the contemporary human condition as they see it, a condition in which we are still living, however exacerbated by extremist politics and the deadly realities of Covid-19.[1]

Falling Man opens as follows:

It was not a street anymore but a world, a time and space of falling ash and near night. He was walking north through rubble and mud and there were people running past holding towels to their faces or jackets over their heads. They had handkerchiefs pressed to their mouths. They had shoes in their hands, a woman with a shoe in each hand, running past him. They ran and fell, some of them, confused and ungainly, with debris coming down around them, and there were people taking shelter under cars.[2]

On 9/11, many of us vicariously lived this scene on television together with the survivors. What DeLillo's nameless man experiences, we have experienced too, though not quite in the same way. "He heard the sound of the second fall, or felt it in the trembling air, the north tower coming down, a soft awe of voices in the distance. That was him coming down, the north tower."[3] Having just crossed Canal Street, the as-yet nameless man is imagining himself as another person descending as the tower breaks apart. "He tried to tell himself he was alive but the idea was too obscure to take hold."[4]

Here and throughout *Falling Man*, the protagonist is caught between what Barthes calls living apart and living together. "Almost all novels," Barthes writes, "contain bits and pieces of material pertaining of Living Together (or Living Alone): little snatches of simulation, like a very clear, fully realized detail."[5] For example, in *Falling Man*, "Someone came out of a diner and tried to hand him a bottle of water."[6] The man and the person (a woman) with the bottle don't know each other, and her opening the bottle and practically throwing it at the man is no more than an act of impersonal humanity. "She said something he didn't hear and he handed back the bottle."[7]

DeLillo's novel is centrally about the depiction of discontinuous states of being-in-the-world, states triggered by 9/11 specifically, but that are nevertheless very recognizable in terms of our own daily lives. Such discontinuous experience is also Barthes's central concern in the seminar he gave in 1976–7 at the *Collège de France*, entitled *How to Live Together*. Barthes searches for answers in Western literary and philosophical texts. Essentially, he is interested in rhetorical tropes that concern living together/apart, tropes we ourselves can find in the four decades after Barthes's death, among them, the falling towers in DeLillo's novel. We need to recall that in *A Lover's Discourse, Fragments* Barthes alphabetized what he considered the most salient tropes of amorous communication, which he saw as fragments rather than elements of a continuous whole. According to Barthes, the figures of love aren't discursive ornaments, but statements (conscious or unconscious), expositions, summaries, plot outlines, invented narratives. "I should add," Barthes notes, the "instrument of distancing."[8] That is, the trope (which can be a setting, conversation, argument, or situation) sets something off or apart in terms of being both rhetorical and imagistic repertoires. Notice, for example, the trope of catastrophe.

Catastrophe / catastrophe

Violent crisis during which the subject, experiencing the amorous situation as a definitive impasse, a trap form which he can never escape, sees himself doomed to total destruction.[9]

The rhetoric of catastrophe in the context of a lover's discourse is broad enough to include gentle versus violent despair ("I love you as one must love, in despair" vs. "I am ... asphyxiated with pain; my whole body stiffens and convulses"), the figure of the abandoning mother, the panic situation ("I am done for"), and, quite relevant to *Falling Man*, the trope of the prison camp inmate who will die apart/together. For the lovesick, Barthes offers the cliché, "when I am without the other ... I am lost forever."[10] Here, of course, being together and apart cannot both coexist. Notable is that in *Falling Man* this final trope is excluded as if it were a taboo, for in DeLillo one is condemned to live together *and* apart. There is no choosing.

In *How to Live Together*, Barthes will repeat the tropological approach to the lover's discourse by again listing main topics or figures in alphabetical order. Considered traits or discontinuous units, the alphabetization of these topoi make up a "non-transitional order" exposing how ways of living are fragmented.[11] Barthes argues that this method concerns a politics of deconstructing metalanguage, which is why he says there will be no sociology at work, no overall account or theory of living together. The tropes in *How to Live Together* will also be distributive and not integrative, synchronic rather than diachronic. Barthes has spoken of this approach as one of investigating "affective culture" that knows no inherent tropological order, because affective culture is largely reactive to incident, which is happenstantial.[12] Tropes of living together/apart are all taken from a shared cultural archive of clichés that we might not immediately notice with the rapidity we would notice the clichés of the lover. No doubt, living together/apart, which so concerns Barthes, could be seen as but another subset within the lover's discourse insofar as loving as living together requires *not* living apart. Toward the end of *Falling Man*, this will be specifically thematized.

From the outset of *Falling Man*, the man who will be known as Keith is not together with people nor apart. A panel truck pulls up to offer him a ride. And only then does he decide where he wishes to go, which is to the apartment of his ex-wife, Lianne. The decision hasn't been thought out. It's the enactment of a possibility, perhaps just a contingency, not a necessity. He doesn't *have* to be with her. The narrative cuts to Lianne who is having vague sexual thoughts some three days later. Some of this pertains to what Barthes would see as what he calls *marked*: "the extended grimness called their marriage."[13] Her mind drifts in and out of what is left incomplete, both in the past and in the present. What does being "with" or "without" someone mean?

Lianne receives a postcard from a friend staying in Rome. It displays the cover of a book: Shelley's *Revolt of Islam*. It is discontinuous with everything else around her, but Shelley's title clearly alludes to 9/11 by mere happenstance. Similarly happenstantial, of course, has been her ex-husband showing up three days prior. "Up from the dead, there he was in the doorway. ... Like gray soot head to toe, I don't know, like smoke, standing there, with blood on his face and clothes." She is talking to her mother with whom her son with Keith is living. Apparently, son and father haven't connected. Justin's grandmother responds disconnectedly: "We did a puzzle, an animal puzzle, horses in a field."[14] The idea was to deflect from the Twin Tower disaster, though Justin will become obsessed with planes crashing into skyscrapers.

Barthes's first topic of *How to Live Together* is Acedy: "boredom or anxiety of heart." "Akedia: prostration <*kedeuo*>: to care for, to take care of, take an interest in. Whence the opposites: *akedeo*: to be unconcerned (effectively the loss of investment); *akedestos*:

abandoned; *akedes*: negligent, neglected."[15] In *Falling Man*, caring for and taking an interest mixes together with feelings of lassitude and unconcern, of letting things drop. Lianne's mother can't fathom why Keith came to Lianne's apartment. "I don't know," Lianne responds, probably because she hasn't been concerned with where Keith has been living, which turns out to be too close to the towers to be habitable, not that even Keith has thought this through. "Why didn't he go straight to a hospital? Down there, downtown. Why didn't he go to a friend's place?"[16] The mixture of concern and unconcern in the mother's voice is palpable. She's suggesting that Keith is to be cared for, but not by them. The conversation between daughter and mother is riddled with holes, silences that cannot be bridged. Keith himself is reticent, which is his way of being-with-others. Not that mother and daughter mind. They don't go so far as to presume connection. Still Lianne is full of questions she would like to ask.

Barthes: "Disinvestment in the loved object: can be a liberation . . . but also a source of distress."[17] But how is this distress lived, apart and together? Keith has been decathected—disinvested—but that presupposes a different prior state of attachment, which may never have existed. The mother and daughter have emotionally disinvested in Keith, though his being a victim of a terrorist attack contradicts the logic of that impulse. All three, as it happens, are living, however differently, in terms of what Barthes calls an asceticism of solitude, a being by oneself. Does Justin live that too? Barthes doesn't point out the extent to which children live apart in their childhood from their parents and the extremes to which their dependency and independence go.

In *Falling Man*, to be together and not together isn't negotiated, only enacted. Keith just shows up. Lianne has fantasies of sexual enjoyment on account of boredom and remains alone. The mother takes a lover who suddenly shows up inconveniently in the middle of the day and Lianne is accosted by the executive editor she works for. "Is this a bad time? [. . .] Because if it is," Carol said, "we can talk whenever."[18] If this is the language of negotiation, Carol isn't really negotiating but pushing herself on Lianne. In this world, living together is a matter of being situated together by means of circumstances that seem to be beyond one's control of which the Twin Tower disaster is most exemplary. This is what Barthes calls the interruption of "incidence."

Of course, there are other figures, or master signifiers, for being together/apart in *Falling Man*. Lianne, for example, conducts group work with Alzheimer's patients who are living together and apart in terms of forgetting and reencountering themselves vis-à-vis their pasts. What does it mean for Lianne to connect with people who aren't so well connected to themselves anymore? Distantly analogous is Keith's sorting through his mail in which he inevitably comes across misspellings of his name which he corrects with a pen. "He wasn't sure when he'd starting doing this and didn't know why he did it."[19] Perhaps he corrects the misspellings in order not to disconnect from himself. By the end of the novel, he will have lost himself to a great extent, but at this early stage of posttraumatic shock he is still trying to hold on to himself in a way distantly analogous to the Alzheimer's patients.

Another telling figure of connection/disconnection is the briefcase that Keith accidentally picked up as his when he fled the distressed tower. "It wasn't his briefcase but he'd carried it out of the tower and he had it with him when he showed up at the door. . . .

He ran his thumb over the padded handle, trying to remember why he'd carried it out of there."[20] Again, there is forgetting. He opens the case and finds various objects, including a wallet, credit cards, and a driver's license. Examining the contents "was somehow morbidly unright." Yet "he was so remote from the things in the briefcase, from the occasion of the briefcase, that it probably didn't matter."[21] Nevertheless, Keith will bring the briefcase and its contents over to Florence Givens, whose name was in the briefcase and whom he looked up in the phonebook. "She was a light skinned black woman, his age or close, and gentle-seeming, and on the heavy side."[22] The meeting is awkward and negotiated mainly by the manners dictated by hospitality. "The cookies were small and awful but he kept nipping into them, unthinkingly, eating only the first baby bite and leaving the mutilated remains to litter the plate." The cookies are figures of the survivors' discourse, symbolizing being together/apart. After much time, Florence recalls, "I was at my screen and heard the plane approach but only after I was thrown down. That's how fast."[23] Impact first, the sound of the plane second, and simultaneously the sprinklers coming on. What follows is the terror and difficulty of getting out of the tower with everyone together and apart, the trope of the stairwell crowded with people all trying to save themselves. "She saw a woman with burnt hair, hair burnt and smoking, but now she wasn't sure she'd seen this or heard someone say it."[24] At times, Florence is having to fend for herself; other times, people are helping her make it out of the building. The story she tells is a tissue of disconnected memories loosely organized and laced with uncertainty about what really had been experienced. This too is not so absolutely different from the Alzheimer's patients remembering/not remembering. Had Keith experienced the same things as Florence? At some point, their memories of the stairwell and the panic cross. Did he see the man she did going up the stairs? "I feel like I'm still on the stairs," she says.[25] At that moment, Keith does too. They are no longer apart.

Barthes speaks of the fantasy of living together as an essentially spatial fact, as is the fantasy of living together "in the same time." "The ultimate sign of Living-Together— to 'talk together.'"[26] Barthes speaks of the pseudo-conjugal, which is what Keith and Florence achieve in what will be their visits together. Such a relation has a consistency of rhythm that is improvised, fugitive, and various even if something is schematically unwavering and retrievable. Barthes cites Nietzsche: "We are nothing more than a succession of discontinuous states in relation to the code of everyday signs, and about which the fixity of language deceives us. While we depend on this code we imagine our continuity, but in fact we live only discontinuously."[27] We do one thing, then another, and then another. Explaining connection requires one to narrate events as if they were inherently related and continuous, an attempt that is made in DeLillo but with considerable self-doubt.

For Barthes, the figure of the anachorite is significant in that it speaks to retreating from the world. "Anachoresis is not a matter of absolute solitude, but rather of this: a way of reducing one's contact with the world + individualism (individualistic asceticism)."[28] Metaphorically anachoresis is a breaking away, "the abrupt jolt of departure." Barthes is thinking of Robinson Crusoe, who in a single stroke is separated. But of anachoresis, Barthes says, "I want to create a life-structure that isn't a life-system."²⁹ We can debate if that is what occurs in *Robinson Crusoe*, but in *Falling Man* one senses that the characters are living apart in a way that refuses any life-system, which is to say, any rigidly organized life, even if parts of everyone's day has structure. Even Keith's eventual escape into the world of professional poker playing ambiguates living by a game's rules with living apart from any determinate sociality. Would these be examples of urban anachoresis? Barthes opens the door to this way of thinking when he says that in the day-to-day world one ought to think of the social distinction between gregariousness and alienation. That certainly suits life at the gaming table. But it also marks the conversations Keith has with Lianne and Florence, talkative but striated with gaps and silences.

Of course, life in New York City, whatever the time, is likely to be a confluence of many sorts of sociality existing side by side and/or interrupting one another. Of much interest to Barthes is the project of distinguishing between various sorts of communities, human and at times animal. What kind of community is a school of fish? Or a nest of insects? What about autarky, "a little 'colony' that requires nothing beyond the internal life of its constituents"?³⁰ This is the world of Hans Castorp in *The Magic Mountain*, of interest to Barthes, in which there is much intradependence and almost no extradependence. "Independence marks the boundary, and so gives the definition, the mode of being of the group."³¹ Jules Verne's Captain Nemo and the *Nautilus* would represent this sort of self-contained existence. Submarine, sanatorium, space station, or outpost would typify autarky.

Another figure of communal living central to Barthes is the idea of the hermitage or monastery in which "each monk is free to live at their own particular rhythm." The major figure here is Athos, a scattering of hermitages that are unregulated, idiorhythmic by nature. In such places, once a year there may be a communal act that would reflect some rule within "a flexible conception of constraint." "Athos: Athonite federation of monasteries, governed by a council, under Greek protection, 1912."³² This speaks to relaxed asceticism, somewhere between hermeticism and monasticism. Here life has a structure that is idiosyncratic, not systematic. For Barthes this represents a denial of being subjected to some outside power, for "the first thing that power imposes is a rhythm."³³ To the contrary, various communities come together in the service of some aim or telos which directs everyone. This aim may be perfection or sainthood. Fraternal organizations may come under this rubric. Christian orders, too. In the Sanatorium, the aim is to get and stay well. Living together obeys rules that have the common aim of avoiding the fate of dying. Barthes wonders: Can groups be maintained in the absence of some telos or some aim to achieve something considered good? How can one be free to experience the idiorrhythmic and yet be adhering to a telos that requires discipline? Barthes also wonders if there could be a community without telos that exists in a happy homeostatic state. "An idyllic view of worldliness: a machine with no goal, where there's no transformation."³⁴ One thinks of Kurosawa's "Village of the Waterwheels" in the film *Dreams*. This is a homeostatic community bonded through Shinto rituals that imply a certain asceticism: to deny material and social transformation. In that sense, homeostasis is itself a coercive power.

Of interest is that *Falling Man* considers more than one sort of sociality, given that DeLillo also depicts the loosely organized group that would execute the 9/11 attacks on America. Whereas the aim of Keith's life has been to work for a company in the Twin Towers in order to support himself, such an aim has been more or less buried within all the particulars of his everyday life that have become more or less routine. Certainly, homeostasis plays a role as an imperative to live and act a certain way, though in general someone like Keith can live outside the system too once he leaves his place of work. For the terrorist Hammad living in Germany, there is the memory of war in the Shatt al Arab fifteen years prior. He recalls watching thousands of boys. "Some carried rifles, many did not, and the weapons nearly overwhelmed the smaller boys." Hammad was a soldier in Saddam's army and the boys were "the martyrs of the Ayatollah, here to fall and die. They seemed to come up out of the wet earth, wave on wave, and he aimed and fired and watched them fall."[35] The boys are more like a school of fish or flock of birds, a herd directed at an enemy seemingly without sufficient purpose. In fact, they are a strategic distraction diverting Iraqi troops from "the real army massing behind front lines," but it took Hammad time to realize that shooting at the boys was pointless. "Most countries are run by madmen," Hammad thinks.[36] Hammad is told by one of the men from his Mosque that "The boys were sounding the cry of history, the story of ancient Shia defeat and the allegiance of the living to those who were dead and defeated. That cry is still close to me, he said. Not like something happening yesterday but something always happening, over a thousand years happening, always in the air." As Hammad listens, he "kept thinking that another woman would come by on a bike, someone to look at, hair wet, legs pumping." For him too, life is disconnected. There is the prayer room, the world outside, the collision of Islam with itself and the West. Islam is unified, however, by Hammad as a struggle against an enemy. This struggle requires sacrifice in order to bring about its aim. Life outside of that concerted struggle is largely meaningless, but it is in the context of this life in Europe that Hammad will meet men who will direct and lead him. "The beard would look better if he trimmed it. But there were rules now and he was determined to follow them. His life had structure. Things were clearly defined. He was becoming one of them now, learning to look like them and think like them." Having lived apart, he is now living more and more together. "This was inseparable from jihad. He prayed with them to be with them. They were becoming total brothers."[37] This is the fraternal group model in which holy war is undertaken as a collective aim, though one that in everyday life isn't entirely linear.

In a session entitled Marginalities, Barthes considers those who are excluded from social-political power, as in the case of Christian martyrs. The monastic orders are themselves born of the marginal religious zones, separated from the world. The monk, Barthes says, is an exceptional individual, even when he lives in a community. In him the sacred is concentrated. But is the same true of the Muslim martyr to be who is living in a precinct of Hamburg? Is that also a case of there being a marginal religious zone? Here, what Barthes calls "living at a distance" may be relevant in that the brotherhood aiming at jihad lives both within and apart from society, functioning within its legal parameters as a matter of form only. To live at a distance in this sense can mean embracing the sort of disconnection with others that makes the socially atrocious become possible as a reality for the sake of martyrdom. Society, not surprisingly, has tended to see marginal zones as subversive and dangerous, wary of denizens who are sometimes viewed as deviant, asocial, and violent. In a parallel vein, set in earlier times, Barthes notes that "Society keeps a close eye on the margin: hermitages get built within the precincts of abbeys, with the hermits now dependent on the abbey, a negation of the basic idiorrhythmic premise, which is to operate outside the remit of any given authority." Barthes adds that "we'd have to append a whole dossier on the social repression of marginalities; the lawful repression of certain abnormalities," communes included.[38]

In *Falling Man*, the marginal zone in Germany is watched but not suppressed, given issues concerning individual rights: freedom of religion, association, and so on. Even in the United States, when the terrorists took flying lessons that excluded how to land a 747, no one bothered to wonder if something abnormal was afoot. In Barthes, the distinction between the normal (the regulated) and the abnormal (the unregulated) is everywhere at issue in the context of living together/apart. What we consider abnormal is in many cases a retreat into a community with a private language, even if it is a community of one. Difference, in this context, concerns withdrawal into an autarchy that cuts ties with the outside world. Does Hammad undertake such a withdrawal? And is that hardly radical given the German social response to Muslim immigrants in their midst as normal-abnormal people?

Rosellen S. suffers from Alzheimer's and is part of the therapy group, a sort of autarchy, moderated by Lianne in East Harlem. Out on her own, Rosellen cannot remember where she lives. "She stood alone on a corner near the elevated tracks, becoming desperate, separated from everything. The world was receding, the simplest recognitions." Moreover, "she was not lost so much as falling, growing fainter. Nothing lay around her but silence and distance."[39] Someone assists her by looking in her handbag for contacts and calls a sister in Brooklyn. Lianne learns this from Dr. Apter and reflects on the growing gap between herself and Rosellen that has been occurring over the weeks. In fact, all the Alzheimer's patients in the group are losing things, which is a symptom of being lost more generally. Lianne's job is to slow down the disease by getting the patients to interact and exercise brain function in the process. To be together requires not being lost, not being surrounded by only silence and distance. Alzheimer's in that context is a figure for what stands apart, alone, and lost. When we are told that Rosellen was not lost so much as falling, we are meant to recall the experience of Florence and Keith in the stairwell with the great press of people pouring in from all the floors. Disoriented, everyone is sort of lost. Florence herself falls down several steps and, for a moment, finds herself apart from the crowd, though still within it. In English, "falling by the wayside" is an idiom that captures Barthes's sense of being isolated in a marginal zone near others. Here, one isn't totally apart, but no longer quite together, either. For Florence, falling by the wayside or margin is a matter of being in a dangerous spot, in the sense of both place and situation. But this is the case for Rosellen, too, who doesn't know anymore where she is or where she lives. Alzheimer's: figure for everyday disintegration.

Barthes: "Let's call 'idyllic' any space of human relations defined by an absence of conflict."[40] Is group therapy idyllic? Lianne's role as group leader is to be supportive of everyone in a way that includes them within a space where conflict is discouraged. Social relations are therefore complementary and respectful in a way that normalizes everyone, despite each person's differences as an effect of Alzheimer's. The idyll, Barthes says, erases social reality.[41] Does group therapy do this as well to some extent? The aim of the group is to stay as healthy as possible, which overrides social reality as stratified and competitive. The therapeutic group is social but not realistically social. In a section Barthes devotes to W. R. Bion, the theoretician of group psychology, we are told that the group leader can be a person or an idea whose role is to protect the group and individuals within it. How individuals pair in groups mattered to Bion, because pairs can work together in order to confront and thereby exist apart from the group as a whole. Last, the group leader meets in order to fight an outside threat or escape from it. Presumably, Lianne serves as protector and fighter. If the group is idyllic, it is also a fortress that protects and defends. But as fortress, the group is suffering what the Twin Towers suffered: disintegration perpetrated by an enemy force that comes unseen and unbidden.

Barthes is interested in pairings, which is part of the reason he mentions Bion. Lianne is oddly paired with Keith both before and after the divorce. She wants strong intimacy—to be together. Yet with respect to Keith's surviving the collapse of the North Tower, she distances herself. He doesn't want strong intimacy but wishes to stand apart, to put space between himself and Lianne. Yet with respect to surviving the collapse, he seeks closeness with Florence, who suffered the same experience. Were they together in the stairwell? Did they actually see one another without realizing it? Upon explaining to Florence that he has taken a job in Jersey, she is concerned about how much space that puts between them. Later we find out that Keith and Florence have been sleeping together.

> "It's only Jersey."
> "Okay," she said.
> He thought she might cry. He thought this kind of conversation was for other people. People have these conversations all the time, he thought, in rooms like this one, sitting, looking.
> Then she said. "You saved my life. Don't you know that?"[42]

Life as Florence knew it came to an end with so many friends dead. "I couldn't see people, talk to people, go from here to there without forcing myself up off the chair." To her, the delivery of the briefcase is motivated by fate. "You ask yourself why you took the briefcase out of the building." The reason is "So you could bring it here. So, we could get to know each other. That's why you took it and that's why you brought it here, to keep me alive." He didn't quite believe this, but believed her. "You ask yourself what the story is that goes with the briefcase. I'm the story," she said.[43] Later we are told that Keith had only seen Florence perhaps four or five times and that without explanation he simply failed to ever contact her again. Yet he will continue to think of her, which raises the question, are they together or apart?

The briefcase is an object of connection, the kind of object that interests Barthes, who mentions lamps and beds. In *Falling Man*, the bed is a figure not just for sex but also for falling together. Keith and Florence are on the ninth floor of Macy's in the bed department. "Florence Givens stood looking at the mattresses, forty or fifty of them, arranged in rows at one end of the ninth floor. People tested the bedding, women mostly, bouncing lightly in seated positions or lying supine, checking for firmness or plushness. It took her a moment to realize that Keith was standing at her side, watching with her."[44] A bit later, we read, "There were tentative women, bouncing once or twice, feet protruding from the end of the bed, and there were the others, women who'd shed their coats and shoes, falling backwards to the mattress, the Posturepedic or the Beautyrest, and bouncing with abandon, first one side of the bed, then the other."[45] In the context of the jumpers on 9/11, this scene of falling bodies on the beds functions as a psychological defense against the horror of what has happened as people fell to their deaths on the pavement surrounding the Twin Towers. There is another echo, too, when Florence notices Keith is with her, for in her mind she has been standing there alone in the mattress department. Naturally, Barthes views the figure of the bed as a signifier of proximity, say, of the body to itself, of one body in relation to another, and so forth. It is also the signifier of fantasy and dream. We have to wonder: Are Florence and Keith lulled into a dreamlike state by all the bouncing bodies in which falling turns into playing and enjoyment? Does the figure of the bed encourage forgetting, distancing, denying what has been experienced as excruciatingly traumatic? Barthes notes: "Bed=site of the subject's fantasmatic expansion."[46] As it happens, in DeLillo the bed is restrictive, a site of fantasmatic exclusion, a sort of memory lapse. The people bouncing on the mattresses are not imagining themselves as victims jumping out of burning skyscrapers. Something akin to this sort of restriction has happened earlier in the novel when Keith and Lianne sleep together and have sex. They forget the past and what has happened between them. The figure of the room also factors into Barthes's considerations of being together/apart. He discusses rooms when they become autonomous spaces in which the scenery becomes the locus for the revelation of confidences and secrets. The room contains the conversation, nurtures it, and allows it to blossom: to reveal fully by giving conversation a space in which to unfold. In *Falling Man*, the room is a place apart in which Florence felt she was dying alone as if in sympathy with her friend who didn't survive. But the room becomes almost conjugal, as Barthes might have said, with Keith's enlivening visits. The room is the mise-en-scène for an interaction that transforms mere survival into living on (*sur-vivance*, in French). Talking, in this context, is saving. Here, the pair (Florence and Keith) and the group (Lianne and the Alzheimer's patients) are pulling against the forces of disintegration. Existence in DeLillo's novel depends upon conversation.

As to Hammad and his compatriots, the time for talking is over. The aim of the terrorists is to carry through on a plan that has been talked through to death. In a training camp in Afghanistan, Hammad "had begun to understand that death is stronger than life. This is where the landscape consumed him, waterfalls frozen in space, a sky that never ended. It was all Islam, the rivers and streams. Pick up a stone and hold it in your fist, this is Islam. God's name on every tongue throughout the countryside." Hammad wears a bomb vest, which makes him feel "ready to close the distance to God."[47] Barthes writes of *anachoresis:* "its foundational act is to break away, the abrupt jolt of departure." *Anachoresis* concerns a way of retreating from the world, fleeing the state, taking up residence in a cell. What Hammad experiences in Afghanistan is the kind of asceticism that closes the gap between him and the sacred. But, as Barthes points out, "anachoresis = an action, a line, a threshold to be crossed."[48] This has to be done collectively and individualistically, according to Barthes. DeLillo writes: "They felt things together, he and his brothers. They felt a claim of danger and isolation. They felt the magnetic effect of plot. Plot drew them together more tightly than ever. Plot closed the world to the slenderest line of sight, where everything converges to a point." This is the fateful pull of "the highest jihad."[49] Hammad has doubts that his friend Amir settles. "This is not suicide by any meaning or interpretation of the word. It is only something long written. We are finding the way already chosen for us."[50] As to the victims who will die alongside the terrorists in the planes, "Amir said simply there are no others. The others exist only to the degree that they fill the role we have designed for them."[51] In Barthes's terms, the terrorists are, in addition to everything else, a fraternal order that lives under a rule or imperative, a plan that is more important than the ones who will carry it out. "The plot shapes every breath he takes. This is the truth he has always looked for without knowing how to name it or where to search. They are together."[52] That it is by means of "the rapture of live explosives" that the terrorists will be bound takes the matter of living together/apart to a radical extreme. Does togetherness require fanaticism? Barthes seems to think it well might. The lover and the terrorist are both fanatical in their own way.

Two last dominant figures of living together/apart in *Falling Man* of importance are the street and the casino. There is a long sequence in the novel in which Lianne is going to meet up with Keith and Justin uptown north of 59th street. "I'm trying to read her mind," Keith says, "Will she walk down one of the avenues? First, Second, Third, or wander a little, here and there?"[53] Keith and Justin are and aren't with her as they guess her movements; moreover, Justin is pulling away from Keith in "a mood of somber opposition."[54] As they walk, Keith begins imagining a conversation with Lianne in which he confesses meeting with Florence. "It was not an affair," he thinks. "There was sex, yes, but not romance."[55] Keith and Justin pass a pharmacy and a travel agency and notice

> a woman crossing the street uncertainly near the intersection. She seemed to stop in midcrossing. A taxi obscured his view for a moment but he knew that something was wrong. He leaned over and gave the kid a backhand tap on the upper arm, keeping his eyes on the figure ahead. By the time she reached the corner on his side of the street, they were both running toward her.[56]

She, meanwhile, has been witnessing a performance artist known as the "falling man," who shows up unexpectedly in various parts of the city to reenact the jumpers who fell to their deaths on 9/11. The man is standing on elevated train tracks and jumps as a train swoops by. This happens to be the spot where Rosellen S. became disoriented.

> [Lianne] felt her body go limp. But the fall was not the worst of it. The jolting end of the fall left him upside-down, secured to the harness twenty feet above the pavement. The jolt, the sort of midair impact and bounce, the recoil, and now the stillness, arms at his sides, one leg bent at the knee. There was something awful about the stylized pose, body and limbs, his signature stroke. But the worst of it was the stillness itself and her nearness to the man, her position here, with no one closer to him than she was.[57]

Lianne is as near as she is remote from the dangling man whose act has terrorized her, so much so that she makes her escape by steadying herself on a nearby wall. Like Rosellen S., Lianne is very disoriented. Though they are far apart, they are, in a certain sense, together.

> She moved now, keeping to the side of the building, head down, feeling her way by hand along the rough surface of the masonry. Her eyes were open but she guided herself by hand and then, once beyond the dangling figure, veered toward the middle of the sidewalk, moving quickly now.... She couldn't seem to walk quickly enough, passing more projects or the same spreading development, one street and then another.[58]

The street, in this case, has suddenly been transformed into the stairwell of the doomed tower in which everyone is disoriented and groping for whatever support is at hand. In place of being paired with Rosellen S., Lianne is now paired with Keith and Florence, having undergone something terrifying and traumatic: the memory of the suspended body recurring as she flees. "She could not think beyond this." Exhausted with running, she meets up as if by accident with Keith and Justin. "She raised a hand so they might see her in the mass of faces, thirty-six days after the planes."[59] She is as if rescued by the only two people in uptown with whom she can be together, all the other human relationships being conducted under the sign of living apart and refusing contact. The figure of the street in this context repeats the contradiction of living together as a function of being apart.

The street has also been the stage for the falling man whose arbitrary performative imposition is experienced as a terrifying happening that ambivalently establishes an identification with both the terrorists and the victims. In repeating the trauma of 9/11, the falling man manifests a disturbing psychological contradiction in which attacker and victim are fused. For Lianne, the falling man is in some sense associated symbolically with Keith, though he is also associated with the street people she encounters—a derelict man, among them. In short, there is a way of seeing that the falling man really is just another urban weirdo whose place is in the street. Such human figures inevitably posit the ambivalence of being apart-together, alien from and close to. In contrast to the terrifying otherness of the jumper who has dangled in such close proximity to her, Lianne is relieved to join with her familiars, Keith and Justin.

No doubt Barthes would have picked out the figure of the casino as another major figure of how (not) to live together in *Falling Man*. After Keith recovers from the immediate trauma of escaping the Twin Towers disaster, he takes on a job for an attorney in New Jersey. Toward the end of *Falling Man*, we find out that he has quit that job in order to pursue what will turn out to be a life of playing poker in mainly Las Vegas. Like the dangling man in the street, who is playing dead, Keith enters a suspended existence in hotels that complement high rollers. At the gaming tables, he is and isn't with others. At one point, he notices a blinking woman across the table, but finds her "hard to see." He becomes aware of the fact that he won't ever wonder who she is or where she will go. "There was nothing outside the game but faded space. She blinked and called, blinked and folded."[60] Full stop. Keith who is still financially viable as a gambler does return from time to time to Lianne and Justin in New York. At one point, Lianne remarks, "I understand there are some men who are only half here." She says she understands this, but adds, "we need to stay together, keep the family going."[61] That is, she accepts being apart-together as a posttraumatic necessity. However, in an attempt to grasp Keith's situation, Lianne has been watching poker tournaments on TV and mentions to him it was like watching a séance in hell. "Tick tock tick tock. What happens after months of this? Or years. Who do you become?"

As a trope, the casino is a hellish place of anomie where life is put on hold, a refuge. Recall Barthes's comment that "anachoresis is not a matter of absolute solitude, but rather of this: a way of reducing one's contact with the world + individualism (individualistic asceticism)."[62] If anachoresis is a breaking away, an "abrupt jolt of departure,"[63] it is the figure of the airplane that instantiates this jolt, which Keith feels as he takes off for Las Vegas. Having reduced his contact with the world, Keith notices that he is flatlining. The rhythm of existentially withdrawing into the rules of the game mean that "Days fade, nights drag on, check-and-raise, wake-and-sleep."[64] In Germany, the terrorists had been living like this too, nihilistically and suicidally. As considerable time passes in the casinos, Keith turns into a fallen man, someone whose dangling has dragged out for much too long. Perhaps the casino is, in the end, not so different from the falling tower: locus of money, chance, and sudden loss. "These were the days after and now the years, a thousand heaving dreams, the trapped man, the fixed limbs, the dream of paralysis, the gasping man, the dream of asphyxiation, the dream of helplessness."[65] In the novel's final chapter, Hammad is experiencing his last moments on the plane before impact, and we seamlessly glide into Keith's tower office. "He thought he saw the ceiling begin to ripple, lift and ripple."[66]

Over the past fifty years, French thinkers have been very keen on analyzing the social relation and what it means to live together as a society, community, or group. In *The Politics of Friendship*, Jacques Derrida famously began with the paradox, "O friends, there is no friend," by which he meant that social relations, even of the closest sort, are aporetic in terms of being together/apart. In *The Inoperative Community*, Jean-

Luc Nancy discussed the idea that community is composed of an interruption of singularities and suspensions. Communication, according to Nancy, is the unworking of work that is institutional, social, economic, and technical. Dissensus, criticism, refusal, withdrawal, asceticism, and suspension characterize being apart. For Maurice Blanchot, who is considered by Nancy, being apart-together speaks to what he calls an unavowable community.[67] Whereas Nancy, Blanchot, and Derrida consider how the social relation and nonrelation are invaginated, Giorgio Agamben takes this a step further in *Remnants of Auschwitz* wherein he constructs an account of community radically without community. Barthes's *How to Live Together* fits into the context of these other thinkers of the social relation for whom that relation is riddled with paradox. DeLillo, for his part, gives us a realistic fictional model that stresses the daily experience of a community lacking sufficient community in the aftermath of terrorist attacks that one should suppose would pull a community together.

Whereas existentialists such as Sartre and Camus considered extreme alienation in which there is active ethical outrage that incriminates the social as antisocial and inhuman, other French literary writers, Maurice Blanchot among them, have depicted a passive attitude that presumes the widespread intercession of nonrelations within personal and impersonal social relations. Indeed, Blanchot, Beckett, Duras, and Robbe-Grillet have explored the nonrelationality of the relation largely from the perspective of the individual—for example, the demobilized soldier in Robbe-Grillet's *In the Labyrinth*, Anne Marie Stretter in *The Vice Consul*, Krapp in Beckett's *Krapp's Last Tape*, or Thomas in Blanchot's *Thomas the Obscure*. DeLillo's *Falling Man* differs in that it multiplies social perspectives and individual experiences wherein living together is hard to distinguish from living apart. Like Barthes, DeLillo dwells upon numerous fragments of social experience that can serve as figures or snapshots for the problematic of how to live together. *Falling Man* in that context is less about Keith than it is about the people who exist in proximity to him, both known and unknown: his wife, her mother, her mother's boyfriend with the shady past, his son Justin, who calls Bin Laden by the name Bill Lawson, Hammad and his brotherhood, Rosellen S. and the other Alzheimer's patients, Florence Givens, the anonymous survivors in the stairwell of the stricken North Tower, the poker players in Las Vegas, the women bouncing on the Beautyrest beds at Macys, the performance artist grotesquely imposing himself on New Yorkers, the fellow survivors in physical rehab, and so on. For all of these persons depicted in the novel, living together paradoxically presumes nonrelationality as the social bedrock upon which community is expected to function. Barthes's seminar on how to live together provides a tropological roadmap for understanding what has become a shared historical reality almost twenty-five years after Barthes began contemplating a book on living together/apart. That is, his seminar, which focuses on literary and communitarian examples, serves as a critical-conceptual approach that enables us to unpack what might go unnoticed, namely the far-reaching social insights of lived experience in our time as DeLillo has depicted them in the aftermath of America's first major catastrophe of the new millennium in 2001. This has now been followed by what is still a much greater catastrophe in progress, Covid-19 in the purposively inoperative and dysfunctional time of the Trump Administration wherein a politics of division has insisted that living together necessarily means living apart, if not dying apart, in ICU hospital beds.

Notes

1. See Callie Ingram, "Counter Narrative Ethics: Don DeLillo's Post 9/11 Novels," in *Critique: Studies in Contemporary Fiction* 60.5 (2019), for an accounting of academic responses to *Falling Man* as insufficiently radical from a progressive left-wing point of view. The domesticity of the novel, we learn, is objectionable in that it is said to depoliticize 9/11. Methodologically, the criticisms of the scholars Ingram cites amount to holding a work of fiction accountable to left-of-center political dogma. This is not very different from conservative Christians condemning novels because they don't uphold Christian values. Ingram herself trivializes the plot of *Falling Man*. The formal features of the novel are overlooked in order to extrapolate a reductive storyline about a couple living in the aftermath of the 9/11 attacks. In contrast, reading the novel from the perspective of Barthes's *How to Live Together* acknowledges the fragmentary and multiaspectual way in which DeLillo is making a significant critique of contemporary society in ways that go far beyond simplistic rubrics of political correctness and content analysis. Also, and perhaps more importantly for us, reading Barthes's seminar by way of *Falling Man* enables one to pull together what is, in fact, a very disparate and fragmented series of notes that would otherwise be very difficult to synthesize usefully.
2. Don DeLillo, *Falling Man* (New York: Scribner, 2007), 3.
3. Ibid., 5.
4. Ibid., 6.
5. Ibid., 13.
6. Ibid., 4.
7. Ibid., 5.
8. Roland Barthes, *A Lover's Discourse, Fragments*, trans. Richard Howard (New York: Hill and Wang, 1978), 5.
9. Ibid., 48.
10. Ibid., 48–9.
11. Roland Barthes, *How to Live Together*, trans. Kate Briggs (New York: Columbia University Press, 2013), 20.
12. See Barthes, *A Lover's Discourse, Fragments*, 7.
13. DeLillo, *Falling Man*, 7.
14. Ibid., 8.
15. Barthes, *How to Live Together*, 21. Barthes's rhetorical question, "Why all the Ancient Greek?" is answered with "Because it slows us down."
16. DeLillo, *Falling Man*, 9.
17. Barthes, *How to Live Together*, 22.
18. DeLillo, *Falling Man*, 20.
19. Ibid., 31.
20. Ibid., 35.

21 Ibid., 36.
22 Ibid., 52.
23 Ibid., 54.
24 Ibid., 55.
25 Ibid. 57.
26 Barthes, *How to Live Together*, 5.
27 Ibid., 19.
28 Ibid., 25.
29 Ibid., 26.
30 Ibid., 37.
31 Ibid., 36.
32 Ibid., 31.
33 Ibid., 35.
34 Ibid., 48.
35 Ibid., 77.
36 Ibid., 78.
37 Ibid., 83.
38 Ibid., 93.
39 Ibid.
40 Barthes, *How to Live Together*, 88.
41 Ibid., 89.
42 DeLillo, *Falling Man*, 108.
43 Ibid., 109.
44 Ibid., 131.
45 Ibid., 132.
46 Barthes, *How to Live Together*, 113.
47 DeLillo, *Falling Man*, 172.
48 Barthes, *How to Live Together*, 25.
49 Delillo, *Falling Man*, 174.
50 Ibid., 175.
51 Ibid.,176.
52 Ibid.
53 Ibid., 165.
54 Ibid., 166.
55 Ibid.
56 Ibid., 167.
57 Ibid., 168.
58 Ibid., 169.
59 Ibid., 170.
60 Ibid., 189.
61 Ibid., 213–14.
62 Barthes, *How to Live Together*, 25.
63 Ibid.
64 DeLillo, *Falling Man*, 226.
65 Ibid., 230.
66 Ibid., 239.
67 See Maurice Blanchot, *The Unavowable Community* (Barrytown: Station Hill Press, 1988).

Bibliography

Agamben, Giorgio. *Remnants of Auschwitz*. New York: Zone Books, 2002.
Barthes, Roland. *A Lover's Discourse, Fragments*. Trans. Richard Howard. New York: Hill and Wang, 1978.
Barthes, Roland. *How to Live Together*. Trans. Kate Briggs. New York: Columbia University Press, 2013.
Beckett, Samuel. *Krapp's Last Tape and Other Shorter Plays*. London: Faber and Faber, 2009.
Blanchot, Maurice. *Thomas the Obscure*. Trans. Robert Lamberton. Barrytown: Station Hill Press, 1988.
Blanchot, Maurice. *The Unavowable Community*. Barrytown: Station Hill Press, 1988.
DeLillo, Don. *Falling Man*. New York: Scribners, 2007.
Derrida, Jacques. *The Politics of Friendship*. Trans. George Collins. New York: Verso, 1997.
Duras, Marguerite. *The Vice Consul*. Trans. Eileen Ellenbogen. New York: Pantheon, 1987.
Harack, Katrina. "Embedded and Embodied Memories: Body, Space, and Time in DeLillo's *White Noise* and *Falling Man*." *Contemporary Literature* 54.2 (2013): 303–36.
Ingram, Callie. "Counter Narrative Ethics: Don DeLillo's Post 9/11 Novels." *Critique: Studies in Contemporary Fiction* 60.5 (2019): 585–99.
Nancy, Jean-Luc. *The Inoperative Community*. Trans. Peter Cooper. Minneapolis, MN: University of Minnesota, 1991.
Polatinsky, Stefan and Karen Scherzinger. "Dying Without Death: Temporality, Writing, and Survival in Maurice Blanchot's *The Instant of My Death* and Don DeLillo's *Falling Man*." *Critique: Studies in Contemporary Fiction* 54.2 (2013): 124–34.
Robbe-Grillet, Alain. *In the Labyrinth*. Trans. Christine Brooke-Rose. London: Calder and Boyers, 1967.
Sumner, Charles. "Don DeLillo's *Falling Man* and the Protective Shield Against Stimuli." *American Imago* 71.1 (2014): 1–27.

14

Barthes

Visual Culture and Homosexual Sociabilities

Magali Nachtergael

Why does it seem so hard to talk about Roland Barthes's homosexuality, and especially for the francophone scholars? Why does he seem so far away from all major changes and gains for the gay community in the 1970s, in contrast with Foucault, who had always been associated with the gay rights movement and its visibility? In an informal discussion, the French queer theorist Sam Bourcier told me that it is because Barthes voluntarily stayed in the closet, in Eve Kosofsky Sedgwick's well-known epistemology, so as to avoid what he called the hysteria of activism. Many scholars have noted that Barthes had never been considered a homosexual writer, even though he prefaced the crude and explicit sexual diary *Tricks* by Renaud Camus. Barthes's homosexuality was a known fact, but not a critical one: as Pierre Joseph Salazar notes, "his life encapsulates, in a way, the changes that affected French, and European, homosociety before the advent of Greenwich Village or the Castro," preferring the use of words such as "desire" and "jouissance,"[1] to blur the gendered lines of same-sex relationships. At the same time, Nicholas de Villiers points out that Barthes had also been, alongside many others, closeted by the critics. During his life, Barthes's critical writings were discreetly but decisively linked to the homosexual community culture, even if directed toward the heterosexual audience. Of course, it would be unfair to say that the gay Barthes has not been accounted for: Harold Beaver, Carol Mavor,[2] Diana Knight, and, more recently, de Villiers and Benjamin Hiramatsu Ireland studied his "homosexual signs," his "boyish" look, the "tricks of the text,"[3] his "queer tactics,"[4] and the question of "race and gender."[5] However, these readings remain underestimated in the reception of Barthes's work, and especially in the construction of a specific network of references rooted in the arts and media culture that he successfully championed to shape in the modern and contemporary cultures of images.

In large part, this cautious, or timid, attitude toward Barthes's homosexuality has to do with the lifelong position that Barthes himself adopted, as much personally as intellectually, of the observer from the margins. First of all, for his mother he kept a chaste silence on the subject of his relationships, which were evidently not following the heteronormative model of a family. Furthermore, in his writings he tended to neutralize gender, as in *Fragment's of a Lover Discourse* or *S/Z*, where the binary vision of sexualized gender was totally overthrown. A key intervention into this debate came from Harold Beaver, who published, a year after Barthes's death, "in Memory of Roland Barthes" the first study to focus exclusively on "Homosexual signs" in Barthes's oeuvre. Ten years later, D. A. Miller eventually decided to "bring out" Barthes.[6] In this slim pamphlet of fifty-five pages, Miller shed light onto the global cultural context in which Barthes developed a truly homosexual network of references. Indeed, from the French tradition of wrestling, "le catch," Queen Christine, "l'euphorie Omo" (a pun on "homo euphoria"), and the famous soap brand in *Mythologies*, to a Wilhelm von Gloeden catalogue, published by a famous Italian editor and collector, Lucio Amelio, notoriously homosexual, Barthes leaves clues or "homosexual signs" everywhere, which makes it all more peculiar that in the francophone context these signs should remain a taboo. Only the controversial biography by Hervé Algalarrondo mentioned Barthes's sexual adventures.[7] However, the biography only satisfies voyeuristic curiosity: homosexual anecdotes were a cruel disappointment, or, as Beaver had put it, only "good for gossip." Prudery of the French may also explain why Barthes enjoyed so much travels abroad, in Morocco, New York, or Japan, where he could express his sexuality more freely, and why he published his most "homosexual" texts outside France, in Geneva (*Empire of Signs*, Skira, 1970) and Naples (*Wilhelm von Gloeden*'s catalogue essay, Amelio editore, 1978).

Barthes, an Observer from the Margins

In France, largely in the wake of the May 1968 student revolt, the gay community started to organize itself into associations and established journals that relayed its claims for equality and social recognition. At this time, Arcadie, founded in 1954 by André Baudry, was the only official homosexual organization in France.[8] It was mainly representing the bourgeois and quite conservative part of the gay community. Following on from the events of May 1968 and Stonewall riots in 1969, the FHAR, the Front Homosexuel d'Action Révolutionnaire (Homosexual Front for Revolutionary Action), was founded in 1971. This faction, which included Françoise d'Eaubonne from Arcadie, and charismatic organizer Guy Hocquenghem, was very active. It used strategies of visibility and shock to conquer the public space, notably through magazines such as *Le Fléau social* and *L'Antinorm*. Years later, the famous magazine *Gai Pied*, established in 1979, openly criticized the establishment and conservative line held by Arcadie and Baudry, who advocated for an inconspicuous integration of homosexuality into heteronormative society. Faced with the rise of visibility of the gay community and a membership that cost 80 francs (€50 in current value), the atmosphere at the "61 de la rue du Château d'eau, à quelques pas du Palace" (a short distance away from The Palace)[9] was far less attractive compared to the lively club ran by Fabrice Emaer, a friend of Barthes who also owned Le Sept, a gay restaurant club on the Right Bank that was one of Barthes's hotspots. Barthes had no known relationships with Hocquenghem and only mentions him to create distance himself from him, accidentally misspelling his name: "not the same homosexuality as Fernandez or Hockenghem [sic]. It is something else I should say, enounce, write."[10] At the same time, as Christian Gury testified, Barthes happened to show up at the gatherings at the Arcadie and goes in the same period to the Palace, in his role of an "observateur" (observer).[11]

Piece by piece, it is possible to reconstruct Barthes's homosexual lifeline, especially thanks to the major biographies published in 2012 and 2015 by, respectively, Marie Gil and Tiphaine Samoyault.[12] Still, the point is not to force Barthes to become a gay writer and thinker. It is worth remembering that D. A. Miller questioned directly his "gayness"[13] and the dim thread of this shadowy gay writing. Nevertheless, time has come to broaden the scope of the reception of Barthes's work and to reintroduce his writings and his visual culture to a specific audience, and the culture induced by his relationships. Just because the company he kept and social circles he frequented had a vital influence on what he valued and chose to write about, Barthes's gay culture cannot be underestimated. It infuses all of his work and orientates some of his major theories, such as the neuter, the living-together, and the notion of the family. These experiences underpin Barthes's position as a writer operating from the margins, decentering his point of view to take the standpoint of an observer with a singular view, a sort of "partial perspective" and knowledge, in anticipation of Donna Haraway's theory.[14]

Aesthetic Choices, Homosexual Taste

As Andy Stafford points out, the issue of gender appeared early in Barthes's writing, notably in his *Michelet par lui-même* in 1954, a volume commissioned for a book series on great French authors. Stafford highlights that "Michelet was attuned to both gender's experiences, collapsing and overcoming divisions, and questioning the marking of structured identity and social function in gender well before Edward Carpenter," adding that these insights prefigured Barthes's considerations on gender developed much later in *S/Z*.[15] If Michelet's writing is genderless, Patrizia Lombardo recalls that Barthes acknowledges Proust's oeuvre as "the reference work, the general mathesis, the mandala of the entire literary cosmogony."[16] The Proustian world is literary, fantasmatic, photographic, and homosemiotic, the keys to understanding of which Barthes gave in his "Discours-Charlus," having chosen the most openly homosexual character of Proust's novel to produce a novel semiotic concept. Barthes had also planned a seminar based upon the visual world of Proust as a part of his literary and photographic project. Much of *The Preparation of the Novel* is supposed to sketch what *Vita Nova*, his novel project, could have been. But considering the draft, edited by Eric Marty in the 2002 *Complete Works*, some chapters look very similar to "Soirées de Paris" or "Incidents," published posthumously. These texts don't have the form of a novel, and resemble the diaristic writing of André Gide, another concealed model for Barthes. François Wahl highlights Gide's connection to Barthes in his preface to *Incidents*: "l'objet n'est pas du tout le Maroc en soi, mais le 'romanesque'" ("the object is not at all Morocco as such but the 'romantic'"). He goes on: "le romanesque, par essence, est fragment" ("romantic, in essence, is the fragment").[17] There is but a small step from this fragmentary writing to the final project of a novel, or what it could have been: a kind of intimate diary, where boys and gigs become the characters in a montage of sketches like photographic snapshots. One example: "Visit from an unknown boy, sent by his friend: 'What do you want? Why are you here?'—'It's nature!' (Another boy, on another occasion: 'It's love!')."[18] If *Incidents* takes the shape of a series of haiku describing living pictures, "Soirées de Paris" arranges longer fragments and then sets them in the context of Parisian gay nightlife.

Barthes's relationship to the world is very much the one of an observer. He likes to frame and cut a piece of real through the lens of the photographs, which testifies to his singular approach.[19] Drawing on his experience as a theater critic, he curates pictures and scenes like the *tableaux vivants*. Since *Empire of Signs*, the layout and scenography of images exemplify what a visual political discourse, in parallel to a text, can be. Jacqueline Guittard's illustrated edition of *Mythologies* brought these associations to the surface and made this visual sphere visible.[20] Photography, as a tool of mediation with reality, prized in theater and cinema, in the realm of visual culture becomes, for Barthes, oriented toward the homosexual community of taste. In "The Third Meaning: Research Notes on Some Eisenstein Stills," Barthes opens his article with a film still showing the young Ivan the Terrible, a desirable executioner, with soft eyes and tender skin, onto which two men pour gold. Barthes focuses on the knowing gazes of "two courtiers, two adjuvants, two supernumeraries"[21] to introduce the concept of the "third meaning," associated with the notion of the "carnival."[22] This mise-en-scène, full of kitsch "rice powder,"[23] becomes a truly camp moment, as Susan Sontag defines it in her 1964 "Notes on Camp."[24] In the "third meaning" concept, Philip Watts recognizes the idea of the search for sexual clues and signs, drawing an explicit comparison with Garbo's face in *Mythologies*,[25] to highlight a "queerness" of such pictures,[26] or a "camp poetics" as stated by the editors of Watts' manuscript.[27] Sometime after Sontag, in 1979, the French writer and editor Patrick Mauriès published a book entitled *Second manifeste camp*.[28] Barthes's intervention through his friend François Wahl, the editor at the Éditions du Seuil, assured eventual publication of this book in the collection Fiction & cie, headed by Denis Roche's. Faced with Von Gloeden's images, Barthes quotes Mauriès quoting Sontag as he wonders if they are "camp."[29] The gay kitsch thematic had been misjudged and downplayed by many by literary critics, even though it received constant support from Barthes to friends and trends.

Around Von Gloeden's Staged Photography

This community of taste and its visible manifestations had been progressively constructed through Barthes's relationships and encounters. French resistance fighter Daniel Cordier was one such key character in Barthes's visual education in art, and especially in contemporary painting. One of his greatest texts on paintings is dedicated to the young minor expressionist artist Bernard Réquichot, who died by suicide aged thirty-two, the day before his opening at the Daniel Cordier's gallery. Eleven years later, Barthes wrote the preface to a catalogue for his retrospective exhibition, an homage to "Réquichot et son corps" (Réquichot and his body). It is a noteworthy fact that Barthes mostly wrote on gay or queer artists: Réquichot, Cy Twombly, Wilhelm von Gloeden, Bernard Faucon, the graphic designer Erté, as well as Eisenstein and Pasolini. He had met some of them through friends, editors, or collectors, such as Franco Maria Ricci and Lucio Amelio in Italy, which Barthes visited often. Amelio knew Joseph Beuys, Andy Warhol, and the Italian avant-garde circle. He invited Barthes to write the foreword for a catalogue comprising pastoral scenes of male nudes staged by the eccentric Wilhelm von Gloeden, whose photographs were collected by Oscar Wilde. Barthes was in constant demand for texts such as this, and his acceptance of such commissions was often reserved for friends whose interests he shared.

In 1964, he dedicated *Essais Critiques* to his then boyfriend, François Braunschweig. A couple of years later, the latter opened, with Hughes Autexier, the TexBraun gallery, specializing in vintage photography. Barthes was introduced to photography, and especially vintage photography, through this gallery, which possessed pictures of Baron von Gloeden.[30] These pictures were well known in the gay community, and Guy Hocquenghem in his 1979 film *Race d'Ep* (a derogatory term for "homosexual" in French, from "pederast") draws a history of homosexual desire that begins with the golden age of von Gloeden's fantasy images. In his foreword, Hocquenghem makes a claim for a right to visibility, and assimilates photography to the history of the gay community: "this is this untold story that the movie wants to make visible [. . .]. Their history goes with the history of photography, those of another memory, another sensitive skin given to beings."[31] In the land and fields, young boys are having sex, showing a problematic preference for "young" bodies. Contrary to Hocquenghem's movie that shares many features with Pasolini's *Salò* (1975), Barthes prefers fictional fantasies to crude depictions. This posture, once again, is indicative of a decision to stand outside; here, outside the struggle for overcoming sexual boundaries, very much at large in the avant-garde of the 1970s in France. Barthes tends to oppose the "lovers discourse," an articulated and imaginary relation to the other, to experimental transgressions.

Still, the pictures of Bernard Faucon cast a different light on the androgyne figure praised by Barthes, which first appeared in Anne-Louis Girodet's *Sleep of Endymion* on the frontispiece of *S/Z*.[32] In Faucon's staged photographs, young boys in their early teens are arranged alongside mannequin dummies to create dreamlike pictures. These ambiguous *tableaux* flirt with the thin line between homoeroticism and the iconography of pedophilia, promoted at the same period of time by the heterosexual visual culture, most noticeably in David Hamilton's photographs or the notorious case of Irina Ionesco's photographs of her daughter Eva. Barthes stresses the uncanniness of these images, but pulls them to their most fictional side, erasing the possibility of "the love for children." He stresses the "trouble," the "violent doubt" caused by these images artificially staged and obviously unreal, in which he prefers to recognize a specter of his own childhood.[33] Did he fully support Tony Duvert's pedophilic novel *Paysage de fantaisie* for the prestigious Medicis Prize in 1973, as told by the press, or as Sebhan reports? Or, did Barthes and Duvert have a violent dispute over the "children's rights" during the cocktail after the award ceremony, revealing profound misunderstanding between the author and the fictional oeuvre?³⁴ Barthes had always exhibited strong empathy for children, as vulnerable people, while at the same time insisting on the power of fiction. But the ages of the "young boys"—not children—he met in Morocco are never clearly stated. If such erotic patterns circulate in artistic and liberal avant-garde culture, Barthes positions himself yet again at their margins.

Nevertheless, the topic of a bucolic landscape can be considered as a strong clue of the homoerotic visual culture.³⁵ Pierre Borhan, in his historical book on homoeroticism in photography, evokes "culturist imagery" that paved the way to Gloeden's success, making a clear link between the "bucolic and antiques codes that create a distance effect and of fictional reconstitution with the Greek world's mise-en-scènes."³⁶ It also emerges in Daniel Boudinet's series of photographs on the subject of which Barthes writes one of his rare monographic texts on photography, "Douze photographies de Daniel Boudinet," *Creatis* (1977). In this utopian and neutralized landscape, no human figures show up, as if the picture was only a realm of potentiality for the imagination. Barthes chose to begin *Camera Lucida* with a blueish curtain that opens slightly to make a window. This photograph by Boudinet would be the only color photograph in the book. By observing the circulation of images, this network of homosociability and taste appears in the editing process, especially when Boudinet's photograph of a night empty square illustrates the cover of the extended edition of Renaud Camus's *Tricks*, the explicit gay sexual diary prefaced by Barthes, and republished in 1982.

A Rendezvous Notebook from Japan

Barthes's photographic gaze was gendered and sexualized. The pleasure of the text is also a "visual" pleasure, to quote the feminist theorist Laura Mulvey on cinema.³⁷ If we think of Barthes's gaze as a site of visual *jouissance*, perusing his illustrated books like picture galleries calls for a search for a third meaning, to unveil the hidden parts of what can be read and seen. As D. A. Miller shows, *Empire of Signs* is what he calls a "Spartacus guide" to Tokyo, with recognizable places and bars for gay visitors. The map sketches lead to the gay neighborhood of Tokyo, Nijo-Chome, which only connoisseurs will find in this little deciphering game.³⁸ The sketchbook from Japan, *Empire of Signs*, was the first of personal Barthes's books, a fantasy, "a new Garabagne," borrowed from Henri Michaux fictional world. This dreamed Japan is mostly populated by his collection of "bromides," popular photo-cards sold in local kiosks. Hiramatsu Ireland calls the book "Memoirs of a gaysha" because it appears as a homosexual fantasy: with its young actors and singers, inhabitants appear as many rendezvous for the gaze.³⁹ Published in the "Sentiers de la création" collection directed by Gaëtan Picon, the book is the portrait of a country by a writer. It is indeed a journal of a journey, complete with a prerequisite travel vocabulary. But words from this vocabulary are essentially useful for cruising. Barthes was invited to Japan by Maurice Pinguet, who worked for the French Foreign Office and lived with his companion in Tokyo. Erick Laurent, who worked on homosexuality in Japan, talks about "liberté-contrainte" (restrained freedom): "In such a context, it seems easy to live as a gay man in Japan [. . .] surely because there is a high tolerance for feeling expressions and homoerotic gestures."[40] The book appears like a journal of sexual encounters in which such rendezvous make up most of the interactions with the Japanese. The portraits in the book, considered with a sexualized gaze, confirm the double language at work behind the pictures. A true erotic of photography unravels, with many actors having an undetermined gender: Kazuo Funaki, whose lips open up sensually between the beginning and the end of the book, as if for a kiss; Nakamura Ganjiro, a bunraku actor playing female roles; the Tigers, idols surrounded by flowers; and Barthes, who suddenly appears, wearing "a japonised mask," to inscribe himself in this imaginary homoerotic world.[41]

Right after *Empire of Signs*, Barthes was invited by poet and editor Denis Roche to write his own "Écrivains de toujours," which becomes *Roland Barthes par Roland Barthes*. This conceptual autobiography contains the first mention of "Goddess H," where "H" stands for homosexuality.[42] Here, he also presents a new kind of family, "famille sans familialisme" ("family without familialism"), which reappears in his posthumous publications, "Incidents" and "Soirées de Paris." After the death of his mother, his circle of homosexual or nonhomosexual friends from the Rue Nicolas-Houël becomes what he calls his "family." It is metaphorically reimagined in *Camera Lucida*, a double place of revelation, to illuminate the photographic "chamber" but also the bedroom (camera) as the space of intimacy. It reveals Barthes homosexual gaze on images that had been suppressed during his jaunts to the wrestling matches with Michel Foucault and his expressions of attraction toward the face of "queen Christine." The homosexual gaze crystallizes around Robert Mapplethorpe's photographs, nothing short of Barthes's favorite photograph. The last pages of *Camera Lucida* leave no doubt: Barthesian photography is homoerotic, queer before queer, that is to say, askew or "obtuse." It is above all positioned at the margins, outside the dominant canon. As Eric Marty noted, the very end of this theoretical novel takes place in a gay nightclub in New York. There, Barthes recognizes the *tableaux vivants* "from which Mapplethorpe has so lucidly derived certain of his photographs,"[43] to extend an insight on how the "the great mutation" of the image is linked to sexual practices: "the anonymous individual (never an actor) who gets himself tied up and beaten conceives of his pleasure only if this pleasure joins the stereotyped (worn-out) image of the sado-masochist: pleasure passes through the image."[44]

Diana Knight shows in her extensive essay on Barthes and utopia, that *Camera Lucida* enhances Barthes's homosexual gaze on images. Knight also raises the question of colonial and racial desire as she comments on Savorgnan de Brazza's portrait with two young black sailors touching him. As Pierre Borhan notes, photography has played a major role in creating an undercover network of visual signs: in the nineteenth century, portraits of homosexual couples were often staged with a hand laid on a shoulder, arm, or leg.[45] This singular gaze, neither gay nor queer, but rather one would say transverse, goes with a history of homosexual visibility of its time, declaring the right to participate to social life, not only without hiding but also without exuberance.

Camera Lucida and the Black Box

The photographic album of *Camera Lucida* was a visual and political project. Singular in its composition, it is no critical work of photographic theory. In extension of his sharp critique of "the great family of man," Barthes's project here was to tackle Steichen's dominant universalism, previously critiqued in *Mythologies*. He carefully chose characters who would coexist with him in the "*camera*," an intimate space. Struck by the loss of his mother, Barthes wanted to dedicate a book to her, to make "the *photo-maman* book," in Barthes's own expression.[46] He invites with him to the "*camera*" a cortege of orphans, rejects, the marginalized, which whom he always empathized, ever since *Mother Courage* and Pic's photography of Brecht. The Barthesian Marxist look on photography where we meet a child of the street, disabled people, black families from Harlem, homosexual boys (of course), a man condemned to death—all those without a place in "great" history.[47] We should recall that Barthes was criticized for not taking part in the May 1968 student protest movement. Perhaps he was not that concerned with this somewhat bourgeois revolution. The following year, in contrast, the Stonewall riots resonated with his personal situation more directly. These riots were sparked by a police intervention at the Stonewall Inn, a New York gay bar, on 27 June.

The homosexual community rebelled, drawing attention to its right to exist. Following these protests, gay pride commemorates a movement based on the process of making homosexuality visible in the public space. Proust would say that the "affiche" won the battle for visibility against "opacity" and "the closet." This underground New York of the 1970s is indeed increasingly visible, and builds communities, not only in San Francisco and Castro Street but also on the beaches. Beaches were also an important cruising place in France: Edgar Morin tells an anecdote about Barthes, reported by Louis-Jean Calvet in his Barthes's biography, which was explicit about his nightly cruising on the beaches of Bayonne.[48] At the time when Barthes wrote his essay on Bernard Faucon's staged photographs in 1978, in the photography magazine *Zoom*, edited by photographer Sophie Ristelhueber, the magazine had published the year before a major photo-essay by Matami, "American *Gay* of Life," showing boys having fun on American beaches and enjoying their lifestyle in broad daylight.[49] The beach is another "locus amoenus" of gay life. It reoccurs again in Barthes's critique of a theater piece entitled *La Plage* (*The Beach*, 1977), written by Cuban painter and writer Severo Sarduy, who was François Wahl's companion. The play shows a series of poetic *tableaux*, memories of moments spent on beaches, focusing on the physical emotions of bodies lying in the sun.

These joyful and openly gay images were circulating as much in the avant-garde milieu as in the mainstream media at the time when Barthes wrote *Camera Lucida*. Intimate pictures, or photographs showing sexual practices, were becoming more and more publicly visible. Barthes discovered these images through many channels: through his friends' reports and his own experiences, recalled in the final pages of *Camera Lucida*, through Camus's *Tricks* or in art galleries, where Robert Mapplethorpe photographs were exhibited. He also encountered such images in films screened at Le Dragon, a famous gay porn cinema close to his home. As he wrote in "Soirées de Paris," he was a regular of this cinema, headed by Jacques Scandelari, also known as Marvin Merkins, author of the mythical *Brigades mondaines* (1978) but above all the cult movie *New York City Inferno* (1978). It was there that Barthes staged his sexual encounters, described in "Soirées de Paris" in the following way: "I leave the house again and go see the new porn film at Le Dragon: as always—and perhaps even more so than usual—dreadful. I dare not cruise my neighbor. . . . Downstairs into the back room."[50] As Patrick Mauriès recalls in a foreword to a collective book on *Les Gays savoirs*, one must not "underestimate the role of cinema in the rise of a gay visibility," a culture that follows what he describes as a "discreet society in which its members recognizes each other, insisting signs just as in the Search of Lost Time."[51] For instance, the cult of *New York City Inferno* is a part of these movies, testifying to what a liberated gay life was like in the nightlife of the Meatpacking District.[52] And it is in this context that Barthes closes his last chapter of *Camera Lucida*, opening a window onto this "porn shop" that is, in reality, a "black box."[53] This description echoes a passage in "Soirées de Paris," where he decides to go to the "dark room" of the cinema, making an analogy between homosexual practices and the photographic dark room. The 1970s were a turning point, articulating a shift from a homosexual semiology, from the practice of reading signs to an assumed visibility. This major shift produced unexpected parodies, such as the gay handbook produced by Hal Fischer in 1977, "Gay Semiotics," which borrowed conceptual art codes as much as semiotic interpretative grids. The time was devoted not to unveiling but to enlightening, a process in which *Camera Lucida* takes part.

In his biography, Hervé Algalarrondo recalls that once Barthes described a Maurice Pialat movie as "abusively heterosexual,"[54] qualifying in opposition as "abusively homosexual" the atmosphere that reigned over the apartment on Rue Nicolas-Houël. This was the base where he met with the moviemaker André Techiné, homosexual too, and who eventually invited him to play a small part in his film *Les Soeurs Brontë* (1979). These relationships ran parallel to his intellectual activity, and sometimes overlapped, as in the case of a radio or TV show or when he went to The Palace or the Sept, led by Emaer, an ex-hustler who organized the hottest nights in Paris at the turn of the 1980s. These encounters provided Barthes with a lot of textual material for what had become his novelistic project, which can be found in his Moroccan diary ("Incidents") or in the chapter outlines of what he called his *Vita Nova*. Barthes spent evenings and nights at The Palace, a giant theater turned into a nightclub where Grace Jones performed for the opening, and which played the best American funk and disco music. The waiters were dressed in futuristic outfits designed by Thierry Mugler that exposed part of their breasts. It was a "theatre for the eyes," as Barthes wrote in an article, "At The Palace, Tonight," published in 1978 in *Vogue Hommes*. Extravagant, creative, interloping, mixed, this spectacular club was a synthesis of many Barthesian utopias: "living-together," pleasure, desire, neutrality (the place was open to everyone); and the panoptic visuality of the theater. All this made it a dreamlike place, setting from Alice in Wonderland, where Barthes exclaims: "How strange is all this!"[55] He may have used the word "queer" rather than "strange," if only it had been in use at the time, since this was a place where transvestites and androgynous people played with gender and codes.

As it was often the case with Barthes, more than the sensuality of homosexual life—in which his own position was one of retreat and a search for neutrality—the mise-en-scène of queerness involves a mixed taste for the ancient and modern, with a hint of strangeness that goes beyond postmodernist schemes and iconologies. One might wonder, as Larry Schehr does, if the neuter status could designate a potential Barthesian queer: "Does it produce the author's idealism as the ground on which a 'happy sexuality' and a 'happy writability' can both simultaneously occur?"[56] Quoted by Schehr, Jane Gallop's hypothesis also designates neuter as a "sensitive zone of Barthes homotextuality."[57] According to Gallop, "it certainly is part of a wish to escape the constraints of bipolar gender differentiation."[58]

Many features converge to suggest a pre-queer theory in Barthes's late writings. This includes a convergence between Barthes's visual tastes and his neutralized practice of the text, as in *A Lover's Discourse: Fragments*, where the narrator has no identified gender. The idea of an identity transcended by the neuter as a third voice, a third sex, was a very common in popular culture and alternative cultures. This is a hypothesis he puts forward in a lesser-known text on the "Romantic Song":

> It is precisely these four family voices which the romantic lied, in a sense, forgets: it does not take into account the sexual marks of the voice, for the same lied can be sung by a man or a woman, no vocal "family," nothing but a human subject— unisexual one might say, precisely insofar as it is amorous: for passion, romantic love—is no respecter of sexes or of social roles.[59]

The success of Barthes's concepts in the visual arts at the turn of the twentieth and twenty-first century is of course linked to his conception of an open semiology, creative, flexible, and labile.[60] The study of "the life of signs in society" that Saussure advocated for is close in spirit to the artistic commitment with its contemporary environment, as much the social than the aesthetic one. It comes as no surprise that concepts such as "living-together" or neuter has regained audience, as it was rooted in standpoint of a minority, and anticipated a more individually engaged art, voicing and performing gendered issues that Barthes managed to set up, quietly but assuredly, in a very heteronormative context.

Notes

1 Philippe Joseph Salazar, "Left Bank, Right Bank. Roland Barthes's Gay Stroll," *Pretexts: Literary and Cultural Studies* 11.2 (2002): 191.
2 Carol Mavor, *Reading Boyishly: Roland Barthes, J. M. Barrie, Jacques Henri Lartigue, Marcel Proust, and D. W. Winnicott* (Durham, NC: Duke University Press, 2008).
3 Diana Knight, *Barthes and Utopia: Space, Travel and Writing* (Oxford: Clarendon Press, 1997), 212–8.

4   Nicholas de Villiers, *Opacity and the Closet: Queer Tactics in Foucault, Barthes and Warhol* (Minneapolis, MN: University of Minnesota, 2012).
5   Benjamin Hiramatsu Ireland, "Queering Photography: Race, Death, and Sexuality in Roland Barthes's *La Chambre Claire* and *Fragments d'un discours amoureux*," *The Modern Language Review* 110.2 (2015): 438–55.
6   D. A. Miller, *Bringing Out Roland Barthes* (Berkeley, CA: University of California Press, 1992).
7   Hervé Algalarrondo, *Les Derniers jours de Roland B.* (Paris: Stock, 2006).
8   Julian Jackson, *Arcadie: La vie homosexuelle en France, de l'après-guerre à la dépénalisation* (Paris: Autrement, 2009), 363, 13.
9   Ibid., 88.
10 "Pas la même homosexualité que Fernandez ou Hockenghem [*sic*]. Ce n'est pas la même chose que j'ai le devoir de dire, d'énoncer, d'écrire." Antoine Idier, *Les Vies de Guy Hocquenghem: Sociologie d'une trajectoire à l'intersection des champs politiques, culturels et intellectuels français des années 1960 aux années 1980*, PhD Thesis, University Picardie Jules Verne (2015), 14. This is a quote from Tiphaine Samoyault, *Roland Barthes: Biographie* (Paris: Éditions du Seuil, 2015), 138). Unless indicated, all translations from French are mine.
11 Christian Gury, *Les premiers jours de Roland Barthes* (Paris: Non Lieu, 2012), 22.
12 Marie Gil, *Roland Barthes: Au lieu de la vie* (Paris: Flammarion, 2012); Samoyault, *Roland Barthes*.
13 Miller, *Bringing out Roland Barthes*, 7.
14 Donna Haraway, "Situated Knowledges: The Science Question in Feminism and the Privilege of Partial Perspective," *Feminist Studies* 14.3 (1988): 575–99.
15 Andy Stafford, *Roland Barthes* (London: Reaktion Books, 2015), 44.
16 Patrizia Lombardo, *The Three Paradoxes of Roland Barthes* (Athens, GA: University of Georgia Press, 1989), 117.
17 François Wahl, "Préface," in Roland Barthes, *Incidents* (Paris: Seuil, 1987), 8.
18 "Visite d'un garçon inconnu, envoyé par son copain": "Qu'est-ce que tu veux? Pourquoi viens-tu?—c'est la nature (Autre, une autre fois: 'c'est la tendresse!')," *Incidents*, 37, trans. Richard Howard (Berkeley, CA: University of California, Press, 1992), 23.
19 See Kathrin Yacavone, *Barthes, Benjamin, and the Singularity of Photography* (New York: Continuum, 2012).
20 Roland Barthes, *Mythologies* (Paris: Seuil, 2010).
21 Roland Barthes, "The Third Meaning Research Notes on Some Eisenstein Stills," *Image-Music-Text*, trans. Stephen Heath (London: Fontana Press, 1977), 52.
22 Roland Barthes, "The Third Meaning," in Roland Barthes, *Responsibility of Forms*, trans. Richard Howard (Berkeley, CA: University of California Press, 1991), 41. I quote both translations, as the meaning is sometimes lost.
23 Barthes, "The Third Meaning," *Responsibility of Forms*, 43.
24 Susan Sontag, "Notes on 'Camp,'" *Partisan Review* 31.4 (1964): 515–30.
25 Philip Watts, *Roland Barthes's Cinema* (Oxford: Oxford University Press, 2016), 52. See also Victor Burgin, "Barthes's Discretion," in *Writing the Image after Roland Barthes*, ed. Jean-Michel Rabaté (Philadelphia: University of Pennsylvania Press, 1997), 27.
26 "He might signal a certain form of queerness." Watts, *Barthes's Cinema*, 60.
27 Dudley Andrew, "Editor's Preface," in Watts, *Barthes's Cinema*, xxi.

28 Patrick Mauriès, *Second manifeste camp* (Paris: Seuil, 1979).
29 Roland Barthes, *Wilhelm von Gloeden* (Naples: Amelio, 1978), 6.
30 Samoyault, *Roland Barthes*, 383.
31 "C'est cette histoire inconnue que ce film veut rendre visible . . . leur histoire accompagne celle de la photographie, une autre mémoire, une autre peau sensible est donnée aux êtres." Guy Hocquenghem and Lionel Soukaz, directors, *Race d'Ep* (1979). The movie was under a censorship ban as a porn movie. Barthes, with Foucault among others, signed a petition to lift the ban (*Liberation*, October 8, 1979). See Antoine Idier, *Les Vies de Guy Hocquenghem*, 319–20.
32 See Yue Zhuo, "Gender Neutral: Rereading Barthes's S/Z and the Figure of the Androgyne," *Word and Text* 8 (2017): 119–35.
33 Roland Barthes, "Bernard Faucon," in Barthes, *Œuvres complètes* (Paris: Seuil, 2002), V, 471.
34 Jérôme Dupuis, "Tombeau pour Tony Duvert," *L'Express*, April 8, 2010, https://www.lexpress.fr/culture/livre/tombeau-pour-tony-duvert_883042.html. Accessed April 9, 2010. See Georges Sebhan, *Tony Duvert, l'enfant silencieux* (Paris: Denoël, 2010), 78–9.
35 Pierre Saint-Amand, Charles A. Porter and Noah Guynn, "The Secretive Body: Roland Barthes's Gay Erotics," *Yale French Studies* 90 (1996): 153–71.
36 Pierre Borhan, *Hommes pour hommes. Homoérotisme et homosexualité masculine dans l'histoire de la photographie depuis 1840* (Paris: Deux terres, 2007), 43.
37 Laura Mulvey, "Visual Pleasure and Narrative Cinema," *Screen* 16.4 (1975): 6–18.
38 Harold Beaver, "Homosexual Signs (In Memory of Roland Barthes)," *Critical Inquiry* 8.1 (1981): 99–119.
39 Benjamin Hiramatsu Ireland, "Memoirs of a Gaysha: Memoirs of a Gaysha: Roland Barthes's Queer Japan," *Barthes Studies* 4 (2018): 2–30, http://sites.cardiff.ac.uk/barthes/article/memoirs-of-a-gaysha-roland-barthess-queer-japan/. Accessed September 10, 2019.
40 "Dans un tel contexte, il paraît aisé de vivre au Japon en tant que gay . . . sans doute parce qu'il existe une grande tolérance vis-à-vis des formes d'expressions de sentiments et actes homoérotiques." Erick Laurent, *Les Chrysanthèmes roses. Homosexualités masculines dans le Japon contemporain* (Paris: Les Belles lettres, 2011), 22.
41 Parts of this analysis had been previously published in French, in Magali Nachtergael, "Roland Barthes à l'heure des Queer et Gay Studies," in *Roland Barthes, continuités, déplacements, recentrements*, ed. Jean-Pierre Bertrand (Paris: Christian Bourgois, 2016), 417–37.
42 Roland Barthes, *Roland Barthes par Roland Barthes* (Paris: Seuil, 1975).
43 Roland Barthes, *Camera Lucida: Reflections on Photography*, trans. Richard Howard (New York: Hill and Wang, 1981), 118.
44 Ibid.
45 Borhan, *Hommes pour hommes*, 40.
46 Roland Barthes, *Mourning Diary*, qtd. by Neil Badmington, *The Afterlives of Roland Barthes* (New York-London: Bloomsbury, 2016), 44.
47 Magali Nachtergael, "*Camera Lucida*'s Iconography or Roland Barthes's Visual Manifesto for Minorities," in *Borders of the Visible: I—Intersections between Literature and Photography*, eds. Luigi Marfè et Giuliana Ferreccio, *Cosmo* 13 (2018). www.ojs.unito.it/index.php/COSMO/article/view/3109. Accessed February 20, 2021.

48 See Louis-Jean Calvet, *Roland Barthes: 1915-1980* (Paris: Flammarion, 1990).
49 Matami, "American Gay of Life," *Zoom* 44 (1977): 67-73.
50 Roland Barthes, *Incidents*, trans. Richard Howard (Berkeley, CA: University of California Press, 1992), 68.
51 "Mésestimer [le] rôle [du cinéma] dans l'émergence d'une 'visibilité' gay." Patrick Mauriès, ed., *Les Gays Savoirs* (Paris: Centre Georges Pompidou, 1998), 14-15.
52 See Judith Benhamou-Huet, *Dans la vie noire et blanche de Robert Mapplethorpe* (Paris: Bernard Grasset, 2014).
53 Barthes, *Camera Lucida*, 118.
54 Algalarrondo, *Les derniers jours de Roland B.*, 47.
55 Roland Barthes, "At the Palace, Tonight," in *Incidents*, 47.
56 Larry Schehr, *The Shock of Men: Homosexual Hermeneutics in French Writing* (Stanford: Stanford University Press, 1995), 114.
57 "It certainly is part of a wish to escape the constraints of bipolar gender differentiation." Schehr, *The Shock of Men*, 115. See Jane Gallop, *Thinking Through the Body* (New York: Columbia University Press, 1988), 113.
58 Gallop, *Thinking Through the Body*, 114.
59 Roland Barthes, "The Romantic Song," trans. Richard Howard, *Responsibility of Forms: Critical Essays on Music, Art, and Representation* (New York: Hill and Wang, 1985), 287.
60 See Magali Nachtergael, *Roland Barthes contemporain* (Paris: Max Milo, 2015).

Bibliography

Algalarrondo, Hervé. *Les Derniers jours de Roland B.* Paris: Stock, 2006.
Barthes, Roland. *Camera Lucida: Reflections on Photography.* Trans. Richard Howard. New York: Hill and Wang, 1981.
Barthes, Roland. *Œuvres complètes.* 5 vols. 2nd ed. Ed. Éric Marty. Paris: Gallimard, 2002.
Barthes, Roland. *Image—Music—Text.* Trans. Stephen Heath. London: Fontana Press, 1977.
Barthes, Roland. *Incidents.* Paris, Seuil, 1987.
Barthes, Roland. *L'Empire des signes.* Genève: Skira, 1970.
Barthes, Roland. *Mythologies.* Paris: Seuil, 2010.
Barthes, Roland. *Responsibility of Forms: Critical Essays on Music, Art, and Representation.* New York: Hill and Wang, 1985.
Barthes, Roland. *Roland Barthes par Roland Barthes.* Paris: Seuil, 1975.
Beaver, Harold. "Homosexual Signs (In Memory of Roland Barthes)." *Critical Inquiry* 8.1 (1981): 99-119.
Borhan, Pierre. *Hommes pour hommes: Homoérotisme et homosexualité masculine dans l'histoire de la photographie depuis 1840.* Paris: Deux terres, 2007.
Calvet, Louis-Jean. *Roland Barthes: 1915-1980.* Paris: Flammarion, 1990.
Camus, Renaud. *Tricks.* Paris: Mazarine, 1979.
Gallop, Jane. *Thinking Through the Body.* New York: Columbia University Press, 1988.
Gil, Marie. *Roland Barthes: Au lieu de la vie.* Paris: Flammarion, 2012.
Gury, Christian. *Les premiers jours de Roland Barthes.* Paris: Non Lieu, 2012.

Haraway, Donna. "Situated Knowledges: The Science Question in Feminism and the Privilege of Partial Perspective." *Feminist Studies* 14.3 (1988): 575–99.

Hocquenghem, Guy and Lionel Soukaz, dirs. *Race d'Ep*. France: Little Sisters Production. 95 min. Released October 24, 1979.

Ireland, Benjamin Hiramatsu. "Memoirs of A Gaysha: Memoirs of a Gaysha: Roland Barthes's Queer Japan." *Barthes Studies* 4 (2018): 2–30. http://sites.cardiff.ac.uk/barthes/article/memoirs-of-a-gaysha-roland-barthess-queer-japan/. Accessed September 10, 2019.

Jackson, Julian. *Arcadie: La vie homosexuelle en France, de l'après-guerre à la dépénalisation*. Paris: Autrement, 2009.

Knight, Diana. *Barthes and Utopia: Space, Travel and Writing*. Oxford: Clarendon Press, 1997.

Laurent, Erick. *Les Chrysanthèmes roses: Homosexualités masculines dans le Japon contemporain*. Paris: Les Belles lettres, 2011.

Lombardo, Patrizia. *The Three Paradoxes of Roland Barthes*. Athens, GA: University of Georgia Press, 1989.

Mauriès, Patrick, ed. *Les Gays Savoirs*. Paris: Centre Georges Pompidou, 1998.

Mauriès, Patrick. *Second manifeste camp*. Paris: Seuil, 1979.

Mavor, Carol. *Reading Boyishly: Roland Barthes, J. M. Barrie, Jacques Henri Lartigue, Marcel Proust, and D. W. Winnicott*. Durham, NC: Duke University Press, 2008.

Miller, D. A. *Bringing Out Roland Barthes*. Berkeley, CA: University of California Press, 1992.

Mulvey, Laura. "Visual Pleasure and Narrative Cinema." *Screen* 16.4 (1975): 6–18. *Roland Barthes contemporain*. Paris: Max Milo, 2015.

Nachtergael, Magali. "*Camera Lucida*'s Iconography or Roland Barthes's Visual Manifesto for Minorities." In *Borders of the Visible: I—Intersections between Literature and Photography*. Eds. Luigi Marfè et Giuliana Ferreccio. *Cosmo* 13 (2018). www.ojs.unito.it/index.php/COSMO/article/view/3109. Accessed February 20, 2021.

Nachtergael, Magali. "Roland Barthes à l'heure des Queer et Gay Studies." In *Roland Barthes, continuités, déplacements, recentrements*. Ed. Jean-Pierre Bertrand. Paris: Christian Bourgois, 2016. 417–37.

Saint-Amand, Pierre, Charles A. Porter and Noah Guynn. "The Secretive Body: Roland Barthes's Gay Erotics." *Yale French Studies* 90 (1996): 153–71.

Salazar, Philippe Joseph. "Left Bank, Right Bank: Roland Barthes's Gay Stroll." *Pretexts: Literary and Cultural Studies* 11.2 (2002): 189–96.

Samoyault, Tiphaine. *Roland Barthes: Biographie*. Paris: Éditions du Seuil, 2015.

Schehr, Larry. *The Shock of Men: Homosexual Hermeneutics in French Writing*. Stanford: Stanford University Press, 1995.

Sebhan, Georges. *Tony Duvert, l'enfant silencieux*. Paris: Denoël, 2010.

Sontag, Susan. "Notes on 'Camp.'" *Partisan Review* 31.4 (1964): 515–30.

Stafford, Andy. *Roland Barthes*. London: Reaktion Books, 2015.

Villiers, Nicholas de. *Opacity and the Closet: Queer Tactics in Foucault, Barthes and Warhol*. Minneapolis, MN: University of Minnesota, 2012.

Watts, Philip. *Roland Barthes's Cinema*. Oxford: Oxford University Press, 2016.

Yacavone, Kathrin. *Barthes, Benjamin, and The Singularity of Photography*. New York: Continuum, 2012.

Zhuo, Yue. "Gender Neutral: Rereading Barthes's S/Z and the Figure of the Androgyne." *Word and Text* 8 (2017): 119–135.

Part III

Glossary

15

Author

Andy Stafford

The author in Roland Barthes's work is most commonly linked to his seminal 1967 essay "The Death of the Author," first published in English in the avant-garde *Aspen Magazine* in the United States (trans. Richard Howard) and delayed in French by the student uprisings of May 1968. There is little doubt that the essay's questioning of an author's authority foresaw the radical events in France that challenged entrenched social, political, and cultural hierarchies. Indeed, the author in Barthes's account can no longer control interpretations of their text: it is up to different readers to valorize their own. Citing as an example *Sarrasine* (1830) by Honoré de Balzac—a short story that Barthes goes on to analyze in his seminars in Paris between February 1968 and May 1969 and which then becomes his 1970 essay *S/Z*—he begins by asking "who is speaking?" The reply is: a "character," a voice, albeit an anonymous one. Implicitly, Barthes was drawing on Ferdinand de Saussure's research on hidden anagrams in texts (Saussure thought he could hear "voices" in biblical as well as modern texts); and the anonymity of the voices was indicative to Barthes that, from the modern period onward, authors had begun to stamp their ownership and their authority on their writing, thereby ushering in a new type of author which replaced "primitive" human communications in which narration had been impersonal, if not multiple. This individualist ideology of an author's "genius" thus lends credence to the modern idea that the author's biography "explains" their text. Against this, Barthes cites Mallarmé, Valéry, Proust, Surrealists as examples of writers and movements that have marginalized the author as guarantor of a text's meaning, as they split the narrator from the author. In the light of the linguistic work of Émile Benveniste, Barthes asserts that language does not need the guarantee of a speaking subject in order for communication to take place: an author does not express ideas; rather, they are inscribed in the text. Even though in 1965 Barthes had been considered as the spokesperson for *la nouvelle critique* by conservative academic Raymond Picard in a bruising public exchange over what literary criticism should aim to achieve, Barthes's essay on the subject, *Criticism And Truth* (1966), was already rejecting the "penetration" of a text's meaning in favor of its "crossing," and "The Death of the Author" went further by discounting any "monologic" reading that is obsessed with discovering a deep "secret" hidden by the author in the text. Barthes's revolutionary move was therefore counter-theological, with God, reason, science, and law as the targets of his critique of authorship. Following both Greek tragedy and Bertolt Brecht's Epic Theatre, Barthes underlined that all texts—whether dramatic or literary—hold ironies that the reader alone can appreciate. Indeed, aware of his own status as author, Barthes seems to illustrate his argument by making his own voice in the essay isomorphic to that in the texts he cites. By using a writing style that puts a distance between himself and the voice of the essayist in 1967–8—a kind of theatrical voice that comes from the wings, almost chorus-like—the essay "The Death of the Author" tries (manages?) to institute a distance between "Barthes-author" on the one hand and the voice without origin on the other. J. C. Carlier argues that it is more like a Menippean satire than an essay, both pedantic and anti-pedantic, but also performative (in the Brechtian) sense, as Barthes institutes a distancing of the voice of the writer, the "voice-off" of a literary critic. This was an important moment in the Barthesian account of the author. Already, in *Writing Degree Zero*, his first essay in 1953, he had argued that the literary form that a writer adopts inevitably signals their political and ethical relationship to the world; and, in "Authors and Writers" in 1960, he had nuanced this unavoidable political stance by suggesting that some "Writers" (as opposed to "Authors") could—or, at least, tried to—defy this logic by pointing to the literary text's occupying a space in between political commitment and refusal of commitment. However, in the wake of the "distance" in "The Death of the Author" instituted between a theory on the one side and its "Author" on the other, Barthes began to divide his own self from his work. In his 1973 seminar, called *Le lexique de l'auteur* (*The Lexicon of the Author*), he rereads all his own writing up until that point and divides his "self" into "RB I" (who has written) and "RB II" (who will write). Opening up questions around the "image" of the author in the media age, this objective, third-person account of self as Author then becomes the strategy deployed in his 1975 biography of himself, *Roland Barthes by Roland Barthes*.

Further Reading

Barthes, Roland. "The Death of the Author." In *Image-Music-Text*. Trans. Stephen Heath. New York: Hill and Wang, 1977. 142–9.

Burke, Sean. *The Death and Return of the Author*. Edinburgh: Edinburgh University Press, 1998.

Carlier, J.-C. "Roland Barthes's Resurrection of the Author and Redemption of Biography." *Cambridge Quarterly* 29.4 (2000): 386–93.

Foucault, Michel. "What Is an Author?" [1969]. In *The Foucault Reader*. Ed. Paul Rabinow. London: Penguin Books, 1986. 101–20.

White, ed. *How to Read Barthes's Image-Music-Text*. London: Pluto Press, 2012. Chapter 7.

Yacavone, Kathrin. "Picturing Barthes: The Photographic Construction of Authorship." In *Interdisciplinary Barthes*. Ed. Diana Knight. *Proceedings of the British Academy 228*. New York: Oxford University Press, 2020. 97–118.

16

Codes

Andy Stafford

Roland Barthes's theorization of codes runs mainly from 1961 to 1970, from his earliest work on press photography in the journal *Communications*, "The Photographic Message" and "The Rhetoric of the Image" (1961 and 1964, respectively, both republished in *Image-Music-Text*), through *Elements of Semiology* (1964) and crowned by the five codes of reading in *S/Z* (1970). Indeed, Barthes became so associated with codes—and decoding—that one detractor, René Pommier, wrote a critique, *Assez décodé* [Enough Decoding]. This period of "high Structuralism" in Barthes's career of the 1960s was prefigured by his early use of Saussure's distinction between denotation and connotation in "Myth Today" (1957); and his work on fashion, clothing history, and vestimentary codes used information theory and Cybernetics (in particular Benoît Mandelbrot's theories), and was doubtless indebted to the pioneering wartime work on code-breaking.

Although Barthes was beginning to use the notion of code in 1960 with respect to cinema and to ancestral, oriental theater, the first full discussion is in relation to the photograph and its message. Already, in the early semiological work on cinema, Barthes was asking, "How does the verbal code assimilate the visual code?"; and in "The Photographic Message," he analyzed this same question for the press photograph, accompanied as it always is by a message (headline, caption, commentary). Here, the code is defined as a "relay," as a language, which needs an "apprenticeship." However, the photograph is a "message without a code"; it is analogical of reality, "continuous" with it and devoid of "signifying units"; and it is to be contrasted with other visual arts (drawing, painting, cinema, theater), which, though visual like photography and using analogical representations of reality in a similar way, nevertheless, develop a second, connotative message which is that of "style." By contrast, the photograph is purely denotative and therefore needs no "cultural" decoding of the connotations of the "style." A code is introduced into a photograph only when language—or "relay" or "second-order message"—is used to describe it and thereby constructs a connotation. The advertisement for Panzani pasta that Barthes analyses in "Rhetoric of the Image" yields up three messages: one linguistic, a coded iconic message, and a noncoded iconic message; the second cultural; and the last perceptual. Between these two essays which assert that photography is a "message without a code," between 1961 and 1964, as White points out, Barthes introduces the spatial-temporal nexus of photography as a crucial element in this codeless medium: to show something that is there before us, but which no longer exists, is to upset normal human understanding of communication and the sign.

Alongside this work on codes and noncodes in visual culture, Barthes develops the use of the code to apply much more widely in his *Elements of Semiology*. In it he reaffirms his view, with André Martinet and *pace* Louis Hjelmslev and Pierre Guiraud, that a code is the language—the formally structured conventions of communication (or *langue* in the Saussurean schema); and speech—the individual language act (or *parole* for Saussure)—is the message; he also uses Roman Jakobson's theory of a "duplex structure" to suggest that message and code can, in certain cases, overlap, such as in *shifters* that transform one language of one code to that of another. Borrowing from Hjelmslev, Barthes suggests the Highway Code as an example of a form of communication that must be a simple set of binaries, and which cannot allow the neutral term, as, otherwise, traffic accidents might then occur, whereas the fashion system can and does use the neutral term (*Elements of Semiology*, 64, 80, 84).

In his study of the language, system, and structure of fashion, *The Fashion System* (1967), Barthes identifies three separate codes: the imagistic code (pictures or photographs of fashion items and combinations), the written code that accompanies the images (captions, descriptions), and the real code (actual clothing). He moves from looking diachronically at clothing as historically and socially coded between classes to considering women's contemporaneous fashion synchronically as a "vestimentary code."

He also begins to look at literary codes. In "The Introduction to Structural Analysis of Narratives" (1966), the narrative is located between two codes, one linguistic and the other trans-linguistic; the functions of narrative underscore a key element in coding: "no unit ever goes wasted"—including those that cover actions, characters, and narratives involving suspense. However, Barthes underlines that, in modern "bourgeois" and "mass culture" society, the codes of narration are hidden as "signs which do not look like signs." Barthes's "Introduction" is for a special number of *Communications* on structural analyses, and Algirdas Greimas's contribution is an early example of codes being applied to narrative. Greimas's 1948 doctorate on fashion using semiology was an important influence on Barthes; and in his contribution on narrative, he applies the anthropology of Claude Lévi-Strauss on primitive codes of food to storytelling, suggesting that a narrative code is general and comparable across human societies. In his 1968–9 seminar in Paris and then in *S/Z*, Barthes applies Greimas's idea to an 1830 short story by Honoré de Balzac, *Sarrasine*, in which he isolates five key codes of reading. Here, structuralism can be seen to pass into post-structuralism and, as described by Stafford (2020), becomes Barthes's "Houdini moment" in which the very constriction of five codes allows for the creative critic all the more to break free of the codes' tight constraints. Made up of short essays, *S/Z* divides Balzac's curious and unsettling tale of a sculptor obsessed with an opera-singer according to five literary codes. The hermeneutic, proairetic, semic, symbolic, and cultural codes are the keys to reading. The enigmatic atmosphere, the suspension of answers, and the red herrings form the hermeneutic code which conveys the suspense and the ironies of the story being told. The suspense is also found in the code of actions, the proairetic. Both these codes are determined by the time of reading—we read a story in a linear fashion, from start to finish—and are analogous to the melody and the harmony in a piece of classical music. The semic code for its part is found in the connotations of the words used, for example "femininity" is connoted by the spelling of the name of the eponymous hero Sarrasine (its "masculine" form would be Sarrazin). The symbolic code seems to approximate—Barthes is not very clear about this—to a deeper version of the semic code. It structures all the antitheses and mediations through which the connotations found in the text pass, for example, the midway point of the position of the narrator (as he tells the young woman his lurid tale), between the outside and the inside of the room where the scene takes place, symbolizes the sexual transgression that Sarrasine's figure of obsession, Zambinella, represents in the story. The fifth and final code of reading, the cultural code, points to the social knowledge that the reader deploys, such as the gnomic dimensions of proverbs, clichés, or popular sayings. The divisions between the five codes are often arbitrary; indeed, in the seminar notes on *Sarrasine*, Barthes hesitates on the number of codes, at one point suggesting there are thousands; for the codes in a tale like Balzac's are all the woven voices which come together, as in a carpet, to form a combined and moving structuration; and the codes exist only at the level of analysis (after rereadings, dismantlings, and reconstructions of the story). The weaving of codes in the literary "text"—a word itself derived from weaving—is but a general picture of how meaning is generated and structured in the perpetual movement of the reader's unfurling understanding of the story; the way in which the five codes are then combined, their relative significance in the structure of the text, is related to their strategic occurrences. How each code relates to all the others is then a determinant in what Barthes calls a text's "readability." This concept in *S/Z* is the one that has raised the most controversy. The proairetic and the hermeneutic codes allow Balzac's text to be "readable" because they are the "two irreversible levels of the classical text." The three other codes are what allow the story to be "writable" by the reader, as they favor the suggestive and active side of reading, the "plural" of the text. Is Barthes suggesting that Balzac (in all his writing? Or only *Sarrasine*?) is simple to read, given how easy it is to extract and name the codes? But surely, it is the act of reading that generates the codes after all, and not the text? What the codes allow Barthes to do is show that, while reading a story, we are constantly rewriting it. We need then to appreciate the plural meanings of a text that are continually generated by the complex interplay of the five codes; this constant interplay then also replays other texts, or "intertexts," which are different for each reader.

In *Empire of Signs* (1970), Barthes explores the ways Japanese culture obviates or modifies our notion of codes; the social greeting of bowing suggests that a "written" code of politeness needs no fixed signified (or meaning) for it to function. Similarly, in his treatise on the language of love, *A Lover's Discourse* (1977), the coded forms of communications between self and (loved) other are constantly reordered by the need to "grasp" and "not-grasp" the loved one.

Further Reading

Barthes, Roland. *The Language of Fashion*. Trans. Andy Stafford. Oxford: Berg, 2006.

Culler, Jonathan. *Structuralist Poetics: Structuralism, Linguistics and the Study of Literature*. New York: Routledge, 1975. 202–37.

Rosenthal, Peggy. "Deciphering *S/Z*." *College English* 37.2 (October 1975): 125–44.

Stafford, Andy. "Barthes's Menippean Moment: Creative Criticism, 1966–1970." In *Interdisciplinary Barthes*. Ed. Diana Knight. *Proceedings of the British Academy 228*. New York: Oxford University Press, 2020. 231–51.

White, Ed. *How to Read Barthes's Image-Music-Text*. London: Pluto Press, 2012. Chapters 1 and 2.

17

Haiku

Brian O'Keeffe

Barthes's interest in haiku dates to *Empire of Signs* (1970), and it's importantly discussed in *The Preparation of the Novel*—a set of lectures delivered at the Collège de France from 1978 to 1980, from which the material below is drawn. Each lecture reflects upon the raw stages of a writer's labor that precede the drafting of an achieved novel. Novelists, Barthes imagines, jot their observations down into a dossier, compile notes that might feed into the finished product. The note: a swift fixing of thoughts or impressions which would otherwise pass the novelist by. For Barthes, the key value of notation is its ability to fix the time that always passes by—the present itself. Haiku prompts such thoughts of notation because it clinches a fleeting moment with exquisite delicacy. "Haiku = exemplary form of the Notation of the Present."

What Barthes values in haiku is the elegant but plainspoken capture of moments as they happen. Haikus are plain but never platitudinous, nor do they force "poetry" upon what occurs: a dewdrop as it beads or a detached petal's soft wilting. Haikus *note* that a petal falls, that a dewdrop forms. That's enough to entrance the mind and draw attention to the discreet miracles that happen around us. And once haiku captures that moment, then we have a poetry which prompts the reaction "That's it!" Haiku triggers that exclamation because haiku's poetic achievement is such that we cannot quibble with the circumstance of that petal's gorgeous withering or that dewdrop's fragile formation on a leaf—there's no need for interpretation or semiotic decoding, just an *assent* to the subtle momentousness we feel when registering that such things occur at all.

"The haiku," writes Barthes, "is an *assent* to what *is*. Here it would be necessary to make a distinction . . . between *assent* and *approbation, adherence, approval* . . . that is to say, between the path of *reality* (haiku) ≠ the path of *truth* (discourse, ideology)." Truth is too grandiose for haiku. Haiku eschews ideology and discourse since both employ rhetoric: the aim is to persuade or otherwise compel us to approve or adhere to whatever is declared a truth (or a prejudice). But haiku gently enjoins assent to something more than any so-called truth—assent to reality, acquiescence to its modest miracles. Thus haiku is capable of an "Effect of the real or rather of *reality* (Lacan)." Lacan is invoked here in order to buttress a notion of *the real* which is to be distinguished from the fictional constructs one sees in the realist novel, for instance.

The realism of Balzac purports to be exact to reality, but Balzac's representations solicit the reader's interpretive desire for the *sens caché*. In Balzac, there is always more meaning to be sought. But haiku is limpid—it doesn't conceal meaning, it isn't aletheic.

"The haiku is basically *realistic*: it believes in the referent." When a haiku refers to a peony, it does not make a sign out of that flower; it intends only to remark the existence of that flower. That's realism. For Barthes, an effect of the real implies "language fading into the background, to be supplanted by a certainty of reality: language turning in on itself, burying itself and disappearing, leaving bare what it says." This is lovely—language as discreet as a good butler, as it were. But it is problematic. Yes, the haiku apparently welds the saying and the said with such utterness that writing becomes transparent, and so reading implies effortless access to that same transparency. But Barthes does not read Japanese—he reads these haikus *in translation*. So as one language, Japanese, withdraws the better to serve the certitudes of the real, another language—French—intervenes, interposes itself, obtrudes. Barthes asks himself, therefore, how translations don't impede his reading experience. "This is how I explain it to myself: the haiku is the conjunction of a 'truth' (not a conceptual truth, but of the *Instant*) and a form." There is seemingly no loss in translation if truth—the truth, now, of an instantaneous event's sheer impact—can convey itself intact across languages. Inasmuch as Barthes can say "That's it!" and regard form itself as unalterable, as if tempered fast by the demands of the event it records, then there is no linguistic gulf between reader and text.

Still, Barthes criticizes French translations that subject haikus to different rhymes and meters. But since he says "all rhythm is *cultural*," one wonders how a translator might yet bridge that cultural gap. Some translations are overpoetic, and "here, in France, our referent-words are very weak; they've become 'literary,' old, and un-poetical; in Japan, there's still a vital connection with the ears of corn, the sparrows, the flowers, the leaves, etc." Perhaps that's true for France, and it might have been true for English poetry (whence Ezra Pound's experiments with "hokku"), but is that true for Irish poetry, for instance? For Seamus Heaney, or Derek Mahon?

What of the Instant? Barthes's credits haiku with the capacity to note down a moment as it happens. Haiku: an "absolute writing of the instant." Beyond Baudelaire's *croquis*, beyond even Mallarmé, haiku can apparently preserve in writing the *punctum* (to use a term from *Camera Lucida*) of time itself. But, Barthes writes, "This *pure*, that is to say, *uncompromised* Instant, which doesn't appear to be compromised by any duration, any return, any retention, any saving for later, any freezing (an absolutely *fresh* Instant) . . . this Instant also seems to be saying: *for the record*, for when I come to read it again." Can an instant remain instantaneous, resist time's repetitions and durations, and also what Derrida would call the "archive," and yet remain available to "record," to the subsequent time when one reads it again?

"Haiku: a new and paradoxical category: 'immediate memory.'" As if memory doesn't lag behind the instant it remembers. As if remembrance—which is to say *writing*—catches up so speedily to the event it recalls that there's no need for Proustian prolongations, those so many pages devoted to the recapture of *le Temps perdu*. Haiku preserves "Time *at once, as-it-happens*; Time is salvaged *at once* = concomitance of the note (of the writing) and what incites it." Haiku happens *just after* the event it records.

It's not belated to what it notes, but perhaps writes itself, there and then, in what one might call the *contretemps* of the time of the instantaneous event itself.

This is apparently possible for haiku, and for two other artforms: music and photography. Of music, Barthes writes: "The privileged art of the instant is music; sound = the *eidos* of the Instant." There is not just one note flying by. Sound *forms* the instantaneity of the note, but music permits the recall of prior notes (the refrain, the melody) even as the present note is sounded. Haiku resembles photography because it "instills the certainty that *this took place*." Assuredly, photographs are more realistic than haiku's "impressionism," but both impress upon us the sense that such and such verily took place. Barthes reserves his awe for haiku and photography for that reason—the utterness of the impression, the certainty of that first "take" on the real: "The haiku and the photograph are *pure authorities* that aren't required to ground their authority in anything other than this: *that has been*." That has been, but it is not gone. The camera's click captures a present in the very moment of its coming to pass; the haiku's note does likewise, thanks to the unalterable qualities of its formal and expressive concision. That is pure authority—authority over the real, and over time itself. When something happens once, haiku ensures that it happens once forever.

Further Reading

Barthes, Roland. *Empire of Signs* [1970]. Trans. Richard Howard. New York: Hill & Wang, 1982.

Barthes, Roland. *The Preparation of the Novel: Lecture Courses and Seminars at the Collège de France (1978–1979 and 1979–1980)*. Ed. Nathalie Léger. Trans. Kate Briggs. New York: Columbia University Press, 2011.

18

Jouissance

Andy Stafford

Jouissance—bliss, orgasm, joy, ecstasy (from the French verb "jouir," to enjoy)—in Roland Barthes's work is usually paired with, and distinguished from, Pleasure. In *The Pleasure of the Text* (1973), *jouissance* is used in its relation to the theories of the French psychoanalyst Jacques Lacan. Lacan famously added to Sigmund Freud's "pleasure principle" (which itself was slightly misnamed as it referred more to avoiding "unpleasure"), by suggesting the notion of *jouissance*, in particular as a way of covering female sexuality and getting beyond the male phallus as "dominant signifier." For this reason, *jouissance* was taken up by French feminism in the *écriture féminine* of Luce Irigaray, Annie Leclerc, Julia Kristeva, and Hélène Cixous. For Barthes, famously interested in—but suspicious of—psychoanalytical categories, *jouissance* had also a Brechtian, political dimension. In *Le lexique de l'auteur* in 1973, just as Barthes is writing again on Brecht after a thirteen-year silence, he underlines the link between *jouissance* and the dialectical in Brecht's theories on the "art of living." For Brecht, he underlines, there is a *jouissance* in theater "of the scientific era" when "surprises" emerge from "logical evolution" or from the "instability of any situation, the humor of contradictions," but also, following Engels, from the "ownership of nature," from Mao's close reading of contradiction, and finally from seeing how human ills are remediable. Barthes stresses that Brecht's is not the *jouissance* of Lacanian theory for whom it signifies the loss of subjectivity in *aphanisis* (or, "fading"), the "deconstruction of the drive." Brechtian *jouissance*, in its suspicion toward overly subjectivist representation and its resultant asociality, is located between pleasure and bliss, in the collective space between the two, in which contradiction is both external and internal to social pleasure—vitality, *joie de vivre*, letting one's hair down—such as that found in the musical, plastic, and poetic "arts"; Brecht's *jouissance* involves considering these daily, people's, "arts of living," in a dialectical fashion (including looking dialectically at dialectics), thereby enjoying the paradox of a revolutionary intellectual considering pleasure and bliss from an "*ethical-aesthetic-political*" position." This is not included in *The Pleasure of the Text*, but it informs the attitude toward pleasure that Barthes is taking, and which might be characterized, as Moriarty suggests (1991), as an attempt "to affirm *jouissance* as a revolutionary force"; except that, as Moriarty concedes, pleasure, especially in reading a text, merely confirms the social construction of self as (falsely) individual, whereas *jouissance* "is a threat to the reader's cultural and psychological identity, tastes and values; it resists language, it is what cannot be spoken." In this sense, pleasure is to *studium* (in Photography) and the *lisible* (the readable, in literature), what, respectively, *jouissance* is to *punctum* (in Photography) and the *scriptible* (the writable). Moriarty points out further that, even though Barthes seems to divide "texte de jouissance" and "texte de plaisir" into avant-garde and revolutionary on the one hand and conformist and classical on the other, "pleasure" refers generally to both *jouissance* and *plaisir*, but then also to cover more narrowly "pleasure" as distinct from "bliss." The crucial point is that there is a mobile division between the two, which, unfixed and not scientific, means that the categories are not reliable nor definitive, but provisional and operative: "the subject is split twice over, between its *plaisir* and its *jouissance*, and one stage further back between its *plaisir* in, and its *jouissance* of, the division."

The "unspeakable" of *jouissance* becomes, in the late Barthes, the bliss of silence, of suspension, of retreat, of the neutral. In photography, it is the experience of seeing an image as ineffable, "Tel!" ("Thus!"). In music, it is the difference between on the one hand playing music, which is outside of semiotics and located within the body, and therefore one of bliss and eroticism, and, on the other, listening to music which is open to the sign system, to communication, and is therefore an act of pleasure. In relation to the Self, both in love and interacting with the Other (see *How to Live Together: Novelistic Simulations of Some Everyday Spaces—Notes for a Lecture Course and Seminar at the Collège de France, 1976-1977* (2013), and *A Lover's Discourse* (1977), respectively), *jouissance* is the assertion of an opacity, even of an intersubjective distance, between lover and loved one, between living with other people but still maintaining a "socialism of distance."

Further Reading

Barthes, Roland. *The Pleasure of the Text*. Trans. Richard Miller. New York: Hill and Wang, 1973.
Gallop, Jane. "Beyond the *Jouissance* Principle." *Representations* 7 (1984): 110–15.
Lacan, Jacques. *The Four Fundamental Concepts of Psycho-Analysis*. Trans. Alan Sheridan. London: Penguin, 1991. Chapters 13–17.
Moriarty, Michael. *Roland Barthes*. Cambridge: Polity Press, 1991. Chapter 8.
Noudelmann, François. "Barthes and Insignificant Music." In *Interdisciplinary Barthes*. Ed. Diana Knight. *Proceedings of the British Academy 228*. New York: Oxford University Press, 2020. 180–7.
Wiseman, Mary Bittner. *The Ecstasies of Roland Barthes*. New York: Routledge, 1989. Chapter 4.

19

The Neutral

Andy Stafford

The Neutral refers to a set of lectures given by Roland Barthes at the Collège de France in Paris, over thirteen weeks between February and June 1978, which, as the second series at the Collège, followed the "How to Live Together" series in 1977. Published posthumously, the lectures on The Neutral represent a central element in what is called Barthes's "late" thought. It refers to two distinct aspects of his writing and research, linguistic and ethological. In linguistic terms, the neutral refers to a third category outside of the traditional binary structures of language, to what Danish philologists Viggo Brøndal and Louis Hjelmslev in the 1940s referred to as the *tertium*, the third "amorphous term." In ethological terms, the neutral is located in primitive societies by Claude Lévi-Strauss in the *mana* whose symbolic value is zero; between the two-term oppositions that structure meaning in linguistics, there is an "unmarked," zero term, which is not a "total absence" but a "significant absence," in which the zero degree "testifies to the power held by any system of signs, of creating meaning 'out of nothing.'" Barthes used these notions of the neutral to inform his first essay in 1953 on the "degree zero" of writing in which he pointed to an Orphean, utopian "writer without Literature," to a form of writing that does not signal its relationship to the literary Institution. Barthes's adaptation of a linguistic idea of the neutral to the literary world of postwar France was a crucial step in his creative form of literary criticism which culminates fifteen years later, in 1968, in his radical reading—and rewriting—of Honoré de Balzac's curious and troubling tale of 1830, *Sarrasine*. Before publishing this in *S/Z* in 1970, Barthes wrote a summary of the gender implications of Balzac's story in "Masculine, Feminine, Neuter" in which nongender and its potential pandemic effects on sexuality are related to the tragedy, narration, and reading of the Balzac tale. The move between the degree zero thesis of literature to the mode of reading literature in *S/Z* that underlines the power of the neutral then becomes one in which the neutral points to a form of acceptable ethics of "How to live together." The idea in *Writing Degree Zero* that it is "impossible to write without labelling oneself" becomes, twenty years later, the growing feeling that it is impossible to interact with the Other without labeling oneself. From the 1973 seminar on *The Lexicon of the Writer* onwards—in which Barthes looked back over his own publications and deemed the existence of two writers in his writing self, "RB I" and "RB II"—he was looking for a third term outside of the binary trap in which he saw himself and other (now, famous) writers. His biography of the self in 1975, *Roland Barthes by Roland Barthes*—as opposed to an autobiography, since it is written in the third person—was the first stage in this search for a neutral existence. Directly opposed to the Neither-Norism that *Mythologies* in 1957 saw as a crucial element of petty-bourgeois and reactionary ideology, Barthes's "neutral" of the 1970s explores the various spaces in which the writer and intellectual can find "non-labelling": in written and spoken discourse; in the image portrayed in the press and the media; in spatial forms of living and even in death. Following his visits to Japan in the late 1960s, Barthes begins to use Far Eastern mysticism—Taoism, Zen Buddhism—to undermine the Western notion of the individual, to decenter and dissolve fixed and eternal conceptions of the "Self." Since it is via language that labeling takes place, the neutral in language is to be found in the no-place, or *atopos*, of nonclassification, involving strategies of suspension of meaning (or *épochè*), of refusal to comment, of stepping back, of instituting silence. The neutral, "no comment" stance is heavily criticized by some on the Left for its seeming abdication, for example in Barthes's refusal to take sides on his return from Maoist China in 1974 in his article on the front page of *Le Monde* "So, How Was China?". However, Barthes's Neutral is neither an abdication nor a concession to oppressive orthodoxies; it is a provisional and experimental attempt to confront power and hierarchy in all their social manifestations, the dream, as Barthes puts it, of "a minimal sociality." Far from a flat or demobilized way of living with others, the Neutral insists on the intensities, the nuances, of life. This is most evident in his 1977 essay on love, *A Lover's Discourse*, in which the lover searches for acceptable ways neither to contain or restrain nor to label the loved one (and by extension the Other). The "NVS"—the no-wish-to-grasp—becomes a key aspect of the Neutral in its silent but corrosive critique not only of how humans interact with each other but also of how different or marginalized cultures can resist being stereotyped and controlled by other, stronger cultures. For these reasons, the Neutral is not only imaginary and nonexistent, it cannot be marketed or easily defined either: its utopian dimensions are inversely proportional to its enforceability.

Further Reading

Badmington, Neil. "An Undefined Something Else: Barthes, Culture, Neutral Life." *Theory, Culture, Society* 37.4 (July 2020). Special number on "Neutral Life: Barthes's Late Work." Ed. Sunhil Manghani.

Barthes, Roland. *The Neutral. Lecture Course at the Collège de France, 1977–1978*. Trans. Rosalind Krauss and Denis Hollier. New York: Columbia University Press, 2005.

Smith, Piers M. "The Neutral View: Roland Barthes's Representations of Japan and China." *IAFOR Journal of Literature and Librarianship* 5.1 (Autumn 2016): 53–60.

Stafford, Andy. "*Classé, surclasser, déclassé*; or, Roland Barthes, Classification Without Class." *L'Esprit Créateur* 55.4 (Winter 2015): 148–64. Special number on Roland Barthes. Eds. Tom Baldwin, Katia Haustein, and Lucy O'Meara.

Villiers, Nicholas de. "A Great Pedagogy of Nuance: Roland Barthes's The Neutral." *Theory & Event* 8.4 (2005). http://muse.jhu.edu/journals/theory_and_event/v008/8.4devilliers.html.

Zhuo, Yue. "Commitment to Degree Zero: Barthes's First Approaches to the Neutral." *Theory, Culture, Society* 37.4 (July 2020).

20

Readerly/Writerly

Warren Motte

In the first pages of *S/Z* (1970), Roland Barthes wonders how to talk about literature, whether to insist upon what every literary gesture has in common with every other or to underscore the particularity of a given text. He thinks about the question of value and about the process of evaluation. How can one determine the value of a text, he asks? He argues that science cannot be relied upon in that task, because science does not evaluate. Nor can ideology avail, because ideology is bound up in representation, rather than production. He concludes that one must rely upon practice, and more specifically the practice of writing. As Barthes thinks through that notion, he suggests that there are two kinds of texts: those that are possible to write and those that can no longer be written. He imagines the latter kind of text as "readerly" (*lisible* in the original French) and the former kind as "writerly" (*scriptible*).

Readerly texts, in his view, constitute the vast majority of our literature; they are fundamentally affirmative rather than interrogative; they seek to persuade us that they are faithful reflections of the world instead of fictional constructions; the role they cast for the reader is that of a passive and essentially idle consumer. In short, they are "classic" texts. (And here, it may be useful to recall Italo Calvino's pithy definition of "classic" literature: they are books about which we never hear people say "I am reading" but always "I am rereading.") Writerly texts, to the contrary, put their constructed nature on display for all to see; they are not things, contends Barthes, but rather processes playing out in a "perpetual present"; they highlight the pleasures of writing and the seductions of the signifier; they seek to enlist the reader in the very practice of writing, no longer a mere consumer but an actual producer of literature. For readerly texts are products rather than productions, Barthes submits, nouns rather than verbs, while writerly texts wager upon flow, difference, and reflexivity.

He returns to that binary a few years later, grafting some new terms onto it. In *The Pleasure of the Text* (1973), he speaks about texts that engender pleasure (*plaisir*) in the reader and texts that produce ecstasy (*jouissance*). He postulates moreover two modes of reading: "horizontal" reading, on the one hand, an activity that is essentially disengaged and plot-bound, and on the other hand "vertical" reading, which demands that the reader recognize the immediate complexity of the text's construction, and wherein he or she exercises considerable agency as a full partner in the production of literary meaning. He argues an impassioned brief for ecstatic texts and vertical reading, for challenge and stimulation—in short, for what he understands as readerly joy.

Seen in their contemporary context, Barthes's arguments can be understood as positions in a new version of the "Quarrel of the Ancients and the Moderns" that inflamed critical debate in the neoclassical period in France. In this iteration of that debate, Barthes takes a stand as a defender of experimental, avant-garde fiction. He was an early champion of Alain Robbe-Grillet and the *nouveau roman*, for instance, and his book on Philippe Sollers (*Writer Sollers*, 1979) stakes claims that are more radical still. The Ancients, as Barthes imagines them, are mostly academics, practitioners of what he calls "university criticism," personified in the figure of Raymond Picard, a professor at Sorbonne who attacked Barthes's *On Racine* when it appeared in 1963, accusing its author of subjectivism, among other high crimes.

As vigorously and heroically as Barthes defended new and challenging forms of writing in the 1960s and 1970s, one notes throughout his career a marked taste for the "well-made" novel and for indisputably canonical texts, from Racine to Chateaubriand, Balzac to Proust. Among other critics, Jonathan Culler has noted the irony of the fact that *S/Z*—the very book in which Barthes postulates the readerly/writerly distinction, and where he promotes writerly literature with such energy—is in fact devoted to a text that is so patently readerly in character. Yet it is legitimate to imagine that, just as he defends new and innovative models of writing, Barthes is likewise clearing away space for new and innovative models of reading. In such a perspective, the analytical techniques that he formulates, whets, and deploys in his analysis of Balzac's *Sarrasine* are calculated to make the text render up currents of meaning that more conventional techniques fail to reveal. Throughout his career, after all, Barthes was fascinated by the question of interpretation, and by problems attendant upon that question. In *S/Z*, he contends that interpretation is principally a matter of recognizing the plurality that literary texts display, and he suggests that the reader must be willing to exercise as much intellectual mobility as she or he can muster in order to come to terms with that plurality. In other words, if Barthes's meditation upon the difference between readerly and writerly texts seems to focus in the first instance mostly upon the process of production, it nonetheless ramifies immediately and inevitably in the domain of reception, calling readers to attention, exhorting us to be as agile, as adroit, and as activist as possible in our engagements with literary texts.

Further Reading

Barthes, Roland. *The Pleasure of the Text*. Trans. Richard Miller. New York: Hill and Wang, 1973.
Barthes, Roland. *S/Z*. Trans. Richard Miller. New York: Hill and Wang, 1975.

Culler, Jonathan. *Roland Barthes*. New York: Oxford University Press, 1983.
Samoyault, Tiphaine. *Barthes: A Biography*. Trans. Andrew Brown. Cambridge: Polity Press, 2017.
Ungar, Steven. *Roland Barthes: The Professor of Desire*. Lincoln: University of Nebraska Press, 1983.

Sign

Dinda L. Gorlée

Roland Barthes's narrative method followed the logical method of Ferdinand de Saussure's lectures on general linguistics at the University of Geneva between 1906 and 1911. Saussure lectured on Sanskrit and Indo-European linguistics, but ventured into general linguistics, which was emerging at that time as a modern science. After Saussure's death (1913), the lecture notes were made public in the *Cours de linguistique générale* (1916), presenting a formal formulation of the linguistic sign. Saussure's lectures were not written as book, ready to be published; rather, the published lectures reflected the impressions of the editors. Therefore, Saussure's *Cours* consisted of fragments of lectures to contribute theoretical sense to the work of his followers.

The linguistic sign is the unitary base of Saussure's method. In the general definition, a sign (such as a word or a phrase) is not a single or unique communicator of "a thing and its name," but it is the "arbitrary concept" of the lexical sign-image (signified, French *signifié*) associated with the mental object (signifier, French *signifiant*). The analysis and cross-analysis between Saussure's binary terminology require personal initiative for special or semioticized reading to find the keywords or semiotic codes of the sign, which strike the sign-receiver's mind as meaningful signs. Then the sign can be deciphered and make sense as the reader's tentative meaning (signification). Saussure believed in mixing up signified in the signifier for the value (sense) of the signification, but not in the complete meaning of the actual sign.

Saussure's linguistics was elaborated with formal phonetics to build the mechanism of opposite contrasts of language units. He distinguished the vocal signs of speech (*parole*), developed into the individual act of writing in language (*langue*). Linguistic units were treated according to the human circumstances of speech: the provisional meaning of the sign is brought out by the element or aspect that is most prominent in the sign, to direct the attention of the sign-interpreter (sign-receiver) to create the internal or external meaning of the sign. The sign may also have other aspects or qualities, such as metaphor and metonymy, to rephrase the two-faced signification of language to suggest a more precise formulation of the sign. The word is the fundamental sign of Saussure's figurative process of human speech (French *parole*), but language does not provide a neutral code of the alphabet; it provides the abstract (or coded) sign of Saussure's sign to be decoded by the interpreter with the mental commentary of the signifier into the signification (sense) of the sign.

For Barthes, Saussure's formulation of special categories not only gave the abstract schema to provide the foundation for his critical work but also produced a crisis for the traditionalists to replace the stylistic reading with the imaginative art of Barthes's freedom from linguistic to the literary sign. Barthes's metaphorical texts dispensed with the old claims of Saussure's firm structure to claim his signifiers (*signifiants*) with unlimited capacities of social and cultural transformations. Barthes's lyrical analysis of his intellectual signifieds (*signifiés*) was his "puzzling" way of reading which became the symbol of French structuralism. His problem was to create from linguistic signs nonlinguistic signs encoded into several codes. He dealt with linguistic signs in the epiphany of unfolding various kinds of signs, such as linguistic or nonlinguistic, natural and artificial, and coded and uncoded signs. Barthes's signifiers classified the complex of sign-and-object into specific sign-functions of signifieds influencing his critical signifier. Barthes's inclusion of multidisciplinary signs inspired his work and that of his followers, mainly Umberto Eco and many other semiotic thinkers.

When Paris was seen as the capital of world fashion, the designers had a vast freedom of visual choice to guide future fashion. Barthes's *The Fashion System* (1967) modified the modish narratives into fashionable myths, that is, conscious and unconscious images of culture. He followed Saussure, who argued that social tradition can make and remake simple and creative changes of dress to signify logical convention; but fashion can also confound the actual designs with illogical ideas of unfashionable speech. Saussure perceived fashion as the social institution of vestimentary signs covering the human body, but fashion is not the same tool as using native language. Fashion presents the "literature" of transforming imaginary artistic signs to exchange previous costume into culturally relevant trends for the future. Clothing determines the psychological changes of culture translated by designers into the consumptionist changes of new and different tastes.

Barthes's image of Parisian fashion was about making alterations to a conventional style of garment. The goal of fashion was to change the sign-function of dress codes expressing, against the traditional folk costume, the cultural figures of fashionable design in details and decoration. Dresses can cover or reveal ladies' legs, so the length of the skirt may vary. Menswear may dispense with the fixed tie or change it into an open shirt. While the fashion journalist's uncritical acceptance of each new style belongs to their professional style, Barthes proceeded critically to express the cultural and countercultural form of fashion codes. In his role of signifier, the writer Barthes decoded the variants of linguistic word and sentences into the invariant models of fashions.

Abandoning the structural codification of Saussure, Barthes paraphrased the synonyms of language into the dialog of parasynonyms. From 1966 to 1968, Barthes lectured in Tokyo and while walking around the metropolis, he discovered as an outsider to Japan the mythological sign-forms of the graphic speech. In the illustrated book *The Empire of Signs* (1970), he interpreted Japanese signs with reasoning-with-sentiment attempting to reconcile the Eastern and Western signs with the different background of culture. As an example, the Japanese kimono was a signifier to dress man and woman. In Barthes's playful texture, the kimono was made in the physical shape of the decorated silk fabric, but the shape was decorated with ample sleeves and a broad belt to outline the magical contours between men's and women's bodies. To operate as a Japanese myth, the object, concept, or person was never seen as a trivial thing but each sign was regarded with the aesthetic and erotic ambiguity of the *object d'art*.

Barthes admired the metaphorical beauty of pictographic characters in Japan, where the ideographs were written vertically and from right to left. He cherished the art-signs of Japanese woodprints with flower and bird arrangements, the visual landscape of Japanese *cuisine*, the formal ceremony of drinking tea, the tranquility of Japanese gardens, and many other signs. He, semiotically, explored the sensory, visual, acoustic, gustatory, and olfactory codes of Japanese signs in Barthes's discourse of signs. Since he treasured Japanese art, photographs, recipes, fashion, and other figurative images, these sign-images left room for the ambiguity of artistic symbols to consider the magical habits of life.

His book *L'Empire des signes* was an interdisciplinary seminar to prepare the Western sign-receiver for the Eastern life and folklore. For the cognitive and emotional significance of signs in his later works, see the cross-fertilization of linguistic and nonlinguistic signs in, Barthes's discourse of *Image-Music-Text* (1977), *Camera Lucida* (1980), and *The Responsibility of Forms* (1982).

Further Reading

Barthes, Roland. *Camera Lucida: Reflections on Photography* [1980]. Trans. Richard Howard. New York: Hill and Wang, 1981.
Barthes, Roland. *Empire of Signs* [1970]. Trans. Richard Howard. New York: Hill & Wang, 1982.
Barthes, Roland. *The Fashion System* [1967]. Trans. Matthew Ward and Richard Howard. New York: Hill and Wang, 1983.
Barthes, Roland. *Image-Music-Text*. Trans. Stephen Heath. London: Fontana/Collins, 1977.
Barthes, Roland. *Mythologies: The Complete Edition, In a New Translation* [1957]. Trans. Richard Howard. New York: Hill and Wang, 2012.
Barthes, Roland. *The Responsibility of Forms: Critical Essays on Music, Art, and Representation* [1982]. Trans. Richard Howard. New York: Hill and Wang, 1985.
Beaugrande, Robert de. "Ferdinand de Saussure." In *Linguistic Theory: The Discourse of Fundamental Works*. London and New York: Longman, 1991. 6–33.
Gorlée, Dinda L. "Paraphrase or Parasite? The Semiotic Stories of Translation." *Chinese Semiotic Studies* 16.1 (2020): 1–46.
Saussure, Ferdinand de. *Course in General Linguistics* [1916]. Trans. Wade Baskin. New York: McGraw-Hill Book Company, 1966.

22

Semiology

Dinda L. Gorlée

As a young man, Roland Barthes was, after receiving his bachelor's degree, struck down by tuberculosis. Tuberculosis was a pandemic, but there was no vaccination to escape the outbreaks of dangerous attacks. Barthes interrupted his studies and spent several years in a sanatorium (1934–5, 1941–5). After those isolated years of constant hardship, he nursed his own fierce love of freedom. His unpublished manuscripts and letters (*Album*, 2015) communicated that he had to educate himself to gain a doctoral degree and become a teacher of French literature and later a professor of literary semiology in Paris.

As a critical theoretician of the new French literature after the Second World War, Barthes opposed the French tradition of Sartre's political texts, the French tradition of Marxism, Freudian psychoanalytical criticism, and Lévi-Strauss's structural mythology. Barthes sought to "reconstitute the message of the work, but only its system, just as the business of the linguist is not to decipher the meaning of the sentence but to determine the formal structure." The rejection of the "New Novel" motivated Barthes's critical efforts to "engineer" the stylistic causes of literary textuality. In his first book *Writing Degree Zero* (1953), he brought into sharpened focus *how* the work was constructed, and *how* the mystery was sharpened in the narrative discourse of criticism.

Barthes's quasi-technical technique was literary semiology, when the theory of rhetoric prescribed the bourgeois *langue cultivée* for literary research in postwar France. Barthes's broader vista of semiological analysis in *Mythologies* (1957) radicalized literary signs into social symbols to theorize current phenomena and events. The figurative thinking of the wrestling match, children's toys, Greta Garbo's face, a new Citroën car, a travelogue, and other "mythological" artifacts were mythical scenes formulated in Barthes's intellectual outlook. The word "myth" was in those days a sophisticated fashionable word, removed from ancient Greek and Roman mythologies. And Barthes was equally alienated from Claude Lévi-Strauss's structural study of myth.

In Barthes's *Mythologies*, the theoretical essay "Myth Today" gave academic prestige to Barthes's evolutionary speech. He traced "in the decorative display of what-goes-without-saying, the ideological abuse which, in my view, is hidden here." By investigating details of the "natural" character of verbal and nonverbal things, Barthes turned mythological reading into "artificial" events. In his speech, Barthes described details with word clues to persuade the readers of the deeper meaning of the whole myth. For Barthes, the myth was larger than the etymological fragment of any rhetorical speech: myths can be decoded and deciphered, since they are encoded with social and psychological signs to be demythologized into symbols of human life.

Barthes's book *Elements of Semiology* (1964) served the pedagogical function to introduce students of the École Pratique des Hautes Études to semiological analysis. Barthes's pioneering term of semiology was derived from Ferdinand de Saussure's *Course in General Linguistics* (1916). Since semiology "would be a part of social psychology and consequently of general psychology," Saussure affirmed that this "science does not yet exist, no one can say what it would be." For Saussure, "Linguistics is only a part of the general science of semiology," pointing out that the "task of the linguist is to find out what makes language a special system within the mass of semiological data." However, "Linguists have been going around in circles: language, better than anything else, offers a basis for understanding the semiological problem; but language must, to put it correctly, be studied in itself; heretofore language has almost been studied in connection with something else, from other viewpoints." Saussure concluded that semiology will exchange the arbitrariness of verbal signs with general laws, but Barthes worked with imperative rules to construct from verbal signs final symbols.

As in Roman Jakobson's linguistic-literary models, Barthes's *Elements of Semiology* elaborated on the twofold classification of Saussure's structural study of language divided between two logical (i.e., associative and systematic) parts of the human brain. In Barthes's writings, the artistic "scenes" (words) consist of the individual "metaphor," while the objective "sequence" (group of words) is the general "metonomy." Barthes's didactic material was the theatrical "connotation" of his narrative voice performed in, for example, the acrobatic expressivity of Charles Chaplin or surrealistic painting, while the technical and collective representation was "denotation" in the narrative world of Homeric epic poetry, the pseudo-world of cinema, and realist art. The shifting emphasis between connotation and denotation is found in Barthes's French stereotypes: the binary (i.e., creative and commercial) combination of the media representation of cultural language in fashion and culinary recipes. Semiological analysis communicates the author's self-image transformed into the role of identifying with social language. This controversial exposure of the semotic self inspired the alien and artificial appearance of his mysterious story-writing shifting between real and imagined, between particular and typical.

Semiology is a synonym of semiotics, but their relationship is a mixed *découpage*. Semiology and semiotics are distinct from each other and have crucial differences. While Saussure's semiology is a static process to organize the arbitrary signs of language into a grammar, Barthes's semiotics stands for a dynamic method, in which linguistic and nonlinguistic signs are received as new signs. Semiotics permits the sign-receiver to reinterpret the received signs into other signs, and so forth. Barthes as a critical thinker followed the semiological formula of Saussure in following his readings of the influence of literary signs upon society, but as creator of works of art, he was a subversive semiologist. Barthes's "semio-criticism," as terrain between linguistics and literature, was a new form to change the ideology of sign theory into social practice.

The *Elements of Semiology* showed that Barthes's early literary interest in semiology was derived from the senior Danish linguist Louis Hjelmslev. Hjelmslev amplified Saussure by postulating in the articles "La structure morphologique" and "Pour une sémantique structurale" (written in 1939 and 1957) the formulation that language was a semiological structure of signs bound in a significative unit to be broadly communicated in the discourse. Yet expression (*forme*) and content (*substance*) do not hold together in Saussure's fixed structure, but involve two independent elements meeting in a *décomposable* unit, translated into each other. The *commutation* of *invariants* to *variants* produces the formal meaning. Instead of Hjelmslev's concept of signs, Barthes preferred cultural symbols as the social key point of the book *S/Z* (1970). With the semiological meaning of the text, Barthes gave rational, irrational, and anti-rational freedom to the critical reading of his speech. His semiotic analysis provided cultural clues to the text, depending on the mood or temper of the reader.

Further Reading

Barthes, Roland. *Album: Unpublished Correspondence and Texts*. Trans. Jody Gladding. Ed. Éric Marty. New York: Columbia University Press, 2018.

Barthes, Roland. "Criticism as Language [1963]." In *The Critical Moment: Essays on the Nature of Literature*. London: Faber and Faber, 1964. 123–9.

Barthes, Roland. *Elements of Semiology* [1964]. Trans. Annette Lavers and Colin Smith. New York: Hill and Wang, 1968.

Barthes, Roland. *Mythologies: The Complete Edition, In a New Translation* [1957]. Trans. Richard Howard. New York: Hill and Wang, 2012.

Barthes, Roland. *S/Z: An Essay* [1970]. Trans. Richard Miller. New York: Hill and Wang, 1974.

Barthes, Roland. "To Write: An Intransitive Verb?" In *The Languages of Criticism and the Sciences of Man: The Structuralist Controversy*. Eds. Richard and Eugenio Donato. Baltimore and London: The John Hopkins Press, 1970. 134–56.

Barthes, Roland. *Writing Degree Zero* [1953]. Trans. Annette Lavers and Colin Smith. New York: Hill and Wang, 1968.

Hjelmslev, Louis. *Essais linguistiques: Travaux du Cercle Linguistique de Copenhague XII*. Copenhagen: Lingvistkredsen/Cercle Linguistique de Copenhagen, 1959.

Krampen, Martin. "Ferdinand de Saussure and the Development of Semiology." In *Classics of Semiotics*. Eds. Martin Krampen, Klaus Oehler, Roland Posner, Thomas A. Sebeok, and Thure von Uexküll. New York and London: Plenum Press, 1987. 59–88.

Lévi-Strauss, Claude. "The Structural Study of Myth." *The Journal of American Folklore* 68.270 (1955): 428–44.

Saussure, Ferdinand de. *Course in General Linguistics* [1916]. Trans. Wade Baskin. New York: McGraw-Hill Book Company, 1966.

23

Structuralism

Dinda L. Gorlée

Roland Barthes's "new criticism" in *Criticism and Truth* (1966) explored a diverse range of methodological concepts to discover new ways to color his texts. He deconstructed the old questions of rhetorical speech, which answered the literary story with close *explications de texte* to cultivate the logical and critical style in etymological speeches. In the second half of the twentieth century, Barthes's *science pilote* reconstructed the postwar France's intellectual power by adopting the semiological analysis, which widened the literary text into a social and cultural complex of multidisciplinary ideas. Barthes engaged his personal identity to struggle with the taboos of public opinion in communicating the intellectual and aesthetic criticism in his dialogue with the readers.

Reading the literary text was broadened into Barthes's mythological activity, in which the historical narratives relate to the contemporary genres of films, theater, sports, and other cultural rituals. Barthes's intimate knowledge of these arts was gathered from the research of literary signs and extended to the display of playing, in his critical fragments, a verbal game. He displayed the nonhistorical criticism of different arts to encourage the readers to read the poetic text with cultural reality mixed with the verbal game of semiotic vocabulary and constructions. Barthes's book *The Pleasure of the Text* (1973) encouraged to think about the double texture in an entertaining, even passionate, way. In his role of critic, Barthes figured out the puzzle of hidden meanings, but to get the cultural readings right, he exploited the web of aesthetic ideas with the creativity of language charged with intrinsic meanings.

Barthes reconstructed and rethought the "formless" elements of the eclectic style of words and sentences translated into pieces of fashion, musical tones, photographs, recipes, and other images. He mediated intelligently between his own work to educate his audience to his intensive discourse to arguing against the quasi-formal approach of Saussure's theory of semiotic signs. Barthes collaborated with French fellow travelers, Michel Foucault, Claude Lévi-Strauss, Julia Kristeva, Jean Baudrillard, Algirdas Julien Greimas, and other thinkers, making that this group founded in Paris the French movement of structuralism. Saussure's formal framework was the *Course in General Linguistics* (1916), which as a textbook could be read etymologically, historically, and metaphorically to transform Saussure's linguistic units into the intellectual logic of French human sciences.

Structuralism was more than just a postwar form of criticism. Rather, it was a cultural movement to change the signifying practice of speech and writing. The structuralists did not give a scientific definition to the common tasks of structuralists, but each structuralist brought together a scientific hypothesis of literary meaning. Instead of a general meaning, Barthes narrowed down the private term "signification" and connected structuralism to Saussure's grammar of words and sentences, but with his own personal differentiation.

The method of "structure" was the modern word for building method and style, in which the structuralist explored structuralist changes in a diverse range of academic fields: linguistics, biology, sociology, ethnology, economics, law, psychology, and medical science. Structuralism followed Saussure, who built in linguistics the rules of the game of chess to "structure" the sixteen pieces of the game. The term "structure" was deeply rooted in the style of French structuralism, in which the notion of structure pointed to the organized capacity of Saussure's semiology of systems, founded on the systematic organization of linguistic units to build the grammatical structure. Saussure wrote about discourse that the "value" of the elements of words to sentences must be determined by the linear rules of the two or more consecutive units according to the general grammar. Alternatively, Barthes as a structuralist regarded the individual "value" of discourse as a balance of the combinative (i.e., linguistic-with-cultural) structure to write his own domain of speech.

For general linguistics, Saussure's two-faced union between a linguistic *signe* (sign) divided in the binary system of the physical or material concept of interpretation in the *signifié* (signified) and the mental activity of the commentary in the *signifiant* (signifier) to govern the total building of vocal and written signs of language. Saussure sought to restore coherence to the system of accepted and denied criteria of written discourse, while his main point was vocal speech. Barthes's literary discourse of Barthes still broadened Saussure's exclusively linguistic sign into nonlinguistic art, including literature, music, photography, fashion, sports, films, and other forms of cultural "information." Barthes dismantled Saussure's terminology to structure his own experiential taste. His critical commentaries resemble Saussure's general theory of signs but are, for Barthes, built expressly for the purpose of the intellectual shape and playful forms of the signifier. By dissecting cultural phenomena into his illuminating figures of metaphor and metonymy, Barthes updated Saussure's grammar to his new field.

Barthes analyzed his working process in the appendix to a letter to a friend, the diplomat Philippe Rebeyrol. He prepared the outlines of "The Postage Stamp" in *Album* (2015) to find his form of meaning. To read Barthes's critical forms of essays, *A Barthes Reader* (1982), selected by Susan Sontag, gives an oversight of Barthes's efforts to fix Saussure's rules of organizing the linguistic structure into the new structure of semio-critical ideas. It seemed that Barthes's later structuralist work both agrees and disagrees with Saussure's theory. Since Barthes's self-criticism has transformed one hypothesis by another into an art-like essay, perhaps his role as a "journalistic" critic invested him with two types of scientific thought and artistic emotions.

Barthes's "semio-criticism" is a relativistic affair by trying to embody the dialogues between the historical linguistics of Saussure and modern texts to communicate with the original text and the audience. Barthes's interests lie mostly in the poetic narrative of language to decipher the living structure of mysteries and modernize the structure to offer a modern resolution. With the active stimulus of Roman Jakobson's development of linguistics to "poetics" and the adventurous contributions of Jacques Derrida, structuralism turned into the subject of dispute, developing into what is later called post-structuralism. See the crucial anthology *The Languages of Criticism and the Sciences of Man: The Structuralist Controversy* (1970) to read Barthes's article "To write: An intransitive verb" (1970). He was happy to merge linguistics and literature in his field of semio-criticism, but Saussure's linguistic theory of symbols remained the anonymous system of language. For Barthes, language was the ambiguity of cultural "myths" (Lavers 1982: 103–27) to the "deep, patient, and often circuitous descent into the labyrinths of meaning" (1982: 141). "Writing" is not the verb of the passive writer, but stands for the active writer to react with semiotic language on the significant events and activities of society.

Further Reading

Barthes, Roland. *Album: Unpublished Correspondence and Texts* [2015]. Trans. Jody Gladding. Ed. Éric Marty. New York: Columbia University Press, 2018.

Barthes, Roland. *A Barthes Reader*. Ed. Susan Sontag. New York: Hill and Wang, 1982.

Barthes, Roland. *Criticism and Truth* [1966]. Trans. and ed. Kathrine Pilcher Keuneman. Minneapolis, MN: University of Minnesota Press, 1987.

Barthes, Roland. *Mythologies: The Complete Edition, In a New Translation* [1957]. Trans. Richard Howard. New York: Hill and Wang, 2012.

Barthes, Roland. *The Pleasure of the Text* [1973]. Trans. Richard Miller. New York: Hill and Wang, 1975.

Bastide, Roger, ed. *Sens et usages du terme structure dans les sciences humaines et sociales* [1962]. The Hague and Paris: Mouton, 1972.

Barthes, Roland. "To Write: An Intransitive Verb?" In *The Languages of Criticism and the Sciences of Man: The Structuralist Controversy*. Eds. Richard Macksey and Eugenio Donato. Baltimore, MD: The John Hopkins Press, 1970. 134–56.

Benveniste, Émile. "'Structure' en linguistique [1962]." In *Sens et usages du terme structure dans les sciences humaines et sociales*. Ed. Roger Bastide. The Hague and Paris: Mouton, 1972. 31–9.

Lavers, Annette. *Roland Barthes: Structuralism and After*. Cambridge, MA: Harvard University Press, 1982.

Macksey, Richard and Eugenio Donato, eds. *The Languages of Criticism and the Sciences of Man: The Structuralist Controversy*. Baltimore and London: The Johns Hopkins Press, 1970.

Saussure, Ferdinand de. *Course in General Linguistics* [1916]. Trans. Wade Baskin. New York: McGraw-Hill, 1966.

24

Studium/Punctum

Andy Stafford

Studium-Punctum, which appears in Roland Barthes's final work, *Camera Lucida* (1980) has become something of a commonplace in accounts of his writing on photography. As often with Barthesian theories, the *studium-punctum* nexus of a photograph constitutes a binary opposition. But, however fixed these binary oppositions, such as *studium-punctum*, might claim to be, in Barthes's work they rarely are; and *studium-punctum* is possibly no exception. It differentiates two ways of reading a photograph, yet implicitly acknowledges that we do both concomitantly, if not simultaneously. In that sense, to deem the *studium* of a photograph as its general, contextual, and social "meaning" on the one side and, then, on the other, to ascribe to the *punctum* the highly individuated wound that the detail in a photograph makes on the viewing self is an artificial, imagined division which is purely operatory. The opposition allows the viewer a possibility of an attachment to one particular image in a sea of photographic clichés. The opposition also gestures toward the photographer's "intentions" in the *studium* on the one hand and to the wholly involuntary detail in the *punctum* on the other. In that sense, the opposition *studium-punctum* neatly characterizes the paradox, or double nature, of photography: both artform (intentionally) *and* pure document (the objective real), the photograph is both general and particular simultaneously. But the "breaking-through," the piercing of a "smooth" photographic record of a moment in the past enacted by the emotional detail, is a *punctum* which allows photography's divided self to become clear. The punctum also underscores the "has-been-ness" of any photographic image, and it is perhaps disingenuous to detach the *punctum* from the certificate of authenticity of the past that Barthes finds in photography.

Indeed, one way to avoid a fetishization of the *studium-punctum* opposition is to point to the clear antecedents in Barthes's work: the essay "The Third Meaning" (1970) on film stills from Sergei Eisenstein's cinema which points to a third, "obtuse" meaning in a photograph (or film still); the analysis of detail in his essay on Roger Pic's photographic record of the Berliner Ensemble production of Bertolt Brecht's *Mutter Courage* (1959); the elevation of the detail in women's fashion in the analysis of the Fashion System; the manner in which the viewer is "scandalized" (or not) by photojournalism in "Photochocs" in *Mythologies* (1957); and, finally, the historiographical way in which Barthes's details the "double grasp" in the work of nineteenth-century historian Jules Michelet.

Already in "The Photographic Message" (1961), Barthes was asking how a press photograph can be at once without a code (denotative) and simultaneously connotative (or coded)? He suggests that "it may one day be possible to reply to that question." In some, even many, ways, the *studium-punctum* opposition is an answer to this "photographic paradox." The photograph is "neutral," "objective," beholden to denotation and naturalness; but also it can be, at once, "invested," "cultural," situated.

The investment involved in being "wounded" by the *punctum* of a photograph might be considered as an element in what has been called the "affective turn." But it is also, as Kathrin Yacavone sees it, indicative of a move in Barthes's work on photography from semiology to phenomenology. However, as we noted earlier, Barthes does not so much abandon the *studium* for the *punctum*, as relativize one to the other (and not necessarily hierarchically). To "double grasp" the semiology and phenomenology involved in viewing a photograph is easier to say than to do; and much of the photography presented in *Camera Lucida* is indeed viewed by Barthes (if only in part) in its *studium*. This relating of part to whole is evident in his much earlier work on photography. When Barthes considers the detail in Roger Pic's photographic record of the Berliner Ensemble (1959), and when he shows how the fashion detail can radically shift the vestimentary code of a fashion ensemble, it is always in relation to the whole (or *studium*). The actor's *gestus* and the costume minutiae in Brecht's dramaturgy, the brooch that radically inflects the overall meaning of a clothing combination, are dialectically linked to their respective *studium* (revolutionary theater in Brecht, overall appearance in fashion).

The key element in the *punctum* of a photograph in relation to its *studium*, however, is the almost violent way in which it suspends language, leaves behind all codes of communication, and rediscovers what Barthes had called in "The Photographic Message" and "Rhetoric of the Image" (1964), a "message without a code." Whereas the *studium* invites the viewer's discursive reaction, the *punctum*—no doubt related to the photograph of Barthes's Mother as a young girl in the Winter Garden image, which he discusses with deep pathos but never displays in *Camera Lucida*—can by contrast only elicit a Zen-like reaction, both short and devoid of linguistic meaning, and summarized in the term Barthes began to use for this "silence": "Thus!."

Further Reading

Barthes, Roland. "Seven Photo Models of 'Mother Courage'" [1959]. Trans. Hella Freud Bernays. *Tulane Drama Review* 12.1 (1967): 44–55.

Batchen, Geoffrey, ed. *Photography Degree Zero: Reflections on Roland Barthes's Camera Lucida*. Cambridge, MA: MIT Press, 2009.

Shawcross, Nancy. *Roland Barthes on Photography: The Critical Tradition in Perspective*. Gainsville: University of Florida Press, 1997.

Tsakiridou, Corrina A. "Roland Barthes Explores Photography 'as a Wound.'" *Paragraph* 18.3 (1995): 273–85.

Yacavone, Kathrin. *Benjamin, Barthes and the Singularity of Photography*. London: Bloomsbury, 2012. Chapter 4.

25

Work/Text

Gerald Prince

Work/Text is another of the numerous binary oppositions—for example, denotation/connotation, readerly/writerly, pleasure/bliss, *studium/punctum*—that Roland Barthes is so fond of and that not only play an important role in his work but also seem to function as veritable engines for it. The opposition is explicitly developed in "From Work to Text" (1971). In conformity with Barthes, one should first note that the conjoined influence of Marxism, psychoanalysis, and structuralism on conceptions of language and literature necessitates, in contrast to the well-established notion of the work, a new notion connected to the toppling of traditional categories, that of the Text. Moreover, one should note that it would be vain to try and distinguish materially the Work from the Text. Though the latter is linked to aspects of modernity, it would be unwise to claim that ancient, classical objects are Works and that modern, avant-garde objects are Texts. Indeed, it is quite possible for there to be "Text" in ancient objects and besides, many modern objects are not Texts at all. The difference between Work and Text is of another kind. The work is substantial and perceptible. It is mentioned in catalogues, displayed and seen in bookshops, and held in the hand. The Text is held in language and experienced in the movement of a production. The work is on the side of *doxa*, of common sense and popular opinion. The Text is paradoxical and subversive. Whereas the work is caught in the closure of a manifest or hidden signified, the Text is open, its realm is that of the signifier, its logic is metonymic, and it practices the endless deferral of the signified. Whereas the work is at best moderately symbolic, the Text is symbolic through and through. The work does not constitute a threat for any monistic system, for any monologism, for the Law. In contrast, the Text is transgressively and irreducibly plural. The work is an object to be consumed while, on the contrary, the Text, which itself has play, is both played with and played. In fact, the Text invites the reader to collaborate and become a coauthor. Last but by no means least, if the work can give pleasure, the Text is tied to *jouissance*, to an (orgasmic) ecstasy or bliss that eliminates metalanguages, hierarchies, and separation.

The Work/Text opposition draws on such thinkers as Derrida (and his critique of centeredness and closure) or Lacan (Barthes's essay explicitly refers to him and makes an analogy between Work/Text and reality/the real). It also finds itself prefigured in some of Barthes's own writings and particularly in "The Death of the Author" (1968) and *S/Z* (1970). Like "From Work to Text" and other pieces by Barthes, "The Death of the Author" compares writing to a tissue. Furthermore, it rejects views of the author as the father of the text. It describes the latter as questioning any and all origins, refusing to close and to arrest meaning, spurning the Law, and constituting a revolutionary space of multiple languages in dialogue and contestation with one another. Above all, it argues that the text finds its unity in its destination, the reader, whose birth is ransomed by the author's death. As for *S/Z*, its famous contrasting of the readerly and the writerly, the *lisible* and the *scriptible*, evokes, of course, the comparison between the work and the Text. As opposed to the readerly text, the writerly text, which is not a thing, is completely and triumphantly plural. A production rather than a product, a structuration rather than a structure, it constitutes an assemblage of signifiers rather than signifieds. It is infinitely open and, indeterminate in origin, it subverts paternity and propriety, nullifies all metalanguages, and makes the reader a producer instead of a consumer.

The Text, as distinguished from the work, is explored in a number of writings by Barthes from the 1970s, notably "Theory of the Text" (1973), first published as an entry for the *Encyclopaedia Universalis*, "Introduction: The Semiological Adventure" ("L'aventure sémiologique," 1974), a lecture given in Milan at the first world congress of the International Association for Semiotic Studies, and *The Pleasure of the Text* (1973). These writings more than suggest the Text's affinity with stereophonies of intertwined languages, networks of puns and wordplays, brash neologisms, anagrammatic disseminations, and audacious incongruities. They stress that the Text is a practice, a set of traces in motion that unsettles all assumptions and defies all institutions and legalities. The Text mixes languages and abolishes metalanguages, it eliminates borders, and, dissolving the distinction between subject and object, it promotes the equivalence of reading and writing. Of note is Barthes's insistence in "Theory of the Text" on Julia Kristeva's contribution to that theory through her emphasis on the text as plural, as productivity, as signifying process and work, as intertext. Of note, too, is the fact that *The Pleasure of the Text*, which distinguishes between readerly objects that provide comfort, enjoyment, *plaisir*, and writerly practices that provoke unruly, disruptive *jouissance*, also points to a displacement of the Text by the claims of desire, the real, and the body.

Roland Barthes by Roland Barthes (1975) confirms the displacement. It makes clear that the Text can lose its freshness, turn into babble, and become paralyzed and that Barthes is ready to move on.

Further Reading

Barthes, Roland. "The Death of the Author [1968]." In *Image-Music-Text*. Trans. Stephen Heath. New York: Hill and Wang, 1977. 142–9.

Barthes, Roland. "From Work to Text [1971]." In *The Rustle of Language*. Trans. Richard Howard. New York: Hill and Wang, 1986. 56–64.

Barthes, Roland. "Introduction: The Semiological Adventure." In *The Semiotic Challenge* [1985]. Trans. Richard Howard. New York: Hill and Wang, 1988. 3–9.

Barthes, Roland. *The Pleasure of the Text* [1973]. Trans. Richard Miller. New York: Hill and Wang, 1975.

Barthes, Roland. *S/Z* [1970]. Trans. Richard Miller. New York: Hill and Wang, 1974.

Barthes, Roland. "Theory of the Text [1973]." In *Untying the Text: A Post-Structuralist Reader*. Ed. Robert Young. London: Routledge and Kegan Paul, 1981. 31–47.

Contributors

Dudley Andrew is Professor Emeritus of Comparative Literature and Film Studies at Yale University. Biographer and translator of André Bazin, he extends Bazin's thought in *What Cinema Is!* (2011) and in the edited volume, *Opening Bazin* (2012). Working in aesthetics and cultural history, he has written several books on French cinema and is preparing *Encountering World Cinema*, featuring European, African, and especially East Asian cinema. Andrew has been nominated in France as a Commandeur de l'Ordre des Arts et des Lettres, and is an elected member of the American Academy of Arts and Sciences.

Thomas Baldwin is Reader in French and Co-Director of the Centre for Modern European Literature and Culture at the University of Kent, UK. His publications include *The Material Object in the Work of Marcel Proust* (2005), *The Picture as Spectre in Diderot, Proust and Deleuze* (2011), *What's So Great About Roland Barthes?* (a special issue of *L'Esprit Créateur* coedited with Katja Haustein and Lucy O'Meara, 2015), and *Roland Barthes: The Proust Variations* (2019).

Jeffrey R. Di Leo is Professor of English and Philosophy at the University of Houston-Victoria, USA. He is Editor of the *American Book Review*, Founding Editor of the journal *symplokē*, and Executive Director of the Society for Critical Exchange and its Winter Theory Institute. He is the author or editor of more than thirty books on philosophy, literature, higher education, book culture, and literary theory. His recent books include *American Literature as World Literature* (2017), *The Bloomsbury Handbook of Literary and Cultural Theory* (2019), *The End of American Literature: Essays from the Late Age of Print* (2019), *Biotheory: Life and Death under Capitalism* (2020, with Peter Hitchcock), *Philosophy as World Literature* (2020), *What's Wrong with Antitheory?* (2020), *Vinyl Theory* (2020), *Philosophy as World Literature* (2020), *Catastrophe and Education: Neoliberalism, Theory, and the Future of the Humanities* (2020), *Contemporary Literary and Cultural Theory: An Introduction* (forthcoming), and *Selling the Humanities* (forthcoming).

Dinda L. Gorlée is a semiotician of applied linguistics (Peirce, Jakobson, Wittgenstein) and a multilingual translation theoretician with interests in the philosophy of language and cultural theory. With a dual PhD in translation theory and semiotics from the University of Amsterdam, Gorlée has worked as a visiting professor of semiotics and translation theory at the Universities of São Paulo, Amsterdam, Ouagadougou, Vienna, and Innsbruck. Her last academic function was Visiting Professor at the University of Helsinki, Finland. Gorlée is Book Editor of Brill's series *Semiotics: Sign of the Times* and works as a general linguist at the Wittgenstein Archives of the University of Bergen, Norway. She is a member of the Collegium of the International Association of Semiotic Studies (IASS). Gorlée's books are *Semiotics and the Problem of Translation: With Special Reference to the Semiotics of Charles S. Peirce* (1994), *On Translating Signs* (2004), *Song and Significance: Virtues and Vices of Vocal Translation* (2007), *Wittgenstein in Translation: Exploring Semiotic Signatures* (2012), *From Translation to Transduction: The Glassy Essence of Intersemiosis* (2015), and *Wittgenstein's Secret Diaries: Semiotic Writing in Cryptography* (2020).

Michael Moriarty is Drapers Professor of French at the University of Cambridge, England, and a fellow of Peterhouse. His publications include *Taste and Ideology in Seventeenth Century France* (1988), *Roland Barthes* (1991), *Early Modern French Thought: The Age of Suspicion* (2003), *Fallen Nature, Fallen Selves: Early Modern French Thought II* (2006), *Disguised Vices: Theories of Virtue in Early Modern French Thought* (2011), and *Pascal: Reasoning and Belief* (2020). He is joint editor of *The Cambridge History of French Thought* (2019). He is a fellow of the British Academy and a Chevalier dans l'Ordre des Palmes Académiques.

Warren Motte is Distinguished Professor of French and Comparative Literature at the University of Colorado, Boulder. He specializes in contemporary writing, with particular focus upon experimentalist works that put accepted notions of literary form into question. He is the author of *The Poetics of Experiment: A Study of the Work of Georges Perec* (1984), *Questioning Edmond Jabès* (1990), *Playtexts: Ludics in Contemporary Literature* (1995), *Small Worlds: Minimalism in Contemporary French Literature* (1999), *Fables of the Novel: French Fiction Since 1990* (2003), *Fiction Now: The French Novel in the Twenty-First Century* (2008), *Mirror Gazing* (2014), and the translator and editor of *Oulipo: A Primer of Potential Literature* (1986; rev. ed. 1998, rpt. 2007). His most recent books are *French Fiction Today* (2017) and *Experimental Literature: A Collection of Statements* (2018, with Jeffrey R. Di Leo). In 2015, he was named Chevalier dans l'Ordre des Palmes Académiques.

Magali Nachtergael is Professor of Contemporary French Studies at the University Bordeaux Montaigne, France. She is the author of three monographs, *Poet Against The Machine. Une histoire technopolitique de la littérature* (Marseille, Le Mot et le reste, 2020), *Les Mythologies individuelles, récit de soi et photographie au 20e siècle* (New York / Amsterdam, Rodopi, 2012), and *Roland Barthes contemporain* (Max Milo, 2015). During the celebration of Roland Barthes's centenary, she curated a series of major exhibitions in France, *Lumières de Roland Barthes (Barthes's Enlightenments)*, and in Seoul, South Korea, *The Family of the Invisibles* with 200 artworks from the National French photographic collections (CNAP). She was granted a research leave at the French National Center for Scientific Research on a gender and sexuality program from 2019 to 2020.

Daniel T. O'Hara, Professor of English and Inaugural Mellon Term Professor of Humanities at Temple University, USA, is the author of nine books: *Tragic Knowledge:*

Yeats's Autobiography and Hermeneutics (1981); *The Romance of Interpretation: Visionary Criticism from Pater to De Man* (1985); *Lionel Trilling: The Work of Liberation* (1988); *Radical Parody: Culture and Critical Agency After Foucault* (1992); *Empire Burlesque: The Fate of Critical Culture in Global America* (2003); *Visions of Global America and the Future of Critical Reading* (2009); *The Art of Reading as a Way of Life: On Nietzsche's Truth* (2009); *Narrating Demons, Transformative Texts: Rereading Genius in Mid-Century Modern Fictional Memoir* (2012); and *Virginia Woolf and the Modern Sublime* (2015). He is also the editor or coeditor of six other books, including *Why Nietzsche Now* (1985); with Gina MacKenzie and Sigmund Freud, *The Interpretation of Dreams* (2005); and with Geoffrey Hartman, *The Geoffrey Hartman Reader* (2005). Currently, he is working on four books, *Roland Barthes and the Revival of Literature, Yeats and Revisionism: A Half-Century of the Dancer and the Dance, The Travesty of Innocence: Thomas Mann's Fictional Ethics,* and *Playing Death: On the Borderless State.*

Brian O'Keeffe is a senior lecturer in the French department at Barnard College and an associate director of the Barnard Center for Translation Studies.

Thomas Pavel is Emeritus Professor in Romance Languages and Literatures, Comparative Literature, the Committee on Social Thought, and Fundamentals at the University of Chicago. His books include *The Lives of the Novel* (2013), *Comment écouter la littérature* (2006), *The Spell of Language: Post-Structuralism and Speculation* (2001), *De Barthes à Balzac. Fictions d'un critique et critiques d'une fiction* (coauthor Claude Bremond, 1998), *L'Art de l'éloignement. Essai sur l'imagination classique* (1996), *Fictional Worlds* (1986), and *The Poetics of Plot: The Case of English Renaissance Drama* (1985).

Gerald Prince is Professor of Romance Languages at the University of Pennsylvania. He is the author of several books, including *Métaphysique et technique dans l'œuvre romanesque de Sartre* (1968), *A Grammar of Stories* (1973), *Narratology: The Form and Functioning of Narrative* (1982), *A Dictionary of Narratology* (1987), *Narrative as Theme* (1992), *Guide du roman de langue française (1901-1950)* (2002), and *Guide du roman de langue française (1951-2000)* (2019), as well as many articles on narrative theory and on modern French literature. Prince is a member of the editorial or advisory board of over a dozen journals (including *Narrative, Style, French Review, Roman 20/50* and *Tangence*). In 2013, he received the Wayne C. Booth Lifetime Achievement Award from the International Society for the Study of Narrative.

Jean-Michel Rabaté is Professor of English and Comparative Literature at the University of Pennsylvania, coeditor of the *Journal of Modern Literature*, cofounder of Slought Foundation, and a fellow of the American Academy of Arts and Sciences. He is the author or editor of more than forty books on modernism, psychoanalysis, philosophy, and literary theory. Recent titles include *Rust* (2018), *Kafka L.O.L.* (2018), *Rire au Soleil* (2019), *Beckett and Sade* (2020), *Rires Prodigues: Rire et jouissance chez Marx, Freud et Kafka* (2021), the edited collections *After Derrida* (2018), *New*

Beckett (2019), *Understanding Derrida / Understanding Modernism* (2019), *Knots: Post-Lacanian Readings of Literature and Film* (2020), and, with Angeliki Spiropoulou, *Historical Modernisms* (2021).

Herman Rapaport is Reynolds Professor of English at Wake Forest University, North Carolina. He is the author of *Milton and the Postmodern* (1983), *Heidegger and Derrida* (1989), *Between the Sign and the Gaze* (1994), *Is There Truth in Art?* (1998), *The Theory Mess* (2001), *Later Derrida* (2004), and *The Literary Theory Toolkit* (2011). His most recent book is *Derrida on Exile and the Nation* (2021), which is an exegesis of the whole of Derrida's foundational seminar, *Fantom of the Other* (1984–5).

Andy Stafford is Senior Lecturer at the University of Leeds. His books include *Sarrasine de Balzac* (2011), *Photo-texts: Contemporary French Writing of the Photographic Image* (2010), *Roland Barthes: The Language of Fashion* (2006, with M. Carter), and *The Modern French Essay: Movement, Instability, Performance* (2005, with C. Forsdick). His new monograph is called *Roland Barthes Writing The Political: History, Dialectics, Self* (2023).

Rudolphus Teeuwen is Professor of English at National Sun Yat-sen University in Kaohsiung, Taiwan. He teaches courses related to eighteenth-century literature and philosophy, aesthetics, the utopian imagination, and literary theory, and has published on these matters, including on Roland Barthes, in journals such as *Cultural Critique*, *Canadian Review of Comparative Literature*, *Theory, Culture & Society*, *Philosophy and Literature*, and *symplokē*. With Steffen Hantke, he edited *Gypsy Scholars, Migrant Teachers and the Global Academic Proletariat* (2007).

Steven Ungar is Professor Emeritus at the University of Iowa, where he taught Comparative Literature, French, and Cinematic Arts from 1976 to 2020. His book-length publications include *Roland Barthes: The Professor of Desire* (1983), *Scandal and Aftereffect: Blanchot and France Since 1930* (1995), *Popular Front Paris and the Poetics of Culture* (2005), *Cléo de 5 à 7* (2008), and *Critical Mass: Social Documentary in France, from the Silent Era to the New Wave* (2018). Ungar is currently completing an English-language edition of Chris Marker's early film criticism.

Zahi Zalloua is the Cushing Eells Professor of Philosophy and Literature at Whitman College and editor of *The Comparatist*. He is the co-author, with Ilan Kapoor, of *Universal Politics* (2021), and the author of *Being Posthuman: Ontologies of the Future* (2021), *Žižek on Race: Toward an Anti-Racist Future* (2020), *Theory's Autoimmunity: Skepticism, Literature, and Philosophy* (2018), *Continental Philosophy and the Palestinian Question: Beyond the Jew and the Greek* (2017), *Reading Unruly: Interpretation and Its Ethical Demands* (2014), and *Montaigne and the Ethics of Skepticism* (2005). He has edited volumes and special journal issues on globalization, literary theory, psychoanalysis, and cultural and trauma studies.

Index

9/11 attacks on America 206–7, 212–19

aclassé 194
actors 18, 22, 36, 94, 229
adaptation 7, 104–12
adhomination 24
Adorno, Theodor 1, 3–4
aesthetics 1, 7, 34, 49, 96, 106–7, 112, 120, 126–7, 151–6, 165–6, 178, 232, 258, 262
affective turn 8, 266
African novel 162–7
Afterlives of Roland Barthes, The (Badmington) 3
Agamben, Giorgio 219
agrammaticality 161–5
À la recherche du temps perdu (Proust) 70, 75, 77, 79, 82 n.59
Album (Barthes) 3, 259, 263
Algalarrondo, Hervé 224
alienation 18–19, 76–7, 89–90, 95, 162, 189, 211, 219
Allar, Neal 191
allegory 16–17, 97, 161
Althusser, Louis 23–4
Amelio, Lucio 224, 227
anachoresis 210–11, 216, 218
analogy 15–25, 176–7
Andrew, Dudley 7
androgyny 227, 232
Angels of Sin, The (Bresson) 94
anthropocentrism 163
anthropology 9, 197, 242
Antony, Mark 87
"Aphorism Countertime" (Derrida) 146
aphorisms 146
Arcadie 224
archives 175, 177, 208, 246
Arendt, Hannah 21
Ascenseur pour l'échafaud (Malle) 93

asceticism 56, 58, 209–11, 216, 218–19
Asianism 122, 124
atopos 194, 251
At the Hawk's Well (Yeats) 176
Autexier, Hughes 227
authenticity 118, 126–8, 137, 153, 265
authors 6–9, 33, 36, 38, 42–3, 45–7, 50, 55–6, 60–5, 155–8, 239–40
autobiography 117, 120–1, 137, 141, 229, 251
autonomy 151, 155
Autres Visages d'Acteurs (Varda) 23
avant-garde 33, 42, 64, 94, 107–9, 123, 227, 239, 249, 254

Badmington, Neil 3
Baldwin, Thomas 6
Barrault, Jean-Louis 23
Barthes, Roland 1, 79 n.1
  Album 3, 259, 263
  alignment of Proust 6
  and Bazin, André 103–12
  biographemes 61–2
  Camera Lucida: Reflections on Photography 2–3, 5, 8–9, 15, 17, 25–6, 62, 86, 140, 142, 144, 173–82, 183 n.6, 228–31, 246, 258, 265–6
  chosisme 8, 151–67
  critique of Pierre 18
  as cruising reader/writer 62–3
  dandyism 63
  "Death of the Author, The" 155–6, 168 n.38, 188–93, 239–40, 267–8
  death(s) 8, 138–48
  and DeLillo, Don 206–20
  designations 3
  distance and proximity in Cayrol, observations about 71–2, 77–8
  Elements of Semiology 2, 6, 241–2, 260–1

Empire of Signs 2, 9, 192–3, 197, 226, 228–9, 243, 245, 257
"Face of Garbo, The" 6, 91–4
Fashion System, The 2, 242, 257
"Fatigue and freshness" 137
film, philosophy of 6–7, 84–99, 103–12
film-based articles (1943-57) 85–99
and film in age of *Mythologies* 84–99
Foucault's assessment of 2
French classics, engagement with 5–6, 42–50
"Garbo's face" 23
gay visual culture and community 9, 223–32
"Harcourt Actor, The" 93–4
hedonism 7, 116–28
homosexuality 9, 223–32
How to Live Together 8–9, 191, 195, 206–9, 219–20, 250
image of himself at work 65
Incidents 3, 121, 127, 225–6, 229, 231
intellectual contributions 2
Kazan's film, remarks on 84–99
"La Bruyère" 5–6, 44–50
La Chambre Claire 103
"La Rochefoucauld" 5–6, 44–50
Le Degré zéro de l'écriture 44, 70
legacies and afterlives 7–9
"Le monde où l'on catche" 104
"Le Pauvre et le prolétaire" 89
Le Plaisir du texte 49
"L'Homme Racinien" 44
literature, philosophy of 6
"Littérature objective" 70–1
living together/apart 206–20
Lover's Discourse, A 3, 9, 34, 62, 177, 194, 207–8, 232, 243, 249, 251
mapping 4–7
with Marx 98
on maxim 46–8
on modern *vs.* classical art 71–2
as moralist 2–3
Mythologies 5–7, 16–18, 21, 23, 25–6, 30 n.35, 84–99, 104, 124, 191, 193–4, 196, 224, 226, 230, 251, 259, 265

"Myth Today" 191–2
on non-vouloir-saisir (no wish to grasp) 9
object-oriented aesthetics 151–67
as observer 224–6, 230–2
Oeuvres Complets 3, 103, 148
"On Gide and His Journal" 125
opacity in work of 186–98
petites mythologies 86–99
as philosopher of culture 3
philosophical legacy 2–4
photography, work on 5, 15–29
"Plaisir aux Classiques" 42–5, 48, 50
plaisir *vs.* jouissance 116–17, 119, 128 n.1
Pleasure of the Text, The 2, 7, 64–5, 116–20, 124, 156, 170, 228, 248–9, 253, 262, 268
"Poor and the Proletariat, The" 18, 94
posthumous publications 3–4
"Power and 'Cool'" 91, 93
Preparation of the Novel, The 225
and Proust, Marcel 6, 70–9
On Racine 5, 33–4, 37, 40, 254
Robbe-Grillet, Alain and 8, 151–2, 158–67
on Robbe-Grillet's poetics of new novel 8, 151
Roland Barthes by Roland Barthes 2–3, 27, 62, 117, 121–4, 127–8, 137, 140, 187, 189, 196, 240, 251, 268
Sade, Fourier, Loyola 6, 55–65, 118, 120
"Sade I" 63–4
"Sade II" 63–4
and search for rigor 5, 33–40
self-irony 8, 173–82
Sontag's assessment of 2
"Sympathetic Worker, A" 7, 84, 94–6, 98
S/Z-essay 2, 75, 118, 124, 192–3, 224–5, 227, 239, 241–3, 250, 253–4, 261, 268
"Tasks of Brechtian Criticism, The" 95, 98
"Third Meaning" 16, 20, 26

"Third Meaning: Research Notes on Some Eisenstein Stills, The" (Barthes) 226
"Visage de Garbo" 104
visual culture 9, 223–32
visual field for 16
Writing Degree Zero 1, 5–6, 63, 140, 189
Barthes Studies (journal) 10 n.13
Bataille, Georges 64
Battleship Potemkin (Eisenstein) 88–9
Baudelaire, Charles 71, 91, 246
Baudrillard, Jean 3
Baudry, André 224
Bazin, André 7, 84, 103–12
   in adaptations 105
   and Barthes, Roland 103–12
   career 105–8
   cinema 105–8
   cultural pieces 104
   death 104
   écriture 106–8
   essays 104–5
   literature 105–8
   neutral style 106–8
   style 108–12
Beaver, Harold 223, 224
Becker, Jacques 91
Benedek, László 98
Bentham, Jeremy 119
Bergson, Henri 55
biographemes 61–2
Bion, W. R. 214
Blanchot, Maurice 159–61, 219
bliss 116–19, 157, 248–9, 267
Bloom, Harold 173
Bob le flambeur (Melville) 93
body 28–9, 50, 56–60, 62, 64, 72–5
Book to Come, The (Blanchot) 159
borderlines 147–8
boredom 122–4, 128, 170, 208–9
Borges, Jorge Luis 15, 107
Bossuet, Jacques-Bénigne 42
Bourcier, Sam 223
bourgeois ideology 24
Brando, Marlon 18, 87, 89–90, 94–5, 98

Braunschweig, François 227
Brecht, Bertolt 18, 21, 84, 89–90, 94–8, 121, 230, 240, 248, 265–6
Bresson, Robert 85–6, 103
Britton, Celia 195–6
Brody, Richard 96
Brown, Clarence 105
Bruckberger, Raymond-Léopold 85–6
Bruckner, Pascal 50, 125
Bryant, Levi 153
Buddhism 93
Burke, Kenneth 1
Burke, Seán 61–2

Cage, John 60
Camera Lucida: Reflections on Photography (Barthes) 2–3, 5, 8–9, 15, 17, 25–6, 62, 86, 140, 142, 144, 173–82, 183 n.6, 228–31, 246, 258, 265–6
camera obscura 28
Camus, Renaud 223
capillarity 99 n.12
Carlier, J. C. 190
Carpenter, Edward 225
Castorp, Hans 211
Catholic Church 93
Cayrol, Jean 6, 70, 72, 104
centipede 162–4
Chamfort, Nicolas 42
Chaplin, Charlie 18–19, 23, 89–90
characters 35–6, 39–40, 44, 86–7, 106–11, 118
chosisme 8, 71, 151–67
   Jealousy's realisms 158–60
   jouissance after death of author/culture/object 155–8
   neo-chosisme 152–5
Christianity 118
cinema 84–5, 94, 96, 105–8
Cinema of Roland Barthes, The (Watts) 103–4
Cinemascope 87–8
classics 4–5, 42–50
classiques 42–50
Clément, René 7, 108–12
Clifford, Charles 28
close reading 2, 7, 9, 84, 206, 248

codes   2, 15–16, 142, 188, 193, 228, 231–2, 241–3
Cohen-Séat, Gilbert   95
Collins, Ray   105
colonialism   16, 159, 191, 197
communism   156, 188, 196, 211
Complete Works (Barthes)   225
Confiant, Raphaël   194
Connor, Steve   151
connotation   16, 49, 241, 260, 266–7
consciousness   71
contrapuntal theory   146–7
Cooper, Gary   98
Copernican Revolution   153
Cordier, Daniel   226
correlationism   152–6
Coste, Claude   48
Counterfeiters, The (Gide)   125–6
Covid-19 pandemic   206, 220
Créole language   187, 194
critiques   90, 96, 151–2, 189–90
   of adjective   193–4
   of authorship   240
   of bourgeois ideology   24
   of everyday life   8
   of *Fruits of the Earth, The*   125
   ideology   24–5, 45–6, 86
   of illusions   49
   of *La Plage*   230
   of liberalism   196
   of looking natural   18
   of mass culture   3
   of *Nekrassov*   44
   of property   196
   of Sartrian transparence   191
   of science   8–9, 187, 193
   of *Si Versailles m'était conté*   88
   of social relations   189, 196
   of textual intentionalism   189
   of *On the Waterfront*   90
   of Western acts of "com-prendre"   9
cruising reading   62–3
Crusoe, Robinson   210
Culler, Jonathan   119, 152
cultural   2, 15–16, 19, 155
cultural criticism   116
cultural imaginary   47–8
cultural studies   4, 7
culture of redemption   179, 184 n.36

dandyism   63
Darrieux, Danielle   22
Dasein   151–2
David, Jean-Louis   20
Davis, Miles   93
death   8, 27–8, 138–49
   of author/culture/object   155–8
   and ghostly presences   141–5
   and name   140–1
   and points in time   145–7
"Death of the Author, The" (Barthes)   155–6, 168 n.38, 188–93, 239–40, 267–8
"Deaths of Roland Barthes, The" (Derrida)   8, 137–48
d'Eaubonne, Françoise   224
de Balzac, Honoré   2, 118, 192–3, 239, 242–3, 250, 254
decadence   91, 122–4
de Certeau, Michel   3
de Chateaubriand, François-René   64
déconstruction   176, 193, 248
de Fontenelle, Bernard Le Bovier   42
de Foucauld, Charles   18
"degree zero" theory   189
de La Bruyère, Jean   43–5, 48–50, 64
de La Rochefoucauld, François   44, 46–8, 50
Deleuze, Gilles   3–4, 76, 146
Deleuzian rhizomatic   8
DeLillo, Don   9, 206–20
Delluc, Louis   22
Delorme, Danièle   22
denotation   16, 49, 241, 260, 266–7
Derrida, Jacques   3, 8, 116, 137–49, 161
   "Aphorism Countertime"   146
   on contrapuntal theory   146–7
   hauntology   140, 144–5, 148
   on ontology   144, 148
   poems   142
   on *punctum*   142–6
   representation of Barthes   141
de Saint-Loup, Robert   76
Descartes, René   24, 119–20
desire   8, 26, 28–9, 34, 61–2, 74–5, 124–6, 128 n.1, 151–67
de Villiers, Nicholas   223
dialectics   28, 45–6, 78, 112, 166–7, 174–5, 186–9, 191, 248, 266

diaries   128
Diderot, Denis   42
Didi-Huberman, Georges   29
Di Leo, Jeffrey R.   7
discharge   57
discourses   7, 9, 33–4, 43, 47, 56–8, 120, 137–8, 143, 147, 156, 245, 263
   of abstract theory   49
   of criticism   259
   of doxa   57
   foreseeable   123
   free indirect   111
   lover's   207–8, 227
   moralist   49
   on photography   26
   semiology   175
   of signs   258
   survivors'   210
   visual political   226
Dmytryk, Edward   96
domestics   58
d'Orsay, Galerie   19
double   26, 139, 189, 191–3
double consciousness   189
double grasp   192–4
Douglas, Charlotte   65 n.2
Douglas, Melvyn   91
doxa   49, 56–7, 63, 267
Doyle, Edie   97–8
drama   5, 16, 18, 37–8, 60, 71, 76, 84, 95–6, 107, 147, 176–7, 192, 240, 266
Dreams (Kurosawa)   211
Du Bois, W. E. B.   189
Du côté de chez Swann (Proust)   76
Duel in the Sun, A (Stevens)   96
Duvignaud, Jean   70

Ecrits complets (Bazin)   103
écriture   7, 103–12
ecstasy   116
"Ego Dominus Tuus" (Yeats)   173–4, 181
Eisenstein, Sergei M.   88–9
electoral photogeny   23
Elements of Semiology (Barthes)   2, 6, 241–2, 260–1
empire   16, 159
Empire of Signs (Barthes)   2, 9, 192–3, 197, 226, 228–9, 243, 245, 257
empruntée   17

encoding   16
ennui   123, 131 n.85
Ensemble, Berliner   84
"Entomologie de la pin-up" (Bazin)   104
Epicureanism   122, 124
Epstein, Jean   22
erotic   56–60, 62, 119–21, 159, 161, 163, 166, 228–9, 249, 258
ethics   187
eudaemonism   122, 124
event   2, 29, 35–8, 70, 91, 96, 112, 145–6, 148, 162, 164, 192, 246–7
Existences (Barthes)   42
existentialism   4, 43–4

face   23
"Face of Garbo, The" (Barthes)   6, 91–4
fakes   22, 29, 243
Falling Man (DeLillo)   9, 206–19, 220 n.1
family photographs   25
fashion   2
Fashion System, The (Barthes)   2, 242, 257
"Fatigue and freshness" (Barthes)   137
Faucon, Bernard   227
ffrench, Patrick   84, 95
films   22, 84–99
   philosophy of   6–7, 84–99, 103–12
Flaubert, Gustave   64, 71
focalization   23–4
Forsdick, Charles   187–8
Foucauld, Charles Eugène   86
Foucault, Michel   1–4, 223, 229
Fourier, Charles   6, 55–65, 66n.24
fragments   3, 9, 49, 63, 78, 107, 120–1, 124, 127–8, 145–6, 162, 164, 178, 187, 207–8, 217, 225–6, 256, 260, 262
freedom   38, 56, 64, 175, 194, 196, 213, 229, 257–9, 261
French classics   5–6, 42–50
   moralistes, rereading   44–50
   questioning   43–4
   reading, pleasure in   42–3
   seventeenth-century   42–3
   writers   42–4
   writings   44
French imperiality   17

Freud, Sigmund 24, 27–8, 46, 58, 118, 248
Freudianism 118
friendship 36, 97, 148, 186
Front Homosexuel d'Action Révolutionnaire 224
Fruits of the Earth, The (Gide) 125–6

Gabin, Jean 93
Gai Pied 224
Gallop, Jane 156–7
Garaudy, Roger 23
Garbo, Greta 23–4
"Garbo's face" (Barthes) 23
Garson, Greer 18
gays 9, 223–32
gay writing 8, 225
gaze 21, 23, 29, 72–6, 78, 88, 152, 159, 162, 165, 228–9
gender 223–5, 228–9, 232, 250
German Romanticism 174
Gide, André 2, 7, 121, 124–7, 225
  Counterfeiters, The 125–6
  Fruits of the Earth, The 125–6
  hedonism 124–7
  Immoralist, The 125–6
  moral philosophy 126–7
  works 124–7
Gielguld, John 18
Gilroy, Paul 189
Giraudoux, Jean 85–6
Girodet, Anne-Louis 227
Glassman, Deborah 85, 89
Glissant, Édouard 8–9, 186–98
  cultural sociology 188
  intentionality, notion of 188–91
  L'intention poétique 190
  opacity 186–98
  on social relations 188–92
  Tout-Monde, notion of 188, 197–8
Godard, Jean-Luc 88
gold 118
Gorleé, Dinda 9
grammar 55, 64, 148, 161–2, 165
Gréco, Juliette 23
Greimas, A. J. 6, 242
Griffiths, Michael R. 188, 190
grisbi 93

Guattari, Félix 76
Guittard, Jacqueline 18
Gury, Christian 225

Hachad, Naïma 188
Haiku 29, 121, 178, 195, 226, 245–7
hallucinations, anthropomorphic 163
Hamilton, David 227
Hamlet (Shakespeare) 139–40
Haraway, Donna 225
"Harcourt Actor, The" (Barthes) 93–4
Harman, Graham 153–7, 166
Harmony 58–9
hauntology 140, 144–5, 148
heautoscopy 26
hedonism 7, 116–28, 131 n.85
  Barthes's revival of 116–28
  boredom, life of 122–4
  Gidean 124–7
  money in 118–19
  for Nietzsche 123–4
  pleasure, overdetermination of 121–2
  sex in 119–21
Hepburn, Audrey 23, 91–2
hermeneutic 2, 152–3, 156–67, 243
high structuralism 192
Hine, Lewis H. 177–8
historians 34, 175
history 212, 227, 229–30
Hitchcocko-Hawksians 96
Hocquenghem, Guy 224
Hollywood 18–19, 95, 97, 105
Holy Shroud of Jesus 29
homosexualities 122, 223–32
homosexual sociabilities 9, 223–32
Horkheimer, Max 3
Howard, Richard 17, 85, 176
How to Live Together (Barthes) 8–9, 191, 195, 206–9, 219–20, 250
Human Comedy, The (Saroyan) 105–6
hypnosis 24

iconography 17, 227
ideology 5, 15–16, 24–5, 56, 63–4, 94–5, 121, 161–2, 166, 187, 191–2, 195
illusion 175

images   5, 15–29, 43, 46, 61, 65, 71–4, 78, 88, 93, 110–12, 142–4, 148, 162, 174–8, 182
imaginary   47–9, 175, 195, 227, 229
Imaginary, The (Sartre)   3
Immoralist, The (Gide)   125–6
Incidents (Barthes)   3, 121, 127, 225–6, 229, 231
indiscutable   17
Infinite Conversation, The (Blanchot)   161
Inoperative Community, The (Nancy)   218–19
intellectuals   33, 63, 98, 110
interpersonal skills of communication   186
In the Labyrinth (Robbe-Grillet)   219
invention   57
Ireland, Benjamin Hiramatsu   223
irony   8, 43, 254
Ivan the Terrible (Eisenstein)   16, 226

Jameson, Fredric   186
Joubert-Laurencin, Hervé   104
jouissance   116–17, 119, 152, 155–8, 169 n.64, 248–9
journals   4, 7, 8, 25, 42, 63, 82, 98, 104–5, 121, 125–8, 224
journal writing   2, 7
Jouvet, Louis   23
Julius Caesar (Mankiewicz)   18, 86, 98

Kant, Immanuel   153
Kaufman, Boris   96
Kazan, Elia   7, 94, 96, 98
Kerr, Deborah   18
Khatibi, Abdelkébir   186
King in New York, A (Chaplin)   19
Kippur, Sara   64
Knight, Diana   223
Krapp's Last Tape (Beckett)   219
Kraus, Karl   1
Kristeva, Julia   3, 116
Kzan, Elia   84

"La Bruyère" (Barthes)   5–6, 44–50
Lacan, Jacques   3, 116
La Chambre Claire (Barthes)   103

Lady in the Lake (Montgomery)   96
La jalousie (Robbe-Grillet)   152–67, 169 n.56
Lang, Fritz   88
language   2, 55–64
  Barthes's   43–9
  characteristic of   59
  of eighteenth-century writing   42
  Fourier's theory of   59
  Ignatius's   56
  philosophy of   3
  photography and   24
  pleasures of   56
  of prayer and devotion   60
  public   56
  of Sade   57–62
  signs of   59
  spurning   6
  state of   47–8
L'Antinorm (magazine)   224
L'Appel du silence (Poirier)   86
"La Rochefoucauld" (Barthes)   5–6, 44–50
Lavers, Annette   85
Le Côté de Guermantes (Proust)   76
Lecture politique du roman (Leenhardt)   158
Le Degré zéro de l'écriture (Barthes)   44, 70
Le Discours antillais (Glissant)   9, 187, 196, 200 n.37
Leenhardt, Jacques   158–9, 161
Leenhardt, Roger   105
Lefebvre, Henri   3
Le Fléau social (magazine)   224
Le Mépris (Godard)   88
"Le monde où l'on catche" (Barthes)   104
"Le Pauvre et le prolétaire" (Barthes)   89
Le Pen, Jean   23
Le Plaisir du texte (Barthes)   49
Le Prat, Thérèse   23, 94
Le rendez-vous (Robbe-Grillet)   64
Le Samouraï (Melville)   93
Les Anges du péché (Bresson)   103
Les Liaisons dangereuses (Laclos)   71–2
Les temps modernes (Sartre)   103
Lettres nouvelles (journal)   86
"L'Homme Racinien" (Barthes)   44
Lincoln, Abraham   89

linguistics   4, 6, 59, 250, 256, 260
L'intention poétique (Glissant)   190
lisible   49, 249, 253, 268
literary object   160-2
"Littérature objective" (Barthes)   70-1
living together/apart   206-20
logothetes   56
Lombardo, Patrizia   225
Lost Continent (documentary)   93
Lost Weekend, The (Wilder)   106
Lovecraft, H. P.   153-5
Lover's Discourse, A (Barthes)   3, 9, 34, 62, 177, 194, 207-8, 232, 243, 249, 251
Lubitsch, Ernst   91

Magic Mountain, The (Mann)   211
Magny, Claude-Edmonde   104, 105
Malevich, Kasimir   55-7, 65 n.1
Malki, Adnan   19-20
Mallarmé, Stéphane   64
Malle, Louis   93
Malloy, Terry   94-5, 97-8
Malraux, Andre   103
Mamoulian, Rouben   91
Manicheaism   122, 124
manifestos   55, 95, 107, 163
Mankiewicz, Joseph   86, 98
Marais, Jean   22
Marker, Chris   7, 84, 96-8, 104
marquis de Vauvenargues, Luc de Clapiers   42
Marty, Eric   195, 225
Marx, Karl   196
Marxism   43-4, 118
masculinity   98, 164, 243
Mason, James   18
mass culture   44, 121
materialism   120
Mauriès, Patrick   226
Mavor, Carol   223
maxim   45-9, 145
Maximes (de La Rochefoucauld)   45-8
media studies   4
mediation   191-3
Meillassoux, Quentin   153
Melville, Jean-Pierre   93
même   143

memory   46, 139, 141-2, 152, 176, 179-81, 212, 215, 217, 224, 227
Mendelsohn, Daniel   98
Mendès-France, Pierre   23
metonymy   143, 145-7, 256, 263
Michelet, Jules   47, 64, 123, 191-2, 225
Miller, D. A.   224-5
Miller, Richard   119
Milner, Jean-Claude   188
mimesis   36, 57, 141, 143
Miracle of Analogy, The (Silverman)   5, 15
modernism   64, 174
Modern Times (Chaplin)   89-90
modern vs. classical art   71-2
money   118-19
monologue   106, 112
monotheism   39
Montgomery, Robert   96
moralist   1-6, 42-50
moralistes   44-50
morality   2, 57, 63, 95, 117, 124-7, 157, 195
moral psychology   5, 40
moral virtues   47
Moreau, Jeanne   23, 93
Moriarty, Michael   5-6
Morrissette, Bruce   158, 161
Motte, Warren   9
mourning   141-2
Murder My Sweet (Dmytryk)   96
Murdoch, Adlai   188
Mythologies (Barthes)   5-7, 16-18, 21, 23, 25-6, 30 n.35, 84-99, 104, 124, 191, 193-4, 196, 224, 226, 230, 251, 259, 265
myths   16-29
"Myth Today" (Barthes)   191-2

Nachtergael, Magali   9
Nadeau, Maurice   86
name, death and   140-1
Nancy, Jean-Luc   218-19
narratives   16-17, 25-6, 28, 64, 84, 86, 95-6, 106-8, 121, 137, 141, 151-2, 158-61, 165, 190, 192, 207-8, 242, 256-7, 259-60, 262, 264
narrator   72-8, 159, 162-5, 169 n.56

native songs 162–7
nature 6, 15–16, 19–21, 24, 27, 29, 45, 47, 56–7, 60, 70–1, 87, 89, 93–7, 104
Nekrassov (Sartre) 44
neo-chosisme 152–5
neocolonial 159, 188, 191
neologisms 62
Neutral, The 250–1
neutrality 18
neutral style 106–8
new novel, Robbe-Grillet's 8, 151, 259
Nietzsche, Friedrich 7, 26, 77, 123–5, 175, 182, 187, 210
Ninotchka (Lubitsch) 91–2
Non-Objective World, The (Malevich) 55–7, 65 n.1
non-vouloir-saisir (no wish to grasp) 9
"Notes on Camp" (Sontag) 226
nouveau roman 64, 70, 151–2, 158, 160, 254
novels 6, 105–7, 111–12, 137, 158–67, 179, 206, 209, 215–18, 220 n.1
Novels of Robbe-Grillet, The (Morrissette) 158
"no-wish-to-grasp" (NVS) 193–6
nuances 64–5

object 8, 151–67
objectivity 15, 55, 60, 106, 111, 153
objectlessness 55–65
Object-Oriented Ontology (OOO) 8, 151–67
obsessions 56
occult modernism 174
Oeuvres Complets (Barthes) 3, 103, 148
O'Hara, Daniel T. 8
O'Keeffe, Brian 8–9
O'Meara, Lucy 195
"On Gide and His Journal" (Barthes) 125
On Photography (Sontag) 3
On Racine (Barthes) 5, 33–4, 37, 40, 254
On the Waterfront (Kazan) 7, 84, 87, 89–99, 104
ontology 104, 139–40, 144–5, 148
  of loss/spectrality 5
  OOO 8, 151–67
  of point 25–9

OOO; *see* Object-Oriented Ontology (OOO)
opacity 186–98
  Barthes's 186–98
  Créole language 187–8
  in "Death of the Author" 190
  definition 195–6
  in dialectic of language 186–9
  double grasp and 192–4
  in *Empire of Signs* 197
  Glissant's 186–98
  in intention 188–91
  mediation in 191–3
  "no-wish-to-grasp" (NVS) 193–6
  in performance 189–91
  practice of 188
  of self 194, 197–8
optimism 7, 105, 124, 197–8
oral culture 190
Orlando (Woolf) 138
Orpheus' music 173
Other, The 74–5, 81 n.32, 186–8, 193–6
overmining 155–7

painting, model of 72, 75
paradigm of pleasure 6, 55–65
Paris Match (magazine) 16–17, 20
parole 242, 256
Pavel, Thomas 5
pedophilia 227
pessimism 7, 121–4, 128, 131 n.85
phantom 25
phenomenology 5, 16, 25, 178, 266
Philippe, Gérard 22
philosophers 1–3, 7, 58, 117, 119, 122, 124, 128, 143, 153
philosophy 1–4, 6–7, 58, 116, 118, 122, 132 n.121, 144, 153
  academic 127
  of film 6
  of free compensation 117
  of involuntary memory 180–1
  of literature 6
  of meaning 117, 157
  moral 124–7
Photogénie (Delluc) 22
photogeny 15–25
  concept of 22

definition 22
electoral 23
photographic ecstasy 176, 179
photography 5, 15–29, 175, 226
 analogy 15–25
 as art/genre 26
 Barthes's analyses 15–29
 in *Camera Lucida: Reflections on Photography* 2–3, 5, 8–9, 15, 17, 25–6, 62, 86, 140, 142, 144, 173–82, 228–31, 246, 258, 265–6
 deictic of 26
 as fake luxury 22
 family 25
 to generality 26
 into kinds of action 175
 madness of 26
 myth of 5, 15–29
 ontology of point 25–9
 operator *vs.* spectator *vs.* spectrum 25–6, 175–6
 photogeny 15–25
 shock effects with 19–21
 social reality and 23–4
 as spectro-graphy 25–6
 studium/punctum of 174–82
 in transubstantiation 29
 von Gloeden, Wilhelm 226–8
Pia, Secundo 29
Pierre, Abbé 17–18
plaisir 116–17, 119, 157
"Plaisir aux Classiques" (Barthes) 42–5, 48, 50
Pleasure of the Text, The (Barthes) 2, 7, 64–5, 116–20, 124, 156, 170, 228, 248–9, 253, 262, 268
pleasures 116–17, 156
 field of 121–2
 money for 118–19
 overdetermination of 121–2
 paradox of 122
 sex for 119–21
 textual 116, 119, 156
 types 116–17
pluralism 122
poetry 142
poiesis 142
pointe 47

points in time 145–7
Poirier, Léon 86
politics 24, 58, 60, 98, 187, 206, 208
Politics of Friendship, The (Derrida) 218
polygamy 39
polytheism 39
"Poor and the Proletariat, The" (Barthes) 18, 94
popular culture 44, 232
post-colonial 9, 163, 187–91
posthumanism 8, 151
postmodernism 4, 153, 157
poststructuralism 242
Poujade, Pierre 23
"Power and 'Cool'" (Barthes) 91, 93
Prendergast, Christopher 141
prendre 187
Preparation of the Novel, The (Barthes) 225
Prince, Gerald 9
proairesis 56
proairetic 2, 242–3
Proust, Marcel 6, 43, 64, 70–9, 179–81, 190, 225, 230, 239, 246
 À la recherche du temps perdu 70, 75, 77, 79
 chosisme 71
 on consciousness 71
 objects, treatment of 72–9
 vs. objects 72–4
 on vision/touch 78
Proust et les signes (Deleuze) 78
provocation 57
psychoanalysis 4, 45, 153, 175, 267
psychology 5, 40, 45, 95, 106, 176, 214, 260
punctum 3, 16, 25–8, 94, 142–6, 175–82, 246–9, 265–6
Pyrrhonism 122, 124

qua writer 48
Queen Christina (Mamoulian) 23, 91, 94
queer 9, 223, 226–32
quotation 42, 137–9, 197

Rabaté, Jean-Michel 5
Rabaté, Maria 23
race 24

Race d'Ep (Hocquenghem)   227
Racine, Jean   43, 64
Rapaport, Herman   9
rapture   116
readerly/writerly   116, 154–6, 160, 163, 166–7, 253–4
reading   163
real   58, 75, 78, 107, 112, 153–4, 167, 181, 212
realisms
   Jealousy's   158–60
   Lovecraft's   153–4
   ontological   153–4
   representational   154
reality   15–16, 23–6, 29, 35, 47, 55, 57, 60, 64, 72–3, 78, 107, 111–12, 126, 153–5, 158–9, 163, 175, 212–14
Rebeyrol, Philippe   123
reception theory   4
referentiality   56, 64
relation as dialectical formulation   188
Remnants of Auschwitz (Agamben)   219
Renoux, René   85–6
representation   161–2
Réquichot, Bernard   226–7
res cogitans   119
Revolt of Islam (Shelley)   208
revolution   19, 57, 70–1, 89–91, 94–8, 153
rhetoric   20, 22, 26, 43–4, 49, 65, 86, 137, 139, 174, 194, 207–8
Ricci, Franco Maria   227
rigor, search for   5, 33–40
Robbe-Grillet, Alain   8, 64, 70–1, 79, 107, 109, 151–2, 158–67, 169 n.56, 219, 254
   art   152
   La jalousie (*Jealousy*)   152–67
   obsession with details   152
Roche, Denis   226
Roger, Philippe   98
Roland Barthes by Roland Barthes (Barthes)   2–3, 27, 62, 117, 121–4, 127–8, 137, 140, 187, 189, 196, 240, 251, 268
Roland Barthes moraliste (Coste)   48
Roland Barthes par Roland Barthes (Barthes)   49

Roland Barthes's Cinema (Watts)   85
romanesque   8, 108, 225–6
Romeo and Juliet   146–7
Roques, Henri   95

Sade, Fourier, Loyola (Barthes)   6, 55–65, 118, 120
"Sade I" (Barthes)   63–4
"Sade II" (Barthes)   63–4
Saillet, Maurice   86
saisir   187
Salazar, Pierre Joseph   223
Salò (Pasolini)   227
Samoyault, Tiphaine   118
Saroyan, William   105
Sarrasine (Balzac)   2, 118, 192–3, 239, 242–3, 250, 254
Sartre, Jean-Paul   2, 5, 25, 44, 74, 189
   Les temps modernes   103
   seventeenth-century literature, view of   44–5
Saussure, Ferdinand   6, 55, 91, 94, 95, 187–8, 232, 239, 241–2, 256–7, 260–4
scandal   20–1
schizophrenia   76
Schopenhauer, Arthur   123–4, 131 n.85
scriptible   49, 249
Second manifeste camp (Mauriès)   226
Sedgwick, Eve Kosofsky   223
Segalen, Victor   195
self   194–5
self-irony   8, 173–82
self-love (*amour-propre*)   46
semantics   2, 26, 59–60, 93–4
semiology   6–7, 175, 259–60
semiosis   57
semiotics   18
Serreau, Geneviève   19
seventeenth century literature   5–6, 42–50
sex   119–21
sign   256–8
signification   21, 47–8, 70, 87, 161, 193, 256
Silverman, Kaja   5, 15
singularity   91, 140–6, 156, 162

skipping 62
Sleep of Endymion (Girodet) 227
Sollers, Philippe 64, 116
Sontag, Susan 1–2, 226
Souls of Black Folk, The (Du Bois) 189
Souriau, Etienne 95
spectacle 6, 23–6, 45, 47, 72–5, 86–8, 127–8, 181–2
Specters of Marx (Derrida) 140
spectrum 3, 25–6, 175–6
speech 16, 24, 57, 63, 154, 187, 194, 242
spirituality 56
Stafford, Andy 8–9, 63, 225, 242
Steichen, Edward 19
Stevens, George 96
Stonewall riots (1969) 224
Stretter, Anne Marie 219
structuralism 187, 192, 262–4
studium 26–7, 144–5, 175–82, 265–6
style 108–12
subject 161–2
subjectivity 34, 43, 45, 111, 119, 153, 248
sudarium 29
suffering 43, 75, 119, 137, 178, 214
Super-Illusion 175
Sur Racine (Barthes) 44, 50
symbolic 2, 43, 46–7, 93, 142, 151, 161, 217, 242–3
"Sympathetic Worker, A" (Barthes) 7, 84, 94–6, 98
syntagm 56, 59, 193
S/Z-essay (Barthes) 2, 75, 118, 124, 192–3, 224–5, 227, 239, 241–3, 250, 253–4, 261, 268

Tableau Vivant 176
Take Arms Against a Sea of Troubles (Bloom) 173
tangibilia 72
"Tasks of Brechtian Criticism, The" (Barthes) 95, 98
Teeuwen, Rudolphus 6
Tel Quel (journal) 42
textuality 2–3
textual pleasure 116, 119
texture 141, 258, 262
text *vs.* authorial intention 5

theater 37–9, 44, 84, 88, 95–9, 108, 120, 176, 190, 226, 230–1
Theophorus, Ignatius 56
Thibaudeau, Jean 42
"Third Meaning" (Barthes) 16, 20, 26
"Third Meaning: Research Notes on Some Eisenstein Stills, The" (Barthes) 226
Thirlwell, Adam 63
Thomas the Obscure (Blanchot) 219
Till, Emmett 19
Tirez sur le pianiste (Truffaut) 93
"Tomb of Edgar Poe, The" (Mallarmé) 181
Touchez pas au grisbi (Becker) 91
tradition 7, 33, 46, 49, 64, 70, 98, 104, 116–23, 127, 158–9, 193, 224
tragedy 18, 35, 37–40, 240
translation 17, 19, 21, 25, 38, 85, 89, 106, 109, 119, 121, 126, 177, 183 n.6
transparence; *see* opacity
transparency 188–9, 195, 197
transubstantiation 29, 141
Tricks (Camus) 223
Truffaut, François 93
truth 35, 39–40, 46, 48, 57, 65, 117, 126, 128, 145–7, 155, 157, 164, 188, 216, 245–6
Tweedie, James 104
Twilight of the Idols (Nietzsche) 81 n.45

understanding 187
Ungar, Steven 7
Unheimlichkeit 74
utopia 56, 138, 174–5, 194, 196, 198, 228–31

Varda, Agnès 23, 94
Ventura, Lino 93
Verne, Jules 64, 211
Vice Consul, The (Stretter) 219
Vilar, Jean 23
violence 39
"Visage de Garbo" (Barthes) 104
visual culture 9, 223–32
visual field 16
visual studies 9

Vita Nuova, Per Amica Silentia Lunae (Dante)   173
Viva Zapata (Kazan)   98
von Gloeden, Baron   227
von Gloeden, Wilhelm   224, 226–8
voyance   176

Wahl, François   225, 226
Watts, Philip   84–5, 99 n.7, 100 n.23, 103–4, 226
weird realism   151–8
Wessing, Koen   26
What is Literature? (Sartre)   189
Wilde, Oscar   125, 227
Wilder, Billy   96, 106

Wild One, The (Benedek)   98
Winter Garden Photograph   28, 147, 177–82, 184 n.40
Woolf, Virginia   138
work/text   267–8
writerly   116, 154–6, 160, 163, 166–7
Writing Degree Zero (Barthes)   1, 5–6, 63, 140, 189
Writing of the Disaster, The (Blanchot)   161

Yeats, W. B.   173–4

Zalloua, Zahi   8
Zola, Émile   64

www.ingramcontent.com/pod-product-compliance
Lightning Source LLC
Chambersburg PA
CBHW052214300426
44115CB00011B/1679